Green Talk

in the

White House

NUMBER ELEVEN
Presidential Rhetoric Series
Martin J. Medhurst, General Editor

Green Talk in the White House

The Rhetorical Presidency Encounters Ecology

Edited by Tarla Rai Peterson

TEXAS A&M UNIVERSITY PRESS ☀ COLLEGE STATION

Library of Congress Cataloging-in-Publication Data

Green talk in the White House : the rhetorical Presidency encounters
ecology / edited by Tarla Rai Peterson.—1st ed.
    p. cm.—(Presidential rhetoric series ; no. 11)
  Includes index.
  ISBN 1-58544-335-2 (cloth : alk. paper)—
  ISBN 1-58544-415-4 (pbk. : alk. paper)
  1. Environmental policy—United States.   2. Environmentalism—
Political aspects—United States.   3. Presidents—United States.
I. Peterson, Tarla Rai. II. Series.
GE180.G75   2004
333.72—dc22   2004005281

To Robert L. Ivie

Contents

Acknowledgments

Numerous colleagues, students, friends, and institutions contributed to this book through critical readings, stimulating conversations, financial support, and less tangible forms of encouragement. First, I thank a special group of people who have assisted me with the challenges presented by cross-disciplinary research. Among those to whom I am most indebted, special thanks go to Markus J. Peterson. He read several drafts of the manuscript, helping immeasurably with corrections, reactions, and friendly encouragement. Conversations with Stephen P. Depoe, Robert L. Ivie, Dennis Jaehne, Susan Senecah, and Bryan Taylor provided helpful ideas regarding the potential connections between environmental and presidential rhetoric. At a time when I despaired of my ability to explain these connections, Lawrence J. Prelli's insight was invaluable.

The idea for this book owes much to the biennial conferences on communication and the environment held in Alta, Utah; Big Sky, Montana; Chattanooga, Tennessee; Cazenovia, New York; Flagstaff, Arizona; Cincinnati, Ohio; and Silver Falls State Park, Oregon. James Cantrill, John Delicath, Stephen Depoe, Dayle Hardy-Short, M. Jimmie Killingsworth, William Kinsella, Christine Oravec, David B. Sachsman, Susan Senecah, Brant Short, and Gregg Walker served as organizers for these conferences. The book's title was a gift from Lt. Col. Stephen W. Starks.

An earlier version of chapter 10 was presented at the 2000 National Communication Association Convention, where it received a top paper award from the Environmental Communication Commission. Earlier versions of chapters 1 through 9 were originally presented at the Third Annual Conference on Presidential Rhetoric, held at Texas A&M University, in 1997. These chapters benefited from the generous assistance of several people, including Moya A. Ball, Thomas W. Benson, Rebecca S. Bjork, Maurice Charland, Stephen P. Depoe, Thomas R. Dunlap, G. Thomas Goodnight, Robert D. Hariman, J. Michael Hogan, Christopher M. Holcomb, Rachel L. Holloway, Robert L. Ivie, M. Jimmie Killingsworth, Elizabeth Macom, John H. Patton, Susan Senecah, James A. Throgmorton, Martha M. Watson, Bruce J. Weaver, and David Zarefsky.

Support for the conference was provided by Texas A&M University's Program in Presidential Rhetoric. In addition to me, program faculty at this time were James Arnt Aune, Vanessa B. Beasley, Leroy G. Dorsey, Martin J.

Medhurst (program coordinator), Enrique D. Rigsby, and Kurt Ritter. The conference was also supported by the Department of Speech Communication, the Center for Science and Technology Policy and Ethics, the College of Liberal Arts, and the Office of the Vice President for Research and Graduate Studies at Texas A&M University. Students who assisted in preparation of the manuscript are TracyLee Clarke, Scott B. Peterson, Tiffanee Peterson, and Lauren Sacks.

The illustrations included in chapter 3 are the property of the J. N. "Ding" Darling Foundation. Contributions to the foundation can be made through Christopher D. Koss, President, J. N. "Ding" Darling Foundation, 785 Crandon Blvd., No. 1206, Key Biscayne FL 33149.

Shortly after I had obtained final copies of the studies and was beginning to prepare this volume, I fell several hundred feet off a mountain in Grand Teton National Park. I spent the next year in a fog of pain, medication, surgery, and recovery. I thank Markus, Wayne, Scott, and the Rescue Rangers in Grant Teton National Park for saving my life that day. I thank Markus, Nils, Wayne, and Scott for supporting me through the extremely difficult year that followed. I thank the authors of these chapters for their extraordinary patience. Finally, the editor of this series is a person of action, one who dislikes unnecessary delay. Thank you, Marty, for waiting.

Green Talk

in the

White House

Introduction

Environmental Communication
Meets Presidential Rhetoric

Tarla Rai Peterson

Presidential rhetoric both constrains and is constrained by political action regarding the natural environment. And our continued existence requires that environment. This collection of studies explores the interaction between presidential rhetoric and environmental debate. Its central purpose is to illuminate the rhetorical significance of crucial environmental discussions the presidency has participated in during the twentieth century. It attempts to achieve this goal by initiating integration between the burgeoning subdiscipline of environmental communication and the tradition of public address scholarship. Although it focuses primarily on environmentalism in the United States, the collection does not attempt to provide a comprehensive history of U.S. environmentalism. Neither does it attempt to analyze every presidential pronouncement related to environmental policy. Instead, it offers in-depth rhetorical analyses of selected key episodes in the history of U.S. environmental policy formation, all of which are inexorably linked to presidential rhetoric.

A second goal of this collection is to encourage a reexamination of basic presumptions guiding the study of presidential rhetoric and to suggest new directions in which it could move. To facilitate this comparative activity, I attempt to position this collection both within the emergent subdiscipline of environmental communication, and as it relates to the more mature research area of presidential rhetoric. This chapter first provides a select review of research in environmental rhetoric. Second, it describes how the scholarship collected in this volume differs from the traditional study of presidential rhetoric, with its grounding in public address scholarship. Third, it suggests three streams of environmental communication scholarship that might enrich the study of presidential rhetoric. Finally, the chapter concludes with a brief guide to the studies in this collection.

Rhetorical Analysis of Environmental Communication

Research on rhetoric and the environment explores the rhetorical motivations within discourse about being at home in the world.[1] In addition to an awareness of symbolic action, it requires an intellectual engagement with questions of social responsibility and the material world. Environmental communication research should enable us to more critically examine our environmental politics. Consistent with the communication discipline's traditional concerns, environmental communication research has attended most closely to symbolic and instrumental messages concerning the environment, and analyses of environmental rhetoric have focused on verbal interactions. The studies in this current volume explore interpretations and political practices associated with the intersection between the environmental movement and environmental policy.[2]

Some publications on rhetoric and the environment are especially relevant to the current collection in that they use rhetorical perspectives and approaches to analyze environmental issues, and they identify with the discipline of communication. In 1992 Jimmie Killingsworth and Jacqueline Palmer's *Ecospeak: Rhetoric and Environmental Politics in America* was published. *Ecospeak,* which integrates concerns from rhetorical studies and technical writing, provides a rhetorically grounded model for theorizing rhetorical practices and strategies that has influenced most subsequent analyses of environmental rhetoric.[3]

Three essay collections explicitly rhetorical in their perspectives and approaches were published in 1996. Star A. Muir and Thomas L. Veenendall's *Earthtalk: Communication Empowerment for Environmental Action* seeks to improve public dialogue by empowering readers to become more effective advocates. The book presents rhetorical strategies and discusses how the media can empower environmental action. Muir and Veenendall take an instrumentalist approach to rhetoric, describing language as a powerful tool for influencing perception and for motivating action to improve the environment. Carl G. Herndl and Stuart C. Brown's *Green Culture: Rhetorical Analyses of Environmental Discourse* adds an exploration of rhetoric's ontological and epistemological function to concerns about strategy and politics. This volume puts a discursive spin on the traditional humanistic quest to discover "what exists, what is good, and what is possible." Herndl and Brown adapt *Ecospeak's* model of environmental communication to organize an excellent discussion of how regulatory, scientific, and poetic discourses contribute to and constrain the environmental dilemma facing Western society. In *The Symbolic Earth: Discourse and Our Creation of the Environment,* James Cantrill and Christine Oravec assert that because we are symbol-using creatures the natural environment we experience is largely a product of how we talk about the world. *Symbolic Earth* examines communication practices that socially construct nature. Its chapters are unified around an attempt to explain how different people facing different circumstances use language to construct the same material environment in radically different ways.[4]

In *Sharing the Earth: The Rhetoric of Sustainable Development* I brought a rhetorical perspective to bear on the increasingly contested term *sustainability*. *Sharing the Earth* uses aspects of Kenneth Burke's critical framework to ground a discussion of how different communities have participated in telling the story of sustainable development. It exemplifies how rhetorical analysis can be used to identify productive points of tension within debates over environmental issues.[5]

In addition to the books described above, rhetorical critics wrote about environmental communication during the 1980s and 1990s. In 1997 Craig Waddell collected examples from these studies to form the first volume of *Landmark Essays on Rhetoric and the Environment*. Environmental communication research can also be tracked through the proceedings of the Conference on Communication and the Environment, which has occurred biennially since 1991. Lawrence Erlbaum is scheduled to publish the first Environmental Communication Yearbook in August 2003.[6]

Juxtaposition of Environmental Rhetoric and Presidential Rhetoric

Martin J. Medhurst delineates the two constructs "rhetorical presidency," and "presidential rhetoric" in his introduction to *Beyond the Rhetorical Presidency*. According to Medhurst, "the primary focus and basic concern of those working within the construct of the rhetorical presidency is largely, if not entirely, institutional. They are most concerned with the nature, scope, and function of the presidency as a constitutional office." He follows Tulis in defining the rhetorical presidency as "the use of popular speech addressed to mass audiences for the purpose of circumventing or bypassing congressional deliberation." Presidential rhetoric, on the other hand, refers to "the principles and practices of rhetoric, understood as the human capacity to see what is most likely to be persuasive to a given audience on a given occasion." In the case of presidential rhetoric, "rhetoric is the subject matter and presidential rhetoric the specific arena of investigation."[7]

Medhurst then sets out broad parameters within which students of presidential rhetoric have worked. Here, he mentions Aristotle's method of topical analysis, his three modes of persuasion (appeals from character, rationality, and emotion), Bitzer's concept of the rhetorical situation, the context within which speaker, message, and audience relate, and the communicative medium. Medhurst follows Theodore Windt in describing presidential rhetoric scholarship as "criticism of single presidential speeches, criticism of rhetorical movements, development and criticism of genres of presidential speeches, and miscellaneous articles on ancillary topics."[8]

The current collection diverges in some ways from more traditional studies in presidential rhetoric. Windt's category scheme is not especially useful for describing the studies in this volume. For example, the closest any of them come to analysis of a single speech is to focus on a single campaign or a single president. Although most analyze certain aspects or dimensions of environmentalism or antienvironmentalism, none seek to encompass the entire movement. None focus on speech genres. It seems, rather, that, according to Windt's schema, these analyses focus on topics that are ancillary to the study of presidential rhetoric.

Neither is this collection best characterized within the traditional parameters of the rhetorical presidency. The studies in this book interpret presidential rhetoric broadly, including presidential advisers and public programs that are connected with presidential administrations, rather than focusing on speeches made by individual presidents. They are more interested in the cultural milieu than in the institution of the presidency. I have no doubt that more institutionally focused analyses would echo Dennis L. Soden's claim that "there is no environmental president." In *The Environmental Presidency,* Soden and contributors seek to "develop a systematic understanding of how presidents have influenced the development of environmental and natural resource policy." The evidence they present indicates that the environment has not provided a driving force in the administrations of any U.S. president, although presidents sometimes have used it as a political issue. Soden's initial hypothesis "that the environmental president is more symbolic than real" highlights a fundamental difference between concerns of researchers of the rhetorical presidency.[9]

For the contributors to this book, differences between the symbolic and the "real" are not so easily distinguished. They would argue that although environmental issues may not have defined the powerful presidential roles of commander in chief, chief diplomat, chief executive, or legislative leader identified by Soden et al., these issues (which became issues through processes that are fundamentally symbolic) are becoming increasingly significant to the presidential role of opinion leader. Further, as powerful technologies enable humans to increase the rate at which we alter the environment and other technologies enable us to monitor the disturbing results of those alterations, environmental issues increasingly impinge on the president's role as chief diplomat. George H.

Bush's decision to run as the "environmental president" in 1988 and Bill Clinton's attempt to claim the title for himself illustrate the increasingly central role of the environment as a political issue.[10] The studies in this volume seek to illuminate the rhetorical significance of such choices, contributing to a systematic understanding of how public figures negotiate conflicts within the public sphere.

Perhaps the disjuncture between the current volume and both presidential rhetoric and the rhetorical presidency occurs because although its contributors are motivated by many of the concerns Medhurst identifies with presidential rhetoric, they also are motivated by an interest in the cultural milieu beyond that traditionally associated with public address (which is related to but distinct from the institutional focus exhibited by studies of the rhetorical presidency). This discovery prompts at least two possibilities. We could decide that, because they do not fit the traditionally accepted schema, these studies are beyond the scope of presidential rhetoric. A more productive alternative might be to suggest a reexamination of the criteria we have used to define and evaluate scholarship in presidential rhetoric. Perhaps the construct could endure strategic expansion without falling into the trap against which Medhurst warns when he claims that an "explanation that accounts broadly for everything, accounts specifically for nothing."[11]

Although Windt's schema is not useful in the context of this collection, another approach might suggest directions for an expanded description of presidential rhetoric. For example, we could divide the studies according to their use of traditional/nontraditional approaches to rhetorical criticism of traditional/nontraditional rhetorical texts. The chapters by Dorsey, Vickery, Short, and Moore use conventional rhetorical approaches to analyze texts that traditionally have been identified as public address, although in most scholarly contexts they would be notable for the careful detail with which they examine the cultural backgrounds for their texts. Other studies can be described as taking traditional approaches to nontraditional texts. The chapters by Daughton and Beasley, Henry, and Prelli use standard approaches to rhetorical criticism to examine texts that are less widely accepted as public addresses worthy of scholarly attention. Daughton and Beasley examine political cartoons, and how they function as a counterpoint to Pres. Franklin Roosevelt's words. Henry almost entirely dismisses the words uttered by President Clinton, focusing instead on the communication of a cabinet appointee who functioned as the president's surrogate during an important public campaign. Prelli uses that most traditional of rhetorical approaches (a topical analysis) to examine the processes whereby a public participation practice (that had no public figures in attendance) constituted democracy. Carcasson's chapter takes a third approach, applying a nontraditional methodology (based in Luhmann's systems theory) to traditional texts (formal speeches by Presidents Bush and Clinton). Finally, two studies apply relatively nontraditional approaches (strongly influenced by cultural studies) to nontraditional texts. Oravec reverses the traditional textual positions by foregrounding the culture of the technoscientific sphere, with its accompanying ideas, and allowing the speech of Theodore Roosevelt to fade into the background. Cox's critical approach combines aspects of relatively traditional rhetorical criticism with postmodern reflexivity. Although he focuses on a president (Clinton), Cox constructs his text from a pastiche of cultural artifacts that include, but are not centered in, Clinton's formal speeches.

Categorizing the chapters in this volume comes with all the attendant weaknesses of any modernist system for describing reality. It oversimplifies relationships among the studies, creating false dichotomies between those that fall into different categories and masking differences among those that fall into the same category. I am certain there is room for argument regarding whether any individual study is best described as using a traditional/nontraditional approach, and whether it examines traditional/nontraditional texts. The point is not to use a Procrustean approach to force studies into particular categories so much as to find a way of organizing the studies that does not leave most of them in a category labeled "miscellaneous." Further, this organizational framework highlights a question suggested earlier. Environmental issues have assumed an increasingly central role within public discourse. The study of presidential rhetoric, with its roots in public address scholarship, has not attended to this discourse. The chapters in this volume focus on environmental communication as it is politically contested. Given that so many of these studies are "nontraditional" in some way, perhaps it is time to rearticulate the tradition.

Significant continuities exist between the current volume and the traditional study of presidential rhetoric. Three studies in *Beyond the Rhetorical Presidency* are especially relevant to this study of intersections between presidential rhetoric and the U.S. environmental movement. The first two, by Bruce Gronbeck and Thomas Benson, argue persuasively that electronic media, which have become as ubiquitous as the spoken word in contemporary society, have fundamentally altered presidential rhetoric. The third, by Robert Ivie, argues for an explicitly expanded notion of rhetoric as "a constitutive force and a source of national identity essential to the operation of the public sphere and the constitution of the polity." Presidential rhetoric then "is equated with the construction of political culture." This collection accepts and works from Gronbeck's and Benson's claims about the ubiquitous nature of electronic media, although not necessarily their interpretations of the influences these media have had. It also takes its cue from the expanded construct of presidential rhetoric as a constitutive cultural force suggested by Ivie. All the studies exemplify to varying degrees the interest in the intersection between communication and culture that increasingly characterizes contemporary rhetorical studies. The subject matter differs, but the analyses in this volume share a fundamental analytical goal articulated in the second volume of Medhurst's presidential rhetoric series: discovering "ways of rhetorically enacting a strong and healthy democratic culture."[12]

This book offers environmental communication scholarship as an example of how the application of multiple perspectives can enrich traditional public address research, thus broadening its appeal for those primarily interested in rhetorical theory, rhetoric of science, applied communication, and other areas within the communication discipline. The practicality of public address studies for citizens has been the traditional and strongest rationale for those studies. This is consistent with public address scholarship's connection with the classical rhetorical tradition dating at least from Aristotle's attempts to systematize an approach that would enable citizens to participate rationally in their own governance.

Contemporary public address scholarship is illuminating, but it is increasingly difficult for the growing number of communication scholars who are not involved in that subdiscipline to imagine how these insights can be translated back to the practical, problem-oriented contexts where political deliberations transpire. Environmental communication is one of these contexts, including debates about energy policy, water use, and wildlife, fishery, forest, and wildland management. The strength of environmental communication studies is their gritty practicality concerning problems confronting a plurality of embodied, situated, interested audiences. Public address scholarship can settle for textual insight and illumination and then promise practicality in some distant future or idealized situation, but environmental communication scholars cannot make that trade-off without undercutting their reason for being. Put otherwise, whereas the appeals to practicality as rationale for public address studies have a highly theoretical quality, environmental communication studies require a more convincing demonstration of practical utility.

The crux of the argument for a book that juxtaposes these approaches to communication research is this: environmental communication studies can help to redeem the promise of practicality for public address scholarship (at least on natural resource issues), while public address scholarship can contribute sophisticated interpretive approaches for understanding the texts from which policies and continued debates transpire. The perspective outlined here is not intended to denigrate previous approaches to the study of presidential or of environmental rhetoric, but rather to enhance both. Perhaps the larger point is that integrating the two approaches offers a different kind of rhetorical analysis—aside from treating different subjects—that could form part of the basis for a more powerful rationale for the study of presidential rhetoric.

Questions posed by this juxtaposition of multiple methods and divergent perspectives are fundamental for practitioners of rhetorical analysis. Do we write rhetorical analyses of political issues, events, and individuals for other public address scholars, for political critics, for decision makers, or for citizens? Should we desire to do so, how can we write rhetorical analyses that respond to the needs of more than one of these groups simultaneously? What qualities have marked rhetorical analyses in public address and in environmental communication? How do they compare and contrast? How can an integration of these diverse approaches to political speech contribute to a more lively public and scholarly debate? Although none of the chapters in this book respond to all these questions, all approach some of them and offer possibilities that could enrich the practice of rhetorical criticism at the same time they enliven the practice of political rhetoric.

Potential for Integration

Environmental communication has been about symbolic practices for constituting human identity and relationships with the earth. It has grown out of an intellectual shift that legitimates rhetoric's epistemic and ontological significance, a heightened awareness and distrust of science and technology, and an increasingly widespread discomfort with visible environmental degradation. It stresses communicative exchange as social engagement among diverse participants who coconstruct their situation. Environmental communication research should enable us to better understand what environmental policy means to society. At least three contemporary streams of environmental communication research suggest opportunities for enriching the study of presidential rhetoric.

The Symbolic and the Material

Kevin DeLuca, whose research focuses on the significance of visual images, has moved toward a theory of critical rhetoric grounded in the visually oriented media event. He also argues that environmental groups must develop strategies and tactics for an electronically mediated age. Daughton and Beasley's analysis of Ding Darling's environmental cartoons (chap. 3, this volume) shows how environmental advocates began developing such strategies during the administration of Franklin Roosevelt. Phaedra Pezullo, whose research focuses on rhetorical strategies used to focus attention on chemical contamination of the environment, cautions against focusing too narrowly on the visual. Since toxic substances frequently are invisible, she advocates that rhetorical scholars attend to a wider range of communicative practices. In arguing for a more embodied sense of rhetoric she turns to Blair and Selzer's concept of material rhetoric, pointing out that, since the material thus theorized often refers to aspects of the physical environment, rich possibilities for cross-fertilization exist.[13]

Pezullo notes as an example of this potential J. Robert Cox's 1982 article "The Die Is Cast: Tropical and Ontological Dimensions of the *Locus* of the Irreparable." Waddell characterizes this study as a defining moment in the scholarship of environmental rhetoric.[14] As Cox explores doing what cannot be undone to a species or a place, he positions materiality centrally for evaluating the arguments of the irreparable and, therefore, of the environment. In my 1998 review of environmental communication scholarship, I further develop the discussion around the relationship between materiality and symbolicity, arguing that "although nature is not inherently a rhetorical text, human actions and social structures associated with it do function rhetorically . . . [and thus] environmental communication must maintain the integrity of both verbal and natural systems since both are essential: our existence depends on nature, and we use language to conceptualize and discuss the natural systems on which we rely."[15] I acknowledge that while invention and symbolicity are important facets of environmental rhetoric, they do not constitute its entire domain. Several of the chapters in this collection discuss the problematic nexus between material and symbolic. Henry's examination of attempts to improve relationships between the U.S. Department of Energy and the public, Cox's alternate readings for Clinton's environmental policy, Prelli's explication of conflicting standards for sustainability, and Carcasson's exploratory analysis of contemporary presidential opportunities (and responsibilities) to participate in international governance are especially relevant to this endeavor.

Science, Technology, and the Rhetoric of Risk

A related site for productive integration is the rhetorical analysis of presidential speech about science and technology issues, which often require the ability to integrate the material and symbolic. Science and technology–based conflicts have become increasingly central to presidential speech since the presidency of Theodore Roosevelt. With its grounding in science and technology, environmental communication studies can lend greater insight to the textual and historical analyses traditionally performed by public address scholars. In turn, the sophisticated approaches to text that have evolved within rhetoric and public address promise to enhance the quality of environmental communication scholarship.

At the center of society's modern political concerns (such as the environment) lie the risks and consequences of modernization, which include irreversible threats to life. Exploring the political rhetoric about environmental issues provides a potentially rich basis for examining questions about the sources and social dynamics of reflexivity with which we might transform the project of modernity.[16] Celeste Michelle Condit's sophisticated insights into the rhetoric of science exemplify these possibilities. For example, Condit has created a highly nuanced narrative of the U.S. debate about genetic research and manipulations by locating its major rhetorical formations in popular magazines, newspapers, and other media.[17]

Ulrich Beck claims that our access to this critical perspective is blocked by a barely recognized myth in which the social thought of the nineteenth century was essentially trapped and which still casts a shadow into the twenty-first century. This myth asserts that the developed nations of the world (best exemplified by the United States), with their patterns of work and life, their production sectors, their understanding of science and technology, and their forms of democracy, are thoroughly modern societies. Expressions of this myth include the claims that history has ended and that democracy requires radical privatization of the economy. Beck argues that although science and skepticism are institutionalized in modern society, skepticism is limited to the external objects of research, while the foundations and consequences of scientific work remain shielded from public scrutiny.[18] Rhetorical analysis of environmental policy could enable a systematic extension of skepticism to the foundations and hazards of scientific work, exposing the discontinuity between its internal and external relations. We are concerned not only with making nature useful and releasing humans from traditional constraints but also with problems resulting from development itself. Political awareness that hazardous side effects pollute the sources of wealth is spreading.

The environmental issues emerging in our industrialized world cannot be sufficiently reinterpreted by better science or more powerful technology. Science itself has limits, for "there is not a single theory which is in agreement with all the facts in its domain."[19] Ecology is perhaps the most integrative of the natural sciences. It attempts to grapple with the whole of nature by taking a systems approach. Inherent in this perspective is the idea of embedded ecological communities. The logical extension is that no ecological explanation is every wholly complete. When one explicitly focuses on normative questions, the insufficiency of the scientific approach becomes obvious. Despite all this, discussions about the destruction of the environment are still conducted dominantly in the terms and formulas of natural science, while social, cultural, and political meanings inherent in scientific formulas remain largely unrecognized.

Rhetorical critiques of environmental discourse can encourage an awareness of conflicting environmental policy options as struggles among rationality claims, some competing and some overlapping. This critical approach presumes that the origin of any critique of science and technology lies not in the irrationality of the critics, but in the limitations of technoscientific rationality. The public refusal to accept the results of scientifically valid risk assessments, then, is not something to be reproached as irrationality. Rather, it indicates that the cultural premises of acceptability contained in technical statements on risks are inappropriate; the risk experts are mistaken in the empirical accuracy of their assumptions regarding what is acceptable.[20] It suggests the need for a rhetorical critique. The contributors to this volume work from the premise that environmental policy serves both a constitutive and an instrumental function. They use presidential rhetoric about environmental policy as a framework within which to examine political responses to the concern for how to prevent, minimize, dramatize, or focus the risks and hazards systematically produced as part of modernization.

Rhetoricizing the Public Sphere

A third topic with strong potential for cross-fertilization between research in environmental communication and presidential rhetoric is the public sphere. Numerous scholars have lamented the breakdown of the public sphere, arguing that an increased reliance on technical reasoning has excluded citizens from involvement in the development of public policy.[21] Public participation in environmental decision making has been an official part of the national agenda since President Nixon signed the National Environmental Policy Act (see chap. 4, this volume). Caitlin W. Toker argues that the pursuit of an ideal public sphere within which this participation can occur has encouraged uncritical acceptance of stakeholder models that promise facilitation of open and free public deliberation according to principles of equality, representation, open deliberation, and consensus.[22] In these forums, stakeholders from all walks of life theoretically come together and engage in open and free deliberation. Through such deliberation, individuals overcome differences to unite in the spirit of the common good and reach a rationally determined consensus. Because decision making occurs through an open competition between interests, the results will be legitimate and fair. Toker's analysis of a stakeholder group created by the Georgia Port Authority demonstrates that stakeholder models work very differently in practice. The consensus process holds participants hostage, allowing powerful institutions to use legal and legislative channels with little disruption. She argues that public deliberation would be better served through an exploration of rhetorical strategies these groups can use to redefine situations, disassociate dysfunctional relationships, and introduce new perspectives.

Robert L. Ivie has suggested shifting the critical focus of the search for the public sphere to celebrate the diversity of participants, languages, types of reasoning, and evidence involved in public debate.[23] Such a shift reveals that, more than their skillful use of technical reasoning, power is what allows the elite to control deliberative processes. One of the weaknesses characterizing stakeholder models is that they ignore power.[24] Public deliberation in the environmental policy context is intensely political and always linked to power relationships and value conflicts. The conditions of public participation always privilege some interests over others. This makes them necessarily partial rather than fully representative. Perhaps more fundamentally disturbing is that rather than creating a safe space for genuine public deliberation, stakeholder involvement processes can create a dangerous space, a quasi- political environment where participants expend their energy articulating public ideals of freedom, equality, and openness while decisions are made elsewhere. Because of their connection to public policy, the studies in this collection speak to the intellectual pursuit of a richer public sphere, and the chapters by Moore, Henry, and Prelli critically analyze various attempts to involve citizens in the development and implementation of public policy.

The Studies

At least since the presidency of Theodore Roosevelt, U.S. presidents have marshaled their rhetorical power to persuade people to support or reject various environmental policies. They have also used the natural environment to vilify political opponents, burnish their own images, and garner support from special interest groups. The chapters in this book are arranged chronologically, beginning with the administration of Theodore Roosevelt, who is identified with the beginning of the conservation movement in the United States.

Environmental Rhetoric and the New Frontier

The conservation movement was consistent with the Progressive Era in its belief that through government regulation people could encourage more rational use of natural resources. Despite the dramatic pronouncements of Theodore Roosevelt and the poetic flights of John Muir, conservation was about using science and technology to develop and implement policies that would encourage rational and efficient use of natural resources; it was not about nature. Nevertheless, conservationists left a significant natural legacy. The magical quality of Roosevelt's unusual sympathy for wilderness conservation, for example, contributed to his ability to set aside eighteen national monuments, enlarge the national forests from 42 to 172 million acres, and persuade Congress to create fifty-one national wildlife refuges.[25]

Theodore Roosevelt is widely identified as both a rhetorical president and as a pioneer for visionary environmental policy in the United States. He called upon the mythos of the American frontier to imbue his environmental policies with the pathos of the American dream. Roosevelt's vision enabled conservation legislation by arguing that the nation's moral strength required the preservation of at least a few acres of untamed wilderness.

In chapter 1 Leroy G. Dorsey analyzes President Roosevelt's rhetorical mission to promote more prudent use of America's "sacred" natural resources. Dorsey argues that by changing the public's frame of reference for the natural environment, Theodore Roosevelt was able to overcome what would have otherwise been impossible odds and create support for a broadly supported conservation ethic. Prior to Roosevelt's conservation crusade, the American public viewed the country's natural resources as essentially inexhaustible. Even when faced with species extinction or deforestation of vast regions, the general response was that such changes were not significant losses. Dorsey argues that Roosevelt changed the public's interpretation of the natural environment from a resource owned by a person or group, to a gift from God. As such, it became the people's moral responsibility to treat nature well and preserve it. It also meant that conservation was everyone's responsibility.

Dorsey further argues that Theodore Roosevelt promoted wilderness as an essence with an intangible quality that enabled communion between God and humanity, fortifying both the body and soul. He built on the belief that the United States was God's chosen land, making Americans a chosen people who were destined to greatness. It was not acceptable for God's chosen people to reject his gift nor to treat it carelessly. Dorsey explains that Roosevelt categorized sins against nature into two categories. First, there was the sin of shortsighted greed, exhibited by business, mainly the timber industry, which was not claiming to practice sustainable forestry at that time. Dorsey demonstrates rhetorical practices used by Roosevelt to dramatize this sin. The second sin against nature was a sin of omission, or indifference, by the American people. Thus members of the public were required to become actively engaged in attempts to stop greedy corporations who threatened to destroy nature.

Dorsey also demonstrates that Roosevelt's rhetoric established links that more contemporary presidents have been less than successful at developing. First, Roosevelt successfully articulated a positive connection between environmental preservation and economic prosperity, which encouraged members of the public who were not likely to be motivated by his religious arguments. He also led the way to federal regulation of environmental issues, asserting that because nature is universal, it falls under the jurisdiction of the federal government. Contemporary presidents continue to struggle with these two issues, which provide important aspects of analysis in other chapters.

Christine Oravec's critique probes more deeply into the relationship between the rhetoric of Theodore Roosevelt, his enigmatic adviser W. J. McGee, and the ever elusive public sphere. Despite Roosevelt's lifelong fascination with science, discussions of his rhetorical contributions to the environmental movement have tended to ignore this influence. Oravec's examination of science and technology rhetoric adds complementary insights to the more traditional analysis of Roosevelt's environmental persona. Relying largely on the rhetorical theory of Michael Calvin McGee and Maurice Charland, Oravec examines how W. J. McGee constructed a public to whom Roosevelt could address environmental appeals.

Her study explains the process whereby Theodore Roosevelt's advisers developed the basis for a political policy of environmental action grounded primarily on scientific and technological premises, then succeeded in popularizing this policy by creating a conception of a conservationist public, which continues to exist in the contemporary political milieu. After reviewing some of the public pressures that encouraged the creation of a movement for effectively coordinating public policy, Oravec explores the rhetorical processes used by advocates of environmental conservation exemplified by W. J. McGee to formulate language that identified conservation as a social movement and justified the advocacy of a social policy based on principles of evolution and the progressive spirit of the "people."

Oravec extends Dorsey's analysis in two directions. First, she shows how conservationists within Roosevelt's administration constructed a continuum for the movement from various concepts and themes present into the public domain and positioned its audience as constituents. Oravec emphasizes the corporate, scientific basis of Roosevelt's conception of national government, shifting the explanatory focus from the archetypical mythic framework discussed by Dorsey toward an emphasis on scientists and technology entrepreneurs whose commodity was the environment as natural resource. The second extension includes her critical analysis of the concept of community, or public, for whom conservationists spoke. While Oravec's analysis confirms Dorsey's claims that civil religion was central to the public created by Roosevelt's rhetoric, she argues that such a mythology does not stand alone as a motivation for public response but is woven into the political, scientific, social, and economic threads of a nation's culture.

Oravec's chapter critically analyzes how Roosevelt's advocacy-oriented advisers combined an artful construction of an activist, conservationist public with scientifically justified calls to action. Her detailed analysis of relevant texts also demonstrates one way an integration of textual analysis techniques often used by public address scholars, contemporary cultural theory, and environmental communication scholarship can enrich the concept of the rhetorical presidency and contribute to a more lively scholarly debate.

Environmental Rhetoric and Political Pragmatism

Franklin D. Roosevelt, Richard Nixon, and Ronald Reagan exemplified a more pragmatic use of the natural environment to achieve specific political ends. Although Franklin Roosevelt's and Nixon's overt pragmatism led to the development of powerful federal conservation agencies, neither engaged the hearts of the people as Theodore Roosevelt's rhetoric had. The materiality of the environmental crisis during the dust bowl and the 1960s, however, provided U.S. citizens with more than sufficient pathos. During Franklin Roosevelt's presidency, the earth itself coated people's throats, burned their eyes, and broke their hearts. Nixon presided at a time when the American landscape exhibited pollution realized from post–World War II prosperity. American rivers were so polluted they caught fire, and our national avian symbol was threatened with extinction. At the beginning of Reagan's presidency, a sense of complacency dominated the environmental movement. The demonstrated ability to clean up polluted air and water, industry's predictions of economic doom, and public anger toward increasing federal regulation of the individual, combined to spur a reaction against federal environmental regulation. Reagan's antienvironmental rhetoric combined the moral force of the American dream with contemporary public anger to effectively constrain enforcement of existing conservation statutes and regulations, which he characterized as anti-individualistic.

Like other social issues, conservation suffered during the 1920s. By the time Franklin D. Roosevelt was first elected (1932), the nation was already suffering from environmental devastation that was as serious as the more publicly present economic disaster. Franklin Roosevelt shared his cousin's positive regard for nature and made his own significant contributions to the conservationist agenda. FDR integrated environmental policy into his New Deal. His environmental legacy can be seen today in agencies such as the Tennessee Valley Authority, the Soil Conservation Service (now the Natural Resource Conservation Service), and the U.S. Fish and Wildlife Service.[26]

Suzanne M. Daughton and Vanessa B. Beasley use the political cartoons of Jay Norwood "Ding" Darling as a basis for their critique of Franklin Delano Roosevelt's conservation rhetoric. Darling served as Roosevelt's first director of the Biological Survey, the precursor to today's U.S. Fish and Wildlife Service. They argue that although the office of the presidency began exerting influence over U.S. environmental policy long before the rhetorical presidency gained ascendancy, presidential involvement in public policies explicitly designed to manage natural resources is of much more contemporary origin. Their study is a rhetorical analysis of environmental controversy within the Roosevelt administration, which established the basic organizational framework within which most contemporary environmental policy is developed and implemented.

Daughton and Beasley's central claim is that the natural environment poses unique political difficulties because of the intrinsic conflicts between the pragmatism of liberal democracy and the moral implications found in most environmental rhetoric. They point out that, despite Theodore Roosevelt's dramatic environmental rhetoric (and his identification with the environmental movement and environmental preservation efforts in the public imagination), most of contemporary U.S. environmental policy is grounded in the political structure developed by Franklin Roosevelt (who is not strongly identified with the environmental movement in the popular imagination). Daughton and Beasley's analysis follows from Oravec's attempt to analyze how successful rhetorical appeals are woven into the political, scientific, social, and economic threads of a nation's culture.

Daughton and Beasley argue that Roosevelt's environmental rhetoric was consistent with his pragmatic approach of "experimenting with a variety of solutions to specific problems and discarding those he did not see as productive." Because he integrated environmental issues into the political, scientific, social, and economic challenges facing his administration, Roosevelt was able to justify the establishment of a vast bureaucracy to ensure conservation of the nation's natural resources. Roosevelt assured the American public that environmental conservation addressed their social and economic desires. Franklin Roosevelt also echoed Theodore Roosevelt's claims that nature itself offered humans a periodic refuge from their frenetic struggle to survive and that given this universal potential, natural resources were appropriately translated into national resources (and therefore subject to federal regulation).

FDR's ability to integrate the desire for short-term economic benefits with the imperative toward a more sustainable future did not, however, eliminate controversy from environmental politics. Daughton and Beasley focus on how Ding Darling's political cartoons functioned as a source of this controversy, which in turn contributed to a perpetual state of negotiation that strengthened Roosevelt's environmental policies. They argue that the environmental rhetoric from his administration had lasting benefits and demonstrates the ubiquity of negotiation within democratic political rhetoric. Their analysis of how arguments within Roosevelt's administration integrated economic, scientific, and spiritual motives into environmental policy suggests ways in which contemporary advocates of environmental protection might enable presidents to more effectively transcend the rhetoric of the economy versus the environment.

During the decades following World War II conservation struggled to maintain a foothold as Americans scrambled for their share of postwar prosperity. Rapid advances in science and technology associated with the war effort were turned to domestic uses. For example, DDT, which had been invaluable in protecting U.S. soldiers from malaria, was sprayed throughout suburban environments, freeing people from the nuisance of mosquitoes and eventually bringing bald eagle numbers to dangerously low levels. Banning DDT resulted in one of environmentalism's rare successes, the recovery of this species.[27] Although a few scientists and conservationists were urging caution, the public was not listening until the publication of Rachel Carson's *Silent Spring* in 1962 brought environmental concerns into the public eye. Although the book was not universally accepted, it was universally noticed. Chemical companies devoted unprecedented resources to publicly demonizing Carson, which only ensured wider awareness of the book. John F. Kennedy read the book, invited Carson to the White House, and began federal investigations of U.S. chemical production. In terms of rhetorical significance, it is difficult to overrate *Silent Spring*. The change from the conservation to the environmental movement is commonly associated with its publication.[28]

The environmental movement was again closely associated with other social issues. By 1970 it had become mainstream. Richard Nixon, who had not identified himself with the protests of the 1960s, responded to the increased public interest in environmental protection by addressing it in his 1970 state of the union address. On April 22 of that year some 20 million Americans took part in the first Earth Day celebration. Although the organizers tended to be former antiwar and civil rights activists, the celebration enjoyed broad participation among every socioeconomic group in the nation. Before middecade President Nixon had signed the National Environmental Policy Act and created the EPA (Environmental Protection Agency). The Clean Air Act was joined by the Clean Water Act, the Ocean Dumping Act, and the Endangered Species Act. The international aspects of environmental problems did not go unnoticed.

In 1972 the United Nations sponsored the Conference on Human Environment in Stockholm, which led to the establishment of the UN Environment Programme.[29]

Micheal Vickery explores how political circumstances converged with Richard Nixon's political identity, administrative agenda, and rhetorical style to constitute the EPA. Vickery claims that, although many people struggle to locate Nixon along a liberal-conservative spectrum, his pragmatism is much more significant. Just as Daughton and Beasley argue that Franklin Roosevelt's environmental policies derived from his political pragmatism, Vickery argues that Nixon's creation of multiple federal agencies with responsibility for environmental regulation was politically expedient. Nixon was, above all else, a political animal, and his support of the EPA exemplified that tendency.

Vickery points out that Nixon became president in a time of raucous public demand for increased environmental protection. Concern for the natural environment enjoyed such broad popularity, particularly among politically active young adults, that it temporarily overwhelmed industry's claims that regulation would stifle the economy.

Vickery cites Nixon's observation that, next to peace, the environment was the major concern of the American people as an example of his awareness of the public interest. Environmental protection was the domestic focus of Nixon's first state of the union address, in which he advocated regulation of industrial pollution. Nixon responded to widespread popular interest in the environment by supporting legislation that enhanced environmental protection and allowing his domestic affairs adviser, John Ehrlichman, great latitude in advocating increased environmental protection. Vickery claims that establishing the EPA as an agency to enforce environmental standards, conduct research, and assist other agencies in recommending new policy was the logical response to public demands of the time. By ensuring that EPA's fiscal operations were overseen by the Office of Management and Budget, the Nixon administration also partially placated industry leaders' concerns that the EPA would interfere with their practices.

Vickery uses his analysis of Nixon and the EPA as a platform for arguing that although public pressures can play an important role in policymaking, rhetorical critics should be cautious about accepting assertions of such influence. He advocates expanding our conception of presidential rhetoric beyond public speeches and other formal discourse (a challenge taken up in many studies included in this collection) as a means for critically exploring the relationship between political realism and rhetorical action. His rhetorical critique of Nixon's relationship with the EPA leads to the conclusion that Nixon used it as a bureaucratic management tool that enabled industry to rationalize the continuation of detrimental environmental practices. Vickery's analysis encourages readers to interpret Nixon's support of the EPA as the skillful use of political power to mediate differing perceptions of reality between factions. He points out that the EPA has enabled preservation of traditional ways in which science and popular desires combine to encourage continued economic expansion at the expense of environmental protection.

The environmental movement's success did not please everyone, and the 1980s marked a significant backlash. When Ronald Reagan was elected, he not only halted the development of government-sponsored measures to protect the environment but also began dismantling those in existence. He appointed antienvironmentalist individuals to key environmental positions, such as James Watt as interior secretary, Ann Burford as head of the EPA, and Donald Hodel as energy secretary.[30]

C. Brant Short analyzes the antienvironmentalist rhetoric of the Reagan administration. Short builds on his previous analysis of Ronald Reagan's participation in the debate over public lands in the United States to evaluate the interaction between the mythology of the frontier and Reagan's environmental rhetoric. He notes Reagan's skillful use of American popular culture to increase his popularity and how his background as an actor enabled him to become known as "the Great Communicator." Short's study is similar to Dorsey's, in that it is focused on how Reagan used historical and cultural forces in his environmental rhetoric. Short demonstrates how Reagan's rhetoric relied on, while simultaneously further legitimating and expanding, the related mythologies of the Puritan errand and the frontier thesis. Short argues further that Reagan's rhetoric helped to develop a public image that identified his personal experience with this mythology, enabling him to more persuasively integrate it into his political rhetoric.

Short asserts that an analysis of Reagan's relationship to environmental policy must include the rhetoric of his flamboyant secretary of the interior James Watt, a born-again Christian who personified the culture of the New Right. Even more explicitly than Reagan, Watt argued that the administration had a mission to restore traditional values, which had been eroded by "the left," which included environmentalists. The four cornerstones upon which Watt's environmental policy was built were that America must have a solid economy in order to care for the environment, orderly development of energy resources was needed to avert a disaster, natural resources should be used for the advancement of civilization, and America has the ability to use and manage the environment wisely. During Watt's tenure, he emphasized that the secretary of the interior's job was to manage the public lands in a way that would enhance national security and encourage economic expansion.

Short demonstrates that Reagan's environmental rhetoric relied on arguments similar to those used by Theodore Roosevelt. Both were technological optimists, assuming that humans could harness natural resources for the betterment of society. Reagan also echoed Roosevelt's association of American values with an entrepreneurial spirit of risk taking and individualism. Reagan's rhetoric emphasized that America was God's chosen land, over which American citizens held stewardship. At this point, however, the rhetoric of the two administrations diverged. Roosevelt extended his religious claim to support pronouncements that Americans were responsible for conserving natural resources and to justify federal regulation of those resources for the communal good. Short argues that Reagan's rhetoric emphasized American's God-given mandate to explore nature for the purpose of developing new energy resources. Further, although Reagan claimed it was appropriate to use natural resources wisely, he not only attempted to reduce environmental regulations but also publicly ridiculed environmental standards designed to protect public health. Through detailed analysis of the public statements made by Reagan and advisers such as Watt, Short demonstrates that, for the natural environment to have any significance within the Reagan administration, it first had to be identified with immediate economic needs or national security.

Sensing an increasing public nervousness about Reagan's antienvironmentalist politics, George Bush promised to be an "environmental president." He signaled his commitment to this promise by appointing William K. Reilly, a respected environmentalist, to head the EPA, but did not take a leadership role himself. For example, in 1989 several states agreed to adopt vehicle emissions standards that were tougher than those recommended by the Bush administration. In 1990 the Bush administration and Congress cooperated to pass amendments upgrading the Clean Air Act to comparable standards. In addition, rather than attempting to integrate the two, Bush struggled to balance environmental and economic concerns. Bush's failure as an environmental president was most obvious in his participation at the 1992 Earth Summit, sponsored by the United Nations in Rio de Janeiro.[31] Carcasson's chapter on global environmental governance examines Bush's rhetoric in greater detail.

The Environmental President Who Wasn't

William Jefferson Clinton promised to reverse the Reagan-Bush record on environmental protection. But Clinton presided at a time when the public was far more concerned with the federal deficit than with the bald eagle. The pragmatism that worked so well for Franklin Roosevelt and Nixon was insufficient to the rhetorical situation in the 1990s, and Clinton's rhetoric lacked the moral conviction of either Theodore Roosevelt or Ronald Reagan. Three chapters focus on Clinton's attempt to become the first environmental president.

J. Robert Cox critiques the rhetorical constraints faced by the Clinton-Gore White House, arguing that a more inclusive model of presidential rhetoric could enrich both the natural world and our public life by reaffirming, refining, and renewing a vocabulary that enhances opportunities for public judgment of conservation efforts. Cox claims that any analysis of motives associated with Clinton's environmental rhetoric must account for his enigmatic appeal to American audiences and his apparent desire to leave a lasting political legacy. He points out that Clinton's choice of Al Gore, who was well known for his environmentalist leanings, as his vice presidential running mate assured him the green vote, while maintaining maximum flexibility for Clinton himself regarding environmental issues. The value of this flexibility continued throughout the years Clinton held office, especially as he faced a Republican Congress that became increasingly confrontational in its opposition to regulation, including environmental regulation. Additionally, this flexibility enabled him to survive when his plans for environmental protection were shot down by competing federal and state agencies, as well as by people within his own administration. Cox asserts that Clinton's republican style of leadership was instrumental in his ability to navigate the stormy relationship between the White House and Congress, as well as his rhetorical self-presentation before the American public.

Cox argues, however, that this leadership style lacked the power needed to support controversial environmental policy decisions. When faced with environmental issues, Clinton followed his general tendency to make political promises without the ability to follow through. The public perception that he surpassed previous presidents in this regard was reinforced when Clinton reneged on his campaign promises to restore and protect the environment. Environmentalists' great expectations for a "real environmental president" quickly turned to disillusionment and a sense of betrayal. They charged that Clinton immediately compromised important environmental questions in favor of polluters and big business. Cox argues that the specter of a hostile Congress waiting to attack further stifled Clinton's feeble attempts to strengthen existing environmental protection policy.

Environmentalists identified Clinton's signing of the 1995 Rescissions Act, which included the now infamous "salvage timber" rider, as the environmental low point of his presidency. By this time, they had labeled Clinton as environmentally irresponsible and an enemy of the environment. Faced with increasingly vocal and widespread public alarm over his apparent antienvironmental stance, Clinton began vetoing Republican-backed antienvironment bills. The

Republican party also began to soften its antienvironmental protection stance, perhaps in response to the same public alarm. Clinton's advisers pointed toward Republic congressmen who were voted out of office, in part due to their poor records regarding environmental protection, and argued that in order to be reelected, Clinton needed the support of environmentalists within his own party and proenvironment Republican women. In order to gain their support, he would have to persuade them that he was serious about saving the earth.

Cox suggests that communication scholarship should contextualize interpretations of Clinton's environmental rhetoric within this general concern for political expediency. From this perspective, Clinton's invitation to the people to "come together" to resolve environmentally based conflicts makes good political sense. Encouraging public involvement in environmental decisions enabled Clinton to appear sympathetic to all parties, as he tried to minimize conflict between environmentalist and opposing factions. Clinton used these public involvement opportunities to emphasize the importance of community, claiming environmental struggles occurred because the people were divided. He viewed environmental conflict as an opportunity to show his commitment to the strengthening of civic community. Thus it made perfect sense for Clinton to declare that in order to renew the natural environment, we needed to renew community.

Cox points out that the American people have shown a strong desire to improve the quality of the natural environment, even including willingness to accept government regulation to achieve that goal. Clinton's republican style of leadership, however, with its overemphasis on community reconciliation as the means to achieve environmentally sustainable public policy, was insufficient to harness this desire. Cox uses a review of the multiple fronts from which Clinton faced opposition to environmental protection policies to help explain why his espousal of republicanism and reliance on community reconciliation were insufficient to support policies that would enhance environmental protection. Cox argues that Clinton sensed the need for public support in order to take effective actions on environmental issues. His republicanism led him to assume people would view public pronouncements regarding environmental protection as binding to the degree that they proclaimed general intentions but not to the degree that they directed how those intentions would be implemented. Thus rather than discussing practical implementation, Clinton retreated to vague pronouncements about civic community.

Cox argues that presidential rhetoric about environmental policy must encourage serious public debate, and rather than focusing on reconciliation, it must encourage citizens to hold public officials responsible for their actions. Because such policy requires a fundamental reordering of many political and social expectations, a strong political vision is necessary but not sufficient. That vision must be translated into a rhetoric of prudence, stewardship, intelligence, and competence. Clinton's civic republicanism was insufficiently credible as a political vision and failed to be translated into a compelling rhetoric.

Mark Moore's analysis of Clinton's spectacular failure to be all things to all people in the Pacific Northwest is a cautionary tale suggesting that successful application of pragmatic politics requires an understanding of the rhetorical situation. Moore points out that many people interpret Clinton's involvement in the controversial 1995 Rescissions Act as just one more example of his disastrous attempts to develop policy for the sole purpose of enhancing his approval ratings. Although Moore does not dispute this possibility, he suggests that, for those who are more interested in understanding how rhetoric functions in the political realm than in either burnishing or denigrating Clinton's personal image, a detailed analysis of rhetorical irony is more fruitful. Viewed from within the perspective set out by Cox, Moore's analytical suggestion seems quite reasonable.

Moore shows that the Northwest timber controversy was incongruous at multiple levels. He argues that Clinton's campaign promises to resolve this issue very likely stemmed from the optimistic belief that, as with other political problems, all that was lacking was a sense of community. He assumed that if someone (and who better than a newly elected president) would provide an opportunity for key disputants to come together, they would develop a sense of community that would enable them to reach a rational compromise. Clinton devoted valuable time and energy to an activity that eventually alienated him from both timber and environmental interests.

Moore explains that the fallout from this political disaster continued to escalate after the public participation was concluded. A salvage act that ignored the recommendations of the citizen groups was proposed in Congress. Realizing that the act flew in the face of what little progress had been made during the public participation attempts, Clinton put off signing it. When he finally did, he telephoned to warn some of those with whom he had proposed building a sense of community that they would need to find a way to stop the results themselves.

Moore also details the incongruity between expected and actual results of the public participation venues Clinton enabled. He points out the irony associated with the timber companies' dire warnings that environmentally motivated stoppages of logging on public lands would destroy the economy of the region, environmentalists' predictions of total ecological devastation, and loggers' self-righteous paranoia. He shows how, through their successful campaign to dichotomize environmental from economic interests and human from nonhuman animals, timber companies unwittingly positioned themselves as responsible for ensuring the continued employment of the laborers they thrust into the public eye.

By ignoring (whether intentionally or accidentally) the rhetorical complexity of the Pacific Northwest timber controversy, Clinton ensured disastrous results. Moore's analysis points out the danger of oversimplifying conflicts and precipitously attempting their resolution, and suggests the utility of detailed rhetorical analysis of environmental conflicts prior to designing management strategies. In this case, only a solution that incorporated the complex ironies within the conflict itself could have offered a reasonable possibility of success.

David Henry writes about a more rhetorically successful attempt by the Clinton administration to encourage public participation, even to serve as a public advocate, in the controversy surrounding the release of information concerning nuclear testing that had occurred between 1963 and 1990. Henry focuses on rhetorical dimensions of responding to demands for disclosure and accountability in a democratic society. He examines surrogate advocacy, where a proxy takes responsibility for discussion and future action while shielding the president from accountability.

Henry examines how Hazel O'Leary, who assumed the role of surrogate, defined the grounds of the discussion, how she attempted to use a deliberative forum, and the role ethics played in this and similar debates. Henry argues that O'Leary's approach to the crisis came from rethinking traditional methods of public advocacy, and responding to demands with induction, personal experience and examples, proofs derived from narratives, and generally personalized rhetoric. She displayed a "feminine" rhetorical style, conveying emotion openly, encouraging self-disclosure from others, and maintaining group harmony. Henry claims that O'Leary wanted to find appropriate solutions and to implement them, which often proved difficult because of public distrust for the Department of Energy. In her presentations she tried to disclose information to the public, to invite independent review, to explain the background of specific situations, to cite examples, and to use illustrations for comparisons of size and amount. Henry also describes the venues O'Leary used for "doing public business in public." He points out their structural requirements (the involvement of stakeholders, open meetings, and increased public discussion), as well as specifically rhetorical aspects, such as the conflict between correct understanding of information and the desire for complete openness and statements concerning moral leadership.

Henry also uses O'Leary's campaign to highlight the potential intersection between ethical and rhetorical concerns. Here, Henry suggests that a rhetorical approach could help negotiate the conflict between the utilitarian ethics of consequences and the ethics of virtue by suggesting a third approach that synthesizes both. He proposes using Nye's "three-dimensional ethics," which evaluates an activity or event's ethical dimensions by examining the relationship among motives, approaches (or means), and consequences. Henry demonstrates that O'Leary was successful as a surrogate advocate and that rhetorical, political, and ethical dimensions all interact in the development of public policy. As Henry argues, O'Leary's short-lived campaign to minimize public fear and loathing toward the U.S. Department of Energy suggests one model for instigating a more collaborative environment for future environmental policymaking.

Presidential Rhetoric and Environmental Governance for the Twenty-first Century

The final section explores new rhetorical opportunities for environmental governance, suggesting that U.S. presidents face audiences that are not content to defer questions of environmental policy to technical experts and are increasingly global in their outlook. Perhaps even more germane to students of rhetoric, public trust in political leadership has eroded along with trust in technical expertise. Increasingly large proportions of the general public demand the right to participate in defining environmental issues rather than simply choosing among options selected by an elite cadre of political insiders. Prelli's and Carcasson's chapters suggest that, within such a lively social context, rhetorical theorists and critics are especially well suited to contribute to the public conversation.

Lawrence J. Prelli provides a detailed examination of a public participation process that grew out of the Clinton administration's preoccupation with community involvement as the means to solve environmental problems. He then shows how traditional rhetorical theory can enhance our understanding of environmental decision making. Prelli begins by reminding us of the difficulties inherent in the development and guidance of collaborative action in the presence of pluralism (such as in the case examined by Moore). He then builds on Cox's claim that sound environmental policy will require rhetoric that exhibits prudence, stewardship, intelligence, and competence. He does this by investigating the problem of judgment within the rhetoric used by citizens who are deliberating environmental policy.

Prelli argues that practical reasoning and situated judgment are essential to environmental debate. He suggests that the rhetorical analyst is well positioned to ask if the rhetoric being used is appropriate to the situation and if it meets practical demands. Pluralism causes complications for those attempting to develop environmental policy, however, because different groups come to the issue with different standards of judgment. Prelli suggests that traditional rhetorical theory can provide a means for discovering acceptable standards such as the taken-for-granted value premise and general patterns of thought that influence decision making.

Prelli examines the rhetoric of the New Hampshire Forest Sustainability Standards Work Team, a group of shareholders who tried to implement sustainability, a concept much celebrated by the Clinton administration. The study demonstrates how the use of different standards can cause a single action to be judged positively or negatively, depending on the standard used. In this case, sustainability was judged in terms of either human utility or ecosystem integrity. Separately each argument appeared valid, yet they contradicted each other. Gradual awareness of this juxtaposition led to the realization of interdependence and the need for mutually agreeable principles of coordinated action. Ultimately, the group provided a variety of options in order to make people aware of better alternatives to their current practices, to allow landowners to retain control of their land, and to avoid the negative response typically associated with additional regulations.

Prelli's chapter reiterates the largely unrealized political potential of rhetorical analysis, as well as suggesting that broad public participation in discussions of environmental policy offers an opportunity to refine traditional rhetorical concepts. His analysis responds directly to Cox's concern with the limitations of civic republicanism as practiced by Clinton. Prelli suggests that while recognition of broad community interests does not solve all environmental problems, it does create opportunities for their resolution. Carefully designed public processes can be used creatively to develop reasoned alternatives. Prelli does not argue that effective public processes enable people to replace personal preferences with community goals. Rather, he argues that rhetorical theory can be used to enhance practical environmental communication and advocacy, and to contribute to a more sophisticated understanding of public processes; an understanding that includes the ability to move beyond personal preferences to collaborative action. In the political culture following from Clinton's civic republicanism, opportunities for public involvement in environmental decision making have expanded far beyond that mandated by the National Environment Policy Act. Prelli emphasizes that, within this realm, effective rhetoric must minimize polarization and emphasize collaborative pursuit of the best alternative as defined by a pluralistic audience.

Martín Carcasson concludes this exploration of presidential rhetoric and environmental policy with a study that expands the notion of the rhetorical presidency to questions of international governance. Carcasson considers the years from 1988 to 2000 and points out opportunities and constraints associated with the rhetoric of George H. Bush and Bill Clinton. The issue of global warming provides Carcasson with a quintessentially rhetorical issue on which to focus his analysis. Although the existence of global warming is not in doubt, its specific causes and its potential sociopolitical significance are the subject of acrimonious debate. It is likely that no other environmental issue so fully represents the increasingly global nature of environmental policy. Not surprisingly, Carcasson's analysis of presidential rhetoric regarding the international environment finds many of the same limitations discovered in rhetoric focused on domestic issues. Carcasson's analysis reveals that both Bush and Clinton fell far short of proposing necessary actions to confront the developing international environmental crisis. Further, despite each president's claims to the contrary, neither demonstrated the ability to minimize polarization and emphasize the collaborative pursuits that Prelli suggests could lead to a more rhetorically informed participation in environmental politics.

Carcasson is interested not in blaming or absolving Bush and Clinton (or any other U.S. president) for this failure, however, but in exploring its contextualization within the contemporary American political system. For this, Carcasson turns to Luhmann's theory of function systems, which identifies six functions that characterize modern society. Using this theoretical framework, Carcasson attempts to clarify how Clinton's and Bush's environmental rhetoric constrains the opportunities for serious responses to environmental problems. He delineates which function systems dominate and which are neglected in their rhetoric.

Carcasson shows how this social structure has constrained political action and then uses his initial analysis as the basis for suggesting new possibilities that could transform the debate into one that enhances opportunities for making public judgments within a pluralistic society, by explicitly including the concepts of prudence, stewardship, intelligence, and competence, as identified by Cox and Prelli. He argues that rhetorical analysis of public controversy (including, but not limited to environmental issues) should identify constraints to action for the purpose of developing appropriate strategies for challenging those constraints. By explicating the systemic social context within which we encounter environmental problems, Carcasson attempts to suggest how environmental advocates can influence the rhetorical situation faced by political actors in ways that enable them to respond more proactively to environmental challenges.

New Directions for Theory and Practice

Perhaps President Clinton's vacillation regarding environmental policy reflects the anxiety of a society entering a new millennium. Exploring the connections between presidential rhetoric and environmental policy provides a means for examining that anxiety and for more fully understanding our relationship (both its material and its symbolic dimensions) with the environment upon which we rely. As we move into the twenty-first century our entire means for making sense of the universe is in flux. Even the cherished taxonomic distinctions between living and nonliving matter are questioned. It is no wonder that the sense of order found in Thoreau's *Walden* or the sublime purity of Muir's Yosemite as interpreted through Ansel Adams beckons. Clarence Glacken claims that the most striking aspect of human conceptions of nature is "the yearning for purpose and order." If it does nothing else, rhetoric provides order to otherwise confused complexity. The very use of the term *environment,* for example, enables us to impose order on nature. Berleant points out that it enables us to reconstruct the earth as "an entity that we can think of and deal with as if it were outside and independent of ourselves." As Kenneth Burke argues, language provides humans with the ability to identify with, and separate ourselves from something or someone else. Thus we turn to the concept of agency to discover that, just as humans have chosen to separate themselves from their natural environment, so can they choose to reunite themselves with it. An explicitly rhetorical approach to environmental issues enables such efforts to proceed within a spirit of friendly skepticism (as opposed to cynicism).[32]

This book illustrates how the incorporation of multiple perspectives and approaches can enhance both our theory and practice by supplying missing strengths and mitigating weaknesses. Although this integration is unusual, it is not unique. Kevin DeLuca's "Trains in the Wilderness: Myths, Corporations, and Environmental Politics" weaves together concepts from political, rhetorical, and critical theory. *Rhetoric and Public Affairs,* the interdisciplinary journal where his study was published, illustrates the new venues that are developing for the crosscutting research this collection seeks to encourage. I hope this volume will provoke readers to think about both presidential rhetoric and environmental communication in new ways, thus providing the spark for an increasingly productive dialogue between public address and environmental communication scholars.[33]

Notes

1. Tarla Rai Peterson, "Environmental Communication: Tales of Life on Earth," *Quarterly Journal of Speech* 84 (1998): 371–93.
2. For overviews of the development of environmental communication within the communication discipline, see James G. Cantrill, "Communication and Our Environment: Categorizing Research in Environmental Advocacy," *Journal of Applied Communication Research* 21 (1993): 66–95; Stephen P. Depoe, "Environmental Studies in Mass Communication," *Critical Studies in Mass Communication* 14 (1997): 368–72; and Stephen P. Depoe, "Talking about the Earth: On the Growing Significance of Environmental Communication Studies," *Rhetoric and Public Affairs* 1 (1998): 435–68.
3. M. Jimmie Killingsworth and Jacqueline S. Palmer, *Ecospeak: Rhetoric and Environmental Politics in America* (Carbondale: Southern Illinois University Press, 1992).
4. Star A. Muir and Thomas L. Veenendall, eds., *Earthtalk: Communication Empowerment for Environmental Action* (Westport, Conn.: Praeger Press, 1996); Carl G. Herndl and Stuart C. Brown, eds., *Green Culture: Rhetorical Analyses of Environmental Discourse* (Madison: University of Wisconsin Press, 1996); James G. Cantrill and Christine L. Oravec, eds., *The Symbolic Earth: Discourse and Our Creation of the Environment* (Lexington: University Press of Kentucky, 1996).
5. Tarla Rai Peterson, *Sharing the Earth: The Rhetoric of Sustainable Development* (Columbia: University of South Carolina Press, 1997).
6. Craig Waddell, ed., *Landmark Essays on Rhetoric and the Environment* (Hillsdale, N.J.: Lawrence Erlbaum Associates, 1997). The Environmental Communication Network (ECN) maintains environmental communication bibliographies at http://www.esf.edu/ecn/bibl.htm; proceedings of the biennial conferences on communication and the environment from 1991 through 2001 are listed at and can be obtained through this site. Susan Senecah, ed., Stephen Depoe, Mark Neuzil, and Gregg Walker, assoc. eds., *The Environmental Communication Yearbook* (Hillsdale, N.J.: Laurence Erlbaum, 2004).
7. Martin J. Medhurst, "A Tale of Two Constructs: The Rhetorical Presidency versus Presidential Rhetoric," in *Beyond the Rhetorical Presidency,* ed. Martin J. Medhurst (College Station: Texas A&M University Press, 1996), xiii, xiv.
8. Ibid., xiv–xx. See also Theodore Windt, "Presidential Rhetoric: Definition of a Discipline of Study," in *Essays in Presidential Rhetoric,* ed. Theodore Ingold and Beth Ingold (Dubuque, Iowa: Kendall/Hunt, 1987), xxiii; Martin J. Medhurst, "American Public Address: A Tradition in Transition," in *Landmark Essays on American Public Address,* ed. Medhurst (Davis, Calif.: Hermagoras Press, 1993), xi–xliii.
9. Dennis L. Soden and Brent S. Steel, "Evaluating the Environmental Presidency," in *The Environmental Presidency,* ed. Soden (Albany: State University of New York Press, 1999), 348; Soden, ed., *The Environmental Presidency,* 2–3.
10. Peterson, *Sharing the Earth,* 6.
11. Medhurst, "Public Address and Significant Scholarship: Four Challenges to the Rhetorical Renaissance," in *Texts in Context: Critical Dialogues on Significant Episodes in American Political Rhetoric,* ed. Michael C. Leff and Fred J. Kauffeld (Davis, Calif.: Hermagoras Press, 1989), 33.

12. Bruce E. Gronbeck, "The Presidency in the Age of Secondary Orality," in *Beyond the Rhetorical Presidency*, 30–49; Thomas W. Benson, "Desktop Demos: New Communication Technologies and the Future of the Rhetorical Presidency," in *Beyond the Rhetorical Presidency*, 50–74; Robert L. Ivie, "Tragic Fear and the Rhetorical Presidency: Combating Evil in the Persian Gulf," in *Beyond the Rhetorical Presidency*,153–78, quotation on 162; Robert L. Ivie, "A New Democratic World Order," in *Critical Reflections on the Cold War: Linking Rhetoric and History*, ed. Martin J. Medhurst and H. W. Brands (College Station: Texas A&M Press, 2000), 262.

13. Kevin M. DeLuca, *Image Politics: The New Rhetoric of Environmental Activism* (New York: Guilford, 1998); Phaedra Pezullo, "Toxic Tours: Communicating the Presence of Chemical Contamination," in *Proceedings of the Sixth Biennial Conference on Communication and Environment*, ed. Marie-France Aepli, John W. Delicath, and Stephen P. Depoe (Cincinnati: University of Cincinnati, 2000), 1–12; Carole Blair, "Challenges and Openings in Rethinking Rhetoric: Contemporary U.S. Memorial Sites as Exemplars of Rhetoric's Materiality," in *Rhetorical Bodies: Toward a Material Rhetoric*, ed. Jack Selzer and Susan Crowley (Madison: University of Wisconsin Press, 1998), 16–57; Jack Selzer, "Habeas Corpus: An Introduction," in *Rhetorical Bodies*, 3–15.

14. J. Robert Cox, "The Die Is Cast: Topical and Ontological Dimensions of the Locus of the Irreparable," *Quarterly Journal of Speech* 68 (1982): 227–39; Craig Waddell, *Landmark Essays on Rhetoric and the Environment*.

15. Peterson, "Environmental Communication," 372; see also Peterson, *Sharing the Earth*, 36–39.

16. Ulrich Beck, *Risk Society: Towards a New Modernity*, trans. Mark Ritter (Newbury Park, Calif.: Sage, 1992); Anthony Giddens, *The Consequences of Modernity* (Stanford, Calif.: Stanford University Press, 1990); Anthony Giddens, *Modernity and Identity in the Late Modern Age* (Stanford, Calif.: Stanford University Press, 1991); Niklas Luhmann, *Ecological Communication*, trans. John Bednarz, Jr. (Chicago: University of Chicago Press, 1989); Peterson, *Sharing the Earth*.

17. Celeste Michelle Condit, *The Meanings of the Gene: Public Debates about Human Heredity* (Madison: University of Wisconsin Press, 1999). See also Thomas Gieryn, *Cultural Boundaries of Science: Credibility on the Line* (Chicago: University of Chicago Press, 1999); Jeanne Fahnestock, *Rhetorical Figures in Science* (New York: Oxford University Press, 1999).

18. Beck, *Risk Society*.

19. Paul K. Feyerabend, *Knowledge, Science, and Relativism* (Cambridge, Eng., and New York: Cambridge University Press, 1999), 146.

20. Peterson, "Subverting the Culture of Expertise: Community Participation in Development Decisions," in *Sharing the Earth*, 86–118.

21. Examples include Celeste M. Condit, "Crafting Virtue: The Rhetorical Construction of Public Morality," *Quarterly Journal of Speech* 73 (1987): 79–97; Walter Fisher, *Human Communication as Narration* (Columbia: University of South Carolina Press, 1987); G. Thomas Goodnight, "The Personal, Technical, and Public Spheres of Argument: A Speculative Inquiry into the Art of Public Deliberation," *Journal of American Forensics Association* 18 (1982): 214–27; G. Thomas Goodnight, "Public Discourse," *Critical Studies in Mass Communication* (1987): 428–32; G. Thomas Goodnight and D. B. Hingstman, "Studies in the Public Sphere," *Quarterly Journal of Speech* 83 (1997): 351–99.

22. Caitlin Wills Toker, "The Vocabulary of Consensus: Struggle and Redefinition in the Georgia Port Authority's Stakeholder Evaluation Group," paper presented at the National Communication Association Convention, Atlanta, Nov. 2001.

23. Robert L. Ivie, "Democratic Deliberation in a Rhetorical Republic," *Quarterly Journal of Speech* 84 (1998): 491–505; see also Nancy Fraser, "Rethinking the Public Sphere: A Contribution to the Critique of Actual Existing Democracy," in *Habermas and the Public Sphere*, ed. Craig Calhoun (Cambridge: MIT Press, 1992), 109–42.

24. Chantal Mouffe, "Deliberative Democracy or Agonistic Pluralism?" *Social Research* 66 (1999): 745–58.

25. Samuel P. Hayes, *Conservation and the Gospel of Efficiency: The Progressive Conservation Movement, 1890–1920* (Cambridge, Mass.: Harvard University Press, 1959); Benjamin Kline, *First along the River* (San Francisco: Acada Books, 2000); Roderick Nash, *Wilderness and the American Mind* (New Haven: Yale University Press, 1982).

26. Peterson, "The Will to Conservation: A Burkeian Analysis of Dust Bowl Rhetoric and American Farming Motives," *Southern Speech Communication Journal* 52 (1986): 1–21; Anna Lou Riesch, "Conservation under Franklin Roosevelt," in *The American Environment: Readings in the History of Conservation*, ed. Roderick Nash (London: Addison-Wesley, 1968); Donald Worster, *Dust Bowl: The Southern Plains in the 1930s* (London: Oxford University Press, 1979).

27. Robert Gottlieb, *Forcing the Spring: The Transformation of the American Environmental Movement* (Washington, D.C.: Island Press, 1993); Philip Shabecoff, *A Fierce Green Fire: The American Environmental Movement* (New York: Hill and Wang, 1993).

28. Rachel Carson, *Silent Spring* (New York: Houghton Mifflin, 1962). For examples of rhetorical analyses *of Silent Spring*, see Craig Waddell, ed., *And No Birds Sing: Rhetorical Analyses of Rachel Carson's* Silent Spring (Carbondale: Southern Illinois University Press, 2000).

29. Gottlieb, *Forcing the Spring;* Kline, *First along the River.*

30. Andrew Rowell, *Green Backlash: Global Subversion of the Environmental Movement* (London and New York: Routledge, 1996); C. Brant Short, *Ronald Reagan and the Public Lands: America's Conservation Debate, 1979–1984* (College Station: Texas A&M University Press, 1989).

31. Peterson, "Sustainable Development Goes to Rio: Implications for Global Environmental Governance," in *Sharing the Earth,* 54–85; Peterson and Kathi L. Groenendyk (Pauley), "George Bush Goes to Rio: Implications for U.S. Participation in Environmental Governance," in *Rhetoric in Intercultural Contexts,* ed. Alberto Gonzalez and Dolores V. Tanno (Thousand Oaks, Calif.: Sage, 2000), 67–90.

32. Henry David Thoreau, *Walden, or Life in the Woods* (New York: Vintage Books/Library of America, 1991); Ansel Adams, *The American Wilderness/The Photographs of Ansel Adams with the Writings of John Muir,* ed. Elaine M. Bucher (Philadelphia: Courage Books, 1997); Clarence J. Glacken, *Traces on the Rhodian Shore* (Berkeley: University of California Press, 1967), 3; Arnold Berleant. *The Aesthetics of Environment* (Philadelphia: Temple University Press, 1992), 3; Kenneth Burke, *A Rhetoric of Motives* (Berkeley: University of California Press, 1969), 19–26, 45–55, 138–41; Kenneth Burke, *Language as Symbolic Action: Essays on Life, Literature, and Method* (Berkeley: University of California Press, 1966), 15–16, 87–89, 301–302.

33. Kevin M. DeLuca. "Trains in the Wilderness: Myths, Corporations, and Environmental Politics," *Rhetoric and Public Affairs* 4 (2001):633–52.

PART I

Environmental

Rhetoric and the

New Frontier

1 Preaching Conservation

Theodore Roosevelt and the Rhetoric of Civil Religion

Leroy G. Dorsey

"The story is told of a congressman who, when pressed to aid in the conservation of his country's natural resources for posterity's sake, retorted, 'What has posterity ever done for me?'" This anecdote reflects the lack of awareness many Americans had regarding the environment and the need for its conservation at the turn of the twentieth century. For the most part, people believed that environmental resources were infinite. This attitude made nature fair game for various industries. For example, coal beds, once thought inexhaustible, were in danger of being depleted. The journalist C. H. Forbes-Lindsay reported that by the mid-1880s "four billion tons were mined by methods so wasteful that more than an equal quantity was either destroyed or left in the ground in such state as to be inaccessible for ever." According to the historian Frank Graham, Jr., the last half of the nineteenth century was dubbed the "age of extermination." "The new technology and the relentless westward march of civilization," Graham observed, facilitated the "hit-and-run raids on the continent's natural resources." Such raids took their toll on many animal species. For instance, the American buffalo once numbered in the hundred millions. Shot for sport by tourists riding past herds on trains and professionally hunted for their hides, the great beasts were nearly wiped out by the late 1800s.[1]

The lumber industry's practices with regard to the nation's forests, however, involved perhaps the most far-reaching consequences for the environment. "With the invention of the circular saw and the steam sawmill in the early 1800s," noted the historian Jack Shepherd, "wholesale deforestation began in earnest." Because of public land giveaways and inadequate homestead laws, loggers moved quickly through the Great Lake states, the Rockies, and the Pacific Northwest "blasting the trees into manageable size with gunpowder, wasting half the timber and burning what was left." Such practices by the timber industry had its costs. Thomas Will, secretary of the American Forestry Association in 1908, warned that unrestrained cutting of forested areas resulted in a host of related problems: by clearing vast areas of trees, trees that acted as natural dams for rainwater, millions of dollars of flooding damage occurred each year. The resulting floods caused billions of tons of soil to be washed into rivers, constituting a loss of fertilizing topsoil estimated at one billion dollars; with the soil clogging the country's waterways, navigation became increasingly difficult and costlier as well.[2]

With this assault on the environment in full force at the turn of the century, Theodore Roosevelt entered the White House in 1901. His background as a rancher, naturalist, and hunter gave him an appreciation for nature and its maintenance. While many advocates attempted to generate interest in conserving the environment, President Roosevelt was among the most successful. The biographer Paul Cutright observed that it was "only after Roosevelt put the full force of his power as president" behind conservation that "it got off the ground."[3]

During his two terms, Roosevelt oversaw an array of conservation initiatives concerning the land, the animals, and the forests. Because of his influence the 1902 Newlands Reclamation Act, which authorized the building of dams to facilitate the irrigation of arid lands, moved through a resistant Congress. As a result of this legislation, thousands of acres of once unproductive land were transformed into agriculturally viable areas. To prevent speculators and corporations from acquiring and using land fraudulently, Roosevelt repealed the Forest Lieu Land Act of 1897; this gave actual settlers more access to public land. In 1906 the president withdrew 66 million acres of land from the public domain to safeguard their development as coal deposits. Concerning animals and their habitats, Roosevelt established the first federal wildlife refuge in 1903 on Pelican Island off the east coast of Florida. This refuge protected birds that were nearing extinction due to plume hunters. Over the next few years he created fifty more wildlife sanctuaries across the United States and Puerto Rico. Perhaps the most significant measure concerning natural habitats came in 1906 with the passage of the Antiquities Act. This bill gave Roosevelt the discretionary power to establish historic areas as national monuments, eighteen of which he created, including California's Muir Woods and Arizona's Grand Canyon. Regarding the forests, Roosevelt placed the management of the forest reserves under the control of the Forest Service headed by his trusted friend Gifford Pinchot. In addition, the Agriculture Appropriations Act that same year gave the Forest Service the means to create new reserves. Perhaps Roosevelt's most well known act regarding forest conservation involved his "midnight proclamation" of 1907. He signed several proclamations that placed 16 million acres of timberland under federal protection just two days before he signed a bill into law that would have prevented him from taking the former action. By the end of his presidency, 150 million acres of forested areas had been safeguarded.[4]

In some cases, the president took unilateral, often untouted action. For example, when Roosevelt created the first federal wildlife sanctuary, there was no attending public fanfare. In determining how to protect the birds of Pelican Island, Roosevelt inquired whether there existed a law that would prevent him from turning that island into a federally protected reservation. According to Cutright, "When assured there was none . . . [Roosevelt] replied, 'Very well, then I so declare it.'" The passage of other initiatives, such as the Newlands Reclamation Act, was sometimes the result of private wrangling between the president and members of Congress.[5]

Stated another way, Roosevelt's public discourse did not have as its subject matter individual legislation. Rather, part of his rhetorical legacy as an advocate of the environment comes from his public messages that attempted to etch the broader notion of conservation—the prudent use of *sacred* natural resources as supervised by the federal government—in the national consciousness. As Donald Bryant might observe, Roosevelt's rhetoric worked to adjust the idea of conservation to the people and the people to the idea of conservation.[6] In this regard the president faced several challenges. The public failed to recognize that the environment was in danger. Roosevelt wrote in his autobiography that the idea "that our natural resources were inexhaustible" was prominent in American culture. Second, some special interests publicly weighed in against conservation. According to Cutright, they "took advantage of the misinterpretation" many people had of the term "forest reserve" to argue that national forest reserves would indeed be sanctuaries "where no timber could be cut and no game shot."[7] Third, Congress resisted the president on many conservation issues. Congress' reasons for its intractability ranged from being lobbied by private interests to protect their economic livelihood to anger at what it considered Rooseveltian arrogance concerning the federal government's role in safeguarding the environment.[8] Given the apathy and outright resistance by the general public, special interests, and legislative leaders, how did Roosevelt publicly promote the protection of the environment to such a degree with these constituencies that he became what one historian called "one of the great conservationist presidents in the nation's history?"[9]

Beyond cursory interpretations of his discourse in various biographies, rhetorical scholarship on Roosevelt's conservation rhetoric is limited.[10] Elsewhere, I argue that the president's campaign for conservation succeeded because he contextualized the issue within a radically altered frontier myth: the traditional conqueror-heroes of the unlimited frontier who marked progress by subduing nature without regard for their successors was replaced by Roosevelt with the yeoman farmers who worked to conserve a finite environment, thus realizing their moral purpose in safeguarding nature's resource for others to use.

This mythic storyline may have helped the president attain short-term gains, but given the lack of prominence in American culture of the farmer-as-hero icon and the misconception of the environment's infinite nature, another explanation for Roosevelt's legacy as a conservation leader is warranted.[11]

That explanation lies in viewing Roosevelt's conservation rhetoric as a manifestation of civil religion. Simply put, despite the edict of a separate church and state, there exists a tangible religious dimension, perhaps even a religion itself, institutionalized in politics. According to the historians Richard Pierard and Robert Linder, the practice of civil religion "involves the mixing of traditional religion with national life until it is impossible to distinguish between the two"; in the process it becomes a "general faith, one that stands in contrast to the particular faith of denominational groups which claim the allegiance of only a segment of the population." The president, especially a rhetorically active one, serves as the chief spokesperson for this religion and can promote a political and social agenda using it. Roosevelt took on this role. Pierard and Linder observed that Roosevelt was one of the "most noted White House 'preachers'" whose "pontifical moral judgments echoed" from the presidential podium he labeled the "bully pulpit."[12]

Specifically, I argue that Roosevelt contextualized the idea of conservation within a civil religious construct, giving that idea a primacy heretofore unseen in the public sphere. To that end, he took his message public and depicted a charitable God that had bestowed upon the nation an environmental wonderland that renewed Americans' physical and spiritual energy, as well as marked them as "the chosen." For the president, such a God-given bounty was sacred and in need of protection. Like a prophet sitting in judgment, Roosevelt chastised those people that disregarded the sacred nature of the environment. He identified two groups of sinners: those business people, particularly the lumber owners, who greedily destroyed the nation's forested areas for economic profit, and the public-at-large, which acted indifferently or slothfully toward the environment. Finally, Roosevelt assumed the role of priest and offered his flock the means for salvation. The nation could achieve civil redemption for its sins if it accepted the idea of a conservation program headed by the federal government. This civil religious construct of God, sin, and redemption allowed Roosevelt to link the environment and conservation to morality and, in turn, to the institutional and cultural values embodied in the national government. In the process, he sanctioned the preeminence of an activist federal government over the individual states.

Civil Religion in American Culture

Sociologist Robert Bellah's 1967 article "Civil Religion in America" stimulated a lively and still-continuing debate concerning religion and politics. Examining the discourse of several American presidents, most notably John Kennedy's inaugural address, Bellah argued that these texts reveal that there "actually exists alongside of and rather clearly differentiated from the churches an elaborate and well-institutionalized civil religion in America." While not necessarily constituting a religion itself, American civil religion invokes "certain common elements of religious orientation" that many people share, providing a "religious dimension for the whole fabric of American life." This "dimension" places the political process under a transcendent goal: that "America be a society as perfectly in accord with the will of God as men can make it." Behind civil religion "at every point," Bellah observed, "lie biblical archetypes: Exodus, Chosen People, Promised Land . . . [and] Sacrificial Death and Rebirth." In other words, civil religion reflects a rhetoric of the sacred as realized through the expression of political ideology. Bellah concluded that civil religion, like traditional religions, has its own prophets (Truman forewarning of the confrontation between democracy and communism); martyrs (Lincoln sacrificed to peace); sacred events (Memorial Day as a ritual expression of national sacrifice); sacred places (Arlington National Cemetery); solemn rituals (the presidential inauguration as the "religious legitimation of the highest political authority"); and symbols (the American flag).[13]

Essentially, Bellah wrote years later, any knee-jerk reaction of disdain for the relationship between politics and religion was unwise. "Religion and morality and politics are not the same things," he admitted, but "cutting all links between them can lead to even worse distortions." With religion as a framework, the nation-state and its citizens could realize such revered concepts as civility, moral purpose, and freedom. Understanding the substance and expression of civil religion, then, is crucial to the development of American culture: "A republic . . . must have a purpose and a set of values. . . . For this reason it inevitably pushes toward the symbolization of an ultimate order of existence in which republican values and virtues make sense. Such symbolization may be nothing more than the worship of the republic itself as the highest good, or it may be, as in the American case, the worship of a higher reality that upholds the standards the republic attempts to embody."[14]

Bellah's articulation of civil religion drew both its staunch supporters and determined detractors. Of the former group, several advocated the pervasiveness of civil religion. The religion and public policy scholar Michael Novak noted that it was natural for the government to elevate itself to the level of a national church. Since "no one church was allowed to become the official guardian of the central symbols of the United States," he observed, "the nation itself began to fill the vacuum" by becoming its "own unifying symbol system, the chief bestower of identity and purpose." In invoking a civil religion, the nation-state tapped into the overarching belief system of traditional religions and promoted a set of values "*as the cohesive force and center of meaning,*" which can unite disparate groups of people. The religion scholar Will Herberg likewise reiterated the relationship between politics and religion realized in what he called "the American Way of Life." Herberg noted that our governing institutions, replete with their political saints and symbols, provide an "organic structure of ideas, values, and beliefs that constitute a faith common to Americans as Americans . . . a faith that markedly influences, and is influenced by, the professed religions of America."[15]

Critics voiced a number of objections to descriptions of civil religion and the depiction of the government as a quasi-religious entity promoting universal norms. For instance, the religion scholar Herbert Richardson warned of the dangers surrounding the belief in civil religion by questioning the nature of its existence. "When any political party identifies its program with a utopian vision and the kingdom of God," Richardson wrote, "the more justified it feels in pursuing this program with unqualified zeal and the less likely it will be to accept criticism or compromise." In other words, dressing policies such as American imperialism with the trappings of religion may unfairly protect them from critical scrutiny. For Richardson, the promotion of civil religion reflects the petty nature of political institutions: "Since modern democratic theories of sovereignty can imagine no alternative institution possessing sufficient universality to claim a general authority to order the whole of society, the state establishes its sovereignty over space, time, property and persons." Similarly, another critic noted the base nature of civil religion and its resemblance to nothing more than what might be called political "dirty tricks." The historian George Kelly concluded that after "all is said and done about American civil religion, it seems to be an artifact of the secularizing process, cloaking profane practices with a sacred terminology and mock-sacred justifications and repudiations."[16]

Ultimately, the debate over civil religion should not stop at whether such a concept should exist, nor necessarily why it exists. From a pragmatic perspective alone, a key question should be how civil religion, this merger of politics and faith, is made real for Americans. According to Pierard and Linder, civil religion's pervasiveness (and hence its persuasiveness) stems from its "politicized ideological base," including the articulation of a God, that that entity's will can be known, and that the nation-state as God's agent represents the primary source of identity for Americans.[17]

That is, a civil religious construct can contain, at its most basic level, three components that find expression rhetorically. First, a rhetorician reveals a divine being which, in turn, provides the framework for those things and ideas that should be considered sacred. Second, given the awareness of what is sacred, the rhetorician can act as a judge who can condemn the community for failing to adhere to God's will. Finally, the rhetorician can offer salvation to the community; in this process of redemption, the transcendent nature of the nation-state is established, the virtues of the republic are affirmed, and the members of the community can once again see themselves in the role of good citizens.

As president and chief spokesperson for the nation's policy initiatives and pious inclinations, Theodore Roosevelt merged the ideas of conservation and religion within a civil religious construct. For him, a charitable God had provided Americans with an environmental bounty that marked it as sacred. To abuse it, as some were doing, he condemned as a sin against God. Ultimately, however, the community could save itself if it accepted the idea of a government-controlled conservation program.

The Beneficent God

Like many officially recognized denominations, civil religion identifies a supreme deity as a focal point for humanity's adoration and angst. "'God' has clearly been a central symbol in the civil religion from the beginning," Bellah observed, and "is just as central to the civil religion as it is to Judaism or Christianity." Furthermore, Bellah noted, this entity, while "somewhat deist in cast" is "by no means simply a watchmaker God," but one that is "actively interested" in American culture. The rhetorical scholar Rod Hart extended Bellah's observation, arguing that chief executives have called upon a pantheon of deities running the gamut from those that directly intervene in human affairs, watch from a distance, and provide counsel as well as rewards to those that deserve but do not demand reverence. In much of Roosevelt's first-term conservation rhetoric, America's God largely resembled what Hart labeled as "God the Genial Philanthropist," a being that dispensed "both material and emotional gifts to the deserving."[18] In this case the supreme entity bestowed its blessing in the form of a magnificent, natural environment. By emphasizing the God-given aspect of nature to his audiences, Roosevelt hoped to establish the sacred nature of the environment.

President Roosevelt wasted no time in establishing the philanthropic disposition of America's God. Early in his first term, on a trip to the western United States in 1903, the theme of the environment as a God-given paradise, as the realization of Eden appeared throughout his rhetoric. "I have been traveling through what is literally a garden of the Lord," Roosevelt declared before a California audience, "in sight of the majestic and wonderful scenery of the mountains."[19] "The lakes, the mountains, [and] the canyons," Roosevelt observed at Yellowstone National Park, resemble a "veritable wonderland" and "make this region something not wholly to be paralleled elsewhere on the globe."[20] On most occasions the president invoked the supreme deity by identifying its eternal essence; in these accounts audiences were reminded that vast stretches of time were involved in the creation of the environment, signifying the hallowed nature of it. Of the Grand Canyon, Roosevelt observed that "the ages have been at work on it" and "man can only . . . mar the wonderful grandeur, the sublimity, the great loneliness and beauty of the Canyon." Days later he remarked to a Stanford University audience that California contained some of the "great wonders of the world" including such marvels as a grove of trees "which it has taken the ages several thousand years to build."[21]

Beyond the visual magnificence of nature, America's wilderness held a special place in religious thought. According to Bellah, the Bible linked the idea of a wilderness with a sense of renewal. Early settlers in North America believed that a "profound personal, ecclesiastical, and world-historical meaning" could be discovered by experiencing the divinity of nature.[22]

Roosevelt's civil religion also emphasized this spiritual dimension of the environment. For him, the wilderness fortified the body and the soul. In his 1901 first annual message he recognized that Americans needed to preserve the "splendid forests and flower-clad meadows" so they could "find rest, health, and recreation." Perhaps more importantly, he declared two years later, nature acted as the catalyst for humanity to reach "the higher life of the intellect, the spirit and the soul." Experiencing the handiwork of the supreme deity allowed Americans to be in direct contact with God. At the Sacramento capitol in 1903 Roosevelt revealed the potential for spiritual fulfillment in nature: "Lying out at night under those giant Sequoias was lying in a temple built by no hand of man, a temple grander than any human architect could by any possibility build, and I hope for the preservation of the groves of giant trees simply because it would be a shame to our civilization to let them disappear. They are monuments in themselves."[23]

By linking nature to God through metaphors, Roosevelt appealed to his audience's moral imagination and defined its ethical responsibility to the environment. The philosophy scholar Mark Johnson observed that humanity's moral understanding should not be viewed as "consisting entirely of the bringing of concrete cases under . . . [absolute] rules that specify 'the right thing to do' in a given instance." Rather, Johnson noted, moral understanding is imaginatively created and metaphors constitute a chief component in that construction: "virtually all of our fundamental moral concepts—cause, action, well-being, state, duty, right, freedom, and so forth—are metaphorically defined . . . [and most] of our moral reasoning is reasoning based on metaphors."[24] When Roosevelt likened nature to a temple, the trees as monuments, the environment as an Edenic wonderland, he not only invested the earth with a special sacredness but also consequently endowed conservation of that sacred space with a moral imperative.

Since the environment represented God's blessing it was sacred and must be preserved. However, the conservation of the environment did not mean it would remain untouched. For Roosevelt, the godly magnificence of nature could be preserved only through its use. He declared that Southern California, a "veritable garden of the earth," had preserved its Eden-like appearance because the people had effectively utilized the waters of that region. "Keep the waters . . . [and] the forests," Roosevelt commanded at the state capitol in California, "so that by the very fact of the use they will become more valuable as possessions." According to the bully pulpiteer, humanity's use of nature perpetuated God's gift: "going over this plain tilled by the hand of man . . . [it] has blossomed like the rose—blossomed as I never dreamed in my life that the rose could blossom." To fully appreciate the environment, then, Americans would be its caretakers.[25]

The president's choice of a munificent God also reflected on the recipients of its generosity. If the supreme being deigned to provide such a majestic bounty, Americans should then consider themselves worthy of such a gift. According to Bellah, this notion that Americans "are an especially choice and chosen people" had existed since the early seventeenth century. Roosevelt continued this line of thinking in his 1905 inaugural address. The "Giver of Good," he declared, has "blessed us with the conditions which have enabled us to achieve so large a measure of well-being and of happiness." God's gifts, he continued, illustrated that Americans were "heirs of the ages."[26] In reminding the nation that "much has been given to us, and much will rightfully be expected from us," Roosevelt confirmed God's benevolence, established the need to piously respect that God-given charity, and reiterated Americans' sense of being a "chosen" people.[27]

The God identified in Roosevelt's conservation rhetoric appeared as a generous entity, which provided a majestic environment that instilled a physical, spiritual, and moral grandeur in American culture. However, this divine link between the supreme deity and the chosen of America, the president assessed, seemed to be at the breaking point.

Transgressions against God

As the chief voice for the nation's civil religion, the president can choose between two varieties of civil religious discourse labeled the "prophetic" and the
"priestly." According to Pierard and Linder, the former term embodies a person who "stands before the people and speaks to them the necessary (and sometimes unpleasant) words from God," while the latter term reflects an individual
who "speaks on behalf of the people" before God.[28] Fundamentally, the prophet
renders judgment and calls for repentance while the priest provides comfort
and praise. These types of rhetoric are not mutually exclusive in traditional
faiths; however, the prophetic mode has been primarily used by presidents since
the beginning of American culture through the mid-1900s and the priestly mode
through the latter half of the twentieth century.[29]

In fulfilling his or her function in speaking the "unpleasant words" from
God, the prophet identified sacrilegious behaviors and subsequently judged
the quality of the relationship between the supreme deity and its people as
wanting. These transgressions, or sins, signaled a broken relationship between
the principal parties.[30] The sociologist Stanford Lyman noted that sin refers to
"humanity's separation from the powers and protections of the gods"; the existence of sinful behavior, then, meant that humankind was essentially alienated from God and doomed to spend an earthly lifetime of loneliness with no
peace of mind.[31] Assuming the role of prophet, Roosevelt declared that Americans had disregarded the sacred nature of the environment. Specifically, the
president identified two major sins being committed against the supreme deity's
gifts: the sins of greed and indifference (also known as sloth).

Greed constitutes a human being's extreme desire for the possession of
material wealth. Given this almost insatiable appetite for riches, sinners faced
the dismal prospect of trying to acquire more and more while realizing that
they could never acquire enough. This state of constant anxiety, Lyman wrote,
illustrated the "especially sinful quality of greed . . . the shift from the worship
of God to the worship of mammon." According to him, the early church's "concern over the worldly desire for money is precisely located in its recognition of
the terrible potentiality for man to place another god, secular and earthly, before the deity rendered sacred by religious authority."[32]

Roosevelt pointed an accusing finger at the lumber industry, which disregarded the sacred nature of the forests. For him greed lay behind the attack on
the environment. He chastised those business people who sinned by worship-
ping the environment solely for its financial worth rather than as a gift from
God. It was the "short-sighted greed of a few," Roosevelt stated in 1901, that
threatened the forests. "We have passed the stage," he charged during a 1903

address in Idaho, "when we can afford to tolerate the man whose object is simply to skin the land and get out." In 1905 Roosevelt condemned lumber barons who authorized clear-cutting, sometimes in an area that spanned thousands of acres: "You all know . . . the individual whose idea of developing the country is to cut every stick of timber off of it and then leave a barren desert for the homemaker who comes in after him. That man is a curse and not a blessing to the country." At the present rate of greed-induced deforestation, he warned, "a timber famine in the future is inevitable."[33]

For the most part Roosevelt's conservation rhetoric concerned the nation's forested areas. He believed the forests were key in maintaining other environmental gifts. In his first annual message he noted the importance of the forests to the land and to the water. Forested terrain not only allowed increases in various animal species but also restrained streams from flooding, which prevented topsoil from washing away.[34] Any abuse of this vital gift, then, had severe ramifications for the entire ecosystem.

As a prophet foretelling an ominous future, Roosevelt warned that greedy Americans were taking the nation down the path China had taken regarding its forests. In his 1908 annual message, one of the first such presidential messages to include photographs, the president revealed that the "ruthless destruction of the forests in northern China" had brought about widespread desolation; as the photographs showed. Once-forested mountains were now "absolutely barren peaks," and as a result, "the soil has been washed off the naked rock."[35] The ruin did not stop there. According to Roosevelt, with no vegetation

the barren mountains, scorched by the sun, send up currents of heated air which drive away instead of attracting the rain clouds . . . . In consequence, instead of the regular and plentiful rains . . . crops wither for lack of rainfall, while the seasons grow more and more irregular; and as the air becomes drier certain crops refuse [any] longer to grow at all. . . . In addition to the resulting agricultural distress, the watercourses have changed. Formerly they were narrow and deep . . . for the roots and humus of the forests caught the rain-water. . . . They have now become broad, shallow stream-beds . . . [and] when it rains . . . roaring muddy torrents come tearing down, bringing disaster and destruction everywhere.[36]

Thus Roosevelt had little patience with American timber barons who believed "as if no great damage would be done by the reckless destruction of our forests" because they were "blinded to the future by desire to make money in every way out of the present." According to the president, the "unrestrained greed" of those individuals who exploited the forests marked them as worthy of nothing but contempt.[37]

For Roosevelt, rapaciousness regarding the environment may have been contemptible, but indifference was intolerable. The greedy timber barons, then, were not the only ones that Roosevelt the prophet called to judgment. Before a meeting of the National Conservation Commission in 1908 he stated that "no man . . . is a good citizen if he does not think of his children's welfare; for there isn't any man whom we despise more than the man who has a good time himself and whose children pay for it."[38] He maintained that the much larger group that threatened to deprive future generations of God's environmental gifts was the American people themselves; their sin, one of indifference.

At first glance indifference, or sloth, appears to be one of the more benign sins. But upon closer examination it represents one of the worst of transgressions in regard to its scope. According to Lyman, sloth "not only subverts the livelihood of the body, taking no care for its day-to-day provisions, but also slows down the mind, halting its attention to matters of great importance"; furthermore, it hinders people in their "righteous undertakings," making them apathetic in "their duties and obligations to God." In other words the physical, mental, and spiritual dimensions of this sin can have far-reaching and devastating consequences.[39]

According to Roosevelt, indifference by the American public explained its lack of prudence concerning the environment. Speaking before the National Editorial Association in June, 1907, the president chided the nation. He stated that the "one characteristic more essential than any other" regarding conservation is "foresight," and "unfortunately . . . it is obviously not a marked characteristic of us in the United States." Instead, the people lived "with an eye single to the present, and have permitted the reckless waste and destruction of much of our natural wealth." This constituted the true offense to the supreme being: Americans had seemingly forsaken their sacred duty to ensure their successors' opportunity to experience the wonders of nature. By the time of his annual message in December, 1907, Roosevelt's rhetoric turned harsher. He still condemned the owners of the "big lumbering company" who "find it to their immense pecuniary benefit to destroy the forests by lumbering" and who sacrificed "the future of the nation as a whole to their own self-interest of the moment." But the bully pulpiteer placed the "heavier blame" on the rest of the country. He railed against the "happy-go- lucky indifference" and the "supine public opinion" that permitted the actions of a few people to go unchecked. In what might be considered his most chilling indictment, Roosevelt labeled the American people uncivilized: "only a savage would . . . show such reckless disregard of the future."[40]

At the Deep Waterway Convention late in 1907, the president articulated the seriousness of the situation in simple terms. As was common in Roosevelt's rhetoric, he gave the country a choice between two alternatives, one worthwhile and the other unimaginable. "It is clear beyond peradventure that our natural resources have been and are still being abused, that continued abuse will destroy them, and that we have at last reached the forks of the road. We are face to face with the great fact that the whole future of the nation is directly at stake in the momentous decision, which is forced upon us. Shall we continue the waste and destruction of our natural resources, or shall we conserve them?" In case anyone failed to grasp the ramifications of the wrong choice, he proclaimed that unless the nation solved the "fundamental problem" concerning the conservation of the environment it would have little reason to solve any other problems. Essentially, Roosevelt the prophet revealed that if the country continued its assault on the environment, whether from avarice or indifference, American culture was doomed.[41]

In his role as presidential prophet Roosevelt advanced a provocative and potentially unpopular line of argument: that the public itself was to blame for the growing environmental problems that faced the country now and, more importantly, in its future. Strategically, however, Roosevelt offered his flock more than despair; he also offered it solace. Just as traditional religions offer followers the means to salvation after their break with God, civil religion can offer its constituents such deliverance. To that end, Roosevelt assumed the role of priest and gave those that he as prophet had judged harshly a chance at civil redemption.

Civil Redemption

In fulfilling the role of priest the chief executive provides a much more hopeful message. Rather than castigate his constituents, the presidential pastor gives them encouragement and direction. The priest, Pierre and Linder wrote, "pronounces words of comfort, praise, and celebration" in affirmation of the national culture. In a larger sense, the political scholar James Fairbanks noted, the priest voices those "values around which society is organized" and from which society can derive its goals. By articulating the means to revere those values and to meet those goals, the priest provides society a chance at redemption.[42]

Redemption constitutes a transformation of character, a rebirth of the "'good' arising from the complete excess of the 'bad.'"[43] According to Kenneth Burke, this transformation reflects a "dramatic change of identity" and provides an individual a sense of "*moving forward*" toward a goal.[44] Essentially, individuals redeem themselves by sloughing off their sinful identity and establish a more repentant character by moving closer to God. To achieve this transformation the priest can provide the means through a "salvation device," which Burke defines as any "conscious or unconscious . . . way of saving one's soul, saving one's hide, or saving one's face."[45] As the nation's priest, Roosevelt offered his audiences a "salvation device": their acceptance of the national government's efforts to protect nature's resources for future generations. A government active in the preservation of the environment seemed appropriate given the president's depiction in his rhetoric of a passive God.

Rather than the God of civil religion described by Bellah as "actively interested" in human affairs, the supreme being as conceived by Roosevelt was largely inactive. Initially, Roosevelt's God assumed the guise of the "Genial Philanthropist," actively, if you will, having bestowed natural resources upon Americans in the past. However, based on the president's rhetoric, the environment was a one-time gift that would not be given again. After that initial bounty, the deity was passive; it did not directly intervene in American culture by renewing its gift or appear as a force with which to reckon when that gift was violated. The "Genial Philanthropist," then, also resembled the entity Hart labeled "God the Witnessing Author"—a "silent, onlooker God" who watched "His creations from afar."[46] Roosevelt's rhetoric created a power vacuum: there was no directly discernible God as active in the protection of the environment as it had been in its creation. This void, the absence of a force upon which the nation could rely for help, would create an expectation and anxiousness for something to fill that gap.

In Roosevelt's rhetoric the federal government filled that void, subtly filling the role left by the nation's beneficent but now inactive supreme entity. The president did not replace the cosmic being he invoked in much of his early rhetoric with a pagan political god. Rather, he simply focused on the government as the entity that could provide the means to safeguard the country's natural resources now and in the future. Like the environment's creator, the federal government appeared powerful, active, and, more importantly, able to provide salvation to the transgressing culture.[47]

Focusing upon the immensity of the task concerning the conservation of the environment, Roosevelt elevated the national government over other likely saviors. Not only was a supernatural being largely absent in much of Roosevelt's second-term rhetoric, the only other contender for this position, the states themselves, were cast as incapable of fulfilling the task. "The highways of the Mississippi and its great tributaries," the president announced to a 1907 St. Louis audience, is a river system that "traverses too many States to render it possible to leave merely to the States the task of fitting it for the greatest use of which it is capable." Instead, this constituted a "national task" involving the "develop-ment of our national resources under the supervision of and by the aid of the Federal Government."[48] In his 1907 Jamestown address Roosevelt again alluded to the inability of any other force, whether it be the states or a supernatural being, to stem the misuse of the environment; only federal agencies were pow-erful enough. "What can be done . . . is now being done," he alleged regarding the prevention of fraud in public land acquisition, "through the joint action of the Interior Department and the Department of Justice."[49]

The philanthropic God had at one time been active in the creation of the environment. Now, Roosevelt asserted, the federal government was working vigorously to protect the country's bounty. According to him in his seventh annual message, national government agencies had been working for years to educate the populace so that it could plan for the "orderly development" of resources "in place of a haphazard striving for immediate profit." Roosevelt cataloged the dynamic behavior of his administration in his address to the National Editorial Association: the Reclamation Service had worked since 1902 to prepare the western states for irrigation; the Department of the Interior worked to ensure that the public would not be overcharged in its use of min-eral fuel; the Forest Service developed plans to stop the devastation of forests.[50]

In order to elevate the federal government in a cosmic hierarchy, it needed to appear as more than a secular entity. So, just as much of Roosevelt's rhetoric revealed the sacredness of the forests and the sin of destroying them, the for-estry service appeared almost divine. When Roosevelt spoke of the men in-volved in it, they took on the persona of ministers attending to a holy mission. "You are engaged . . . in a calling whose opportunities for public service are very great," Roosevelt declared to the Society of American Foresters in 1903; "treat the calling seriously" since it "touches the Republic on almost every side, political, social, industrial, commercial." Like ministers revealing the word of God, the foresters were called upon to "convince the people of the truth" and to instill "ideals into the mass of [their] fellowmen" so the nation would take care of the forests.[51]

Taking care of nature, particularly the forests, meant using them resource-fully so future generations could experience God's bounty. To gain the coop-eration of business concerns, Roosevelt the priest blessed the link between the forests and financial gain. "Forestry," Roosevelt stated in 1903, "is the preser-vation of the forests by wise use"; to that end, the foresters needed to commu-nicate to their flock that by preserving some forests, other forests could be used to increase the prosperity of the nation. "The forests . . . should be used for business purposes," Roosevelt claimed at Stanford University, "in a way that will preserve them as permanent sources of national wealth." The president explained during an address in Sacramento, California, that some trees would be preserved "because they are the only things of their kind in the world," but "I do not ask that lumbering be stopped at all." Rather, he called for the forests to be used in such a way "that not only shall we here . . . get the benefit for the next few years, but that our children and our children's children shall get the benefit."[52]

Traditionally, while the sin of greed reflects the worship of material things instead of God, in Roosevelt's later rhetoric, the supreme being had virtually disappeared. With no God, then, greed as originally depicted by the president was no longer valid. Essentially, as long as the lumber industry utilized the environment so that future generations would have the opportunity to experience nature, it could worship the environment for the economic benefit it provided. This line of thinking reflected Roosevelt's offer of redemption to business concerns: if they could temper their passion long enough to follow the dictates of the Forest Service regarding "wise use," they would help to perpetuate an environmental legacy for the nation's descendants; otherwise, the lumber industry would "hand over" to the children a "heritage diminished in value" and truly be damned as greedy sinners.[53]

This was not Roosevelt's only attempt to help Americans find redemption. In 1908 he offered selfish private interests and an indifferent public another chance for salvation. The site for this public absolution occurred in the East Room of the White House on May 13 when the president gave the opening address at the governors' conference on conservation. The president had announced the conference on conservation seven months earlier at the Deep Waterway Convention in Memphis. "It ought to be among the most important gatherings in our history," he contended, "for none have had a more vital question to consider." To that end, the Roosevelt administration worked to turn the three-day conference into a highly successful and highly touted media event. It invited all the country's governors, the Supreme Court justices, members of Congress, industrialists, scientists, foreign dignitaries, and scores of newspaper and press associations (with many from each group attending).[54] The administration inundated the media with advance material that, according to Chief Forester Gifford Pinchot, made it "front-page news all over the United States" and practically silenced opposition, making conservation the "commonplace of the time" and an "inseparable part of the national policy." Thus Roosevelt captured the public's attention for his message of redemption.[55]

At the governors' conference the president delivered his address, what one biographer called Roosevelt's "testament of faith" and "statement of hope."[56] In it he attempted to establish the transcendent place of the federal government in protecting the environment. Roosevelt did not deify the national government; rather, he elevated it above the public's possible mundane conception of it. In the process he illustrated that by accepting the federal government and the principles it reflected, Americans could move beyond their individual and selfish desires to attain a sense of community. In other words, by accepting the idea of conservation and its enactment through the national government, they could find personal redemption for their past sins.

According to Hart, civil religious rhetoric exhibits a "nostalgic nature": it "tends to turn in upon itself" by using "its own ancestral rhetorical forms to provide itself with both a rationale and psychological momentum."[57] In one sense rhetoricians using this type of discourse look to the past, reminding the audience of its hallowed origin in order to lessen the audience's anxiety regarding contemporary challenges. As the nation's priest, Roosevelt comforted his constituents by taking them back to the past, tracing the use of natural resources in early American history.

From the beginning, Roosevelt maintained, Americans had utilized the environment and had recognized its importance to the nation's development. "When our forefathers met in Independence Hall . . . mining was carried on fundamentally as it had been carried on by the Pharaohs." Likewise, in 1776 wooden boats with sails carried products from Boston by water just as the "wares of the merchants of Nineveh and Sidon" had been transported during the Roman Empire. Ironically, during George Washington's time, Roosevelt observed, the "forests were regarded chiefly as obstructions to settlement and cultivation," and the "man who cut down a tree was held to have conferred a service upon his fellows." Despite the fact that early Americans knew little about the vast resources of the environment, they realized their significance. In fact, according to the president, the development of natural resources had led directly to the creation of a national government. Roosevelt observed that "Washington clearly saw that the perpetuity of the States could only be secured by union, and that the only feasible basis of union was an economic one; in other words, that it must be based on the development and use of their natural resources. . . . It was in Philadelphia that the representatives of all the States met for what was in its original conception merely a waterways conference; but when they had closed their deliberations the outcome was the Constitution that made the States into a Nation."[58] History revealed that to safeguard the country and its use of natural resources, something more than the individual states were needed. Thus Roosevelt not only reaffirmed the Constitution's status as a sacred text in American culture but also established the national government's preeminent role in conservation.

Since the federal government was born out of safeguarding nature's resources, it now needed to fulfill its destiny. Roosevelt declared that "the Nation began with the belief that its landed possessions were illimitable" and "capable of supporting all the people who might care to make our country their home." However, due to thoughtlessly allowing "the right of the individual to injure the future of all of us for his own temporary and immediate profit," the country faced shortages of land, forests, and minerals. Now was the time for change, Roosevelt commanded; now was the time to recognize the national government as a guardian of the future in the "essential matter of natural resources." Thus conservation, as practiced by the government, constituted an issue of morality. Invoking Supreme Court justice Oliver Wendell Holmes's opinion, Roosevelt illustrated how one of the country's most august representatives described the nature of state guardianship of the country's resources. Holmes, said Roosevelt, observed that the "State as quasi sovereign . . . of the interests of the public has a standing in court to protect the atmosphere, the water, and the forests within its territory, irrespective of the assent or dissent of the private owners of the land most immediately concerned." This, concluded the president, was a "dictum of morals." As such, this state policy was of "vital importance" to the entire country. Extending the high court's ruling in support of federal government control of the environment, Roosevelt maintained that any policy pursued by his administration would also "preserve soil, forests, [and] water power as a heritage for the children and the children's children of the men and women of this generation." Essentially, the president borrowed the justice's argument about state responsibility to promote the fact that the national government similarly stood ready to serve its moral purpose.[59]

Roosevelt's invocation of morality reflected one of the distinctive features of civil religious discourse: its "emotional simplicity." According to Hart, such discourse is "normally uncomplicated inventionally," relying on the "relatively straightforward commonplaces" in order to engage "the listener's most basic motivations." Stated another way; political rhetoricians can use simple, universally understood (yet undoubtedly ambiguous) concepts to engage an audience's emotions regarding policy matters. Roosevelt invoked two other simple, provocative topics: foresight and patriotism.[60]

Whereas Roosevelt the prophet indicted the country in 1907 for its lack of foresight regarding the environment, Roosevelt the priest offered a more comforting message in 1908. For him, saving the future appeared to be a simple matter of commonsense, a trait that "civilized men" like the audience were capable of exhibiting. "We should exercise foresight now," he charged, "as the ordinarily prudent man exercises foresight in conserving and wisely using the property which contains the assurance of well-being for himself and his children." Roosevelt claimed that forethought alerted the country to conserve the mineral, forest, and water resources in order to ensure the perpetuation of those resources for the next generation. But this task of irrigation, canalization of rivers, and protecting forests proved to be an immense task. To realize the prescient vision of the populace, the federal government was necessary: "all these various uses of our natural resources are so closely connected that they should be coordinated, and should be treated as part of one coherent plan."[61] Roosevelt did not specify the mechanics of that plan but his intent was clear: such a plan could only be coordinated by one overarching agency, the national government.

To engage the audience further, Roosevelt revealed that the federal government would not act alone. According to the president, the administration needed the public to fulfill its duty as well, the "patriotic duty of insuring the safety and continuance" of the country: "When the People of the United States consciously undertake to raise themselves as citizens . . . to the highest pitch of excellence in private, State, and national life, and to do this because it is the first of all the duties of true patriotism, then and not till then the future of this Nation, in quality and in time, will be assured."[62] Just as the Constitution attained a hallowed place in the culture, patriotism likewise reached the status of a politicoreligious virtue: Americans exhibiting that quality illustrated their reverence for the government and consequently its attempt at conserving the environment. Ultimately, by behaving in a principled, prudent, and patriotic manner, Americans would receive personal absolution through the "salvation device" Roosevelt offered. In the process they would redeem themselves, turning away from their sinful ways and assuming new identities as good citizens.

Traveling across the United States and generating media exposure, Roosevelt took his message regarding conservation public. Cutright concluded that the "most decisive factor" in protecting the environment was the educative function of Roosevelt's rhetoric: "Sensing from the beginning that the fate of the forests and other natural resources depended upon education," the president brought "the conservation message into homes of farmers and merchants, factory workers and professionals."[63] Employing what he called the presidential "bully pulpit," Roosevelt preached a sermon in the civil religious tradition, merging symbols of sacred concepts with ideas of a secular nature. In his early rhetoric he invoked a powerful and benevolent God that had blessed Americans with a magnificent environmental bounty. Americans needed to act as caretakers to safeguard the sacred nature of the environment. However, Roosevelt judged the nation as wanting in its responsibility. According to Roosevelt the prophet, greedy businessmen disregarded the environment's hallowed nature. Specifically, the lumber owners' transgression against God resulted in far-reaching and almost irreversible environmental problems. Compounding the private interests' sin of greed, the rest of the public sinned through indifference to these problems. Having condemned his flock as the prophet, Roosevelt then assumed the role of priest and gave the national community an opportunity to receive remission for its sins. To redeem itself, the nation needed to accept the federal government as the environment's savior. The president observed that history illustrated that the national government was the only force powerful enough to protect the environment and that it now needed to fulfill its destiny, with the public's blessing. By accepting the governing institution that embodied such values as morality, foresight, and patriotism, and its efforts to safeguard nature for future generations, Americans would receive civil redemption.

In large part, Roosevelt's civil religious construct focused attention on the environment, and humanity's responsibility to it, as part of the transcendental design of the cosmos. This sanctification of the environment represents a concept that continues today in the public consciousness. For example, the rhetorical scholar Susan Senecah noted that the campaign to prevent dams in the Grand Canyon in the 1960s capitalized on the fact that the canyon had become a "sacred symbol" in American culture.[64] Given the contextualization of the environment as sacred, a concept given force by Roosevelt's sermons almost one hundred years ago, why is it that nature continues to be assaulted?

One answer may lie in the conception of God, both the cosmic entity and the earthly one, that Roosevelt established. While this powerful being had at one time created unparalleled wonders, it now appeared largely inactive. Unlike some depictions of a supreme being as wrathful and retributive in nature, this God of the environment offered no threat of punishment. Thus why should people fear retribution when they violated the deity's gift? Furthermore, Roosevelt articulated an irreconcilable dilemma. The sacred nature of the environment appeared questionable because of its limitations. In other words, could the public truly accept a being of infinite power creating something so finite in nature? In many religions God constitutes an omnipotent force; in Roosevelt's civil religion, the supreme being appeared much weaker and perhaps less awe inspiring. In another sense, by making the national government the savior of the environment, Roosevelt may have inadvertently perpetuated a sense of indifference in the public. Americans could easily find civil redemption by simply allowing the federal government to act in their behalf, thus absolving them of any further responsibility toward nature.

Yet another answer may lie in Roosevelt's addition of business enterprises to a hierarchy of power that no longer featured a supreme being. "The problem with the environment is that it is both everywhere and nowhere," the rhetorical scholar Dennis Jaehne wrote, an "essentially contested concept" that "needs to be explicitly linked to some notion of *specific place*" for it to be a useful symbol.[65] Roosevelt designated that "specific place" as business to ground the esoteric sacredness of the environment. The president always maintained that natural resources were to be conserved through their "wise use"—an *economic* use that would buoy the material foundation of the country. To that end, he virtually eliminated the God that had initially bestowed nature's treasures on the United States so that the lumber owners' use of the forests could no longer be considered a sin. As a result, the zeal of loggers became a virtue under the institutional god Roosevelt established with his civil religious discourse. In fact, the diligence of any industry to make a profit from the environment within certain guidelines, and thus provide the nation with a solid material foundation, would be blessed by the national government.

Perhaps the most telling answer involves Roosevelt's linking of the sacred environment to earthly profits; essentially, he linked God and mammon. This disconcerting imagery might best be understood as a representation of the "grotesque." The historian Frances Barasch observed that this term "emerged as a designation for the stylized mingling of flora and fauna" in sixteenth-century Italy, as well as a description of the "fantastic creatures which were found in the antique frescoes" of the Roman catacombs. Its common usage entails that which is incongruous or strange. The president's pairing of God with business (the serpent in the garden) created what the art scholar Philip Thomson might label as "a violent clash of opposites." Such imagery becomes unpalatable and is rejected by the audience. Thomson noted that when "something which is familiar and trusted is suddenly made strange and disturbing," people try to escape that discomfort; in other words, the "effect of the grotesque can best be summed up as *alienation*."[66] As a result, Americans rejected the absolutely sacred nature of the environment as well as the need to fulfill their responsibility to it.

Roosevelt's merger of the supernatural with the secular, forging a God/Devil grotesquerie, created a tension that effectively corrupted, and continues to corrupt, the environment's supposedly hallowed nature. As Senecah noted, "national park officials at the Grand Canyon found that the average visitor spends over one and one half hours at the Grand Canyon but of that, spends only 7 minutes at the rim and this at a very small portion of the 218 mile long rim. The rest of the time is spent in curio shops [and] restaurants."[67] In the early twenty-first century the tension between the pious and the profane that Roosevelt called attention to shows no sign of weakening. The president as chief spokesperson for the nation's civil religion has an opportunity to mediate that tension and inculcate the requisite values necessary for the environment to last for future generations. Unless the president-as-pastor is careful, he or she may very well anoint the prophets of profit and prevent our heirs from experiencing their environmental heritage.

Notes

1. The anecdote is quoted in Paul R. Cutright, *Theodore Roosevelt: The Making of a Conservationist* (Urbana: University of Illinois Press, 1985), 211; C. H. Forbes-Lindsay, "Taking Stock of Our National Assets: The Far-Reaching Significance of the White House Conference," *Craftsman* 14 (July, 1908): 378; Frank Graham, Jr., *Man's Dominion: The Story of Conservation in America* (New York: M. Evans, 1971), 14, 18.
2. Jack Shepherd, *The Forest Killers: The Destruction of the American Wilderness* (New York: Weybright and Talley, 1975), 14–15; Thomas E. Will, "The Conservation of Natural Resources," *Independent* 64 (April, 1908): 947–48.
3. Cutright, *Theodore Roosevelt*, 213.
4. See Cutright, *Theodore Roosevelt*, 213–27; William H. Harbaugh, *The Life and Times of Theodore Roosevelt*, rev. ed. (New York: Collier Books, 1967), 306–15; Lewis L. Gould, *The Presidency of Theodore Roosevelt* (Lawrence: University Press of Kansas, 1991), 40–42, 202.
5. Cutright, *Theodore Roosevelt*, 223; Harbaugh, *Life and Times*, 306–307.
6. The actual quotation reads "the rhetorical function is the function of adjusting ideas to people and people to ideas." See Donald C. Bryant, "Rhetoric: Its Functions and Its Scope," in *Contemporary Rhetoric: A Reader's Coursebook*, ed. Douglas Ehninger (Glenview, Ill.: Scott, Foresman, 1972), 26.
7. Theodore Roosevelt, *An Autobiography* (New York: Charles Scribner's Sons, 1929), 395; Cutright, *Theodore Roosevelt*, 221.
8. See Cutright, *Theodore Roosevelt*, 220; Carl E. Hatch, *The Big Stick and the Congressional Gavel: A Study of Theodore Roosevelt's Relations with His Last Congress, 1907–1909* (New York: Pageant, 1967), 10–15.
9. Gould, *The Presidency*, 40.
10. For interpretations of his discourse, see Harbaugh, *Life and Times*, 304–18; Cutright, *Theodore Roosevelt*, 210–30.
11. See Leroy G. Dorsey, "The Frontier Myth in Presidential Rhetoric: Theodore Roosevelt's Campaign for Conservation," *Western Journal of Communication* 59 (Winter, 1995): 1–19; Daniel O. Buehler, "Permanence and Change in Theodore Roosevelt's Call for the Conservation of Natural Resources," paper presented at the Speech Communication Association Convention, San Antonio, November 18–21, 1995, 7–8.
12. Richard V. Pierard and Robert D. Linder, *Civil Religion and the Presidency* (Grand Rapids, Mich.: Academie Books, 1988), 23, 20, 26–27. For analyses of presidents using civil religion to promote various policies, see Rita K. Whillock, "Dream Believers: The Unifying Visions and Competing Values of Adherents to American Civil Religion," *Presidential Studies Quarterly* 24 (Spring, 1994): 375–88; David S. Adams, "Ronald Reagan's 'Revival': Voluntarism as a Theme in Reagan's Civil Religion," *Sociological Analysis* 48 (Spring, 1987): 17–29; Rachel L. Holloway, "'Keeping the Faith': Eisenhower Introduces the Hydrogen Age," in *Eisenhower's War of Words: Rhetoric and Leadership*, ed. Martin J. Medhurst (East Lansing: Michigan State University Press, 1994), 47–71.
13. Robert N. Bellah, "Civil Religion in America," *Daedalus* 96 (Winter, 1967): 1, 3–4, 9–18.
14. Robert N. Bellah, "American Civil Religion in the 1970s," in *American Civil Religion*, ed. Donald G. Jones and Russell E. Richey (San Francisco: Mellen Re-

search University Press, 1990), 271; Robert N. Bellah, *The Broken Covenant: American Civil Religion in Time of Trial,* 2d ed. (Chicago: University of Chicago Press, 1992), 176.

15. Michael Novak, *Choosing Presidents: Symbols of Political Leadership,* 2d ed. (New Brunswick, N.J.: Transaction Publishers, 1992), 107, 127; Will Herberg, "America's Civil Religion: What It Is and Whence It Comes," in *American Civil Religion,* 77–78.

16. Herbert Richardson, "Civil Religion in Theological Perspective," in *American Civil Religion,* 165, 178; George A, Kelly, *Politics and Religious Consciousness in America* (New Brunswick, N.J.: Transaction Books, 1984), 247.

17. Pierard and Linder, *Civil Religion,* 25.

18. Bellah, "Civil Religion in America," 15, 7. Hart has labeled these gods the Inscrutable Potentate, the Witnessing Author, the Wise and the Just, the Genial Philanthropist, and the Object of Affection; see Roderick P. Hart, *The Political Pulpit* (West Lafayette, Ind.: Purdue University Press, 1977), 70–72.

19. Theodore Roosevelt, "Address at Pasadena, California, May 8, 1903," in *California Addresses by President Roosevelt* (San Francisco: California Promotion Committee, 1903), 24.

20. Theodore Roosevelt, "At Laying of Cornerstone of Gateway to Yellowstone National Park, Gardiner, Montana, April 24, 1903," in *Presidential Addresses and State Papers of Theodore Roosevelt* (New York: Kraus Reprint, 1970), 1:324–25.

21. Theodore Roosevelt, "Address of President Roosevelt at Grand Canyon, Arizona, May 6, 1903," in *Presidential Papers Microfilm: Theodore Roosevelt Papers,* series 5C, reel 427 (Washington, D.C.: Library of Congress, 1969), 2; Roosevelt, "Remarks at Leland Stanford Jr. University, Palo Alto, California, May 12, 1903," in *California Addresses,* 68–69.

22. Bellah, *The Broken Covenant,* 12.

23. Theodore Roosevelt, "First Annual Message, December 3, 1901," in *The Works of Theodore Roosevelt: State Papers as Governor and President, 1899–1909,* national ed. (New York: Charles Scribner's Sons, 1926), 15:104; Roosevelt, "Remarks at Leland Stanford Jr. University," 64; Theodore Roosevelt, "Address at the Capitol Building, Sacramento, California, May 19, 1903," in *California Addresses,* 140.

24. Mark Johnson, *Moral Imagination: Implications of Cognitive Science for Ethics* (Chicago: University of Chicago Press, 1993), 4, 193.

25. Theodore Roosevelt, "Remarks at Los Angeles, California, May 8, 1903," in *California Addresses,* 30; Roosevelt, "Address at the Capitol Building," 141; Roosevelt, "Address at Pasadena," 24.

26. Bellah, *The Broken Covenant,* 41; Theodore Roosevelt, "Inaugural Address, March 4, 1905," in *Presidential Addresses,* 3:269.

27. Roosevelt, "Inaugural Address," 269–70. This reference by Roosevelt constitutes the only clear invocation of the supreme being Hart labeled as "God the Object of Affection," one who deserved but did not demand obedience. According to Hart, this is one of the least invoked gods; see Hart, *Political Pulpit,* 72–73.

28. Pierard and Linder, *Civil Religion,* 24.

29. See Martin E. Marty, "Two Kinds of Civil Religion," in *American Civil Religion,* 145–51; Pierard and Linder, *Civil Religion,* 24.

30. Richard Stivers, *Evil in Modern Myth and Ritual* (Athens: University of Georgia Press, 1982), 54.

31. Stanford M. Lyman, *The Seven Deadly Sins: Society and Evil* (New York: St. Martin's Press, 1978), 271.

32. Ibid., 232, 234.

33. Roosevelt, "First Annual Message," 104; Theodore Roosevelt, "Address of President Roosevelt at Boise, Idaho, May 28, 1903," in *Presidential Papers Microfilm,* series 5B, vols. 6–11, reel 425, 1. Theodore Roosevelt, "The Forest in the Life of the Nation, January 5, 1905," in *Proceedings of the American Forest Congress* (Washington, D.C.: H. M. Suter Publishing for the American Forestry Association, 1905), 4, 9. For a discussion of timber-cutting practices, see Shepherd, *The Forest Killers.*

34. Roosevelt, "First Annual Message," 104–105.

35. Theodore Roosevelt, "Eighth Annual Message, December 8, 1908," in *The Works of Theodore Roosevelt,* 520.

36. Ibid., 521.

37. Ibid., 517; Theodore Roosevelt, "At Raleigh, N.C., October 19, 1905," in *Presidential Addresses,* 4:470.

38. Theodore Roosevelt, "Address of President Roosevelt at the General Meeting of the Joint Conservation Conference at the Belasco Theater, December 8, 1908," in *Presidential Papers Microfilm,* series 5B, vols. 12–13, reel 426, 5.

39. Lyman, *Seven Deadly Sins,* 5–7.

40. Theodore Roosevelt, "Address of President Roosevelt before the National Editorial Association, at Jamestown, Virginia, June 10, 1907," in *Presidential Papers Microfilm,* series 5C, reel 427, 8–10; Roosevelt, "Seventh Annual Message, December 3, 1907," in *The Works of Theodore Roosevelt,* 449–51.

41. Theodore Roosevelt, "Address of President Roosevelt to the Deep Waterway Convention at Memphis, Tennessee, October 4, 1907," in *Presidential Papers Microfilm,* series 5C, reel 427, 42–44.

42. Pierard and Linder, *Civil Religion,* 24; James D. Fairbanks, "The Priestly Functions of the Presidency: A Discussion of the Literature on Civil Religion and Its Implications for the Study of Presidential Leadership," *Presidential Studies Quarterly* 11 (Spring, 1981): 224.

43. Kenneth Burke, *The Philosophy of Literary Form: Studies in Symbolic Action,* 3d ed. (1941; Berkeley: University of California Press, 1973), 431.

44. Kenneth Burke, *Attitudes toward History,* 3d ed. (1937; Berkeley: University of California Press, 1984), 318; Burke, *The Philosophy of Literary Form,* 203.

45. Burke, *Attitudes,* 319.

46. Hart, *Political Pulpit,* 71.

47. My point here is that Roosevelt did not directly anoint the federal government as God nor specifically subordinate it as an agent of God. In Roosevelt's second term he discussed the government in ways similar to those he had used when invoking God during his first term. The implication, then, is that the government would be seen as powerful enough (a god in some sense) to continue the works of *the* being that was now inactive.

48. Theodore Roosevelt, "Address of President Roosevelt at St. Louis, Missouri, October 2, 1907," in *Presidential Papers Microfilm,* series 5C, reel 427, 8–9.

49. Roosevelt, "Address of President Roosevelt before the National Editorial Association," 29.

50. Roosevelt, "Seventh Annual Message," 443; Roosevelt, "Address of President Roosevelt before the National Editorial Association," 12, 20–22.

51. Theodore Roosevelt, "At a Meeting of the Society of American Foresters," held

at the residence of Mr. Gifford Pinchot, Washington, D.C., March 26, 1903, in *Presidential Addresses*, 1:254, 250, 256.

52. Ibid., 251; Roosevelt, "Remarks at Leland Stanford Jr. University," 69; Roosevelt, "Address at the Capitol Building," 140.

53. Roosevelt, "At Raleigh, N.C.," 469

54. Roosevelt, "Address of President Roosevelt to the Deep Waterway Convention," 45. See Stephen Ponder, "'Publicity in the Interest of the People': Theodore Roosevelt's Conservation Crusade," *Presidential Studies Quarterly* 20 (Summer, 1990): 552; Cutright, *Theodore Roosevelt*, 228

55. Gifford Pinchot, *Breaking New Ground* (New York: Harcourt, Brace, 1947), 353.

56. Harbaugh, *Life and Times*, 317.

57. Hart, *Political Pulpit*, 82.

58. Theodore Roosevelt, "Opening Address by the President," in *Proceeding of a Conference of Governors in the White House, Washington, D.C., May 13–15, 1908* (Washington: Government Printing Office, 1909), 5–6.

59. Ibid., 7, 10–12.

60. Hart, *Political Pulpit*, 103–104.

61. Roosevelt, "Opening Address," 8, 10.

62. Ibid., 12.

63. Cutright, *Theodore Roosevelt*, 218.

64. Susan L. Senecah, "The Sacredness of Natural Places: How a Big Canyon Became a Grand Icon," in *The Conference on the Discourse of Environmental Advocacy*, ed. Christine L. Oravec and James G. Cantrill (Salt Lake City: University of Utah Humanities Center, 1992), 203.

65. Dennis Jaehne, "Issues in the Intersection of Environmental Discourse and Policy Discourse: A Critical Response," in *Conference on the Discourse of Environmental Advocacy*, 149–50.

66. Frances K. Barasch, *The Grotesque: A Study in Meanings* (The Hague: Mouton, 1971), 13; Arthur Clayborough, *The Grotesque in English Literature* (Oxford: Clarendon, 1965), 70–71; Philip Thomson, *The Grotesque* (London: Methuen, 1972), 11, 59.

67. Senecah, "The Sacredness of Natural Places," 220.

2 Presidential Public Policy and Conservation

W. J. McGee and the People

Christine Oravec

In 1890 the U.S. Census Bureau declared an end to a century of unlimited development by announcing the closing of the frontier.[1] Eighteen years later the railroad baron James J. Hill, a speaker at the White House Conference of Governors on the conservation of natural resources, associated the end of the frontier with the potential shortage of arable land: "We now turn to the only remaining resource of man upon this earth, which is the soil itself. How are we caring for that, and what possibilities does it hold out to the People of future support? We are only beginning to feel the pressure upon the land. The whole interior of this continent, aggregating more than 500,000,000 acres, has been occupied by settlers within the last 50 years. What is there left for the next 50 years? How long will the remainder last? No longer can we say that 'Uncle Sam has land enough to give us all a farm.'"[2]

This and similar statements at the conference evinced public concern over the apparently dwindling reserve of materials necessary for the nation's economic welfare.[3] However, the emerging public concern demonstrated at the White House conference did not alone create the climate necessary for formulating public policy on the rapid consumption of natural resources. To some, the only adequate response to a problem of such magnitude appeared to be the creation of a fully developed national movement for conservation, a movement that expressed the concern of the public over diminishing supplies of vital goods and advocated organized action.

Until recently, few scholars of communication had attempted to explain how a movement for conservation was initiated and sustained. But in the winter of 1995 Leroy Dorsey wrote an article for the *Western Journal of Communication* entitled "The Frontier Myth in Presidential Rhetoric: Theodore Roosevelt's Campaign for Conservation." In this article he explained that the myth of the frontier hero, once a conqueror of western lands, had to be reduced to the dimensions of a domestic agriculturist for such a conservation movement to be created. Dorsey further argued that Roosevelt conceived of the movement for conservation as a moral as well as an economic imperative, much like Jeremy Bentham's "greatest good for the greatest number," while appending the phrase, "for the longest time."[4]

I have no quarrel with Dorsey's accurate and well-articulated analysis of the reworking of the frontier myth. In this chapter I offer two extensions of Dorsey's argument. The first extension is an attempt to balance the explanatory framework of the archetypical yeoman farmer myth with the conception of natural resources held by entrepreneurs, scientists, and social theorists of the time. Informed by the foundational work of Samuel P. Hays and Alan Trachtenberg, my interpretation attempts specifically to account for the conservationist dimensions of President Roosevelt's progressivist form of national government. These two eminent social historians present the case for perceiving social and political movements of the late nineteenth and early twentieth century as corporate and scientific rather than popular or cultural in nature. In so doing, they prevent naive readings of the political rhetoric of the time and supply crucial material detail.

Yet a study of a resource-based movement such as conservation should address both ends of the spectrum, the scientific and the cultural, to fully account for its popularity. Hays and Trachtenberg stop short of explaining the kind of public enthusiasm accompanying these movements that, as Dorsey recognizes, can only come from a shared cultural mythos. By drawing from these historians' scientific and political basis, but without dismissing the force of cultural mythology, I aim to show how conservationist political power was forged through an intricately articulated combination of culture, science, and social theory. For example, the conservationists' popular mythology included but transcended Jefferson's notion of the "yeoman farmer" by including the entire public within the movement. And in terms of social science, they went beyond Frederick Jackson Turner's famous stages of Western civilization by incorporating evolutionary theory in their version of national history.[5]

The second extension of Dorsey's work is a more thorough examination of the concept of the community, or public, for whom the conservationists expended their efforts. Their notion, located in both the evolutionary science and the progressive politics of the time, confirms Dorsey's insistence upon the moral or spiritual qualities of the community. My position, however, is that myths do not stand alone as instigators of public action; they are woven into the political, scientific, social, and economic threads of a nation's culture. Therefore one should expect of the conservation movement not only a spiritual imperative but also a scientific and bureaucratic rationale for the placement of its followers within the confines of the myth itself.

The theoretical justification behind this extension of Dorsey's argument is derived from two seminal studies in the construction of the public within social movements—those of Michael Calvin McGee and Maurice Charland. Charland's approach to constitutive rhetoric is particularly illuminative because the leaders of conservation essentially fabricated a social policy compatible with their policy toward natural resources. As James J. Hill said, a concept of a "People" to whom the resources of the United States belonged.[6] Created within a period of a few months, and promulgated during the tenure of a two-term presidency, this concept of the public derived substantially from the writings of a single, relatively unknown ideologue within that bureaucracy—a man named W. J. McGee. His concept of "the People" proved instrumental in constituting conservation as a powerful, wide-ranging movement that effectively positioned a broad cross section of the American population within its boundaries and justified unprecedented presidential policy-making power.

Noted speakers and writers, borrowing heavily from the ideas of W. J. McGee if not employing him directly as a speechwriter, developed a comprehensive social movement and a governmental policy for the conservation of natural resources. McGee interwove his conception of the conservationist public from many contextual threads—scientific theory, technological practice, social studies, and most decidedly, cultural mythology. Since conservationist discourse based on McGee's ideology drew upon all these resources, it proved to be a remarkably thoroughgoing and perhaps even definitive foundation for political and bureaucratic policy. One might say that McGee's concept of the public has consistently served the conservationist cause, for better or for ill, from its historical origins up until today.

To explicate how the process of constituting a conservationist public came about, I provide an example of how such writers and speakers as Theodore Roosevelt, Gifford Pinchot, and W. J. McGee himself formulated specific language to construct just such a social reality, in this case the entity of "conservation" as a social movement. Then I examine in detail how McGee employed the three "discursive efforts" Charland claims are essential to constituting a people: first, identifying their essence or nature; second, fabricating their history; and third, providing them with the "illusion of freedom" of action that exercised their moral or spiritual qualifications.[7]

In the course of this examination, I hope to show how conservationists constructed a rhetorical tapestry for the movement from various concepts and themes present in the public domain and in the course of doing so interpolated their audience into the role of constituents. Further, by employing Charland's three discursive efforts as a loose structural framework, I illustrate how political rhetoric may be less skeptically regarded and more easily understood. In fact, a study of McGee's ideological discourse may demonstrate that public policy often requires a constitutive subtext theorizing the existence of the kind of public required to justify and implement a given course of action. These constituted publics are not falsehoods per se but fabrications, the function of which is to provide extant political subjects with the discursive scaffolding necessary for constructing a collective identity, a history, and a direction for future action.

Constituting Identity: Conservation as Self-Designation

"Conservation," a word that has become so commonplace that politicians of all persuasions lay claim to it, was originally a contested term. The requirements of justifying their cause forced early conservationists to choose a particularly tenuous middle path between those who would have had national resources opened for general use and those who would have preserved the land from use. These conservationists needed to demonstrate nothing less than the endorsement, or at least the understanding, of a major part of the public, including supporters both of businessmen and "nature lovers." In addition, conservationists needed to create a movement broad enough in its appeal to be identified neither as the creation of scientific specialists alone nor the promotion of a particular political administration.

The Conference of Governors of 1908, almost universally recognized then and now as the key event in the history of conservation, was the first of a series of well-publicized commissions that confirmed the existence of an ongoing movement.[8] In the wake of the commissions, speakers for the movement claimed with some justification that nearly every individual in the United States had somehow been exposed to the terms and principles of conservation.[9] Furthermore, the doctrine of the movement pervaded such major magazines throughout the nation as the *Century, Outlook, World's Work,* and *McClure's.*[10] By the end of the first decade of the twentieth century the movement had received if not support, then at least recognition from a significant portion of the American public and represented for many the "public interest" of America in its natural resources.

The growth of the movement depended upon premises concerning nature and society that were embedded in its philosophical position and its communicative style. Specifically, conservationists succeeded in identifying the term "conservation" with the interests of a growing social and political movement, transforming it from a scientific term to a word designating the moral and spiritual resources of a people. Speakers for the movement unilaterally decided that the single term "conservation" best served this need for self-identification.

However, "The word 'conservation' in its present sense did not come into official use until the Theodore Roosevelt administration," claimed writer and editor Paul Brooks.[11] Narrowly construed, conservation stood for such specific goals as preventing the waste of natural resources, using resources wisely, and distributing national wealth among the whole people.[12] Even so, the connotations of the word were also broad enough to include moral and ethical justification for collective action, in the process transforming an ostensibly neutral term into powerfully evocative discourse.

The primary technical function of the term conservation was to identify two differing standards for managing natural resources under one overarching principle. The first standard was the temporary withdrawal of natural resources from immediate use, to allow for long-range planning and minimizing of waste. The second was the development of plans for the gradual use and development of the resources in the interest of the general public. Gifford Pinchot, in his book of essays *The Fight for Conservation,* described the two standards as follows: "The first great fact about conservation is that it stands for development. There has been a fundamental misconception that conservation means nothing but the husbanding of resources for future generations. There could be no more serious mistake. Conservation does mean provision for the future, but it means also and first of all the right of the present generation to the fullest necessary use of all the resources with which this country is so abundantly blessed."[13]

Pinchot's initial phrase may sound shocking to readers in the twenty-first century because the lines between multiple use and preservation have been drawn firmly by the environmental conflicts of the 1970s and 1980s. We no longer take for granted the progressivist assumption that growth and progress can enhance our store of resources or benefit the environment in any fundamental way. Pinchot, however, was reacting to the wanton waste and destruction of resources declared to be finite by Frederick Jackson Turner's announcement of the end of the frontier in 1890. The closest contemporary equivalent for what Pinchot had in mind might be a crude conception of "sustainable development," enhanced by scientific principles and ever more efficient technology. At the same time, Pinchot recognized that reserving resources for future generations to use, rather than asserting nature's inherent right to exist, was the most socially acceptable way to defend halting unchecked development and justifying government intervention.[14]

A coordinate function of the term was to regulate differing policies for managing natural resources, such as minerals, water, and forests. Scientists soon discovered that conservation fulfilled this function admirably. The first college textbook of conservation claimed: "Conservation is not a simple subject that can be treated with reference to a single resource, independently of the others;

it is an interlocking one. The conservation of one resource is related to that of another. Thus the conservation of coal is to be accomplished in a large measure by the substitution of water as a source of power. The conservation of the metals is to be largely accomplished by the substitution of cement and stone and brick and other products."[15] To the scientists and technicians involved in the new movement, the power of conservation lay not so much in the originality of its particular techniques as in its broad comprehension of many independent problems. Conservation was presumed to take an organic approach toward the environment that was all encompassing. The term designated a paradigm for thought that approached the certainty of a natural law.

Yet conservation was used to function as a unifying principle not only for achieving technical coherence, but also for motivating a social movement. Conservationists needed to employ the term not only as part of a scientific paradigm but also as a fundamental ethical principle or natural truth that evoked human compliance. According to Gifford Pinchot, in an article for the periodical *Agricultural History,* conservation implied an ethical attitude toward the use of natural resources:

> I was riding my old horse Jim in Rock Creek Park one day—I think it was February 1907—when suddenly the idea . . . occurred to me . . . that all these natural resources which we had been dealing with as though they were in watertight compartments actually constituted one united problem. That problem was the use of the earth for the *permanent good of man* . . . . The idea was so new that it did not even have a name. Finally Overton Price suggested that we should call it "conservation" and the President said "O.K." So we called it the conservation movement.[16]

The significance of Pinchot's homey anecdote is underscored by the frequency with which it was cited in conservationist literature. His moment of epiphany conjures up revelatory images such as Saint Paul's conversion on the road to Damascus or Moses' conversation with a burning bush. The emphasis on human morality also echoes such imperatives as the Sermon on the Mount and the Ten Commandments. Combined with an offhand, folksy style of communication, Pinchot's explanation of the origins of "conservation" infuses the term not with scientific precision but with a backwoods preacher's earnestness and a chosen prophet's self-aggrandizement.

With the social imperative playing an important part in identifying the objectives of the movement, conservation also firmly linked political and administrative considerations with the management of natural resources. Because individual bureaus often became identified with the natural resources they regulated, conservation came to be viewed as a basic and natural principle of government as well as of efficient regulation of nature.[17] Theodore Roosevelt's address to the conference of governors, for example, made explicit the connection between efficient management of resources and governmental efficiency. In a phrase later quoted frequently in the literature of the movement, Roosevelt exhorted his listeners to "remember that the conservation of natural resources, though the gravest problem of today, is yet but part of another and greater problem to which this Nation is not yet awake, but to which it will awake in time, and with which it must hereafter grapple if it is to live—the problem of national efficiency, the patriotic duty of insuring the safety and continuance of the Nation."[18]

In a similar vein, Pinchot related that his work with "more bureaus than any other man in Washington" made it the most "natural thing in the world that the relations of forests, lands, and minerals, each to each should be brought to my mind."[19] If unity, coherence, and organic interrelationship were integral parts of nature's law, then all human activities, the political included, were also products of that law. Governmental organization, particularly the Rooseveltian view of government centralized in the federal bureaucracy, both reflected and stimulated a view of nature itself as an organic whole.[20]

Eventually, the concept of conservation so effectively united the scientific and political goals of the movement that some began to think of it as the "true moral welfare," which was the ultimate goal of society and humankind. As a principle of moral welfare, conservation evoked values of order and harmony with nature, values not significantly different from those of romantic philosophical idealism or Victorian sentimental religion. W. J. McGee, in an article for the Mississippi Valley Historical Association, asserted the association of conservation with religion, an association that also appeared in the messages of Pinchot and Roosevelt. For McGee, the ethical doctrine of conservation— the greatest good for the greatest number—"was better expressed in an utterance of two millenniums past—'A new commandment give I unto thee, that ye love one another.' . . . Whatever its material manifestations, every revolution is first and foremost a revelation in thought and spirit."[21] The direct reference to Christianity's "new" commandment to love everyone underscored McGee's belief in an easily perceived equivalency between religious commandments and Jeremy Bentham's economic theory. He assumed that true understanding of the principles of conservation came about through spiritual revelation, much like Pinchot's experience in Rock Creek Park.

The religious mode of conversion served the conservationists' goals precisely because of its strong implications for social action, particularly the impetus to convert the unbeliever. Indeed, Gifford Pinchot appealed directly to the evangelical spirit in his book *The Fight For Conservation*: "Among the first duties of every man is to help in bringing the Kingdom of God on earth. The greatest human power for good, the most efficient earthly tool for the future uplifting of the nations is without question the United States."[22] The leaders of the movement encouraged each individual to promote the conservation gospel, "second only . . . . to the great fundamental questions of morality," by applying Christian virtue to the common good.[23] With missionary zeal rivaling Roosevelt's aggressive militarism, conservationists framed their movement as a force for civilizing and refining those people and nations who had not yet reached the level of enlightenment bequeathed to the United States.

Conservation as a concept was particularly useful in transforming what could have been perceived as a technical, bureaucratic reorganization or a scientific procedure into a movement that engaged the moral and even spiritual responsibility of the individual to the public good and the United States to the world. As Samuel P. Hays wrote, the tenor of the discourse "tinged the conservation movement with the emotion of a religious crusade."[24] Nevertheless, conservationists continued to justify the new and revolutionary principles of conservation by further characterizing its constituency, placing the movement firmly within a temporal context, and conferring upon it a long-term and respectable claim to agency.

Constituting Identity: The People as a Designation of the Public

The concept of conservation indeed served well to identify and unify the scientific, ethical, and political themes of the movement. When opponents questioned the legitimacy of progressivist political policy, however, conservationists needed to further justify their assumption that the federal government was the best manager of natural resources. In response to such opposition, the conservationists developed a functional national policy from the evolutionary principles of science and the social theories that emerged from those principles, and as a result they demonstrated the right of the government to act in the general public interest.

In developing a political policy, speakers for conservation placed the entire conservation movement within a temporal framework encompassing the technological and intellectual history of humankind, as well as the history of the nation. Historical justification was a particularly appropriate mode of argument for the conservationists because their ideology was rooted in the scientific and social premises of progressive evolutionary thinking. Note, for example, this excerpt from Theodore Roosevelt's introductory speech at the conference of governors:

The steadily increasing drain on these natural resources has promoted to an extraordinary degree the complexity of our industrial and social life. Moreover, this unexampled development has had a determining effect upon the character and opinions of our people. The demand for efficiency in the great task has given us vigor, effectiveness, decision, and power, and a capacity for achievement which in its own lines has never yet been matched. . . . [I]t is safe to say that the prosperity of our people depends directly on the energy and intelligence with which our natural resources are used. It is equally clear that these resources are the final basis of national power and perpetuity. Finally, it is ominously evident that these sources are in the course of rapid exhaustion.[25]

From the conservationists' evolutionary viewpoint, natural resources not only existed as an organized system but also exerted a force inevitably modifying the characteristics of future generations. Furthermore, to lend immediacy to their warnings, advocates of conservation constructed a history of wasteful consumption that began in the ancient past, continued into the present era, and made every subsequent conservation measure urgent and necessary. The following paragraph from the president's speech underscores such urgency:

This Nation began with the belief that its landed possessions were illimitable and capable of supporting all the people who might care to make our country their home; but already the limit of unsettled land is in sight. . . . We began with an unapproached heritage of forests; more than half of the timber is gone. We began with coal fields more extensive than those of any other nation . . . and many experts now declare that the end of both iron and coal is in sight.[26]

It may not be a coincidence that the last half of the nineteenth century witnessed an unprecedented level of scientific discussion concerning not only natural resources but also large groups of extinct species, from dinosaurs to Native American tribes. In the case of American civilization, a glorious history of human development would be brought to a sudden and devastating end if citizens ignored the increasing depletion of the very raw materials that fostered that history.

The scientific theory supporting such ideas was labeled "neo-Lamarckianism," after Darwin's famous but wrongheaded predecessor whose theories were still quite popular at the turn of the century. Lamarck hypothesized that variations in the characteristics of members of a species came about through encounters with the environment. Hence, in a famous example, the need to survive by eating the leaves on taller and taller trees resulted in the gradual lengthening of the giraffe's neck, a characteristic subsequently passed down to its offspring. Indeed, since no one, including Darwin, was certain of the source of species variation, such an explanation seemed plausible until the phenomenon of genetic mutation was discovered. Therefore, those species that could alter the conditions under which they dwelled could also take an active role in altering their own characteristic qualities, presumably for the general improvement of the group. For conservationists, neo-Lamarckianism associated the evolutionary development of a species with the pressing need and the inherent capability to direct and regulate that development. Conservation was a law of nature that insured that survival of the most developed species required not merely strength but also ingenuity, foresight, and even benevolence.

The concept of neo-Lamarckian evolution was fully articulated by the early 1900s. But the language that most effectively communicated both the temporal inevitability of conservation and the immediate urgency of its tasks permeated the writing of one man, the ethnologist, geologist, and popularizer of science, W. J. McGee (1853–1912). As acknowledged intellectual leader of the movement (Pinchot labeled him the "scientific brains" of conservation and attributed to him the creation of the formula "the greatest good for the greatest number for the longest time"), McGee remained comparatively unknown to the majority of those becoming conscious of the growing movement, as his influence was exerted primarily from within the bureaucracy. His most influential appointments, for example, were as vice president and secretary of the Inland Waterways Commission, editor of the Proceedings of the Conference of Governors, leader of the Bureau of Ethnology, and president of the National Geographic Society.[27] His more scholarly publications were unavailable to the majority of those aware of conservation, though he did publish some of his ideas in such outlets as the *World's Work, American Review of Reviews,* and *Conservation* magazine.[28]

Despite McGee's relative obscurity, his influence appears to have pervaded the conservationists' most public literature. According to the historian Whitney Cross and Pinchot's own testimony, McGee collaborated with Pinchot in anonymously composing many of the official published statements of conservation, including several of Theodore Roosevelt's addresses.[29]

A close reading of McGee's idiomatic discourse confirms this claim. Indeed, McGee built a requirement for a successful rhetorical appeal into the very fabric of his ideology. As Charland has pointed out, by identifying, historicizing, and motivating the construction of the political public, McGee was the writer who most insistently infused "freedom of choice" into an already positioned population. Conservationists repeatedly evoked his idea of the American people to lend credibility to their claims. In doing so, they reinforced the perception of their social movement, not as a special interest group or bureaucratic creation but as a natural evolutionary trend representing all the American public.

In official statements and individual writings, McGee promulgated portions of his sophisticated and complex view of the relationship between humanity and nature, a view that appears nowhere in its entirety. Excerpts, however, show that McGee viewed the conservation movement as the culminating phase of a great evolutionary pageant rooted in the well-known but still debatable principles of neo-Lamarckian evolution.[30] As early as 1894 McGee's papers before the Smithsonian Institution raised controversy by insisting that "the characters of organisms are determined through interaction with environment."[31] Distinct from social Darwinists, whose notion of the "battle of the fittest" meant a conflict among individual members of a given species, neo-Lamarckians located the battle upon an environmental backdrop, with species of every kind struggling to adapt themselves to the conditions provided them by nature.

The importance of McGee's contribution to conservationism came in his direct application of evolutionary principles to humanity's relationship with the environment. According to McGee, mankind as a species was unique on two counts: first, the effect of environmental influences exerted upon humanity was primarily spiritual rather than physical, and second, humanity exhibited the particularly distinguishing trait of active adaptation, the ability to modify at will the immediate confines of environmental influence.

> The failure of the law [of the environment producing physical variation], when extended to mankind, is apparent only. The desert nomads retain common physical characteristics, but develop arts of obtaining water and food, and these acts are adjusted to the local environment; dwellers alongshore do not suffer modification in bodily form, but their arts are modified and they become fishermen and sailors; the mountaineers do not acquire the physical characters of the subhuman animals of the mountains, but learn to use weapons and to protect themselves from bodily injury by artificial devices. . . . Thus development, differentiation, transformation, are no less characteristic of the human genus than of lower organisms—indeed, it is in this noblest of organisms that plasticity or adjustability to diverse conditions culminates—but the differentiation is intellectual rather than physical, cerebral rather than corporeal.[32]

McGee's characteristically dense prose at times obscured his point. But the upshot of his claim for humanity's unique adaptive characteristics was a construction of human nature that satisfied social reformers' desire to differentiate humankind from animals, and supported the argument that human action need not always be selfish or defensive in nature. Human nature itself, according to McGee, was shaped by its historical interaction with the forces of the environment, and that struggle could have morally progressive results.

One additional factor, besides spirituality and adaptability, ultimately differentiated mankind from animals—and distinguished McGee's variety of evolutionary thought. Instead of viewing the individuality of humanity as its most important trait, producing virility, independence, and perhaps conflict and struggle, McGee emphasized the adaptability of the *cooperative* or *social* tendencies. "The essential unit is the organization rather than the organism," McGee stated, and society was the chief means of adapting to, or conquering, the natural environment.[33] He even claimed that the rough and ready mountaineering character, exemplified by many others with reference to the independent Swiss, did not create competition among individuals but produced a "regard for neighbor," an "altruistic government," and a true "nationhood," through "ceaseless strife against rocks and ice."[34] McGee's interest in the social implications of evolution transformed the figure of the isolated mountaineer directly confronting the wilderness into a representative of the collective spirit shaping and manipulating its natural surroundings. For McGee, the primary virtues ultimately resulted from societal development and institutionalization. "Justice, truth, mercy, and probity," derived not from individual experience but from socially productive organization.[35] The scientific designation of individual human beings as members of a species became the social-scientific designation of humans as part of a people.

Consequently, as a continuing society with its roots in primal history and its future contingent upon the American destiny, for McGee "the People" was itself a sociobiological entity, the most adaptive unit of human organization and development possible. But why not recognize, his critics might ask, that active adaptation in the form of social organization contained the potential for depletion of the very resources that provided humanity its character? McGee's response was measured: Given its biological foundation, the human urge to conquer nature was neither good nor evil but itself a temporary stage in the evolutionary development of the people. As society developed throughout successive stages, its very existence depended upon a blend of primitive and progressive forces—a "balance between impulse and responsibility"—that came about only if the people overcame their impulse to conquer nature and gradually turned their energies toward cooperation with each other and with their environment.[36]

This evolution of character was only possible if society developed an intelligent and self-reflective awareness of humankind's place in the natural flow of history, a perspective that McGee consistently attempted to provide throughout his historical review. "All our national extravagances are shocking to sensibilities once awakened," McGee stated, and he hoped that the response of civilized society would be a sense of self-consciousness that would motivate it to curb its lust for material gain.[37] Again, the similarity of these ideas with the basic tenets of neo-Lamarckian evolutionary theory is apparent. Human beings, at the apex of the biological order, were the only species whose cognitive faculties were developed enough for them to be aware of their own fate. As a result, moral attitudes toward natural resources required intelligence, self-reflection, and a remarkable degree of self-control.

Finally, through his concept of "the People," McGee prepared the way for viewing the future of the American people as a stirring patriotic and even spiritual consummation of the gospel of conservation. As always, the source of patriotic pride remained the environment, the North American landscape that overwhelmed its discoverers and overcame any natural wonder Europe could boast. However, in the grand evolutionary pageant of conservation, the various elements of the environment of the United States were elevated to characters of epic proportions that acted out their parts on the stage of human history. As a result, the new environmental consciousness became part of a civic ritual: "Just as the Land for which the Fathers fought was at once the tangible basis and the inspiration for patriotism in an earlier day, so in this day the birthright Land, the soil-making Forests, the native Minerals, and the life-giving Waters inspire Patriotism anew. Each is well worthy of story and song and shrine; and each inspiration is warmer and the whole are knit in closer union by reason of each other." The United States took its national identity not from its civilized products of art and culture, as did the worn-out countries of Europe, but from the very material elements that formed and shaped its character. Further, America was destined to be the quintessentially evolved nation, primarily because of its recognition "in story and song and shrine" of its own material origins.[38]

Significantly, the consummation of the civic ritual praising the natural environment evoked a spiritual "exaltation," much like the exaltation of the sublime response. If there were to be a national religion, it was to be based upon near-worship of natural resources at the shrine of perpetual conservation: "A new Patriotism has appeared. . . . Its object is the conservation of national resources; its end the perpetuation of People and States and the exaltation of Humanity. The keynote of its cry unto the spirits of men is the *Greatest Good for the Greatest Number for the Longest Time*." As individual human beings eventually died, the only conceivable form of eternal life was the continuity of collective existence. Only conservation would ensure a form of eternal life for the biological entity called "the People," and the measure of that vitality was the kind of aroused popular opinion that Gifford Pinchot later called "public spirit."[39]

The conservationist view of humanity as both user and preserver of natural wealth assumed that humans were intelligent, self-perceptive, and able to modify their actions in the course of time. However, to confirm its claims to ultimate truth, the conservationist impulse required more than rational self-awareness and self-control; it also required wide recognition from the American public. Hence the arousing of an "exaltation" or "public spirit" among its popular audience was a primary goal of the major conservationists. Certainly a social movement of considerable force would legitimate the actions already taken by the government and provide a counterforce to the attitude of "free giving" and monopoly that were perceived as threats to the remaining resources.[40] But more importantly, the conservation movement required popular as well as institutionalized support because it based its very concept of truth upon the role of a public in control of its own destiny; that is, as a people possessing the "illusion of freedom." In sum, it may be said that the form of the movement—as an organization with a popular base—was prepared in advance to correspond with its basic ideological premises through the constitutive power of conservationist discourse.[41]

The Discursive Construction of a Conservationist People

The creation of a movement that could demonstrate its claims for public support depended at its base upon the expressed belief of its leadership in the efficacy of public opinion—in Pinchot's term, "public spirit." This belief was transformed into media of communication intended to reach a widespread public. The story of how the public actually stepped into the activist role sketched by Pinchot, Roosevelt, and McGee lies beyond the scope of this chapter. But extensive documentation supports the claim that Pinchot, in particular, took up McGee's conceptions and transformed them into widely distributed and persuasive popular discourse. Using circulars, bulletins, articles, and other easily available writing composed in a distinctive style, the leaders of the conservation movement established links between the central organization and its public audience. The resulting success of the movement finally depended upon its use of convincing rhetoric to place the public into the position of the conservationist conception of the people, and as a result to forge a bond between public spirit and the public interest.[42]

Nonetheless, it is still possible to make a general estimate of the more ideological outcomes of the movement by way of summary and conclusion. From a broad perspective, the movement for conservation may be seen as a part of the continuing development in public attitudes toward appreciation of nature that began in the mid-nineteenth century. From this broader view, conservation diverged sharply from the entrepreneurial attitude of exploration and development that had reigned since the nation's beginnings. In Dorsey's terms, the myth of the frontier hero had indeed been replaced by the myth of the yeoman farmer, but a particularly well-informed, rational, and efficient yeoman farmer. With evangelistic zeal, adherents promoted the idea that a new level in the evolutionary history of the American people as a species had been reached through cultural mythology, intellectual self-consciousness, and Rooseveltian bureaucracy. Indeed, the model for efficiency and organization in government was Gifford Pinchot's Forest Service, in particular, and government conservationism in general. Modern historians tended to agree with the movement's proponents that conservation was a veritable revolution in human political and social arrangements as well as in the human spirit.

Conservation, however, was not so removed from its historical and cultural roots as its proponents often wished to imply. A closer reading of conservationist discourse reveals that the policy of social change manifest in conservationist rhetoric drew directly from several cultural conceptions prevalent by the first decade of the twentieth century in America. Those conceptions, based in neo-Lamarckian evolution, progressivist social consciousness, flourishing American nationalism, and barely secularized spiritualism, were combined to create a unifying and organic model of public action. Thus the thematically precise fabrication of the people determined to a considerable degree both the constitution of the movement and its incorporation into governmental structure. Conservation in this more specific view can be seen as a reformist, middle-of-the-road orientation toward public policy typical of other progressive movements of the turn of the century. It certainly was not revolutionary in comparison to such conceptions of the environment as preservationism, a movement that advocated the perpetuation of nature for its own sake.

Yet regardless of the evaluative perspective one might take, retelling the story of conservation can make a definitive contribution to our understanding of communication, particularly its conceptual basis. This chapter may better serve to illustrate the ideological foundations of political and social discourse than to answer the question of whether conservation itself was either groundbreaking or ameliorist. As the rationale of a nationwide social movement that ultimately merged with a governmental bureaucracy, conservation derived its greatest level of integration and potential influence from the discursive construction of its own constituency. This discourse, manifested in the rhetoric of Theodore Roosevelt, Gifford Pinchot, and W. J. McGee, inserted a collective human figure, "the People," into the largest tapestry of time available to thinkers of their age. It was a figure that required of its readers and its listeners the acceptance of an inevitable position within that framework of time and a voluntary willingness to adopt that position.

Further, the figure of the people demonstrated the truth of its own scientific and social premises to the degree the policy itself was supported by the public. The concept of the people acting freely to constrain their consumption of resources was built into the very fabric of conservationist language, thus providing a rationale and a directive to those citizens who wished to behave in accordance with natural law. It may not be claiming too much that movements of any size or type require this kind of constitutive figuration, not only of potential audiences and followers but also of leaders, strategies, and the environments that serve as scenic background. If so, the threads that make up such a tapestry will be discovered nowhere else but in the details of rhetorical discourse, for there the concepts of the mind find their tactile manifestation.

Notes

The author thanks Tarla Rai Peterson and two anonymous reviewers for elucidating the potential of this study. It was originally delivered under the title "Presidential Public Policy and Conservation: W. J. McGee and the People" at the Conference on the Presidency and Environmental Policy, Texas A&M University, College Station, Texas, Feb. 28–Mar. 2, 1997. Portions of the material were later included in a book chapter entitled "Science, Public Policy, and the 'Spirit of the People': The Rhetoric of Progressive Conservation," in *Rhetoric and Reform in the Progressive Era*, ed. J. Michael Hogan (East Lansing: University of Michigan Press, 2002). The chapter presented here contains additional conceptual development and textual analysis. It is dedicated to the memory of Michael Calvin McGee.

1. Roderick Nash, *Wilderness and the American Mind*, 3d ed. (New Haven: Yale University Press, 1982), 143. The culminating statement on the closing of the frontier was Frederick Jackson Turner's reference to the census bulletin of 1890 before the 1893 meeting of the American Historical Association: "'Up to and including 1880 the country had a frontier of settlement, but at present the unsettled area has been so broken into by isolated bodies of settlement that there can hardly be said to be a frontier line. . . .' This brief official statement marks the closing of a great historic movement." Turner's further claim that "the existence of an area of free land, its continuous recession, and the advance of American settlement westward, explain American development" pointed up the urgency of retaining areas of underdeveloped land for the sake of preserving the particular character of American life (Turner, "The Significance of the Frontier in American History," in *The Frontier in American History* [New York: Henry Holt, 1948], 1).

2. Conference of Governors, *Proceedings*, ed. W. J. McGee, May 13–15, 1908, (Washington, D.C.: Government Printing Office, 1909), 67; for similar sentiments, see also 7 and 74. Hereafter cited as Governors' Conference.

3. Governors' Conference, 32, 40, 148, 179–80.

4. Leroy Dorsey, "The Frontier Myth in Presidential Rhetoric: Theodore Roosevelt's Campaign for Conservation," *Western Journal of Communication* 59 (1995): 1–19.

5. Samuel P. Hays, *Conservation and the Gospel of Efficiency: The Progressive Conservation Movement, 1890–1920* (New York: Atheneum, 1974); and Alan Trachtenberg, *The Incorporation of America: Culture and Society in the Gilded Age* (New York: Hill and Wang, 1982).

6. The general outline for the "constitutive" components of the development of "the People" is derived from Maurice Charland, "Constitutive Rhetoric: The Case of the *Peuple Quebecois*," *Quarterly Journal of Speech* 73 (1987). See also Trachtenberg, *The Incorporation*, 180–81.

7. Charland, 41.

8. Robert Gottlieb, *Forcing the Spring: The Transformation of the American Environmental Movement* (Washington, D.C.: Island Press, 1993), 24; Stephen Fox, *John Muir and His Legacy: The American Conservation Movement* (Boston: Little, Brown, 1981), 130; Charles R. Van Hise, *The Conservation of Natural Resources in the United States* (New York: Macmillan, 1926), 67; Gifford Pinchot, *The Fight for Conservation* (New York: Doubleday, Page, 1910), 1; Treadwell Cleveland, Jr., *Forest Service Circular: A Primer of Conservation*, no. 157 (USDA, 1908); J. Leonard Bates, "Fulfilling American Democracy: The Conservation Movement, 1907 to

1921," *Mississippi Valley Historical Review* 44 (1957): 32; Samuel Eliot Morison and Henry Steele Commager, *The Growth of the American Republic,* 4th ed. (New York: Oxford University Press, 1950), 2:399–401. Frank E. Smith in *The Politics of Conservation* (New York: Pantheon-Random, 1966), 108, stated only that "a much publicized Governors' Conference on Conservation was held at the White House . . . but it changed few votes in Congress."

9. Pinchot, *Fight for Conservation,* 41.

10. Roy M. Robbins, *Our Landed Heritage: The Public Domain, 1776–1936* (New York: Peter Smith, 1950), 311–12, and Robert Underwood Johnson, *Remembered Yesterdays* (Boston: Little, Brown, 1993), 278–313, discuss the particularly influential work of the *Century* editorialists during the early years of the forest reserves. The shift in popular interest from the "genteel" magazines to more topical, reform-oriented magazines after 1890 did not reduce the popularity of conservation; advocates published in *McClure's* and *Collier's* as well as the *Century.* Roosevelt himself was on the staff of the *Outlook* for a short period, and Pinchot used the *World's Work* as an outlet for his more popular writings. See Frank Luther Mott, *A History of American Magazines, 1865–1885* (1938; rpt., Cambridge, Mass.: Harvard University Press, 1957), 3:1–14, 430–31; and Mott, *A History of American Magazines, 1885–1905* (Cambridge, Mass.: Harvard University Press, 1957), 4:779.

11. Quoted in Paul Russell Cutright, *Theodore Roosevelt: The Making of a Conservationist* (Urbana: University of Illinois Press, 1985), 238.

12. Pinchot, *Fight for Conservation,* 42–47.

13. Ibid., 42.

14. For a thorough discussion of contemporary concepts of sustainable development, see Tarla Rai Peterson, *Sharing the Earth: The Rhetoric of Sustainable Development* (Columbia: University of South Carolina Press, 1997).

15. Van Hise, 362.

16. Gifford Pinchot, "How Conservation Began in the United States," *Agricultural History* 11 (1937): 262–63; emphasis added. The importance of this event in the history of conservation is underscored by Pinchot in his biography *Breaking New Ground* (New York: Harcourt, Brace, 1947), 322–26.

17. Bates, 31; Hays, 72.

18. Governors' Conference, 12. See also *National Conservation Association: What It Is* (N.p.: n.p., n.d.), 1, and Trachtenberg, 194.

19. Pinchot, *Breaking New Ground,* 322.

20. John R. Ross, "Man over Nature: Origins of the Conservation Movement," *American Studies* 16 (Spring, 1975), 52; Hays, 72.

21. W. J. McGee, "The Conservation of Natural Resources," *Mississippi Valley Historical Association Proceedings, 1909–1910* (Cedar Rapids, Iowa, 1911), 378.

22. Pinchot, *Fight for Conservation,* 95.

23. Governors' Conference, 3.

24. Hays, 145.

25. Governors' Conference, 7.

26. Ibid., 7.

27. Pinchot, *Breaking New Ground,* 325–26; Smith, 101; and Gottlieb, 25. The only biography I have been able to locate was written by McGee's sister, Emma R. McGee, *The Life of W. J. McGee; Distinguished Geologist, Ethnologist, Anthropologist, Hydrologist, etc. in Service of United States Government with Extracts from Addresses and Writings* (Farley, Iowa: Torch Press, 1915). This small volume of reminiscences

contains a useful bibliography of his more scientific publications. W. J. McGee insisted that no periods follow the two initials in his name, in order to conserve ink. He also characteristically capitalized many words, particularly "the People," which makes tracing much of his influence upon other authors and speakers a relatively forthright task.

28. In addition to McGee's conservationist writings, which are cited throughout this chapter, there was a short series in the magazine *Science* reporting on the official conferences and policies of the movement (see, for example, "Recent Steps in the Conservation Movement," *Science* [April 2, 1908]: 539–40; and "Current Progress in Conservation Work," *Science* [March 26, 1909]: 490–96); an article entitled "Water as a Resource," in the conservation issue of the *Annals of the American Academy of Political and Social Science, 1909* (Philadelphia, 1909): 521–50; and such articles in *World's Work* as "Our Great River," Feb. 1907, 857–84; and "How One Billion of Us Can Be Fed," Feb. 1912, 443–51.

29. Whitney Cross, "W. J. McGee and the Idea of Conservation," *Historian* 15 (Spring, 1953): 159, 161–62; Pinchot, *Breaking New Ground*, 188, 328, 346, 350; Graham, 133; Hays, 129, 140.

30. Increasingly, the neo-Lamarckian flavor of evolutionary theory in the United States in the later part of the nineteenth century is being recognized. See, for example, Peter J. Bowler, *Darwinism* (New York: Twayne, 1993). One index to the influence of neo-Lamarckian thought such as that of McGee's upon the non-technical literature of conservation is reference to noted authorities in the field. For example, Nathaniel Shaler, a famous neo-Lamarckian, is mentioned by Pinchot in *Fight for Conservation*, 9; James J. Hill in his Governors' Conference speech, 64; Van Hise, in "Patriotism that Counts," *Century* (July, 1908): 475; and C. H. Forbes-Lindsay, "Taking Stock of our National Assets: The Far-Reaching Significance of the White House Conference" (July, 1908): 377.

31. W. J. McGee, "The Relation of Institutions to the Environment," *Annual Report of the Board of Regents of the Smithsonian Institution, 1895* (Washington, D.C.: Government Printing Office, 1896), pt. 1, 704; Cross, 152; Ross, 52.

32. McGee, "Relation of Institutions," 704–705.

33. Ibid., 705.

34. W. J. McGee, "National Growth and National Character," *National Geographic Magazine,* June, 1899, 195. McGee was a hydrographer and a geologist, so it is not surprising to find him attributing the highest levels of human development to migratory wandering and intermingling between coastal and highland desert peoples, as he does in the 1895 Smithsonian address. However, the influence of Americans' more than sixty-year identification with mountaineering figures led McGee in the *National Geographic* article to make an obligatory comparison between the Swiss and the American characters.

35. McGee, "Relation of Institutions," 711.

36. McGee, "Conservation of Natural Resources," 366.

37. McGee, "Conservation of Natural Resources," 374. In the campaign for national organization and efficiency and against waste, the Rooseveltian conservationists paradoxically found themselves attacking individualism under the leadership of a president noted for that very trait. See the attacks on individualism in Pinchot, "Foundations of National Prosperity," *North American Review,* Nov., 1908, 748; Van Hise, "Patriotism and Waste," *Collier's,* Sept. 18, 1909, 41; and George L. Knapp, "The Other Side of Conservation," *North American Review,* April, 1910, 465–81.

38. McGee, "The Cult of Conservation," *Conservation,* Sept., 1908, 472.
39. McGee, "The Cult of Conservation," 469.
40. Smith, 108.
41. Van Hise, *Conservation of Natural Resources,* 394; Bates, 39; Grant McConnell, "The Conservation Movement—Past Present," *Western Political Quarterly* 7 (1954): 463–78.
42. For further discussion of the dissemination of conservationist discourse through the media and an account of its persuasive effect, see Christine L. Oravec, "Science, Public Policy, and the 'Spirit of the People': The Rhetoric of Progressive Conservation," chapter 3 in *Rhetoric and Reform in the Progressive Era,* ed. J. Michael Hogan, vol. 6 of *A Rhetorical History of the United States,* ed. Martin J. Medhurst (East Lansing: University of Michigan Press, 2002).

PART II

Environmental

Rhetoric

and Political

Pragmatism

3

The President
and the Reformer

Rhetoric, Politics, and the Environment
under Franklin Delano Roosevelt

Suzanne M. Daughton and Vanessa B. Beasley

Zachary Taylor is not remembered as an environmentalist. In fact, the nation's twelfth president is probably not remembered today for much of anything at all. Taylor's relative obscurity may be the result of his brief term; he served just over one year as chief executive, dying in 1850 after eating tainted cherries at a July Fourth celebration. Yet at least one of Taylor's actions has had lasting effects. In 1849 he named Thomas Ewing as the first national secretary of the interior, and in so doing, formally brought environmental issues into the purview of the federal government and its executive branch.

To be sure, the types of environmental issues the Department of Interior has concerned itself with have varied greatly since Taylor's day. In the mid-1800s the department's most active agency was its Bureau of Indian Affairs, with the offices citizens are presumably more familiar with today—including U.S. Fish and Wildlife, Bureau of Land Management, and the National Park Service—being more recent additions. As this federal department's responsibilities have grown, so too has citizens' interest in the environment. Nongovernmental organizations such as the Sierra Club have acted repeatedly to influence federal legislation on parks, wildlife, and other natural resources during the twentieth century.

If the natural environment has become increasingly politicized since Taylor's presidency, then U.S. politics has had to become more and more environmental.[1] Over time, presidents have had to think—and talk—more often about such matters, even though the natural world has been a difficult subject for many of them, as some of the chapters in this volume reveal. In the United States this difficulty is exacerbated by the apparent clash between the pragmatism driving the liberal democratic system and the moral imperatives implicit in most environmental rhetoric.[2] Politicians, it seems, are motivated by the pathologies of their present constituents, while the environmentally minded frequently seek to ensure a better future—not only for human beings, but also for "animals, plants, and possibly even for the Earth itself."[3]

If politics and environmentalism make strange bedfellows, it is perhaps odd that one chief executive, is remembered today as a champion of both. The ultimate pragmatist and consummate politician Franklin Delano Roosevelt is also widely credited with initiating some of the most significant conservation-oriented programs and policies in U.S. history. As part of his earliest New Deal legislation, the president approved unprecedented amounts of federal spending on public relief and appropriated large sums to resource development and conservation.[4] Under his guidance, A. L. Riesch Owen has noted, the American conservation movement "came into maturity" and "triumphed."[5]

Perhaps because none of his presidential successors have matched FDR's prolific record, many historians and biographers seeking insight into his environmental initiatives have attributed them to his personal love of nature. "[B]iographers all agree that he held a lifelong belief in the necessity for conservation," FDR Library director Herman Kahn once observed. His "keen interest and considerable knowledge" of the environment, Frank Freidel has written, began early in his youth under the watchful eyes of his uncle Theodore and his associate Gifford Pinchot. The noted FDR scholar James MacGregor Burns suggested that this love of nature motivated Roosevelt to pass an impressive number of farm and conservation bills while serving as a state senator in New York. Throughout Roosevelt's political career, Kahn argues, his "main emphasis" was "the conservation of all the natural resources of the nation."[6] FDR was "most interested in, and most eloquent about, the devastation of our forests, the destruction of our soil, and the needless spoliation of our great scenic and wilderness areas."[7]

After reading these descriptions, one might suppose that Franklin Roosevelt was the ideal Green politician, unilaterally exercising his senatorial, and later, presidential power on a crusade to protect the environment. This assessment, however, would not be entirely complete. While there is ample evidence that Roosevelt was genuinely interested in the natural world (and specifically forests), he was also an astute student of American politics. As such, he knew, perhaps, that citizens in democracies have to make difficult choices about how limited resources will be used.[8] While this political truth is always significant, it was particularly relevant when Roosevelt occupied the White House. Why would citizens support efforts to conserve the environment when, during the Great Depression or the early years of World War II, for example, they were presumably much more worried about preserving themselves?

In a series of presidential speeches and messages, Roosevelt gave citizens and legislators good reasons to do so.[9] Instead of talking about the need to preserve or even appreciate nature for its own sake, Roosevelt repeatedly argued that conservation made good economic sense for the United States. In its name FDR created jobs (via the Civilian Conservation Corps, [CCC] for example) and promised more efficient management of natural resources (such as the Tennessee Valley Authority). In this chapter, we explore how Roosevelt crafted such a politically efficacious environmental discourse. Specifically, we argue that Roosevelt successfully associated ecological action with the country's economic needs, thereby furthering conservation initiatives in the 1930s and '40s.

Not everyone thought Roosevelt went far enough in these efforts, however. One of the best- known conservationists of the era, Jay Norwood "Ding" Darling, was particularly critical of Roosevelt's brand of environmentalism, even though he himself was briefly a member of the FDR administration. To recover this alternative, and frequently neglected, critique of Roosevelt's conservation rhetoric, we also discuss Darling's reactions to FDR, represented through his private correspondence with the president as well as his public, Pulitzer Prize–winning cartoons. By using Darling's work to represent the more ideologically pure, but presumably less politically viable, rhetorical path FDR chose not to take, we hope to show that Roosevelt's environmental rhetoric was born out of a negotiation between political compromise and environmental commitment—a middle course with both benefits and limitations.

Roosevelt's Challenge

Even if FDR had wanted to convince Congress and U.S. citizens to value the environment for its own sake, the president presumably would have had difficulty making such an argument. Historically, the American people have repeatedly chosen short-term, economic benefits over long-term, environmental ones in their decisions about natural resources. Even the colonists did so; acutely aware of American timber's value on the international market, they passed the nation's earliest conservation legislation solely to protect this valuable crop.[10] Citizens' seemingly insatiable appetite for forestry products grew at such a rate during the nineteenth century that Noah Webster predicted "the improvidence of the people of this country for timber would some day be regretted."[11]

As long as environmental resources have appeared plentiful, however, most such warnings have repeatedly been eclipsed by popular calls for more immediate gratification. Even during times of environmental hardship, when citizens might be expected to endorse future conservation efforts, their leaders (including FDR) have advocated a "continuing and overwhelming faith in the logic of expanding production." Similarly, Christine Oravec has pointed out that even some of the past arguments for environmentalism have been framed largely in terms of social utility. Although these scholars and others have lamented the ways in which these rhetorics may prevent the American people from viewing the natural world as inherently valuable, the logic underlying such talk shows no signs of abating.[12]

Avarice alone might be too simplistic a characterization of an attitude many citizens may simply view as their birthright. In addition to historical precedent, the American people also share some philosophical beliefs that influence their relationship with the natural world. Some observers have noted, for example, that U.S. citizens' use of natural resources stems from a religious belief in humanity's dominion over nature.[13] Other scholars have expanded upon Frederick Turner's notion of a quintessentially American "New Western" spirit by suggesting that such impulses drive citizens to seek control over new frontiers.[14] More recently, some feminists have argued that Americans' disregard for the environment is merely another manifestation of a patriarchal culture.[15]

If American citizens are somehow socialized against thinking in terms of the environment's intrinsic value, then they would have presumably been even less inclined to do so during the FDR years. The historian Doris Kearns Goodwin has followed Eleanor Roosevelt's lead in labeling the latter years of Roosevelt's presidency as "no ordinary time," but from an ecological standpoint, the same could be said of all his terms.[16] When FDR assumed office in 1933, the country was reeling from the economic devastation of the Great Depression. Environmental crises exacerbated such worries during the 1930s, as severe droughts and the subsequent dust bowls plagued residents from the plains to the East Coast. By 1940 the American people were increasingly turning their attention to the mounting hostilities abroad; by 1942 citizens were probably more interested in conserving their food rations than anything else. In the face of all these competing exigencies, FDR still managed to enact historic environmental legislation, referring to conservation as "one of the primary responsibilities of the federal government at all times."[17]

Roosevelt's Response

Lest this reference reveal too much of a philosophical commitment to environmentalism, however, Roosevelt was quick to point out that he did not subscribe to any one specific way of thinking. Asked once by a young reporter about his philosophy (after the president had rejected the labels of Communist, capitalist, and socialist), a puzzled Roosevelt replied, "Philosophy? Philosophy? I am a Christian and a Democrat, that's all."[18] Although committed to liberalism in general, Roosevelt often combined a liberal approach with elements of conservatism in his policies and in his discourse, delivering messages that sounded liberal but had conservative policy implications, and vice versa. This practice infuriated opponents on both the right and the left because it frequently kept them off balance, wondering how to oppose someone who rarely stayed in one place for long. Indeed, his cabinet choices alone provide a miniature portrait of his affection for diversity and have for years frustrated historians seeking an underlying logic.[19]

FDR's philosophy (or antiphilosophy) of governing can perhaps best be summed up by saying that he believed in experimenting with a variety of solutions to specific problems and discarding those he did not see as productive. As president, he often sought a course of action that was visible only in the rearview mirror as the midline between zigs to the left and zags to the right.[20] Even then, this path was sometimes only visible to the driver as a "middle road." Despite his constant changing of directions, Roosevelt saw his efforts as all part of the "science of government," a discipline aimed primarily at learning "how to understand people [and] how to influence them."[21]

FDR-as-rhetorical-scientist crafted an appeal for conservation that might influence people by addressing their economic and social problems. Human needs, he argued—especially during times of crisis—were best served by careful, "systematic husbandry" of nature's bounty.[22] This was a position he had advocated previously as a New York senator, when he had joined Republican progressives on state development of water power.[23] Yet the phrase "systematic husbandry" is telling in its implications of the planned human intervention into natural processes that FDR would advocate throughout his presidency. His argument about the necessity of such intervention manifested itself most visibly and dramatically in his public talk about *natural* resources as *national* resources.

In our analysis, we noticed that Roosevelt used both "natural resources" and "national resources" frequently, and we looked for the distinctions, if any, in his use of the phrases. We found that virtually all his discourse included discussion of "national resources," whether the specific topic was wildlife, forestry, soil conservation, or parkland. He always conflated natural resources *into* national resources, characterizing the virtues of the trees, soil, water, and animal life on the basis of what they could offer the country's population.[24]

But for the president, "national resources" included the skills of the populace as well (1935:8, 60). In an early address to Congress, Roosevelt spelled out the rationale for his choice of the term "national resources," providing insight into his strategy of stressing the interdependence of humans and the environment.

> Men and Nature must work hand in hand. The throwing out of balance of the resources of Nature throws out of balance also the lives of men.

We find millions of our citizens stranded in village and on farm—
stranded there because Nature cannot support them in the livelihood
they had sought to gain through her. We find millions gravitated to
centers of population so vast that the laws of natural economics have
broken down.

If the misuse of natural resources alone were concerned, we should
consider our problem only in terms of land and water. It is because misuse extends to what men and women are doing with their occupations
and to their many mistakes in herding themselves together that I have
chosen, in addressing the Congress, to use the broader term "National
Resources."

For the first time in our national history we have made an inventory
of our national assets and the problems relating to them. . . .

In this inventory of our national wealth we follow the custom of prudent people toward their own private property. We as a Nation take stock
of what we as a Nation own. We consider the uses to which it can be
put. . . . We think of our land and water and human resources not as
static and sterile possessions but as life-giving assets to be administered
by wise provision for future days. We seek to use our natural resources
not as a thing apart but as something that is interwoven with industry,
labor, finance, taxation, agriculture, homes, recreation, and good citi-
zenship. The results of this interweaving will have a greater influence on
the future American standard of living than all the rest of our economics
put together. (1935:8, 60–61)

Clearly, Roosevelt's depiction of land and water as assets owned by the nation
and meant to be used justifies a sense of entitlement that can quickly become
problematic and has certainly done so in our own time. Yet this imagery enabled Roosevelt to capitalize on the combination of short-term economic goals
and long-term environmental concerns to further immediate conservation
efforts in ways a less pragmatic rhetoric might have been unlikely to achieve.

In a substantial number of cases (more than one-quarter of the speeches
studied here), FDR actually spelled out the economic benefits of his proposed
conservation measures or used economic metaphors (such as "inventory" and
"assets" in the quotation above) that demonstrated the benefits of a proprietary interest in nature. For example, Roosevelt discussed the "agricultural
wealth" of New York State (1934:64, 194), described the soil as "our basic asset" (1937:25, 102), and called a federal irrigation project "a good investment"
(1937:116, 377). He talked about forest fires as "a frightful waste" of "our forest
wealth" (1937:80, 288), and drawing on his personal experience as a tree farmer

at Hyde Park, asserted that "Forestry pays from a practical point of view" (1944:101, 382).

Indeed, whether the topic was "national resources" or "natural resources," the noun being described (resources) implies that the item being talked about is to be *utilized* for some purpose beyond its own existence. Thus forests are not good in and of themselves but because of the benefits that accrue to humans. Trees become "crops" to be used as lumber, first for domestic needs and later for building boats for the war effort (1944:101, 380).

Soil conservation is essential for producing food for the people in the cities and for maintaining property values. In a fireside chat following his drought inspection trip in 1936, for example, Roosevelt lays out the following scenario: "If, for example, in some local area the water table continues to drop and the topsoil to blow away, the land values will disappear with the water and the soil. People on the farms will drift into the nearby cities; the cities will have no farm trade and the workers in the city factories and stores will have no jobs. Property values in the cities will decline" (1936:120, 333). By stressing the interrelatedness of the land and its people (and, of course, the people and their land), Franklin Roosevelt justifies the use of precious economic resources for conservation during a time of human suffering: "Spending like this is not waste. It would spell future waste if we did not spend for such things now. . . . That is why it is worth our while as a Nation to spend money in order to save money" (1936:120, 333).

Water, for example, can be controlled and used for power, as well as flood and drought prevention. In a campaign address in 1936 the president quotes himself during an earlier drought: "before American men and women get through with the job, we are going to make every ounce and every gallon of water that flows from the heavens and the hills count before it makes its way down to the Gulf of Mexico" (1936:159, 447). And what constitutes making every ounce count? Why, making it "work for the people of all the states through which [it] run[s]," of course (1936:159, 447).

And in its quest to be useful to the American people, wildlife becomes game. In one of the most telling examples, the president urges legislation to conserve reindeer herds in Alaska not because of the value of biological diversity but "to preserve for the future the only controllable food supply [for native peoples] for which the tundra areas of Alaska are suitable" (1939:95, 388). He speaks of a "reindeer industry" and reminds his audience that reindeer were imported "to replace . . . the indigenous food supply of the natives, which had been depleted by the expansion of American commerce and industry" (1939:95, 389). Essentially, then, whenever Roosevelt discusses nature he does so in terms of its national economic value. Nature is never valued in and of itself.

Indeed, Roosevelt would not even concede that nature was always a positive force, economically or otherwise. FDR expressed Americans' ambivalence toward nature in his use of metaphors of conflict.[25] At times, conservation-minded citizens fought to protect nature from the wicked ways of other, more exploitative human forces, as Roosevelt noted when recalling that "more than thirty years ago we, as a Nation, began a great battle to save our forest resources" (1937:80, 287). However, for Roosevelt and presumably for the American people, nature itself was sometimes the enemy, particularly when natural disasters threatened to destroy the gains in resources achieved by "developing" and thus "improving" on nature. In a greeting to the National Reclamation Association, Roosevelt says, "Many of these [irrigation projects] will serve as additional protection from the onslaught of nature for lands already developed" (1937:116, 376).

The closest FDR comes to expounding on the inherent worth of nature is in his discussion of "preserving the beauty" of parkland, which, of course, is still "useful" for the recreation of the American people (1936:81, 240). In his address at the dedication of Shenandoah National Park, Roosevelt provides one of the most telling examples of his characteristic appeals for an environmentalism that will bear economic fruit. Praising the work of "local and State and Federal authorities . . . engaged in preserving and developing our heritage of natural resources," he quickly equates this work with a higher purpose: the "conserving of our priceless heritage of human values by giving to hundreds of thousands of men the opportunity of making an honest living" (1936:81, 238). Here even Roosevelt's most "priceless" *human* values are economic, a theme that becomes more significant as the speech continues.

Alluding to the CCC members who have worked in the park, for example, FDR equates their previous unemployment with the land's. "The involuntary idleness of thousands of young men ended three years ago when they came here to the camps on the Blue Ridge. Since then they have not been idle. Today they have ended more than their own idleness, they have ended the idleness of the Shenandoah National Park. It will be a busy and useful place in the years to come, just as the work of these young men will, I am confident, lead them to busy and useful lives in the years to come" (1936:81, 238–39). Fortunately, then, through the work of the Civilian Conservation Corps, the park has now been rescued from its disgraceful shirking and can provide its highest service to the American people. Citizens who visit will "forget the rush and the strain of all the other long weeks of the year, and for a short time at least, the days will be good for their bodies and for their souls" (1936:81, 239). For FDR, the cycle of environmental benefits will then be complete, with the natural world providing rest and perspective for the American people, and presumably reinvigorating them to return to their "honest living" of productivity back at home.

Similarly, economic appeals for the conservation of all resources was a major focus of Roosevelt's rhetoric, appearing as a specific topic in most (nearly 80 percent) of the discourse we examined. And consistent with the focus described above, Roosevelt's version of conservation is often justified for its foresight regarding our children's inheritance; he talks in terms of "our heritage of natural resources" (1936:81, 238). Near the end of the Shenandoah National Park speech, FDR pledges, "We seek to pass on to our children a richer land—a stronger Nation" (1936:81, 240).

In the late 1930s, as national and international attention focused increasingly on the war in Europe, FDR spent less time talking specifically about the environment. When he did talk about issues of conservation, it was usually in terms of how prudent rationing of particular resources (especially those that were already industrially processed) could substantially aid the Allies' war effort. By the 1940s conservation of rubber, oil and gas, and food (and the growing of victory gardens) had all but replaced discussion of reforestation, water power and irrigation efforts, and soil and wildlife conservation.

For Roosevelt, the nation's bounty includes natural resources and more. His proprietary emphasis on the use of resources applies not only to plants, animals, water, and minerals but also to the people and their talents. The apparent arrogance of assuming that nature provides materials for our use is closely combined with a more humble look at ourselves as tools for the betterment of society and the environment.

Responses to Roosevelt

Measured in terms of program and policy creation, FDR's rhetoric does seem to have contributed to short-term betterment. The Civilian Conservation Corps, Public Works Administration, and Works Progress Administration, along with other agencies established under 1933's National Industrial Recovery Act all facilitated the immediate benefits that FDR sought to provide during his first years in ofice, with many of these efforts seemingly successful at linking conservation with economic relief in the public consciousness.[26]

FDR's rhetorical and legislative efforts influenced other politicians as well. At the beginning of his presidential term, with partisan politics minimized by the country's dire economic condition and the Democrats' landslide victory, Roosevelt's conservative efforts "suffered little to no partisan attack." By the 1936 election, when Republicans were challenging the New Deal more vocally, they remained relatively silent regarding its conservation policies, particularly since their constituents continued to battle flooding and dust bowls in their home states. Indeed, during this time period, Roosevelt's brand of conservation began to be viewed as something of a nonideological universal good. In 1937 congressional representative A. Willis Robertson summarized his political colleagues' sentiments on both sides of the aisle when he suggested that "conservation . . . is a nonpolitical activity in which we can unite." By the end of the 1930s, Owen writes, "conservation was a word the politicians loved."[27]

For Roosevelt, who wanted his conservation policies to continue long after his administration, this bipartisan affection was welcome.[28] Not everyone was enamored with Roosevelt's efforts, however. The president may have received credit for influencing most voters and politicians to see the benefits of the "systemic husbandry" of the natural world, but one American citizen remained leery of this reasoning throughout the FDR years. Unlike Roosevelt, Jay Darling had no bully pulpit from which to argue for his alternative brand of environmentalism, but he did have some political connections, a vicious wit, and an equally sharp pen.

The Politician and the Reformer

Jay Norwood Darling, better known as "Ding," was a two-time Pulitzer Prize–winning editorial cartoonist who made it his mission to prick the public conscience about conservation issues. A combination of social critic and environmental prophet, Ding was a self-taught artist who came to conservation through his college studies in biology. (Darling would later credit one professor at Beloit College with changing his life's course by showing him "the functional relationship of biology to man's existence.") From that point on, biographer David Lendt writes, "the desire to preserve life had become his occupation."[29]

An active outdoorsman, Jay Darling's dream was universal conservation education in order to ensure the environmental protection necessary for the health and well-being of all species. He served as a founding member of the Iowa Fish and Game Commission in the early 1930s, and he was influential nationwide through the syndication of his editorial cartoons, which appeared in more than one hundred major newspapers. In fact, Ding was one of the early mass media celebrities: His name was a household word and he became the foremost ecologist and conservationist of his day.[30]

Of his chosen profession, Darling said, "Every cartoon should contain a little medicine, a little sugar-coating and as much humor as the subject will bear." However, as the editor of a collection of his conservation and wildlife cartoons drily notes, Ding "sometimes forgot the sugar."[31] Not only are Ding's cartoons enlightening examples of political rhetoric from the first half of this century, they continue to speak to us today. For example, Darling was one of the first people in the United States to worry about fossil fuel shortages with a 1948 cartoon forecasting this predicament decades before the oil embargoes of the 1970s (fig. 1).[32] The cartoon, captioned "It's Nice Somebody Can Enjoy It," depicts life at the "Horse Retreat for Discarded Horse Power." In the background, an over-the-hill horse limps along on crutches. Several other crotchety old nags (literally "out to pasture") are seated on a bench and staring, startled, at the tuxedo-clad horse in the foreground. This "tycoon horse" is reclining in a comfortable rocking chair with his hooves on a stool, neighing with laughter as he scans the headlines in the "Extra" edition of the equine newspaper, "The Horse's World." They trumpet "Petroleum Famine On The Way," "World's Supply Inadequate for Expanding Uses," "End of Cheap Gasoline in Sight for Motorists, Farm Tractors and Power Plants," and "Big Hearted Uncle Sam is Living Way Beyond His Natural Resources." The photograph above the fold shows a stranded motorist, his eyes bugging out, his hat coming off his head, and his hair standing on end to illustrate his alarm as he literally screams "Bloody Murder!" Clearly, Darling could see a trend in the making, and took this opportunity to point out America's overdependence on fossil fuel and where it would lead.

An influential and farsighted public figure, Ding had some serious reservations about Roosevelt's conservation efforts. To be sure, some of the cartoonist's suspicions stemmed from a general and long-standing distrust of politicians' motives. As a fish and game commissioner in Iowa in 1931, Darling repeatedly voiced his "distress" over political interference in environmental matters. According to Lendt, Darling believed that "because of short-term political considerations, [politicians] could not institute what seemed to be only moderate and sensible programs for the long-term maintenance of America's natural bounty." Darling would have preferred, Lendt notes, to "see the politician's hands removed from the natural resources cookie jar."[33]

Yet Darling seemed especially critical of FDR. A lifelong conservative Republican, Ding was a great fan of the first President Roosevelt but suspicious of the second from the start. The cartoonist was a personal friend of President Hoover's and a delegate to the 1932 Republican National Convention, where he gave such rousing speeches (for Hoover and against Prohibition) that he was widely encouraged to run for Congress. Darling felt, however, that political office would be "a personal and professional tomb" and that his goals could be met more effectively in other forums.[34] Although he could not have known it in 1931, one of the most influential forums for Darling's conservation work would be, ironically, a position in the FDR administration.

IT'S NICE SOMEBODY CAN ENJOY IT

Figure 1. In this 1948 cartoon Ding Darling forecast petroleum
shortages decades before oil embargoes of the 1970s.
Courtesy J. N. "Ding" Darling Foundation.

After the 1932 presidential election, word of Darling's intellect, environmental commitment, and oratorical talent spread quickly. In the months that followed, Darling resumed cartooning and his work with the Iowa Fish and Game Commission, successfully relieving its sorely understaffed scientific team by recruiting (and personally funding) one of Aldo Leopold's best doctoral students. During this time Darling was also outspoken in his criticism of the new chief executive—both in his personal comments as well as in his cartoons. As figure 2 shows, the welfare state was an unnatural state, unfit for adults. This 1934 cartoon (one of Ding's favorites) depicts half a dozen students in a schoolroom. A smug schoolmaster, looking suspiciously like Uncle Sam without the stars and stripes, holds the rod over them. Only the youngest pupil, a boy of about age seven, looks delighted, raising his hand eagerly as he reads from a book entitled *How Not to Work*. The adult learners beside him scratch their heads in puzzlement. Their garb reveals that they have previously come from a variety of occupations, but now they are being required, apparently against their better natures, to study from the likes of *Learn How to Play, How to Use Your Spare Time,* and *Benefits of Idleness.* Lendt reports that Ding "saw in Roosevelt's policies the destruction of private initiative and enterprise and the beginnings of a welfare state."[35] Should readers miss the barb, the caption reads "We Must Learn to Employ Our Idle Time with Other Things Than Work, or, Introducing the New Franklin D. Roosevelt Theory of Economics and Education."

In January 1934, at the same time that Roosevelt was initiating much of his New Deal and resource management legislation, the president also appointed a special committee to devise a "wildlife program that would dovetail with his submarginal land elimination program."[36] Despite his reservations about Roosevelt, Darling agreed to serve on this committee, where he was later joined by Aldo Leopold. There, after observing that the current Biological Survey was "a very poor thing" and continually arguing for its improvement, Darling found himself and Leopold charged with its renewal. By March, 1934, Ding Darling, stalwart critic of FDR, was curiously in that same president's employ as head of the U.S. Biological Survey, the forerunner of today's U.S. Fish and Wildlife Service.

According to Lendt, Darling suspected at times that Roosevelt had appointed him more to silence his criticisms than to forward the aims of conser-

Figure 2. First published in *Collier's* magazine, this 1934 cartoon was one of the artist's favorites. Courtesy J. N. "Ding" Darling Foundation.

vation. Indeed, some of Darling's first experiences working for FDR confirmed such fears; he reported exasperation once upon hearing a rumor that an important Biological Survey report had been spotted far underneath the president's bed. Yet Darling also acknowledged later that the dreaded New Deal Democrat had done far more for wildlife than his Republican predecessor Hoover.[37]

Darling served as head of the Biological Survey for twenty months, from March, 1934, to November, 1935. From the beginning of his term, Ding was explicit in his frustration with Roosevelt's refusal to provide $1 million to fund the survey as he had promised.[38] Funding eventually came as a result of some inspired political discourse during the Senate floor discussion of the Duck Stamp Act—an episode that sheds light on the political yet almost haphazard machinations that went into at least one of FDR's most notable environmental "successes," a victory that almost certainly would have not been possible without Darling's intervention.

The Duck Stamp had been designed by Ding as one of his first duties upon appointment. Its required purchase by hunters would provide financing for wildlife refuges and for the enforcement of migratory bird regulations. In need of a political ally, the artist found a friend in South Dakota senator Peter Norbeck, who used a creative rhetorical technique in order to make the Biological Survey's long- promised funding a reality. Norbeck, who had a heavy Scandinavian accent, capitalized, albeit in a somewhat perverse fashion, on the ancient canon of delivery. He took out his false teeth so that no one could understand him, then urged and got unanimous support for a measure to fund the Biological Survey to the tune of not $1 but $6 million.[39]

In the meantime, Roosevelt had been alerted by Ding that in order for the bill to go into effect in time for hunting season, it would need attention before the president left on vacation, and so he signed the measure without inspecting it closely. This set the stage for a rather unusual exchange of letters between the two men the following year. Upon hearing from Rex Tugwell (Roosevelt's deputy secretary of agriculture) that FDR was planning not to release some previously promised additional funds to the survey, Darling sent the president an illustrated letter (fig. 3).[40] Figure 3 depicts an alarmed and frustrated Ding jumping up and pulling at what is left of his thinning hair, yelping "HEY! LOOK OUT WHAT YOU'RE DOIN'!" As always, brilliantly illustrating figures of speech by literalizing them into visual metaphors, the artist shows that the financial ground is being cut from beneath him by a caricature of a grinning, self-satisfied Roosevelt. The instrument of such destruction is of course the budget pencil, which bisects the picture and focuses the viewer's attention. FDR is shuffling other papers on his desk, but taking a moment from his busy schedule to draw a clean, deadly line through "MY $4,000,000.00 (OR SO REX TELLS ME.)" In

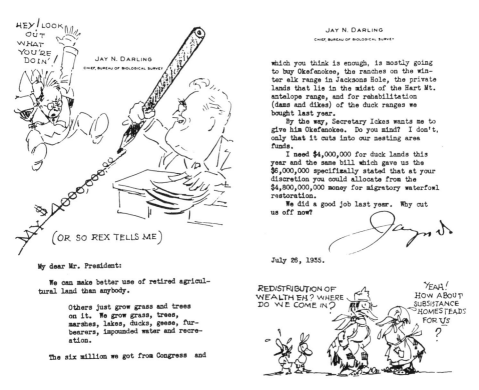

HEY! LOOK OUT WHAT YOU'RE DOIN'!

JAY N. DARLING
CHIEF, BUREAU OF BIOLOGICAL SURVEY

$4,000,000

(OR SO REX TELLS ME)

My dear Mr. President:

We can make better use of retired agricultural land than anybody.

Others just grow grass and trees on it. We grow grass, trees, marshes, lakes, ducks, geese, furbearers, impounded water and recreation.

The six million we got from Congress and

JAY N. DARLING
CHIEF, BUREAU OF BIOLOGICAL SURVEY

which you think is enough, is mostly going to buy Okefanokee, the ranches on the winter elk range in Jacksons Hole, the private lands that lie in the midst of the Hart Mt. antelope range, and for rehabilitation (dams and dikes) of the duck ranges we bought last year.

By the way, Secretary Ickes wants me to give him Okefanokee. Do you mind? I don't, only that it cuts into our nesting area funds.

I need $4,000,000 for duck lands this year and the same bill which gave us the $6,000,000 specifically stated that at your discretion you could allocate from the $4,800,000,000 money for migratory waterfowl restoration.

We did a good job last year. Why cut us off now?

July 26, 1935.

REDISTRIBUTION OF WEALTH EH? WHERE DO WE COME IN?

YEAH! HOW ABOUT SUBSISTANCE HOMESTEADS FOR US?

Figure 3. This 1935 letter from Darling to the president was written on official Bureau of Biological Survey stationery and adorned with Darling's trademark cartoons. Courtesy J. N. "Ding" Darling Foundation.

the text of the letter, which begins much more formally and respectfully with "My dear Mr. President," Darling enumerates the achievements and justified the expenditures of the Biological Survey, concluding "We did a good job last year. Why cut us off now?" As a sort of visual postscript, Ding sketches a pathetic family of ducks, the babies crying while the parents, wearing patched and tattered clothing, mutter "Redistribution of Wealth, eh? Where do we come in?" and "Yeah! How about subsistence homesteads for *us*?" The indignation, outrage, cynicism, and suspicion of motives implied in the illustrations create a rich interplay with the more conventional (and perhaps slightly overdone) formality of Darling's salutation. His letter itself can be read as belligerent, plaintive, or simply straightforward, but it offers no closing, just his final question that hangs on the page like a challenge, iterated more specifically by the duck voices.

Roosevelt's reply was also artful, but in the linguistic rather than the visual sense.[41] In his letter to Ding the president referred to his head of Biological Survey as "the only man in history who got an appropriation through Congress, past the Budget and signed by the president without anybody realizing that the Treasury had been raided." Taking as his due the privilege of rank and familiarity, and perhaps also illustrating in his own way that he can take a joke at his expense, Roosevelt begins, "Dear Jay," a salutation that cuts nicely between "Hey!" and "My dear Mr. President" (see fig. 3). "You hold an all-time record," FDR continued: "In addition to the six million dollars you got, the Federal Courts say that the United States Government has a constitutional right to condemn millions of acres for the welfare, health, and happiness of ducks, geese, sandpipers, owls and wrens, but has no constitutional right to condemn a few old tenaments [*sic*] in the slums for the health and happiness of the little boys and girls who will be our citizens in the next generation!" In addition to offering some amusing insight into the behind-the-scenes workings of the executive office, this letter sheds light on Darling's and Roosevelt's different approaches to environmentalism. For Darling, the (relative) ideological purist, the president's commitments seemed to be untrustworthy, constantly shifting, and overshadowed by other demands on his time. No matter how impressive Roosevelt's rhetoric about planning for the future sounded to the public, Darling suspected from his administrative days with the Iowa Fish and Game Commission that politicians adhered to no such long-term views and that their positions were less grounded in moral stances than in the political zeitgeist.

In figure 4 Darling gives vent to his frustration with governmental overplanning of natural resources as economic resources. The caption reads "Our Engineers Plan Water Uses for Everything Except Nature's Objectives," and the U.S. Army Corps of Engineers is shown amid a desert of their own making. As a single drop of rain falls from the sky, and fish and cattle skeletons litter the ground, a thirsty cow opens her mouth and sticks out her tongue in anticipation. But the chief engineer is ahead of her, and shouts "Quick, men! The steam shovel! There's another drop of water!" Nearby, his four associates argue amongst themselves, offering four alternative uses for the water, each more ludicrous and environmentally disastrous than the last. To the avowed environmentalist, Roosevelt's talk about the economic benefits of the environment presumably illustrated the very same purely pragmatic and utilitarian impulses that endangered the natural world in the first place. Indeed, all this talk must have seemed exactly that—mere talk—when FDR balked at providing additional funding.

Although we know little about Roosevelt's interpretation of the exchange of letters with Ding, it is safe to assume that it left him somewhat exasperated.

Figure 4. No fan of the U.S. Army Corps of Engineers, Darling depicted the corps in the midst of a desert of its own making. Courtesy J. N. "Ding" Darling Foundation.

For the president, the survey's unexpected additional congressional funding presumably meant he could waver on his previous promise and distribute the money elsewhere. After all, as his letter indicates, FDR had slums filled with "little boys and girls" to worry about; why should their welfare be slighted to ensure the happiness of "ducks, geese, sandpipers, owls and wrens"? No matter how sincere his commitment to conservation, the president of the United States had other commitments as well.

And so it went for the two men. Darling criticized Roosevelt for not putting his money where his mouth was; Roosevelt tweaked Darling for demanding money for safe habitats for wildlife when the same were unavailable to the poorest Americans. Issues of life and death for human beings and for the land presented both motive and opportunity for ongoing conflict between Roosevelt and Darling.

This type of discord would continue throughout much of Darling's tenure at the Biological Survey. When Darling resigned in the fall of 1935, he commented to a colleague, "it's been a great war." He attributed his achievements to the fact that by "telling everybody to go to hell," he had been able to lead the scientists and administrators in the survey into constructive action. One important "somebody," apparently, was President Roosevelt. Years after leaving Washington, Ding wrote that "whenever I hear anyone boasting of Franklin D. Roosevelt as a conservationist I think of how little the public knows of the political crimes committed in the name of Conservation."[42]

Having recovered Darling's perspective, what are we to make of Roosevelt as conservationist? Does his rhetorical savvy account for—or perhaps even discount—some of his alleged transgressions? In other words, was Roosevelt's characteristic pragmatism simultaneously his most effective but also most environmentally "criminal" rhetorical trait?

Constraints Associated with Roosevelt's Middle Course

Such questions bring to mind the intrinsic tensions between politics and environmentalism. From a political, pragmatic standard, Roosevelt could not afford the luxury of ideological purity. At the beginning of his presidency, he needed to provide relief to the American people, and even if his interest in nature meant he had a predilection for environmental projects, he could not justify the programs in those terms alone. As Darling himself pointed out shortly after leaving the U.S. Biological Survey, the realities of politics made it impossible for Roosevelt and other politicians to fulfill the genuinely conservationist urges they did have, because the "exploiters of natural resources are always organized and conservationists never."[43] Ding made this point in a cartoon as well (fig. 5).

Figure 5. Darling believed conservation organizations needed to join together if they were to influence national policy. Courtesy J. N. "Ding" Darling Foundation.

Figure 6 is a two-panel sequence that shows the benefits of coalition building. In the first panel, captioned "It Is Hard To Start A Fire With One Stick of Wood," ten different environmental interest groups are symbolized by ten individual campers, each attempting vainly to coax a campfire to life. Each has a dozen or so spent matches scattered beside the kneeling figure, and a single log announcing his or her concern: Garden Club, Independent Club, Horticulture, Parks, Water Conservation, Soil Conservation, Forests Conservation, and Wild Life Conservation. In the second frame, headlined "But If You Could Ever Get the Fire Wood Together In One Pile—," the environmentalists have realized their shared interests and joined together. A huge covered pot, labeled "Conservation Clearing House," bubbles away above a roaring fire, as the assembled workers laugh and cheer, "Boy! She's A'Cookin' now!" A strength of Roosevelt's environmental rhetoric, then, is that in balancing ecological and economic arguments, it does seem to have created space to enable conservationists (including Darling) to organize and flourish in the 1930s and '40s.

Even now, lasting benefits can be felt from the conservationists' and Roosevelt's efforts alike. The Duck Stamp Act did provide much-needed revenue for federal environmental projects. Similarly, the CCC did create, restore, and maintain parklands and forests in a manner that citizens can still enjoy, and the Tennessee Valley Authority did provide power *and* profits to extremely impoverished areas. In addition, FDR was elected to four terms as chief executive, initiating countless other social and environmental programs with lasting effects.

In one sense, then, Roosevelt's "middle road" between the public's need for economic relief and the environmentalists' growing demands for conservation was masterful. In its attention to both the economy and the environment, Roosevelt's rhetoric foreshadowed the current interest in sustainable development and, perhaps more importantly, reminds us that all democratic political rhetoric—on all topics—is born of negotiation, marked by the Bakhtinian multivoicedness of its diverse constituencies and their often competing needs.

Perhaps this rhetoric's most significant weakness, however, is related to its pragmatic focus. In its responsiveness to the political zeitgeist of its era, Roosevelt's rhetoric may have stood less of a chance of altering it. While justifying environmental action almost solely in terms of economic gain, for example, Roosevelt said very little about why the natural world might be valuable for other reasons (or even in its own right).

Lest this critique seem revisionist, it is worth remembering that this is exactly the charge Darling leveled repeatedly at Roosevelt and his secretary of the interior Harold Ickes. Building a dam might put people back to work and provide an additional power source, but it was also apparent to scientists and

Figure 6. Environmentalists in the twenty-first century are still trying to convey the importance—and intrinsic value—of healthy ecosystems. Courtesy J. N. "Ding" Darling Foundation.

conservationists even of Roosevelt's era that such construction would do irreparable damage to the local ecosystem. "Once the ecology was destroyed, it was destroyed forever," Darling claimed when arguing in public with his boss.[44] Indeed, much of his lifelong frustration with politicians came from his inability to get them to see this "big picture." But he draws it quite clearly in figure 6, which presents a shocking image of the entire world in the grip of huge destructive machinery (the "U.S. Natural Resources Rendering Works"). The crater that used to be the North American continent is being ground up into cash and waste. The slaughterhouse language and the two tiny human figures evoke despair. One peers over the edge into the depths of the "U.S. Mine of Natural Resources," his bulging eyes, leaping hat, and exclamation points displaying his horror and alarm. The other man, pictured next to the huge pile of coins and bills, covers his eyes as he wails, "All the Money in the World—But Nothing to DO, NO FOOD and No Place to GO!" The caption poses a rhetorical question, "How Rich Will We Be When We Have Converted All Our Forests, All Our Soil, All Our Water Resources And Our Minerals into Cash?" As environmentally minded citizens struggle to get their elected representatives to take this same view, further investigations of previous relationships such as Darling and Roosevelt's may yield even more clues about the nature of politics, and, conversely, the politics of nature.

Notes

1. Throughout this chapter, we use the term "environmental" in a broad sense to connote a relationship with or concern for the natural world. We do not use it to suggest any specific political campaign or social movement.

2. See Freya Mathews, introduction to *Ecology and Democracy,* ed. Mathews (London: Frank Cass, 1996), 1–12.

3. Paul Lucardie, introduction to *The Politics of Nature,* ed. Andrew Dobson and Paul Lucardie (London: Routledge, 1995), x.

4. Frank Freidel, foreword to *Conservation under F.D.R.,* by A. L. Riesch Owen (New York: Praeger, 1983), viii.

5. Freidel, foreword to *Conservation under F.D.R.,* vii.

6. Herman Kahn, foreword to *Franklin D. Roosevelt and Conservation, 1911–1945,* ed. Edgar B. Nixon (New York: Franklin D. Roosevelt Library, 1957), 1:vii; Freidel, foreword to *Conservation under F.D.R.,* viii; James MacGregor Burns, *Roosevelt: The Lion and the Fox* (New York: Harcourt, Brace and World, 1956), 46.

7. Edgar B. Nixon, introduction to *Franklin D. Roosevelt and Conservation,* xi.

8. See Bronwyn M. Hayward, "The Greening of Participatory Democracy: A Reconsideration of Theory, " in Mathews, *Ecology and Democracy,* 215.

9. See select bibliography for list of messages examined. We included public speeches (delivered over the radio and in person); messages to Congress; letters to governors, committee chairs, and a telegraph to union leaders; press conferences; White House statements; and executive orders. We selected most of these from the public papers based on their classification under the rubric of "national planning," which included most issues we would classify as environmental and then added messages that seemed from their titles to promise relevance. Discussion of these issues occurred with the greatest frequency early in FDR's presidency, with 1934 to 1937 as the peak years. (Not coincidentally, Jay Darling's tenure as chief of the Bureau of Biological Survey occurred during this time.) We did not focus on specific projects such as the Tennessee Valley Authority, the Agricultural Adjustment Act, or the Civilian Conservation Corps except when they overlapped with more explicit environmental concerns (most notably, conservation of wildlife and natural resources).

10. Freidel, *Conservation under F.D.R.,* vii.

11. Webster quoted in Ernest A. Engelbert, "American Policy for Natural Resources: A Historical Survey to 1862," Ph.D. diss., Harvard University, 1950, 137.

12. Tarla Rai Peterson, "The Will to Conservation: A Burkeian Analysis of Dust Bowl Rhetoric and American Farming Motives," *Southern Speech Communication Journal* 52 (1986): 9; Christine Oravec, "Conservationism vs. Preservationism: The 'Public Interest' in the Hetch Hetchy Controversy," *Quarterly Journal of Speech* 70 (1984): 444–58.

13. See, for example, Lynn White, Jr., "The Historic Roots of Our Ecological Crisis," *Science* 155 (1967): 1203–1207, and David and Eileen Spring, eds., *Ecology and Religion in History* (New York: Harper and Row, 1974).

14. See, for example, Henry N. Smith, *Virgin Land: The American West as Symbol and Myth* (Cambridge: Harvard University Press, 1950), and Janice Hocker Rushing, "Evolution of the New Frontier in *Alien* and *Aliens:* Patriarchal Co-Optation of the Feminine Archetype," *Quarterly Journal of Speech* 75 (1989): 1–24.

15. See, for example, Elizabeth Dodson Gray, *Green Paradise Lost* (Wellesley, Mass.:

Roundtable Press, 1981), and Lynn Stearney, "Feminism, Ecofeminism, and the Maternal Archetype: Motherhood as Feminine Universal," *Communication Quarterly* 42 (1994): 145–59.

16. Doris Kearns Goodwin, *No Ordinary Time: Franklin and Eleanor Roosevelt: The Home Front in World War II* (New York: Simon and Schuster, 1994).

17. Donald Worster, *Dust Bowl: The Southern Plains in the 1930s* (New York: Oxford University Press, 1979), 4; Owen, *Conservation under F.D.R* , 3.

18. Nathan Miller, *FDR: An Intimate History* (Garden City, N.Y.: Doubleday, 1983), 343.

19. Burns, *Roosevelt*, 234–46, 148–50, 24; Miller, *FDR: An Intimate History,* 351–52.

20. Burns, *Roosevelt*, 46, 403; Miller, *FDR: An Intimate History,* 343–44, 325, 345–52.

21. Burns, *Roosevelt*, 46.

22. "The President Presents a National Plan to the Congress for the Conservation and Development of Our Water Resources," *Public Papers and Addresses of Franklin D. Roosevelt,* comp. Samuel I. Rosenman, 13 vols. (New York: MacMillan, 1941), 1938: 138–41. Hereafter, quotations from messages are identified parenthetically in the text by the year in which the message was delivered, the item number in the *Public Papers,* and the page number, for example, (1938:32, 140).

23. This economic focus thus bears out Peterson's claim that capitalism served as a "god term" for much of the dust bowl–era rhetoric. See Peterson, "The Will to Conservation."

24. Arthur Schlesinger relates how the term "national resources" originated: "At a meeting with Roosevelt in June 1934, the [newly formed National Planning Board] discussed how its mission could best be defined. The President groped for a phrase like 'land and water planning.' [Charles W.] Eliot [II, the board's executive officer] suggested natural resources, and [Wesley C.] Mitchell commented that human beings were perhaps America's most important resource. [Charles E.] Merriam then suggested the phrase 'national resources.' The President repeated the phrase several times, liked its sound and remarked, 'That's right, friend Eliot, get that down, because that's settled.'" Arthur M. Schlesinger, *The Age of Roosevelt: The Coming of the New Deal* (Boston: Houghton Mifflin, 1958), 350, citing National Planning Board Minutes (June 25, 1934), National Archives.

25. As Ryan notes, "FDR had an affinity for metaphor." Halford R. Ryan, *Franklin D. Roosevelt's Rhetorical Presidency* (New York: Greenwood Press, 1988), 162.

26. Owen, *Conservation under F.D.R.,* 85.

27. Ibid., 163–64.

28. Ibid., 86.

29. David L. Lendt, *Ding: The Life of Jay Norwood Darling* (Ames: Iowa State University Press, 1989), 14.

30. Ibid., 63; Christopher D. Koss, foreword to *The Prints of J. N. Darling,* by Amy N. Worthen, 2d ed. (Ames: Iowa State University Press, 1991), 5, 7. Although Ding's cartoons are no longer part of the contemporary political landscape, most of us have probably seen at least one lasting example of his work, for he designed the symbol of the flying Canada goose that is displayed at every federal wildlife refuge in the country. Darling received both the [Theodore] Roosevelt Medal and the Audubon Medal for his conservation efforts.

31. Lynette Pohlman, preface to *The Prints of J. N. Darling,* by Worthen, 4; *J. N.*

"Ding" Darling's Conservation and Wildlife Cartoons (Key Biscayne, Fla.: J. N. "Ding" Darling Foundation, 1994), 8.

32. See Lendt, album, in *Ding,* n.p. Many other environmental issues that may seem to be relatively new problems associated with late twentieth and early twenty-first century excess—including the hazards of pesticides and overpopulation, the ecological disruption caused by the building of dams, and the need for wetland preservation—were subjects Darling warned about in the 1910s, '20s, '30s, and '40s.

33. Lendt, *Ding,* 49.

34. Ibid., 53–54.

35. Ibid., 59, 62.

36. Ibid., 63.

37. Ibid., 67, 70, 85, 63.

38. Ibid., 75.

39. Ibid, 75–77.

40. Jay N. Darling to Franklin D. Roosevelt, Washington, D.C., July 26, 1935, in Lendt, album, *Ding,* n.p.

41. Franklin D. Roosevelt to Jay N. Darling, Washington, D.C., July 29, 1935, in Lendt, album, *Ding,* n.p.

42. Lendt, *Ding,* 78–87.

43. Ibid., 96. Darling himself was instrumental in creating such associations, arguing in a 1935 speech for the federation or centralization of the hundreds of groups then in existence. His efforts led to the creation of, among other organizations, the National Wildlife Federation, with Darling serving as its first president. See Lendt, *Ding,* 85; *J. N. "Ding" Darling's Conservation and Wildlife Cartoons,* 29.

44. Lendt, *Ding,* 83.

Select Bibliography of Messages by
Pres. Franklin D. Roosevelt (in chronological order)

1933 Public Papers and Addresses of FDR, Vol. 2
"Establishment of the Rio Grande Wild Life Refuge. Executive Order No. 6086."
(March 28), 90–91.
"The Thirty-seventh Press Conference (Excerpts)." (July 28), 312–16.
1934 Public Papers and Addresses of FDR, Vol. 3
"Extemporaneous Speech at the Subsistence Homes Exhibition." (April 24), 193–200.
"A Typical Act of Protection and Conservation of Wildlife by Providing Suitable Ref-
uges." (June 29), 320–21.
"The National Resources Board Is Established." (June 30), 335–36.
"White House Statement on the Establishment of the National Resources Board."
(July 3), 336–38.
"Radio Address Delivered at Two Medicine Chalet, Glacier National Park." (Aug. 5),
358–62.
"The One Hundred and Sixtieth Press Conference (Excerpts)." (Nov. 23), 465–77.
"A Typical Executive Order (No. 6910) on Withdrawal of Public Lands to be Used for
Conservation and Development of Natural Resources." (Nov. 26), 477–79.

1935 Public Papers and Addresses of FDR, Vol. 4
"A Request for State Cooperation in Forest Conservation." (Jan. 2), 25–26.
"'Men and Nature Must Work Hand in Hand'—A Message to the Congress on the use
of Our National Resources." (Jan. 24), 59–62.
"The National Resources Committee Is Created. Executive Order No. 7065." (June 7),
242–48.
"A Recommendation to the Congress to Approve the State Compact to Conserve Oil
and Gas." (Aug. 9), 319.
"Extemporaneous Remarks at Celebration of Fiftieth Anniversary of State Conserva-
tion at Lake Placid." (Sept. 14), 362–66.
"Address at Dedication of Boulder Dam. 'The National Benefits of This Project Will Be
Felt in Every One of the Forty-eight States,'" (Sept. 30), 397–402.
"A Letter on the North American Wildlife Conference Called by the President." (Dec.
20), 500–501.
"The Two Hundred and Fifty-eighth Press Conference (Excerpts)." (Dec. 22), 502–503.

1936 Public Papers and Addresses of FDR, Vol. 5
"A Greeting to the North American Wildlife Conference," (Feb. 3), 77.
"A Presidential Statement on Signing the Soil Conservation and Domestic Allotment
Act." (March 1), 95–102.
"A Request for Ratification of the Migratory Bird Treaty with Mexico." (March 5), 107–
108.
"The President Suggests Cooperation by Farmers in the Soil Conservation Program in
Their Individual and National Interest." (March 19), 135–38.
"'We Seek to Pass on to Our Children a Richer Land, a Stronger Nation'—Address at
Dedication of Shenandoah National Park." (July 3), 238–40.
"The First 'Fireside Chat' of 1936, Following the Drought Inspection Trip—'We Are
Going to Conserve Soil, Conserve Water, Conserve Life.'" (Sept. 6), 331–39.

"The President Creates a Committee to Recommend a Long-Term Program for the Utilization of the Resources of the Great Plains Area." (Sept. 19), 369–70.

"Campaign Address at Denver, Colo. 'We Have Sought and Found Practical Answers to the Problems of Industry, Agriculture, and Mining.'" (Oct. 12), 443–49.

"Campaign Address at Providence, R. I. 'We Believe That the Material Resources of America Should Serve the Human Resources of America.'" (Oct. 21), 516–19.

1937 Public Papers and Addresses of FDR, Vol. 6

"A Message to the Congress Transmitting a Six-Year Program of Public Works for the Nation Prepared by the National Resources Committee." (Feb. 3), 30–34.

"The President Urges the Adoption by All States of a Uniform Soil Conservation Law." (Feb. 26), 102–104.

"The President Transmits to the Congress a Report on Control and Use of Headwaters to Conserve Water and Control Floods." (May 12), 193–96.

"The President Recommends Legislation for National Planning and Development of Natural Resources Through Seven Regional Authorities." (June 3), 252–56.

"Presidential Statement Urging Cooperation to Prevent Forest Fires." (July 2), 287–88.

"Presidential Statement on the Report by the National Resources Committee on Technological Trends and Their Social Implications." (July 12), 298–99.

"A Recommendation for Legislation Approving the Interstate Compact to Conserve Oil and Gas." (July 19), 309.

"Presidential Statement on the Report of the National Resources Committee on 'Our Cities—Their Role in the National Economy.'" (Sept. 20), 367–69.

"A Greeting to the Convention of the National Reclamation Association." (Sept. 23), 376–77.

1938 Public Papers and Addresses of FDR, Vol. 7

"The President Presents a National Plan to the Congress for the Conservation and Development of Our Water Resources." (March 10), 138–41.

"'America Needs a Government of Constant Progress Along Liberal Lines.' Address at Oklahoma City, Oklahoma." (July 9), 442–45.

1939 Public Papers and Addresses of FDR, Vol. 8

"Transmitting the Report of the National Resources Committee on 'Research: A Natural Resource.'" (Jan. 23), 100–101.

"The President Transmits to the Congress a Comprehensive Study of the Energy Resources of the United States as a Basis for Future Legislation." (Feb. 16), 137–39.

"The President Recommends Legislation to Conserve Reindeer Herds in Alaska." (July 19), 388–89.

"The President Recommends Legislation for a National Policy on Oil Conservation." (July 22), 398–99.

"A Recommendation for Rehabilitation of Parts of the Northern Lakes States Region." (July 31), 399–401.

1940 Public Papers and Addresses of FDR, Vol. 9

"The President Transmits to the Congress the Progress Report of the National Reclamation Association." (Jan. 11), 36–37.

"The President Calls Attention to the Many-Sided Program of the Tennessee Valley Authority." (Jan. 15), 37–39.

"'We Will Extend to the Opponents of Force the Material Resources of This Nation; and, at the Same Time, We Will Speed Up the Use of those Resources So That We Ourselves May Have Equipment and Training Equal to Any Emergency,' Address at the University of Virginia." (June 10), 259–64.

1942 Public Papers and Addresses of FDR, Vol. 11
"The President Transmits to the Congress a Report on Development of Natural Resources." (Jan. 14), 52–54.
"The President Appeals to the State Governors to Conserve Rubber by Reducing Speed Limits." (March 14), 162–64.
"The President Addresses a Letter to the Rubber Director and the Price Administrator Urging Prompt Establishment of the Rubber Conservation Program." (Nov. 26), 494.

1943 Public Papers and Addresses of FDR, Vol. 12
"The Eight Hundred and Eightieth Press Conference (Excerpts)." (Feb. 16), 94–100.
"The President Telegraphs Union Leaders Directing Them to the Rubber Strike in Akron." (May 26), 225–27.

1944–45 Public Papers and Addresses of FDR, Vol. 13
"The President Urges the Growing of Victory Gardens." (April 1), 116–17.
"Informal, Extemporaneous Remarks at Clarksburg, West Virginia." (Oct. 29), 378–82.
"The President Urges Conservation of Food." (Jan. 22), 525–26.

4 Conservative Politics and the Politics of Conservation

Richard Nixon and the Environmental Protection Agency

Micheal R. Vickery

Many who came of political age during Richard Nixon's presidency view him as an archetypal political "conservative." This perception is rooted, of course, in the cultural and political legacies of the Vietnam War and Watergate. Yet for others who have reflected on the broad scope of his administration's foreign and domestic policy initiatives, Nixon's location on the liberal-conservative spectrum is not so consistently clear. For example, Howard Phillips, a staunch conservative Republican activist during the Nixon era, complained that, "Nixon was a liberal; there is no question about it." Phillips cited Nixon's economic policies, his support for wage and price controls, support of national endowments for the arts and the humanities, and his creation of the Legal Services Corporation and the Environmental Protection Agency (EPA) as proof of a "whole cultural and social portfolio at the White House."[1] Phillips attested, in fact, that he helped organize Conservatives for the Removal of the President in 1974, in part because, "There was no principle to which Nixon was really committed" and "he did not have firm opinions. . . . [M]ost of his policies in the domestic area were brokerable."[2]

Other observers of the Nixon presidency, however, saw Nixon as a pragmatic, conservative politician. Gerald and Deborah Strober's extensive oral history of Nixon's presidency led them to argue that, although he was not as ideologically rigid as some other operatives in the conservative wing of the Republican Party, he was clearly a "conservative pragmatist." The Strobers reported a high degree of consensus in the views of those who worked with Nixon that he consistently articulated the virtues of "new federalism" as a governing philosophy. New federalism encompasses a core belief in limited government and a primary political goal of transferring governmental authority away from Washington to state and local government. The new federalism was, in fact, the centerpiece of the "six great goals" Nixon espoused in his second state of union address in 1971.[3] One index of the proportional significance this governing philosophy held in Nixon's political calculation was that his discussion of the six great goals of his administration occupied sixteen columns in the *Public Papers of the President* and almost one-third of that rhetorical space was devoted to the topic of returning power to the states.

That Nixon consistently espoused the goal of reducing the power of the federal government while his administration participated in the creation of many new federal regulatory agencies, including the Environmental Protection Agency, is perhaps a key reason that Nixon's legacy has flustered both the left and right of the American political spectrum. Perhaps it is also why another former Nixon associate would state simply that, "Nixon was an almost completely political animal: he was neither moral nor immoral, but was amoral; he made decisions based on how they affected him politically; not based on whether they were right or wrong—I don't think right or wrong entered into it, although he did use those words quite frequently."[4]

Historian Stephen Ambrose writes that, "Nixon was better than any politician in America at bowing to the inevitable; he was also a man who, as he often said, when he changed policy, liked to leapfrog the next position in line."[5] From the accounts of journalists and other observers of the Nixon years, environmental policy may be a perfect illustration of Nixon's pragmatic use of an expedient political issue. It is even arguable that the birth of U.S. environmental policy during the decade of the 1970's would have been driven by expediency rather than philosophy, no matter who had won the White House in 1968. Tom Wicker and Samuel Hays both contend that despite the presence of the well-known proenvironmental senator Edmund Muskie running for vice president on the Democratic ticket, the campaign of neither Richard Nixon or Hubert Humphrey gave more than cursory attention to environmental issues during the 1968 campaign. Joan Hoff too has observed that even though polls were beginning to show by 1968 that the environment was gaining steam as a public issue, environmental legislation was virtually nonexistent on the newly elected president's list of priorities for his administration.[6] Many observers have attributed both the urgency and the substance of the Nixon administration's remarkable record of environmental legislation to Domestic Affairs Adviser John Ehrlichman, Deputy Assistant to the President John Whitaker, and Russell Train, undersecretary of the interior, who became chairman of the Council on Environmental Quality. Wicker, for example, writes that, "Richard Nixon was no more an environmental than a racial activist when he entered the White

House; he had only a dim view of the environment as a political issue and delegated the subject largely to [John] Ehrlichman."[7]

Whatever the impetus, the environmental issue was the domestic focus of Nixon's first state of the union address in 1970. The president asked in the speech whether a 50 percent increase in wealth over the following ten years would equate to a 50 percent increase in happiness and whether increasing urbanization would yield only traffic, smog, polluted water, noise, and crime. He went on to assert that

[t]he great question of the seventies is, shall we surrender to our surroundings, or shall we make our peace with nature and begin to make reparations for the damage we have done to our air, to our land, and to our water? Restoring nature to its natural state is a cause beyond party and beyond factions. It has become a common cause of all the people of this country. It is a cause of particular concern to young Americans, because they more than we will reap the grim consequences of our failure to act on programs which are needed now if we are to prevent disaster later. Clean air, clean water, open spaces — these should once again be the birthright of every American. If we act now, they can be. . . . Now, I realize that the argument is often made that there is a fundamental contradiction between economic growth and the quality of life, so that to have one we must forsake the other. The answer is not to abandon growth but to redirect it. For example, we should turn toward ending congestion and eliminating smog [with] the same reservoir of genius that created them in the first place. Continuous vigorous economic growth provides us with the means to enrich life itself and to enhance our planet as a place hospitable to man.[8]

Passages such as this are perhaps one reason that there is a lack of consensus on the "real" political identity of Richard Nixon. Certainly one of the more curious residues of the 1960s and 1970s is that a federal bureaucracy to regulate industrial pollution was established by an ostensibly conservative Republican president and administration. In this chapter I examine the discourse and the context in which the Environmental Protection Agency was constituted and consider the legacy of this moment of rhetorical and political invention for understanding the generative forces that have helped shaped environmental policy in the United States. The focus of the chapter is the mosaic of discourse from Richard Nixon, academic policy analysts, and chroniclers of the Nixon presidency. This discourse not only yields evidence of the ways in which political identity, administrative agenda, and rhetorical style intersected to produce the country's legacy of environmental policy but also extends our understanding of the forms of presidential rhetoric. Surely the texts and contexts of Richard Nixon's public pronouncements and justifications of the EPA offer significant insight into the way conflicted political and social agendas of a unique historical epoch were manipulated by a unique president. More importantly, the rhetorical moments in which the EPA was constituted yield important opportunities for insight into the way the conflicted cultural forces of capitalism and environmentalism may be imprinted on presidential rhetoric and public policy. The creation of the EPA reveals much about the way a president may attempt to manage these forces to fit his or her governing philosophy and political agenda. For it is not only through public utterance but also through the administrative power to constitute bureaucratic channels of communication between the public and private sectors that a president may exercise rhetorical power to influence the trajectory of civic life.

The Genesis of the EPA

Richard Nixon and Spiro Agnew defeated Hubert Humphrey and Edmund Muskie in the general election of 1968 and the new Republican administration was sworn into office in January, 1969. Barely a year later, on January 1, 1970, the National Environmental Protection Act was signed into law creating the White House Council on Environmental Quality. President Nixon stated in his first state of the union address on January 22 that the environment, "next to our desire for peace, may well become the major concern of the American people in the decade of the seventies." On February 10, 1970, President Nixon delivered a special message to Congress on environmental quality in which he asserted the goal of fighting pollution and touted the Council on Environmental Quality as "the keeper of our environmental conscience and a goad to our ingenuity." Then the White House transmitted Reorganization Plan 3 of 1970 to Congress in the summer of the same year, calling for the creation of the Environmental Protection Agency, which would demonstrate, "a profound commitment to the rescue of our natural environment, and the preservation of the Earth as a place both habitable by and hospitable to man." Reorganization Plan 3 became effective on December 2, 1970, and the EPA came into existence with William Ruckelshaus as its first director. The roles and functions of the EPA as they were articulated in the reorganization plan included the establishment and enforcement of environmental standards "consistent with national environmental goals," conducting research on pollution, assisting other unspecified agencies "through grants, technical assistance and other means," and assisting the Council on Environmental Quality in recommending new policy.[9]

As President Nixon approached the end of his second full year in office, the National Environmental Protection Act of 1969 had been passed, the White House Council on Environmental Quality had been established and had presented its first report to Congress, the EPA was almost a year old, and the president had used his first state of the union address to mark the environment as a centerpiece of his administration's domestic agenda. These would seem to be powerful rhetorical and political markers of a committed proenvironment administration. Yet on January 4, 1971, only eighteen days before the second state of the union address in which environmental policy would again be affirmed as one of the "six great goals" of the Nixon administration, representatives from the four major television networks (ABC, CBS, NBC, and PBS) had an on-the-record conversation with the president during which none of the reporters asked a single direct question about environmental policy or environmental issues. And again, in January, 1972, a year after the identification of environmental policy as a significant goal of his administration, Nixon had another conversation, this time with Dan Rather of CBS, in which he was not asked a single question about environmental issues.[10]

As odd as the seeming disinterest of the media in the White House's championing of environmental issues might seem, odder still is the apparent disinterest in these issues by the White House staff itself. For example, only two days before the 1971 state of the union address, no mention of environmental policy issues was recorded during the first part of the staff meeting open to the press nor was it mentioned in the summary that the president's press secretary provided at the press briefing following the closed portion of the meeting. This might be less interesting had it not turned out to be a harbinger of the place that "the environment" took in the memoirs and recollections of key members of the Nixon administration. For example, there is no discussion of the environment or the EPA in the index to the almost 700 pages of Robert Haldeman's memoir. John Ehrlichman mentions the environment but only in his description of meetings in which the possibility of moving William Ruckelshaus from directing the EPA to another administrative position was discussed and in discussing strategies for getting Congress to take the blame if it overrode Nixon's veto of the 1972 Clean Water Act. The most curious of Ehrlichman's revelations with respect to the administration's commitment (or lack thereof) to environmental issues was his direct assertion of Nixon's fundamental disinterest in the subject. Curious as it is, Ehrlichman's observation is merely a recapitulation of Nixon's own reflection on the administration; neither the environment nor the EPA are even indexed as a topic in the 1,120 pages it took Richard Nixon to write his own memoirs. The omission of "the environment" from so many records and memoirs of an administration that did so much to embed "environmental protection" into the structure of the government is remarkable. One may legitimately wonder at how to reconcile what the administration of Richard Nixon did with regard to environmental policy and what those who did it said and failed to say about the importance of environmental issues in their memoirs.[11]

Environment as an Issue in the Nixon White House

In his study of the evolution of environmental policy in the United States, Samuel Hays argues that Richard Nixon became president at just the time when a government response to environmental issues was virtually required. Economic growth and lifestyle changes following World War II created the conditions for intensified debate involving "natural-environment values." Hays argues that between 1957 and 1965 increased concern for recreation, wetlands, parklands, and other aesthetic pleasures of the natural environment led to the first phase of federal legislation. In the midst of this first phase, concern also began to increase about adverse effects of industrial development, especially with regard to air and water pollution. These concerns marked the beginning of a second phase in environmental policy, between 1965 and 1972, in which the focus shifted to issues of ecological degradation and human health and safety. Consequently, Hays argues, "The full force of the drive to control the waste products of modern industry was felt by the new Nixon administration." Even if the new president were not particularly interested in environmental issues, at least some members of the new administration did realize their political significance. Hays argues that despite an apparent lack of genuine sympathy for the environmental movement, there was a very significant *political* drive toward environmental goals that gave rise to the significant action taken by the Nixon administration.[12]

> By all accounts, Nixon made a quick study of the political implications of an environmental policy initiative and he literally pounced on the issue when confronted with two distinct political realities. The first was that popular support for environmental legislative reform, especially among American youth, was growing rapidly. This support was marked by poll data that showed a doubling of the public's concern about pollution as a major issue: Prior to 1969, the concern about the environment was limited to a relatively small, better-educated, more affluent segment of the population. . . . But public opinion surveys conducted in the 1960s showed a rising popular concern about environmental pollution. The percentage of people who believed that water pollution was a "very seri-

ous" problem doubled from 13 percent in 1965 to 27 percent in 1968, and the percentage that viewed air pollution as a very serious problem increased from 10 percent to 25 percent. Only 17 percent mentioned pollution as one of the three most important problems requiring government action in 1965, but by 1970, 53 percent mentioned [it] as one of the top three issues.[13]

This comports with the fact that only 1 percent of respondents to a private White House poll in 1969 identified the environment as the most important issue facing the new president but a survey in 1971 showed that number had increased to 25 percent. The first Earth Day celebration on April 22, 1970, is credited by some observers with boosting public concern, increasing the general level of environmental activism, and putting pressure on the government to respond. Tom Wicker writes, "After the Earth Day demonstrations, Richard Nixon, pragmatic as always, moved not to flee or thwart but to seize upon that environmental consensus. Indeed, barely two months after Earth Day, Nixon proposed in a special message to Congress his plans to create the Environmental Protection Agency in order to "'rationally and systematically' organize the government's efforts to study, set standards, monitor, and enforce regulations controlling pollution issues."[14]

That political thinking had more to do with the adoption of new, stringent federal environmental regulations than did ecological thinking is a position argued by other scholars of environmental policy as well. In the face of increasing public concern about pollution, both the Democratic and Republican Parties began to look for expedient ways to address issues of environmental policy. These concerns and the increasing pressure for the federal government to act were fueled, in large part, by popular frustration with ineffective state and local government initiatives to address water and air pollution problems.[15] For these reasons and others perhaps, the Nixon administration did act, but the rhetorical action through which the administration executed its response to the political exigency of the environment was convoluted.

In his August, 1971, message to Congress transmitting the second annual report of the Council on Environmental Quality, Nixon stated the national importance of having reformed environmental policy and created the Council on Environmental Quality and the Environmental Protection Agency. Nixon went on to state the administration's desire to create a new Department of Natural Resources, "with unified responsibility for energy, water, and natural resource programs" that would "provide wide and coordinated management of all our natural resources so that man can live and work in greater harmony with the natural systems of which he is part." However, the message's closing section provides a quick check on any unreflective joy at the president's commitment to activist government or to environmental values. The final section is subtitled "A Sense of Realism" and in it, the president warns that "we should not expect environmental miracles. Our efforts will be more effective if we approach the challenge of the environment with a strong sense of realism."[16] Nixon made it clear that neither environmental rhetoric nor moral dedication would be achieved without costs and that the costs that mattered were direct, short-term economic ones.

> How clean is *clean enough* can only be answered in terms of how much we are willing to pay and how soon we seek success. The effects of such decisions on our domestic economic concerns—jobs, prices, foreign competition—require explicit and rigorous analyses to permit us to maintain a healthy economy while we seek a healthy environment. It is essential that we have both. It is simplistic to seek ecological perfection at the cost of bankrupting the very taxpaying enterprises which must pay for the social advances the nation seeks. . . . We must develop a realistic sense of what it will cost to achieve our national environmental goals and choose a specific level of goal with an understanding of its costs and benefits.[17]

That Nixon's rhetoric and his administration's actions are internally inconsistent will surprise no student of public political discourse. It is the explanation and the legacy of these inconsistencies that must be understood if we are to understand the rhetorical making of public policy.

Pragmatic Realism in Nixon's Environmental Record

Virtually no one would attribute the remarkable record of environmental legislation during the Nixon administration to concord between Richard Nixon and "environmentalists." As one writer has put it, Nixon's decision to champion the environment as a core domestic issue in his new administration "reflected political expediency rather than agreement with environmental objectives."[18] Other observers claim that Nixon's advisers were able to convince him to use environmental issues as an expedient means of reaching out to young, middle-class voters, thereby helping to counteract the unpopularity of the Vietnam War with that segment of the electorate.[19]

That the White House's early and aggressive use of the environment as an issue may have been nothing more than basic campaign strategy is supported by Richard Cohen's analysis of the way the White House saw the reelection campaign of 1972 shaping up. Cohen reports claims by Nixon adviser (and first chairman of the Council on Environmental Quality) Russell Train that the White House was very sensitive to the fact that Edmund Muskie was the leading contender to be the Democratic Party nominee in the 1972 election. Muskie was seen as a formidable potential adversary in that he had name recognition from his run as vice president in 1968. But Muskie's longstanding interest in environmental legislation made him a further threat, especially in light of what the polls were saying about the ascendancy of pollution as a salient public issue.[20] As Robertson and Judd so bluntly put it, "Muskie's political ambitions prompted President Nixon to become an environmental advocate." Muskie himself, after his retirement from politics, observed that "Nixon saw me emerging as a potential presidential candidate and he knew of my interest in environmental issues. . . . So, he created the EPA. He tried to preempt the issue from me."[21]

Joan Hoff provides an interesting perspective on the way the White House constructed their view of the challenge posed by Muskie. She argues that, despite the likelihood of Muskie as an opponent and the obvious power of the environment as an issue for Muskie, Nixon was not inclined to do just anything in order to steal the issue. He was unwilling, his advisers said, to try "to 'out-clean' Mr. Muskie; there's no way you can do it." Out-cleaning the opposition may not have been an option but other options were certainly entertained. Two weeks before he died, Muskie received a copy of a March 1971 memo from Pat Buchanan to Richard Nixon. The memo articulates Buchanan's view that, if Muskie "is not cut and bleeding before he goes into New Hampshire" he would likely win the Democratic nomination. The remedy, Buchanan said, was "to go down to the kennels and turn the dogs loose on Ecology Ed."[22]

John Ehrlichman explicitly repudiates any claim that Richard Nixon had anything other than a political interest in environmental issues: "The fact was that [Nixon] didn't much care about the subject of environmental conservation or what I did about it, so long as I didn't create any political problems for him." Ehrlichman's memoir is among many sources that support the perception that Richard Nixon was a thoroughgoing pragmatist. For example, Ehrlichman discusses a long memorandum he wrote to Nixon in the fall of 1970, arguing that advice Nixon had been getting about steering a more rigidly conservative course into the 1972 elections was wrongheaded. Ehrlichman's memo argues that the proper electoral strategy would be to steer a center course: "Very few initiatives will be truly in the center. They will fall on one side or the other. Our domestic policy job, as I have understood it up to now, was to insure some *balance*. As we can, consistent with the Social issues concept, we will try to co-opt the opposition's issues (e.g., Muskie's environment) if the political cost is not too great."[23]

Roderick Hart's analysis of modern presidential rhetoric leads him to claim that "Richard Milhouse Nixon was more aware of practical communication than was any other president," that "[c]lear headed American pragmatism resounded throughout his speeches," and that Nixon had a marked "capacity to size up an issue and reduce it to its pragmatic understructure." Hart claims that Nixon not only depended on persuasion, as all presidents must, but also was acutely aware of this dependence. Hart labels him a "metarhetorical president."[24]

Hart's analysis of Nixon's presidential speeches led him to conclude that Nixon was a thoroughly practical politician, a devotee of detail, an untiring pursuer of documentation, and a huge fan of the tactical political stratagem. Hart argues that Nixon's essential pragmatism is revealed through the consistent and preponderant presence in his speeches of names, dates, concrete language, a focus on the present, and a penchant for argument from expediency. The essential markers of Nixon's rhetorical style, Hart argues, are *realism,* measured by the presence of "expressions referring to tangible, immediate, and practical issues"; *activity,* measured by the presence of "statements referring to motion, change, or the implementation of ideas"; and *familiarity,* measured by the presence of the "terms most frequently encountered in everyday speech."[25]

According to Hart, Nixon's extraordinary reliance on realism and activity combined with a colloquial, unembellished, familiar style and a staccato delivery contributed to a kind of rhetorical demagoguery. Hart paints this picture of Nixon's style: "These stylistic features reveal a man . . . who gets things done, who finds (and honors) the bottom line . . . who runs the presidency as the good Republican corporation the forefathers intended it to be. He was . . . certainly not a president to get mired down in a philosophical discussion." When we look at Nixon's justifications of the environmental policies his administration put into place, we find much to confirm Hart's observation that Nixon's pragmatic style was especially notable when the president attempted to justify policy decisions.[26]

Conservative Presumption in Nixon's Environmental Rhetoric

Analysis of the characteristic features of liberal and conservative political discourse suggests that both genres of discourse are marked by a speaker's tendency to espouse acceptance of societal structures, but whereas liberal discourse tends to also espouse a broader citizen participation in government, conservative discourse tends to reject influences that might threaten existing instruments of social control. Analysis of public argument also suggests that liberal and conservative political arguments are predicated on different presumptions. Liberal argument is predicated on the presumption of change as an inevitable force and an acceptance of abstract values. Conservative argument is predicated on the presumption of permanence (e.g., the status quo) and on the social primacy of concrete values. According to Perelman and Olbrechts-Tyteca, abstract values like truth and justice are universally valid no matter how instantiated through individual and particularly situated action, whereas concrete values are attached to a specific social group, a particular object, or even an individual.[27]

Given these differentiations of liberal and conservative discourse, it is possible to separate Nixon's positions from the presumptions that underlay his arguments in support of environmental regulation. Nixon's explicit statements in support of environmental values and his support for creation of the EPA are prima facie "liberal" in the sense that his administration did, in fact, propose and implement a great many changes in the structures and agencies of the government. But Nixon's justification of his environmental policies, espoused throughout the first two years of his first administration, are certainly not dissertations on abstract ecological values.

A telling rhetorical moment occurs in Nixon's comments on January 1, 1970, the same day he signed the National Environmental Policy Act of 1969. The act established the Council on Environmental Quality in the executive office of the president to recommend environmental policies. Nixon asserted that "[t]he past year has seen the creation of a President's Cabinet committee on environmental quality, and we have devoted many hours to the pressing problems of pollution control, airport location, wilderness, preservation, highway construction, and population trends." He went on to say that the reclamation of pure air and water was a now-or-never proposition, commended Congress for passing the new act, and asserted, "We are most interested in results. The act I have signed gives us an adequate organization and a good statement of direction. We are determined that the decade of the seventies be known as the time when this country regained a productive harmony between man and nature."[28]

These comments are interesting insights into how Nixon perceived the "problem" of the environment. Whatever those problems might be, they had not merited days or weeks or months of analysis, only hours. And as helpful as the new council of advisers was expected to be in addressing those problems now rather than never, "adequate organization" and "good statement of direction" are hardly ringing phrases of endorsement. These statements and others reveal Nixon's fundamental view of the environmental problem as a structural issue of politics-as-usual. The human values that are implicated by this way of defining the threats to the environment are the concrete values of continued economic expansion and effective political management of the instruments of government as they impinge on economic activity. The rhetorical attributes of the arguments proposed by Nixon are clearly conservative.

Nixon's public pronouncements on the environment and environmental policy at times expressed an imperative to preserve and protect the natural environment. But moments of idealistic vision are muddled and sometimes contradicted by claims and arguments in the same speeches in which they occur. However, these contradictions and complexities may not, as they first seem, be inconsistent with the core and constant qualities of Nixon's rhetoric or his governing philosophy. As analyses of Nixon's rhetorical style and the political exigencies of the moment suggest, the more philosophical, abstract, and evocative aspects of Nixon's talk about the environment have less to do with ecology and conservation than with a practical attempt to adapt a political agenda to the shifting American attitudes about the environment. Reading Nixon's rhetorical legacy on the environment, one has the clear sense that he was a man working a political angle. There is much in the post-Nixon record to suggest that this was indeed the case.

Aspects of Nixon's participation in creating the White House Council on Environmental Quality, the Clean Air Act of 1970, and the Environmental Protection Agency seem diametrically opposed to his espousal of new federalism and the goals of shifting regulatory control to state and local governments. Yet upon closer examination, Nixon's environmental agenda seems consistently pragmatic, political, and conservative.

In his message to Congress announcing his intention to create the EPA, Nixon directly addressed the contradiction between this action and his avowed political principles: "In proposing that the Environmental Protection Agency be set up as a separate new agency, I am making an exception to one of my own principles: that, as a matter of effective and orderly administration, additional new independent agencies normally should not be created. In this case, however, the arguments against placing environmental protection activities under the jurisdiction of one or another of the existing departments and agencies are compelling." The compelling reasons Nixon gave for the creation of the EPA came down to the need for the agency to maintain objectivity in its assessment and standard-setting functions and independence in its role as a regulatory agency. Nixon affirmed that "in this case a strong, independent agency is needed," but the agency would also need to work closely with and draw upon expertise of other agencies. Conflicts inherent in attempts to reconcile "objective" views of ecological and economic data and to balance industrial and community interests were not explicitly recognized in Nixon's remarks. But these conflicts were not left to chance.[29]

As constituted, the fiscal operations of the EPA were placed under the control of the Office of Management and Budget. This virtually insured that the EPA would never have the budgetary freedom to confront the powerful economic and political interests the agency was charged with regulating. The questionable efficacy of such an arrangement did not go unnoticed. Environmental activist Barry Commoner stated in a speech at Hofstra University that the cost-benefit analysis implied by the imposition of OMB authority over the EPA, "meant that unless the economic benefits outstripped the costs of an environmentally sound action, it should not be taken"[30]

Hays's study of the history of environmental politics in the United States leads him to argue that the ultimate legacy of U.S. policy has not been as substantive as it might have been because the core tension between economic growth and ecological science was resolved in favor of "managing" the affairs of the economy. Hays writes:

> Among institutional leaders in government, in business, and in the scientific and technical professions environmental values never took deep root. Those leaders were far more preoccupied with more traditional forms of economic growth. They emphasized production rather than newer forms of consumption, the creation of jobs rather than the enhancement of intangible environmental values. Many of these institutional leaders perceived the environmental movement as emotional rather than rational, a phenomenon of national hysteria rather than of sound action. The more sober ones felt that although the environmental movement reflected legitimate public desires, it also expressed demands the economy could not afford to meet.[31]

By placing the Council on Environmental Quality under direct control of the White House and the EPA under budgetary control of OMB, Nixon was apparently aware of the conflict between ecological values and traditional economic values. The bureaucratic structure into which the EPA was embedded can be seen as an explicit effort to manage that conflict in a way that favors traditional economic cost-benefit analysis.

Certainly, concern for a traditional industrial model of economic costs and benefits are found in Nixon's stated fears that environmental regulation would get out of control. Nixon put the matter quite starkly in a remark to a speechwriter: "In a flat choice between smoke and jobs, we're for jobs."[32] In a speech before the Economic Club of Detroit in 1971, less than two years after his first state of the union speech in which he asserted that the environment had to be protected regardless of the cost, Nixon stated:

> It is vitally important . . . that more attention . . . be given to the cost factor as well as to the factor that we are all interested in—of cleaning up our air and. . . . water. . . . [W]hen the Congress, or an administration carrying out the will of the Congress, sets certain standards . . . we must weigh against that: How many jobs is it going to cost? And, if it is going to cost a disproportionate number of jobs . . . then we have to reevaluate the decision. . . . We are committed to cleaning up the air and. . . . water. But we are also committed to a strong economy, and we are not going to allow the environmental issue to be used sometimes falsely and sometimes in a demagogic way basically to destroy the system—the industrial system that made this the great country that it is.[33]

In a note affixed to a memo John Ehrlichman had sent him addressing the negative economic implications of environmental activism, Nixon clearly revealed his affinity for conserving regular political and economic order. Nixon's note read, "I completely agree—We have gone overboard on the environment—and are going to reap the whirlwind for our excesses."[34]

Environmentalists were not, to put it mildly, seen by Nixon as equal stakeholders in the great enterprise of rescuing the "natural system" from the ravages of economic development. The audiotape recording devices in the Oval Office captured the following comments by Nixon to Henry Ford II and Lee Iacocca on April 27, 1971:

> President: Whether it's the environment or pollution or Naderism or consumerism [we] are extremely probusiness. Uh, we are fighting, frankly, a delaying action. . . . [W]e can't have a completely safe society or safe highways or safe cars and pollution-free and so forth. Or we could have, go back and live like a bunch of damned animals. . . . [A]nd, boy this is true. It's true in, in the environmentalists and it's true of the consumerism people. They're a group of people that aren't one really damn bit interested in safety or clean air. What they're interested in is destroying the system. They're enemies of the system. So, what I'm trying to say is this: That you can speak to me in terms that I am for the system"[35]

What can we make of Nixon's role in the development of U.S. environmental policy? What accounts for the conflicted look and feel of Nixon's own discourse, the conflicted memories of his role as committed new federalist, closet liberal, and amoral political survivalist? Part of the problem in trying to get a clear understanding of the relationship between Nixon and environmental policy is that, in the final analysis, it seems that the environment mattered only as a political issue to Nixon and mattered not much at all to his advisers. Neither did it seem to mean much to the mainstream press at the time.

The purity of Nixon's motives are surely questionable, but his administration did in fact create the first federal bureaucracy to be charged with making and enforcing environmental regulations. The EPA continues to be a source and a site of conflict between political and economic interests that seek to either regulate or stimulate the American industrial democracy. The EPA was and continues to be something that the conservative Nixon probably did not approve of in terms of political philosophy. But because it was created and continues to provide a governmental mechanism through which to discipline and channel "environmental activism," it served the ends of the pragmatically conservative Nixon. Nixon established the EPA in a way that guaranteed no federal regulatory action regarding natural resource conservation and pollution control could be taken without being disciplined by the capitalist political economy. This was the political elegance with which the ideals of ecological philosophy were co-opted by embedding them in the coordinating bureaucratic structure of the EPA.

What can we learn from examining Richard Nixon's role in formulating environmental policy and creating the Environmental Protection Agency? First, external social pressures play an important role in the policymaking arena. There is no news in this, only confirmation. Nixon's response to a growing social consensus about the importance of strong environmental policy is a virtual case study of the power of political expediency in producing public policy. Second, rhetorical elements of what Hart has labeled realism and activity ought to be looked at closely in attempts to assess the efficacy of executive rhetoric.

A third lesson is that a president's rhetoric and the actions of an administration must be read more deeply than the descriptions and justifications offered by key actors, even in retrospect. The sociopolitical context and the underlying cultural presumptions of the policy discourse must also be interpreted. Critics have to look at the resources of value, belief, and secular political faith that underpin the arguments made in the discussions and explanations of policy issues at the time policy is being rhetorically constituted. Understanding the relationship between a president's rhetorical habits, political agendas, and the forms that policies take requires access to more than just the formal speeches and texts of a presidency. These reveal much but not all. A president's speeches and formal documents fit within a mosaic of discourse out of which public policy is not just discussed but constituted. Critics can learn from the primary rhetorical texts of public speeches, but they should also engage secondary and even tertiary forms of discourse. Such discourse, even if it occurred behind closed doors at the White House, can contribute to our understanding of the public talk. This point is made very nicely in Joan Hoff's description of her own research into the Nixon presidency:

> Over a decade of painstaking research into his presidential papers and tapes has convinced me that a confluence of conditions in the country in the late 1960s and advice from his closest aides contributed as much, if not more, to the successes and failures of Nixon's presidency as his individual psyche. These factors often determined the substantive agenda he pursued in domestic and foreign policy. Even in the best of times, but particularly in times of turmoil like the late 1960's and 1970's, presidential policies seldom reflect exclusively the ideas or personality of any given president. They are, instead, the collective product of his aides and various divisions of the executive branch and his own personal administrative mode of operation."[36]

To Hoff's observation should be added this: a president's rhetorical skills as an administrator should be considered a principle mode of operation. A president must channel an individual psyche, an interpretation of contingent social conditions, and a political agenda into rhetorical artifacts that effectively address real and multiple audiences. Public rhetoric tells us much about *how* a president thinks, not just what he or she thinks about. We learn also from these data how thinking is turned into publicly accessible forms. These forms include not just speeches and other formal statements of policy but also the forms of bureaucratic control through which administrative actions are taken.

The contradictory, if not disingenuous, elements of the Nixon administration's response to environmental issues reveals the deep cultural tensions that lie at the heart of these issues. Action in the domestic arena of environmental policy was for Richard Nixon politically expedient and rhetorically efficacious. By examining how he talked about the environment, we come to know something important about Richard Nixon as well as the American audience to which his policies and the EPA were addressed. We can reasonably conclude that President Nixon was prepared to be perceived as a pragmatic, conservative manager of the affairs of an industrial, capitalist state. The EPA was, from this perspective, constituted by Nixon as a bureaucratic management tool and Nixon wanted environmentalists and industrialists to know it.

As such, the EPA would please neither constituency well but would serve Nixon perfectly as a way to manage liberal antibusiness interests and discipline environmental science under the regime of American industrial democracy.

The policies the Nixon administration put forward and the contradictory interpretations of Nixon's motives in pursuing them are both culturally interesting and understandable. Nixon's actions toward environmental policy are excellent illustrations of what Robertson and Judd refer to as the "reluctant activism" characteristic of Republican presidents who have had to balance traditional disdain for strong federal government with the interdependent relationship between private business and the public sector that grew out of World War II.[37] For Nixon, rising popular worries about the environment constituted a situation into which he had to fit the agencies of conservative, probusiness Republican politics. The EPA, as an expression of this reluctant activism, is also an embodiment of the conservative presumption at the core of Nixon's politics and his rhetoric. The agency was an instrument useful in preserving the conventional cultural and political arrangements through which science and popular desires are wedded to the goal of economic expansion. The EPA functioned for Nixon and for the American people as a kind of condensation symbol into which could be collapsed the conflicts between liberal political doubts about Nixon's interest in the environment and conservative political fear that an expansionist philosophy of government regulation would strangle business and industry.

Placed in context, Richard Nixon's message transmitting the first annual report of the Council on Environmental Quality to Congress reveals much about Nixon's rhetorical and political proclivities as an "environmental president." The text of the president's message places heavy emphasis, in Nixon's characteristically practical style, on the objective nature of environmental issues and the virtues of "managing" those problems. In his message, the president portrays the environment not as an issue to be viewed in purely abstract, aesthetic, or personal terms but as a system that needs to be managed:

> . . . the active participation of the business community is essential. The government's regulation and enforcement activities will continue to be strengthened. Performance standards must be upgraded as rapidly as feasible. But regulation cannon do the whole job. Forward-looking initiatives by business itself are also vital—in research, in the development of new products and processes, in continuing and increased investment in pollution abatement equipment. . . . In dealing with the environment we must learn not how to master nature but how to master ourselves, our institutions, and our technology. We must achieve a

new awareness of our dependence on our surroundings and on the natural systems, which support all life, but awareness must be coupled with a full realization of our enormous capability to alter these surroundings. Nowhere is this capability greater than in the United States, and this country must lead the way in showing that our human and technological resources can be devoted to a better life and an improved environment for ourselves and our inheritors on this planet

Our environmental problems are very serious, indeed urgent, but they do not justify either panic or hysteria. The problems are highly complex, and their resolution will require rational, systematic approaches, hard work and patience. There must be a *national* commitment and a *rational* commitment. . . . The newly aroused concern with our natural environment embraces old and young alike, in all walks of life. For the young it has a special urgency. They know that it involves not only our own lives now but also the future of mankind. For their parents, it has a special poignancy—because ours is the first generation to feel the pangs of concern for the environmental legacy we leave our children.

At the heart of this concern for the environment lies our concern for the human condition: for the welfare of man himself, now and in the future. As we look ahead to the end of the this new decade of heightened environmental awareness, therefore, we should set ourselves a higher goal than merely remedying the damage wrought in decades past. We should strive for an environment that not only sustains life but enriches life, harmonizing the works of man and nature for the greater good of all.[38]

The mechanistic definition of environmental problems and the faith Nixon seemed to place in entrepreneurial values is unmistakable. It helps us understand how "the environment" was used by Nixon as a salient rhetorical token and how this token was translated into policies and institutional structures consistent with Nixon's core political philosophy. Nixon indicated in a number of places his interest in making the EPA part of an overall management strategy for dealing with the pressures from both business and social activists to do something about the environment.[39] By layering environmental issues within industrially and politically controlled structures of influence, such actions effectively controlled the forms of "rationality" that might be brought to bear in formulating responses to environmental problems.

The faith that dispassionate technical expertise and rational decision making can solve human problems is at the core of the American mythos. The liturgy of this faith was followed in Richard Nixon's justifications of his administration's environmental policy. But it is clear that Nixon did not really believe that facts, reason, and good will would resolve environmental controversies in ways consistent with his conservative political beliefs. It is perhaps more accurate to see the creation of the EPA as the actions of a president who had a core belief that political power would always be needed because agreement between experts and cooperation between government and other interest groups would always be problematic in the arena of environmental policy.

Perhaps there is no universally acceptable way to determine whether the EPA was the product of inspired interest in protecting the environment or craven interest in protecting the bases of economic power. I simply note in this regard that it is instructive to look at Nixon's rhetoric through a wide lens. To do so is to observe a rather astounding irony. For at the same time that Nixon was espousing the virtues of devoting technological resources to the betterment of human life on the planet, carpet bombing and defoliation of the Southeast Asian ecosystem was being pursued as formal government policy. Out of such paradoxes, perhaps, are revealed what Rod Hart labeled the "manifold complexities" of Richard Nixon.[40] In the discourse through which Nixon created the EPA and discussed his manifold views on environmental issues, we also see revealed the way conservative political beliefs were used to discipline the ideals of ecological conservation and preserve the economic status quo in a culture that is deeply conflicted about its ecological values.

Notes

1. Gerald S. Strober and Deborah H. Strober, *Nixon: An Oral History of His Presidency* (New York: HarperCollins, 1994), 108, 111.
2. Ibid., 109, 111.
3. Ibid., 109; Richard M. Nixon, "Annual Message to the Congress on the State of the Union, January 22, 1971," *Public Papers of the Presidents* (1971), 50–58.
4. Strober and Strober, *Nixon*, 110.
5. Stephen E. Ambrose, *Nixon, V2: The Triumph of a Politician, 1962–1972* (New York: Simon and Schuster, 1989), 458.
6. Tom Wicker, *One of Us: Richard Nixon and the American Dream* (New York: Random House, 1991); Samuel P. Hays, *Beauty, Health, and Permanence: Environmental Politics in the United States, 1955–1985* (Cambridge: Cambridge University Press, 1987); Joan Hoff, *Nixon Reconsidered* (New York: Basic Books, 1994).
7. Wicker, *One of Us,* 507.
8. Nixon, "State of the Union," *Public Papers of the President* (1970), 12–13.
9. Nixon, "Annual Message to the Congress on the State of the Union, January 22, 1970," *Public Papers of the Presidents* (1970), 8–17; Nixon, "Special Message to the Congress on Environmental Quality, February 10, 1970," *Public Papers of the Presidents* (1970), 96–109; Nixon, "Special Message to Congress about Reorganization Plans to Establish the Environmental Protection Agency and the National Oceanic and Atmospheric Administration," July 9, 1970, *Public Papers of the Presidents* (1970), 578–86.
10. "A Conversation with the President: Interview with Four Representatives of the Television Networks, January 4, 1971," *Public Papers of the Presidents* (1971), 6–23; "A Conversation with the President: Interview with Dan Rather of the Columbia Broadcasting System, January 2, 1972," *Public Papers of the Presidents* (1972), 1–17.
11. Nixon, "Remarks at a White House Staff Meeting on the Second Anniversary of the President's Inauguration, January 20, 1971," *Public Papers of the Presidents* (1971), 44–47; H. R. Haldeman, *The Haldeman Diaries* (New York: G. P. Putnam, 1994); John Ehrlichman, *Witness to Power: The Nixon Years.* (New York: Simon and Schuster, 1982), 325–26, 70; Nixon, *The Memoirs of Richard Nixon* (New York: Grosset and Dunlop, 1978).
12. Hays, *Beauty, Health, and Permanence,* 54, 57–58.
13. David Brian Robertson and Dennis R. Judd, *The Development of American Public Policy: The Structure of Policy Restraint* (Glenview, Ill.: Scott, Foresman, 1989), 323.
14. Wicker, *One of Us,* 509; Nixon, "Reorganization Plan to Establish the EPA, July 9, 1970," *Public Papers of the Presidents* (1970).
15. Robertson and Judd, *Development of American Public Policy,* 335–43.
16. Nixon, "The President's Message," *Environmental Quality: The Second Annual Report of the Council on Environmental Quality* (Washington, D.C.: Government Printing Office, 1971), v–xi.
17. Ibid., xi; emphasis in original.
18. Hays, *Beauty, Health, and Permanence,* 58.
19. Richard E. Cohen, *Washington at Work: Back Rooms and Clean Air* (New York: Macmillan, 1992); Hays, *Beauty, Health, and Permanence;* Robertson and Judd, *Development of American Public Policy.*

20. Cohen, *Washington at Work.*
21. Robertson and Judd, *Development of American Public Policy,* 335; Cohen, *Washington at Work,* 13.
22. Hoff, *Nixon Reconsidered,* 23; Liz Chapman, "Muskie Got Copy of Buchanan Memo Just before He Died," (http://www.maine.com:80/dems/muskie .htm#memo, visited Jan. 12, 1997). Print version available from author.
23. Ehrlichman, *Witness to Power,* 70, 217.
24. Roderick P. Hart, *Verbal Style and the Presidency* (New York: Academic Press, 1984) 127, 130, 132.
25. Ibid, 16–17.
26. Ibid, 130–31.
27. Thomas D. Clark, "An Analysis of Recurrent Features of Contemporary American Radical, Liberal, and Conservative Discourse," *Southern Communication Journal* 44 (Summer, 1979): 399–422; G. Thomas Goodnight, "The Liberal and the Conservative Presumption: On Political Philosophy and the Foundation of Public Argument," in *Proceedings of the Summer Conference on Argumentation,* ed. Jack Rhodes and Sara Newell (Annandale: Speech Communication Association, 1980), 304–37; Chaim Perelman and L. Olbrechts-Tyteca, *The New Rhetoric: A Treatise on Argumentation,* trans. John Wilkinson and Purcell Weaver (South Bend: University of Notre Dame Press, 1969).
28. Nixon, "Statement about the National Environmental Policy Act of 1969, January 1, 1970," *Public Papers of the Presidents* (1970), 2–3.
29. Nixon, "Reorganization Plans to Establish EPA, July 9, 1970," *Public Papers of the Presidents* (1970), 581–82.
30. Hoff, *Nixon Reconsidered*; Robertson and Judd, *Development of American Public Policy;* Commoner cited in Wicker, *One of Us,* 513.
31. Hays, *Beauty, Health, and Permanence,* 60.
32. Wicker, *One of Us,* 515.
33. Quoted in Wicker, *One of Us,* 514.
34. Ambrose, *Nixon, V2,* 460.
35. Wicker, *One of Us,* 516.
36. Hoff, *Nixon Reconsidered,* 5.
37. Robertson and Judd, *Development of American Public Policy,* 140.
38. Nixon, "Message to the Congress Transmitting the First Annual Report of the Council on Environmental Quality, August 10, 1970," *Public Papers of the Presidents* (1970), 660; emphasis in the original.
39. For example, Nixon appointed a group of corporate executives to a National Industrial Pollution Control Council operating out of the Department of Commerce. See Hays, *Beauty, Health, and Permanence.*
40. Hart, *Verbal Style,* 147.

5 Conservation Reconsidered

Environmental Politics, Rhetoric, and the Reagan Revolution

C. Brant Short

Most analysts do not consider the Reagan presidency as a high point in the study of environmental politics. But the eight-year legacy of the Reagan administration has a significant place in the study of environmental history. Reagan presented a powerful vision that countered the conservation consensus of the previous twenty years and offered an alternative ideological paradigm to understand nature, wilderness, natural resources, and public land management. Although the candidate Reagan seemed uninformed about many environmental issues during the 1980 campaign, President Reagan and his advisers presented an agenda that challenged the core values that had guided environmental politics in the 1960s and 1970s. To casual observers, Reagan's status as the Great Communicator explained his rise to power, his election to the presidency, and his efforts to dismantle "big government" and "return" power to the people. But in dealing with Reagan, deeper forces are at work than wit and eloquence. While many have called Reagan a master in using "symbolic politics," they often fail to address the depth and scope of Reagan's discourse. It is "not enough to delineate Reagan's issue and ideological coalition in strictly political terms," argued Combs. Instead, scholars must identify and evaluate the "broader political context of mythological themes in American culture that Reagan embodies."[1]

Reagan's environmental agenda, most forcefully articulated by himself and his first secretary of the interior, James G. Watt, provides a useful vehicle to consider the Reagan revolution in American politics. In this chapter I discuss Reagan's ideological rhetoric and how it shaped his environmental agenda. I also consider the historical and cultural forces that guided Reagan's environmental rhetoric and follow Combs' charge to evaluate the cultural myths that gave Reagan's discourse both substance and meaning.

The significance of public advocacy in shaping environmental policies in American history seems self-evident. Thoreau, Muir, Theodore Roosevelt,

Leopold, Carson, Abbey, and many others demonstrate a tradition of advocacy in public efforts to define nature, landscape, and wilderness. The importance of rhetoric, however, becomes even more salient when considering another fact. There is "one glaring omission" in the Constitution according to historian Donald Worster: "Nowhere in all the sections, articles, and amendments is there any mention of the American land and our rights and responsibilities pertaining thereto. I find the word 'land' appearing only once, and then it refers to the capture of prisoners 'on Land and Water.' Otherwise, the subject is never mentioned: no reference to any role the government has in acquiring, holding or regulating the use of land."[2]

On the other hand, the Constitution provides for the protection of private property in the Fifth Amendment. The writers of the Constitution, concluded Worster, had two distinct ideas regarding land in the new country. First, they believed that land should be owned by as many people as possible and second, "to make the nation grow in richness and power the land and its products should be treated as commodities, put up for sale to the highest bidder in the marketplace."[3] Of course, the framers did not envision the vast western public lands that would alter the nature of private property and generate a new role for the federal government. The silence of the Constitution, coupled with cultural assumptions promoting property and economic privileges as the highest good, affirm the need to study the rhetorical constructions of the American landscape and its relationship to government.

I contend that Ronald Reagan's environmental discourse fused two powerful American myths, the Puritan errand and the frontier thesis, into a unified ideological statement of how the nation's public lands should be defined, managed, and owned. This vision of landscape provided a means of assessing environmental issues beyond property and wilderness, such as hazardous waste, acid rain, and pollution. To more fully understand Reagan's environmental discourse, I consider three topics: first, reviews of the Reagan administration's environmental record; second, Ronald Reagan's orientation toward nature and the environment; and third, Reagan's environmental discourse and its place in environmental history.

The Reagan Administration and Environmental Politics

Even before he left the White House, Ronald Reagan was under the scrutiny of journalists, politicians, activists, and scholars. Although a number of observers have already evaluated Reagan and suggested his place in history, his environmental record receives little attention. For example, in a 1988 volume edited by *Washington Post* reporters Sidney Blumenthal and Thomas Edsall, the only mention of James Watt in the entire book concerned his credentials as a New Right conservative. In his assessment of Reagan's long-term impact as president, William Schneider identified five fundamental changes in American politics (taxes; defense spending; budget deficit; federal judges; party realignment). Reading this account, one would believe that Ronald Reagan had no environmental agenda. Another book on the Reagan presidency, from a group of political scientists, similarly ignored environmental politics in favor of national defense, taxes, and political realignment. The editors of this volume concluded that Reagan's legacy was that of an "incomplete revolution" because of three factors: failure to complete the New Right's social agenda; the continued existence of the New Deal welfare state; the failure of New Federalism proposals.[4]

Among those observers specifically interested in environmental issues, several have critiqued Reagan's environmental policies. Considering the modern president's power to act independently of Congress and the courts with broad administrative mandates, two books have assessed the Reagan administration's use of institutional authority in shaping environmental policies.[5] Other accounts have looked at the administration's record from a historical-political orientation. The most significant legacy of the Reagan years, concluded David Vogel, "may be the complete absence of any fresh regulatory initiatives. Reagan's election wrote *finis* to the exuberance of the 'environmental decade.'" In assessing Reagan's first term, Samuel P. Hays observed that Reagan's policies actually "strengthened support for environmental organizations." Hays notes that environmentalists grew in numbers, raised more money, and identified new initiatives in direct reaction to administration policies. In fact a new burst of energy fostered local and state environmental organizations. In another assessment of Reagan's first term, Norman Vig concluded that the president's economic agenda defined environmental policies: "More than in any previous administration, government policies across the board were subordinated to a few overriding economic and political objectives," wrote Vig. "Thus, programs such as those for the environment received relatively little independent attention and were largely viewed as targets for deregulation efforts." Reagan's first term "was a failure if the goal was to achieve major deregulation or changes in the basic framework of environmental law," claimed Vig. "The 'administrative strategy' of seeking changes through executive agencies while bypassing Congress and ignoring environmental constituencies and public opinion largely backfired. . . . As conservatives have since pointed out, the opportunity for reforming environmental regulation was squandered amidst these political controversies and the pro-environmental backlash that resulted."[6]

Turning to Reagan's second term, Vig observed that Reagan took "no obvious leadership on environmental issues" and that the president "appeared even less involved in the details of domestic policy than in the first term." In the second term, Congress reauthorized several significant pieces of environmental legislation (Superfund; Clean Water Act); the Environmental Protection Agency returned to its original mission under the leadership of William Ruckelshaus and Lee Thomas; and a new national park and several million acres of wilderness were added to the public lands.[7]

Turning to the primary figures who presented the Reagan administration's environmental agenda, the president and his first secretary of the interior, there is an unusual silence regarding environmental affairs in their assessments of the Reagan revolution. In his autobiography, *An American Life*, Ronald Reagan did not mention James Watt, the Department of Interior, the Environmental Protection Agency, the "Sagebrush Rebellion," national parks or wilderness areas, or any other topic related to his environmental legacy. Instead Reagan stressed foreign affairs and his success in stopping Communism and winning the cold war. The New Right rhetoric of 1980 that presented a detailed blueprint for the Reagan presidency is nowhere to be found in the autobiography. Even more striking than Reagan's omission of environmental issues in his autobiography is James Watt's scant reference to them in his 1985 book *The Courage of a Conservative*. Watt took the lead in 1981 in making environmental reform the core of his tenure as secretary of the interior. Fired after thirty months in office, Watt returned to Wyoming and produced a book defending the conservative revolution in America. After having discussed foreign affairs, race relations, economic liberty, crime, and other topics for two hundred pages, Watt finally presented a single paragraph about environmental issues: "We had brought a revolution to the department. We had successfully implemented policies, regulations, manuals and orders that would last for decades. I was very proud of our accomplishments. The president's agenda had been put in place, restoring our parks and wildlife areas, making energy resources available, and defusing the 'Sagebrush Rebellion.'"[8]

What can one make of Reagan's and Watt's reticence regarding environmental politics? Is their silence an attempt to mask a failure, to ignore a discussion of accountability? Or does the lack of attention to an environmental legacy indicate that other issues were of greater importance to them? In their effort to define and defend their ideology, Reagan and Watt demonstrated that environmental politics were subsumed by a larger agenda. In stressing his record on governmental regulation, private enterprise, energy policy, and even national defense, Reagan revealed that the perception that he was disinterested in environmental policymaking was probably accurate. In Reagan's vision of how to run the federal government, environmental policies were the servant of a larger ideology. This orientation toward the environment was aptly stated in a policy memorandum to Reagan in August, 1979. Economic adviser Martin Anderson designed the document to help Reagan develop campaign themes and arguments: "Energy policy is intimately connected to economic policy, environmental policy, and social policy. If policies are pursued in these areas without concern for their effects on energy, they will be self-defeating. We need an optimum blend of sound national policies that will allow reasonable, fair trade-offs between our energy needs and our economic, environmental, and social concerns. Having clean air and low gasoline princes will be of small consolation in the midst of rolling blackouts, rising unemployment, and mile-long gasoline lines."[9]

Ronald Reagan campaigned for the presidency in 1980 with a clear statement of how he planned to revolutionize government. Embedded within that vision were significant changes in America's energy policies. Indeed, energy was the critical link between domestic and foreign policies for Reagan and his supporters: a plentiful supply of energy promoted economic expansion at home and, at the same time, it promoted a stronger defense posture in the world, assuring foreign suppliers of energy that the United States was a trusted ally. Economic reform and energy development were the pillars of Ronald Reagan's vision for his presidency; the nation's environmental policies had to be consistent, and indeed, support the Reagan revolution.

Ronald Reagan's Orientation toward Nature

The foundation of Reagan's rhetoric as a candidate and as president goes beyond New Right thinkers who emerged in the late 1970s offering a series of books, speeches, and seminars on a new political paradigm. In searching for the core of Ronald Reagan's environmental rhetoric, I was struck by his ability to enlist and interconnect two different American myths: the Puritan errand into the wilderness and Frederick Jackson Turner's frontier thesis. Although the myths have been dissected, critiqued, and even rejected by some observers, they are rhetorically compelling and continue to speak to Americans who seek a collective cultural orientation. Much of the power of Reagan's rhetoric came from his ability to simultaneously *symbolize* both myths through his life experiences and *integrate* them into his political discourse. Few individuals in history have been able to portray the American mythos literally and figuratively. Reagan did both.

The Puritan errand into the wilderness is the oldest American myth; it became a historical narrative, a theory of culture and politics, and a point of inspiration for generations of Americans, all at the same time. The wilderness became integral to creating a new cultural identity, removed from English/European origins. "The forests of New England acquired a moral function in the Puritan cosmology" noted Michael Kammen, "and their agonies of primitive life served to reinforce the Puritan's view that they were God's chosen people."[10]

But the errand offered more than a theological justification for continued migration, settlement, and development. The migration to the New World fulfilled a prophecy, and this prophecy became "an unlimited license to expand." The acceptance of the errand also transformed the culture's view of time from a "sacred past to a scared future" and rejected the Old World ideal of a vertical society with class harmony. The errand provided the "ideology of a nascent free enterprise culture." Sacvan Bercovitch found that the errand gained consensus as the colonies moved toward independence. After the revolution, the errand took a "self-enclosed *American* form. Independence from England completed the separation of the New World from the Old. Henceforth, Americans could direct the process of migration toward its proper goal, the conquest of a continent." Probably most important in the evolution of the new country was the errand's ability to "consecrate the practice and theory of democratic capitalism." The errand became the most important part of defining the American experience. Bercovitch concluded that "the story they told was broadcast through the land every July Fourth, the high holy day of American civil religion. A new era, so the story went, had begun with the discovery of the New World, and the Revolution confirmed it, just as Christ had confirmed the new era of faith."[11]

The errand became a narrative that manifested itself in many avenues of American life. It provided a theological and historical lens for viewing the immense and mysterious American landscape; the concept of wilderness was invested with visions of private property, capitalism, agricultural development, and harvest of natural resources. And most significant for the evolving American identity, the errand was more than a journey, it was a pilgrimage. "For each Puritan saint, the venture into the wilderness had an inward and private end," wrote Bercovitch. "It was a journey of the soul to God, the believer's pilgrimage through the world's wilderness to redemption."[12]

The second American myth that provided currency for Ronald Reagan was the frontier thesis. Presented in 1893 by Frederick Jackson Turner, the thesis had an overwhelming impact among academics as well as the general public. The frontier thesis, concluded historian William Cronon, "remains the foundation not only for the history of the West, but also for much of the rest of American history as well. Textbooks still follow the basic outline which he and his students established in their lecture courses." Indeed, Turner's famous dictum,

"The existence of an area of free land, its continuous recession, and the advance of American settlement westward, explain American development," remains a central part of most historical accounts of the West.[13] As Dorsey (chap. 1, this volume) points out, Theodore Roosevelt based his conservationist appeals on a rendition of the frontier myth.

The rhetorical impact of the frontier thesis has been thoroughly discussed by Ronald Carpenter, who concluded that the thesis "achieved a profound impact over the years over our national psychology." Paul Rodman and Michael Malone supported this claim, observing that Turner's thesis had a "remarkable impact upon both the profession [of history] and upon the literate public, for its message of American distinction ideally suited an era in which a proud and successful United States was emerging as an industrial and globally expansive power." For Turner, the foundation of American history was the process by which Europeans were transformed into Americans. "The struggle with the wilderness turned Europeans into Americans," observed Patricia Nelson Limmerick, "a process Turner made the central story of American history."[14]

Although historians have critiqued the frontier thesis in recent decades and identified its analytical shortcomings, its rhetorical vision has remained powerful throughout the twentieth century and the beginning of the twenty-first.[15] Turner's thesis created a lens that altered the explanation of how American identity emerged and evolved. No matter how much scholars recognize Turner's "*analytical* shortcomings, we still turn to him for our *rhetorical structure*," wrote Cronon. Indeed, the lasting power of the frontier thesis "is its simplicity and its sense of movement, its ability to shape and set in motion so many of the mere *facts* that American historians need to narrate."[16] Turner's study helped displace prevailing intellectual attitudes of nineteenth-century America and, in turn, suggested that the "novel attitudes and institutions produced by the frontier, especially through its encouragement of democracy, had been more significant than the imported European heritage in shaping American society."[17]

Ronald Reagan and the American Landscape

Ronald Reagan's life story resonates comfortably with the frontier thesis, and his political oratory appropriated both the Puritan errand and Turner's thesis. In combination, these two American myths formed the core of Reagan's views toward nature, landscape, and environment.

Born, raised, and educated in the American heartland, Ronald Reagan transcended his Illinois heritage to become America's first cowboy president (at least since Theodore Roosevelt). Reagan lived on a "ranch" in California; he rode horses and did ranch work on vacations; he acted in a number of Hollywood Westerns; he hosted a televised Western program, announcing on air his intention to enter politics; and he was a friend of the most famous cowboy in American history, John Wayne. Reagan's ranch was a part of his persona, a place where he spent nearly a full year of vacation time during his eight years in the White House.[18] Indeed the Secret Service gave Reagan the codename "Rawhide." It is understandable that observers have linked Reagan's popularity to his ability to appropriate and project symbols of the American West.[19] Yet such a viewpoint only touches upon the periphery of Reagan's mythic stature. It seems to me that Reagan embodied Turner's frontier thesis as an individual; in other words, Reagan's personal history paralleled Turner's cultural narrative. So instead of being just another frustrated cowboy who moved to the West, rode a horse, and wore boots and a hat, Ronald Reagan lived out the frontier thesis.

Part of Reagan's ability to symbolize the American West (and thus Turner's westward American experience) lies in his film career. Although Reagan did not act in many Hollywood Westerns, he desperately wanted to be part of this genre. After World War II, he recalled, "I was back in pictures and loving it." But the parts were typically "drawing-room comedies." Reagan wrote, "But I did wish Jack Warner would think of me on the back of a horse wearing a cowboy hat. . . . But when I'd ask Jack to put me in a western, he'd cast me in another movie in which I'd wear a gray-flannel suit." Reagan renegotiated his exclusive contract with Warner Brothers, which allowed him to work in other film studios. According to his autobiography: "As a free lance, I agreed to make one picture a year for three years at Warner Brother and was also able to make pictures at Paramount, MGM, RKO, and Universal. I finally got to some westerns. Among them two of my favorites were *The Last Outpost* and *Cattle Queen of Montana*, with Barbara Stanwyck. In *The Last Outpost*, I teamed up with my favorite horse, Baby."[20]

Reagan made the transition from movies to television in the 1950s, hosting *GE Theatre*, a dramatic anthology series. But he continued to love the Western, and in 1964 he became the host and an occasional actor on the syndicated television series *Death Valley Days*. In another connection between the symbolic Western and his daily life, Reagan remembered his work on the show: "If I wasn't scheduled to act in a show, I'd drive down to the studio from our ranch, spend an hour or so taping an introduction for the next show, then drive home; some days, I didn't have to get out of my ranch clothes for the filming."[21]

One of Reagan's most powerful connections to popular conceptualizations of the frontier thesis came from his public friendship with John Wayne. Although Reagan and Wayne never appeared in any films together, they seemed to be cut from the same cloth. Wayne "was a hero to Ronald Reagan, who once made a pilgrimage to Wayne's birthplace in tiny Winterset, Iowa, and told visitors to the White House that 'Wayne understood what the American spirit is all about.'" In a eulogy for John Wayne written for *Reader's Digest,* Reagan praised "the Duke" for his friendship, patriotism, and anti-Communism. But within the eulogy, we see the story of Ronald Reagan as well. Two young men from the Midwest, who loved sports, find their future in a new industry in the American West. Two actors with families both wanted to fight in World War II but could not because of physical problems. And finally two men who believed that political truths could be found and reinforced in popular culture. Reagan concluded his eulogy by acknowledging the relationship between films, truth, and ideology: "'There's right and there's wrong,' Duke said in *The Alamo.* 'You gotta do one or the other. You do the one and you're living. You do the other and you may be walking around but in reality you're dead.' Duke Wayne symbolized just this, the force of the American will to do what is right in the world. He could have left no greater legacy." Reagan even turned to the Duke in his campaign for the presidency in 1980. "What other presidential candidate, on election eve," observed Laurence Barrett, "could cite John Wayne as the essence of the American hero—and even quote the late Duke's wisdom—in what purported to be a serious half-hour television speech."[22]

As the Reagan biography emerged, each facet of his life story was a reaffirmation of Turner's ideal American. Like Turner, Reagan was a child of the Midwest and was profoundly shaped by the populist spirit of his day. Reagan traced his values to a small town upbringing in central Illinois. "His public memories of boyhood are transformed into a 'Huck Finn–Tom Sawyer idyll' and the simple gifts of small town life" wrote Combs. But if the public biography of Reagan's happy childhood may "have little actual validity, the fact that many were willing and able to share the fantasy attests to its remarkable salience at this late date in American history." Reagan also came from the economic lower class of society and understood the importance of education in being able to participate in the American dream. The democratizing power of communication is also part of Reagan's biography. His leadership of a student protest at Eureka College, and his recognition of his oratorical prowess, are central parts of Reagan's life story.[23] As American society embraced technology in various facets of life in the first half of the twentieth century, so did Ronald Reagan. He first turned to radio as a career, which led him to the American West and a new opportunity in motion pictures. From films he moved to television and became a national spokesman for a powerful technological force, the General Electric Corporation and the "all electric" home of the future. The Reagans even lived in a specially designed electric home, where they filmed a three-minute television advertisement for GE.[24]

Entering politics in 1964, again through the agency of television, Reagan brought with him a twentieth-century life that reified the fundamentals of the frontier thesis: American values emerge from one's interaction with the landscape (Midwest; small town; California); individualism and risk taking are rewarded (radio; films; television; politics); technology can harness the forces of nature to benefit society (radio; television; electric appliances); and finally American democracy is open to anyone who wants to participate.

Christianity clearly forms a significant part of Reagan's ideological orientation. In 1980 Reagan declined to identify himself as a born-again Christian, suggesting that it was counter to his upbringing.[25] Moreover Reagan did not regularly attend church services, prompting questions of his convictions. Regardless of the nature of his personal faith, Reagan embraced Christianity in the New World tradition of the Puritan errand. "For all of his studied casualness about religion," claimed Combs, "Reagan became identified as no Presidential figure since William Jennings Bryan with a politics of popular redemption." Combs concluded that "Reagan's power over the faithful, then, stemmed from his ability to summon up a world of memory and illusion and to equate divine and national purposes in an overarching world mission. He urged us to come, love the beloved republic and God would bless America. . . . God would bless America again because of our moral exceptionalism, and thus our innocent predestination, in a world of otherwise power-exercising states." Reagan's theology, claimed Garry Wills, is rooted in optimism and the ability of humans to make wise choices. In contrast to Jimmy Carter's belief in "original sin" and the need for limits and self-denial, Reagan's Christianity called for "a dutiful innocence and optimism."[26]

Ronald Reagan's Environmental Rhetoric

In a search for President Reagan's environmental rhetoric, few texts are available. A sitting president must discuss many topics on a daily basis, and a single issue cannot be the focus of any administration. Also, a president may transfer the responsibility for creating a public mandate to another level of government, to a general, a cabinet secretary, or a member of Congress. In the case of Ronald Reagan, one must consider the rhetoric of James Watt as well as the president to assess the administration's environmental agenda.

Reagan's environmental rhetoric begins with his campaign for the presidency. Certainly one of the most important moments in the campaign came on July 17, 1980, when he gave his nomination acceptance speech at the Republican National Convention. Reagan told the audience that the campaign's central issue is the "political, personal, and moral responsibility" of the Carter administration of the "unprecedented calamity which has befallen us." Defining his vision of progress through a contrast with the Democratic vision, Reagan proclaimed: "They tell us they've done the most that humanly could be done. They say that the United States has had its day in the sun, that our nation has passed its zenith. They expect you to tell your children that the American people no longer have the will to cope with their new problems; that the future will be one of sacrifice and few opportunities."[27]

Reagan reminded his listeners of a group of families who, in 1620, "dared to cross a mighty ocean to build a future for themselves in a new world." In their creation of the Mayflower Compact, these families "set the pattern for what was to come." And for Americans in 1980, Reagan asked, "Isn't it once again time to renew our compact of freedom; to pledge to each other all that is best in our lives; all that gives meaning to them—for the sake of this, our beloved and blessed land." Reagan offered his plan to save the economy, repeating his theme that conservation of natural resources was not the answer. Calling for greater exploration for oil, coal, and natural gas, Reagan presented his view of how people and the environment should be connected, announcing that "we are going to reaffirm that the economic prosperity of our people is a fundamental part of our environment.[28]

Reagan then recalled the many people he had met during the campaign, noting, "It is impossible to capture in words the splendor of this vast continent which God has granted as our portion of our creation. There are no words to express the extraordinary strength and character of this breed of people we call American." In a striking peroration, Reagan returned to the idea of the Puritan errand: "Can we doubt that only a Divine Providence placed this land, this island of freedom, here for a refuge for all those people in the world who yearn to breathe free?" And then Reagan pointed to the place of God in the campaign: "I'll confess that I've been a little afraid to suggest what I'm going to suggest. I'm more afraid not to. Can we begin our crusade joined together in a moment of silent prayer? God bless America"[29]

An account of Reagan's ability to combine the frontier thesis and the Puritan errand within a single discourse is described by Elizabeth Drew. On Memorial Day, 1980, Reagan campaigned at the Western Deserts Gospel Sing, held at the San Bernardino County Fairgrounds. Before his speech, Reagan held a press conference in an open stable, with bales of hay placed behind the candidate as a prop. Reagan spoke on a stage in the rodeo field and was seated in front of a large wooden wagon wheel on which his name was painted. Dale Evans, wife of Roy Rogers, appeared at the rally, where Reagan received a plaque in appreciation of his "Christian testimony and recognition of gospel music." In his speech, Reagan asked "whether this nation can continue. This nation under God." Drew described Reagan's speech in this manner: "He talks, as he often does, about the 'loss of confidence, a great concern and worry on the part of the American people.' He attributes the loss of confidence to inflation. He cites 'our lack of confidence with regard to the energy crisis' and the 'doom-criers in the land who tell us that we will never again have things as good as we've had them, that we must learn to live with scarcity.' He says, 'I don't believe that,' and he is applauded. He says, 'I think this country is hungry for a spiritual revival—one nation, under God, indivisible,' and he is applauded."[30] Within this single event during a few hours of the 1980 campaign, Ronald Reagan symbolically embraced symbols of the frontier experience (rodeo grounds; wagon wheel; Dale Evans; a stable and bales of hay) and the Puritan errand (God's people; spiritual revival; one nation under God) and suggested that America's future was linked to concerns regarding energy and scarcity.

A different view of Reagan's environmental vision in 1980 emerges from a speech he did not deliver. On October 7, in two speeches to unemployed steel and coal workers in Ohio, Reagan planned to present his plan for reforming the Clean Air Act, but "the candidate did not stick to his written speeches. Instead, he made off-the-cuff remarks about air pollution that later touched off a flurry of angry newspaper editorials, and denunciations from environmentalists." According to the *Congressional Quarterly* account, the "written speech, which was not delivered, said that air pollution had been 'substantially controlled.'" The speech would have outlined a plan for clean air reform, including cost-benefit analyses for new regulations. Instead of the prepared text, Reagan "quipped that the Mount St. Helens volcano had probably dumped more sulfur dioxide into the air than is released in 10 years of 'automobile driving or things of that kind.'"[31] Reagan's decision to ignore a policy statement in favor of ridiculing environmental standards for clean air demonstrated his abiding preference for minimizing governmental involvement in the environment. The unemployed steel workers and coal miners were probably more sympathetic to a criticism of the system than to a statement offering reforms of policies they believed were hurting their future.

As president, Reagan gave few speeches directly related to environmental policymaking, allowing James Watt great freedom during 1981 and 1982 to articulate the administration's vision of environmental reform. In 1983 Reagan used his weekly radio message to defend Watt's actions (June) and then to discuss Watt's "resignation" (November) as interior secretary. In July, 1984, Reagan used the radio message to review his environmental and natural resource policies, "one of the best-kept secrets in Washington." After listing specific policy successes in his first term, Reagan reminded the public: "We came to Washington committed to respect the great bounty and beauty of God's creation. We believe very strongly in the concept of stewardship, caring for the resources we have so they can be shared and used productively for generations to come."[32]

Two speeches presented by Reagan in June, 1984, provide an overview of his environmental rhetoric. In signing legislation designating wilderness areas, Reagan opened by observing that "God has blessed the American people with vast and beautiful land, a land of mountains and prairies, lakes and forests that reach from sea to shining sea." And in concluding his remarks, Reagan observed that in future generations, parents would take their children to these "woods to show them how the land must have looked to the first Pilgrims and pioneers. And as Americans wander through these forests, climb these mountains, they will sense the love and majesty of the Creator of all that."[33]

In a much longer address to dedicate a new building for the National Geographic Society, Reagan delved into the philosophy guiding his views of the environment. He opened by acknowledging that members of the National Geographic Society are concerned about the environment, "You are worried about what man has done and is doing to this magical planet that God gave us," he said. "And I share your concern." Reagan then claimed that modern conservatives in America "want to protect and preserve the value and traditions by which the Nation has flourished for more than two centuries." Reagan continued by stating that Americans must protect and conserve the "land on which we live. . . . This is our patrimony. This is what we leave our children. And our great moral responsibility is to leave it to them either as we found it or better than we found it." At that point Reagan added this important qualifier to his commitment to preservation: "We want, as men on Earth, to use our resources for the reason God gave them to us—for the betterment of man. . . . [W]e must keep in mind the word 'balance'—a balance between the desire to conserve and protect, and the desire to grow and develop; a balance between concern for the good earth, and concern for the honest impulse to wrest from the earth the resources that benefit mankind."[34] Reagan's view of the environment stressed the "wealth" associated with nature and the responsibility to use it appropriately (for economic prosperity and growth) and then pass it to the next generation for their use. Significantly, Reagan reminded Americans of the Puritan errand, pointing to God's reason for giving people the gift of nature: "for the betterment of man."

The most powerful advocate in the Reagan administration's first term for a revolution in environmental policymaking was James Watt. As the only bona fide member of the New Right, and the only self-proclaimed born-again Christian in the Reagan cabinet, Watt sensed a special mission to change government and restore traditional American values. In another work, I detail Watt's personal and political background and explain his rise to power as a critic of American environmentalism.[35] He spoke regularly during his thirty months in office, and in many ways he reiterated the basic themes of Reaganism, albeit without Reagan's humor and self-deprecating manner.

In his first major speech as interior secretary, presented on March 23, 1981, to the North American Wildlife and Natural Resources Conference, Watt identified the "four solid cornerstones in this Administration's conservation policy":

1. America must have a sound economy if it is to be a good steward of its fish and wildlife, its parks, and all of its natural resources.
2. America must have orderly development of its vast energy resources to avert a crisis development which could be catastrophic to the environment.
3. America's resources were put here for the enjoyment and use of people, now and in the future, and should not be denied to the people by elitist groups.
4. America has the expertise to manage and use resources wisely, and much of that expertise is in State Government and in the private sector.[36]

In combination, the four cornerstones closely paralleled Reagan's environment discourse and reflected Watt's evangelical Christian view of natural resources. The Puritan errand is most obvious in Watt's claim that resources "were put here for the enjoyment and use of people, now and in the future." God gave Americans vast wealth in resources that should be used today and tomorrow; time does move from the "sacred past" of the Old World theology to that of a "sacred future" in the New World vision. By using "expertise" the nation can "orderly develop" natural resources for the good of all.

Three months later Watt spoke to a group of outdoor writers where he told his audience that "man is a key component in the environmental equation. Too often in the recent past, there has been a strong tendency to write people out of the equation." For Watt, outdoor recreation really meant to "re-create one's soul," thus government must provide greater sensitivity to resource users. Watt concluded, "Now new keys of access to the Reagan Administration have been passed out to all the hunters and fishermen and to all groups and people who believe in managing the lands, the waters, and the wildlife for the benefit of all Americans, not just a select few."[37]

For Watt, as well as Reagan, the nation's public lands were keys to economic growth, national security, and improvements in the quality of life. Claiming that the "greatness of a nation is determined by how it manages its human resources and natural resources," Watt assessed America's energy problem as representing a lack of faith, not a lack of natural resources. "We do not have a shortage in energy resources," Watt explained in October, 1981. "We have a shortage in the will to manage those resources for the benefit of America and Americans." Watt repeated a claim in this speech that appeared in most of his speeches: "It is my job to manage all of these lands and to manage them in a way that will improve *our national security, protect the environment, and create jobs.*"[38] Watt continued to articulate the connection between the American land-scape and freedom and prosperity; indeed he could not envision a policy that did not combine all three. Watt's mission to be the oracle of the political New Right in the Reagan administration, combined with questionable policy decisions, led to his resignation in October, 1983. With the 1984 elections upcoming, and a number of controversies surrounding the Interior Department, Watt's successor William Clark returned public discourse on the environment to the back pages of the nation's newspapers.

Reagan presented few major public statements on the environment in his second term, but when he did address some aspect of environmental policy-making, he returned to the core themes he campaigned on in 1980. In a 1986 message to Congress accompanying the annual report of the Council on Environmental Quality, Reagan reviewed the administration's successes in pollution control and wilderness preservation. But he also reminded Congress that his environmental philosophy rested on two fundamental propositions: "The first is that the spirit, creativity, and personal drive of individual Americans will be this Nation's greatest resource. It is the human genius that turns physical substances into resources, and human creativity in a free society is never exhaustible. Second, human institutions can encourage or constrain the ability of people to make the best use of their resources and to solve environmental problems." Reagan concluded the message by recalling the past generations who had built a strong nation on the principles of individual initiative and private institutions. According to Reagan, "They worked to turn our abundant natural resources to productive use and they learned to love their new land with its grand vistas, its mountains and forests, its fertile fields, and its bustling cites."[39]

Two years later, as his second term of office neared completion, Reagan sent another message to Congress with the annual report of the Council on Environmental Quality. In some ways, this message was Reagan's attempt to create an environmental legacy for his administration. He opened with the nation's founders, claiming that for the settlers who came to America by ship in the seventeenth century, "this new land promised a New World, and a new chance to make possible the oldest of dreams—the dream of personal liberty." The settlers and explorers found "an abundance of land—virgin forests, untouched meadows, bountiful streams, and sweet-smelling air—that vastly exceeded anything the kings of the old world could have ever imagined." But there was so much land in the new country, "that there was no way to restrict it to a privileged few." The founding fathers made ownership of the western lands available to anyone "brave enough to take the risk, to grasp the main chance, and to hope for a better tomorrow." The migration and settlement of the frontier created a nation of "hope, opportunity, experimentation, mobility, and personal freedom." After reviewing the history of wilderness preservation in the United States, Reagan turned to his administration and its success in environmental policymaking. He argued that his administration "has understood the necessary relationship between freedom and opportunity, between opportunity and growth, between growth and progress, including progress in restoring and maintaining the quality of the human environment. The same spirit of creativity and innovation that has created 17 million jobs has also benefited the land itself, making America the beautiful more beautiful still."[40]

Clearly significant strands of the Puritan errand and the frontier thesis are at work in Reagan's review of his environmental agenda. One cannot understand his mission without acknowledging the Puritan migration to New England; this reference reinforces the theological connection between human activity and a divine plan. Definitions of landscape must consider the idea of prophecy and the need to "conquer and use" the wilderness to fulfill God's plan. But Reagan comfortably moved to the second American myth in his worldview, showing that the vast American frontier promoted intellectual and material prosperity. The frontier allowed the founders to reject property rights for the privileged classes in place of property rights for all Americans willing to work hard, take responsibility, and develop the nation's abundant resources. Reagan's pride in "restoring and maintaining" the quality of the human environment reiterates qualities within the Puritan errand and the frontier thesis. Both myths reaffirm the power of landscape in shaping human progress. Whether one defined progress in economic or political terms, the American wilderness offered the vehicle for continued evolution of the human condition.

For Reagan, the nation's vast public lands had to be connected with the American people to have meaning. Reagan's epigram in his October, 1988, message to Congress summarized his vision of the nature, culture and politics: freedom is necessary for opportunity; opportunity is necessary for growth; growth is necessary for progress; and finally progress restores and maintains the "quality of the human environment." Nature cannot have meaning without connection to culture in Reagan's orientation. More directly, the environment served as the primary agent in the American experience.

If Ronald Reagan articulated a vision of landscape so directly connected to the nation's cultural and social fabric, why do observers suggest a failed environmental policy? The answer may be found in what Robert G. Gunderson called "the oxymoron strain" in American discourse, a "rhetorical balancing of transcendental and pragmatic values" that has characterized American society since the Puritans arrived.[41] Although many of the specific goals that his administration sought were ultimately rejected, Reagan still claimed success in environmental leadership as he left office in 1988. For Reagan, embracing the transcendental values of America's mission was meaningful on its own terms, even when pragmatism dictated actions that seemed at odds with his worldview. The Reagan revolution failed to significantly alter the conservation consensus of the 1960s and 1970s, which reflected a deep public commitment to the values of environmental integrity and wilderness preservation. But in assessing his environmental legacy, Ronald Reagan measured his success in terms of America's renewed faith in its leadership, a greater appreciation of its history and heritage, and a sense that progress would continue unabated. In each of these areas, Reagan invoked the Puritan errand and the frontier thesis and presented an inspirational vision of the American character closely connected with the nation's landscape.

Reagan's environmental legacy may be more important for its symbolic reconstruction of how nature and wilderness should be viewed in the United States. Reagan offered a vision of the environment that rejected the conceptions of time and space central to the ideology of the environmental movement. In terms of time, environmentalists looked to the future as a guide to making policy; Reagan asked Americans to look to the past to recapture the power of wilderness to bring out the best in its citizens. In terms of space, environmentalists created a vision that asked Americans to look at planet Earth as a single, complex and fragile ecosystem; Reagan looked to the nation's public lands as useful for recreation, wealth, and spiritual renewal. Although Reagan left the presidency in 1989, his vision was embraced by the wise use movement of the 1990s, and it finds adherents among many in George W. Bush's administration. For these reasons, Reagan's rhetorical presidency continues to resonate in environmental politics and the Reagan revolution remains a substantive ideological framework for the present and the future.

Notes

1. James Combs, *The Reagan Range: The Nostalgic Myth in American Politics* (Bowling Green, Ohio: Bowling Green State University Popular Press, 1993), 5.
2. Donald Worster, *The Wealth of Nature: Environmental History and the Ecological Imagination* (New York: Oxford University Press, 1993), 96.
3. Ibid., 99.
4. William Schneider, "The Political Legacy of the Reagan Years," in *The Reagan Legacy,* ed. Sidney Blumenthal and Thomas Byrne Edsall (New York: Pantheon Books, 1988), 53–59; Dilys M. Hill and Phil Williams, "The Reagan Legacy," in *The Reagan Presidency: An Incomplete Revolution?* ed. Dilys M. Hill, Raymond Moore, and Phil Williams (New York: St. Martin's Press, 1990), 239.
5. Robert F. Durant, *The Administrative Presidency Revisited: Public Lands, the BLM, and the Reagan Revolution* (Albany: State University of New York Press, 1992); Robert A. Shanley, *Presidential Influence and Environmental Policy* (Westport, Conn.: Greenwood Press, 1992).
6. David Vogel, "The Politics of the Environment, 1970–1987," *Wilson Quarterly* 11 (1987): 67–68; Samuel P. Hays, *Beauty, Health, and Permanence: Environmental Politics in the United States, 1955–1985* (New York: Cambridge University Press, 1987), 505; Norman Vig, "Presidential Leadership: From the Reagan to the Bush Administration," in *Environmental Policy in the 1990s,* ed. Norman Vig and Michael E. Kraft (Washington, D.C.: Congressional Quarterly Press, 1990), 36, 41.
7. Vig, "Presidential Leadership," 42–44.
8. Ronald Reagan, *An American Life: The Autobiography* (New York: Simon and Schuster, 1990); James Watt with Doug Wead, *The Courage of a Conservative* (New York: Simon and Schuster, 1985), 197–98.
9. Martin Anderson, *Revolution: The Reagan Legacy* (Stanford, Calif.: Hoover Institution Press, 1990), 461.
10. Michael Kammen, *People of Paradox: An Inquiry Concerning the Origins of the American Civilization* (New York: Vintage Books, 1972), 22.
11. Sacvan Bercovitch, "The Rites of Assent: Rhetoric, Ritual, and the Ideology of the American Consensus," in *The American Self,* ed. Sam Girgus (Albuquerque: University of New Mexico Press, 1981), 9–10, 13, 14, 17.
12. Ibid., 9.
13. William Cronon, "Revisiting the Vanishing Frontier: The Legacy of Frederick Jackson Turner," *Western Historical Quarterly* 18 (1987): 160, 157.
14. Ronald Carpenter, "Frederick Jackson Turner and the Rhetorical Impact of the Frontier Thesis," *Quarterly Journal of Speech* 63 (1977): 117; Paul Rodman and Michael Malone, "Tradition and Challenge in Western Historiography," *Western Historical Quarterly* 16 (1985): 31; Patricia Nelson Limmerick, *The Legacy of Conquest: The Unbroken Past of the American West* (New York: Norton, 1987), 21.
15. For critiques of the frontier thesis, see Limmerick, *Legacy of Conquest,* Rodman and Malone, "Tradition and Challenge," and Worster, *The Wealth of Nature*; on its rhetorical vision, see Carpenter, "Frederick Jackson Turner"; Carpenter, *The Eloquence of Frederick Jackson Turner* (San Marino, Calif.: Huntington Library, 1983).
16. Cronon, "Revisiting the Vanishing Frontier," 170.
17. Henry Nash Smith, *Virgin Land: The American West as Symbol and Myth* (Cambridge, Mass.: Harvard University Press, 1970), 250.

18. Michael Schaller, *Reckoning with Reagan: America and Its President in the 1980s* (New York: Oxford University Press, 1992), 3.

19. Barry Alan Morris, "The Ponderosa Presidency: Reagan's Western Melodramatic Form," *Speaker and Gavel* 19 (1981): 31–37. In an insightful study written after Reagan's first election as president, Morris examines Reagan's use of the "western melodramatic form." Morris notes that Reagan incorporated each of the dominant themes of the West into his rhetoric: virtue of martial superiority, rugged individualism, dominance of man over nature, and respect for traditional roles.

20. Reagan, *American Life*, 104, 118.

21. Ibid., 138.

22. Richard Grenier, "The Cowboy Patriot," *National Interest* (Fall, 1996): 84, retrieved from Infotrac electronic data base; Reagan, "Unforgettable John Wayne," *Reader's Digest*, Oct., 1979, 119; Laurence Barrett, *Gambling with History: Reagan in the White House* (New York: Penguin Books, 1984), 41.

23. Combs, *Reagan Range*, 33; Garry Wills, *Reagan's America: Innocents at Home* (Garden City, N.Y.: Doubleday, 1987). Reagan's leadership of a student strike at Eureka College is well documented. Protesting the elimination of classes due to a budget cut, Reagan spoke in favor of a student strike. Wills devotes an entire chapter to this episode. The importance of the strike for Reagan is that he found the power of oratory in the event: "I discovered that night that an audience has a feel to it and, in the parlance of the theater, the audience and I were together" (48).

24. According to Wills, "Reagan was not only made the host, occasional star, and part-time producer of the successful new show; he became a symbol and spokesman for the entire GE endeavor, what a publicist called the company's ambassador of goodwill to the public at large. His very mode of life was turned into an advertisement for living well electrically" (*Reagan's America*, 278).

25. Elizabeth Drew, *Portrait of an Election: The 1980 Presidential Campaign* (New York: Simon and Schuster, 1981), 173.

26. Combs, *Reagan Range*, 123, 129; Wills, *Reagan's America*, 384–85.

27. Reagan, "Acceptance of the Republican Nomination for President,," in *Contemporary American Voices: Significant Speeches in American History, 1945–Present*, ed. James R. Andrews and David Zarefsky (New York: Longman, 1992), 341.

28. Ibid., 341–42.

29. Ibid., 345–46.

30. Drew, *Portrait of an Election*, 174–75.

31. Kathy Koch, "Philosophical Split Divides Candidates on Environment," *Congressional Quarterly* (Oct. 18, 1980): 3132, 3162.

32. Reagan, "Environmental and Natural Resources Management," Radio Address, July 14, 1984, reprinted rptd. in *Ronald Reagan's Weekly Radio Addresses: The President Speaks to America*, ed. Fred Israel (Wilmington, Del.: Scholarly Resources, 1987), 1:227.

33. Reagan, "Remarks on Signing Four Bills Designating Wilderness Areas," *Papers of the President: Administration of Ronald Reagan* (June 19, 1984), 879–80.

34. Reagan, "Remarks at Dedication Ceremonies for the New Building of the National Geographic Society," *Papers of the President* (June 19, 1984), 875.

35. C. Brant Short, *Ronald Reagan and the Public Lands: America's Conservation Debate, 1979–1984* (College Station: Texas A&M University Press, 1989), provides a biographical account of James Watt, explores his rise to power in the environ-

mental debates of the 1970s, and reviews his tenure as secretary of the interior
from 1981 to 1983.

36. James G. Watt, "Secretary Watt Outlines Conservation Policy to Avert Crises
and to Serve Present and Future Generations," speech presented to the North
American Wildlife and Natural Resources Conference, March 23, 1981, Washington, D.C.

37. Watt, "New Policies Make Man Key Component in Environmental Equation,
Interior Secretary Watt Tells Outdoor Writers Association," speech presented to
Outdoor Writers of America Association, June 15, 1981, Louisville, Ky.

38. Watt, "Speech to the Associated Press Managing Editors," Oct. 23, 1981, Toronto,
Canada; emphasis in original.

39. Reagan, "Message to the Congress Transmitting the Annual Report of the Council
on Environmental Quality," *Papers of the President* (Feb. 19, 1986), 226–27.

40. Reagan, "Message to the Congress Transmitting the Report of the Council on
Environmental Quality," *Papers of the President* (Oct. 3, 1988), 1272–73.

41. Robert G. Gunderson, "The Oxymoron Strain in American Rhetoric," *Central
States Speech Journal* 28 (1977): 94.

PART III

The Environmental

President

Who Wasn't

6

The (Re)Making of the "Environmental President"

Clinton/Gore and the Rhetoric of U.S. Environmental Politics, 1992–1996

J. Robert Cox

"If Bill Clinton is anything," Whillock suggests, "he is an enigma to the public, a mass of contradictions." Admired by generations that have grown up in the post–baby boom period for his postmodern conversational style, scolded by the *Los Angeles Times* for abdicating Teddy Roosevelt's bully pulpit, and excoriated by archdruid environmentalist David Brower, for doing "more to harm the environment and to weaken environmental regulations in three years than Presidents Bush and Reagan did in 12 years," Pres. William Jefferson Clinton presents scholars an opportunity for deconstructing the "enigma" of his public rhetoric.[1]

On July 9, 1992, candidate Bill Clinton, speaking from the governor's mansion in Little Rock, announced his choice for vice president. With Al Gore at his side, he pledged, "together we will finally give the United States a real environmental president." Yet Clinton as president has been widely viewed as discovering, with Dick Morris's help, the "environment" only as a foil for the antienvironmental 104th Congress and as a wedge issue to attract Republican female voters in the 1996 presidential election. Both perceptions may be true.[2]

I should also disclose something of my own location, as a critic whose view of Clinton-as-orator reflects an ambivalence from participating in much of the politics of the environment during the first Clinton/Gore term. When the president signed the now infamous "salvage timber" legislative rider in July, 1995, I spoke on behalf of the Sierra Club's half million members of a "depth of disappointment, disbelief, and anger over a President's action on the environment [that I had not seen] in many, many years" and of a leader who had "betrayed the trust of Americans who care about the environment and our forests." One year later, in fall 1996, I also participated in the national Sierra Club's decision to endorse Bill Clinton for a second term in office.[3]

It is tempting, therefore, to approach the topic of a rhetoric of the Clinton environmental presidency from what Wander called a moral or external standard of consistency, a perspective that "lends itself to cynical and bitter commentaries" as critics observe contradictions between what a president said and what he (or his administration) did.[4] Or, viewed more favorably, such a stance would simply chronicle, in Clinton's case, a heroic struggle with a recalcitrant Congress, a Congress that would have defunded the Environmental Protection Agency and opened Alaska's Arctic National Wildlife Refuge for oil drilling.

In one sense, Clinton's own rhetoric invites the former stance: "This must be a campaign of ideas, not slogans," he announced from the steps on the Old State House in Little Rock in 1991. "I'm going to tell you *in plain language* what I intend to do as President." Critics who would account for the charges of hypocrisy associated with this "plain language" would inquire into the reasons and conditions that destabilize this relationship, between the saying and the doing of environmental policy. But while this gives us important context and constraints, I suspect our task is more than this. It must also be an effort to probe the sources within Clinton as rhetorical performances themselves that begin to explain the aporias of this president's leadership.[5]

I argue, therefore, that Clinton's environmental presidency is constituted in, and constrained by, the style he deploys to construct political authority, what Hariman has called the "the republican style." Clinton's public rhetoric, I suggest, enables a republican effort to "form the virtuous political community" but also defers its rhetorical competence; both within the president's rhetoric and as Clinton fails to recognize and mediate deeper structural and institutional resistance in the presidential (administrative) "body." These failures suggest a republican style of leadership better able to invite a political community to "come together" than to nurture its performance in critical debates about the environment.[6]

A Drama in Three Acts: Public Narratives of the Clinton "Environmental Presidency"

Any understanding of the rhetoric of the first term of the Clinton/Gore administration (1993–96) now begins simply within the textual space of the president's speeches. Critics inevitably, and to their frustration, first encounter a wider social text inscribing this president's words and deeds, and the public's response, on the environment. By early fall 1995 public perceptions and White House image making had converged in what has become an entrenched narrative of Bill Clinton's "environmental presidency." Roger O'Neil's report for NBC "Decision '96" is typical:

O'Neil: It's one of the pillars of his campaign. [Vice Pres. Al Gore, with Pres. Clinton at his side, releases Bald Eagle at Patuxent Naval Air Station, July 4, 1996.]

Vice Pres. Al Gore: Please welcome America's environmental president, Bill Clinton!

Pres. Clinton: We can and we must protect the environment while advancing the prosperity of the American people and people throughout the world.

O'Neil: It's a pristine picture. But not entirely a true reflection of the president's environmental record.

Unidentified Crowd: (In unison) Clinton, repeal the clear-cut deal!

O'Neil: In the Pacific Northwest, after promising reform, Clinton's worst environmental blunder was reopening some forests to logging. [Scene of old-growth tree falling, after being cut.]

Unidentified Speaker: It's about time that President Clinton stopped saying one thing and then doing another.

O'Neil: Clinton also backed down on promises to reform mining and grazing laws when special interests in Congress objected. Clinton didn't really become a "green" president until two years ago, seizing on a public backlash from a perceived Republican effort in Congress to weaken environmental laws, including clean air and clean water. So, Clinton began defending the environment and ended up earning high marks in a report card NBC News asked five environmental groups to grade. From air, to water, to protecting wildlife and federal lands, mostly A's and B's.

Mr. Jim Wyerman (Defenders of Wildlife): As compared to Congress, whatever grade you give Clinton, we think Congress deserves an F.

Ms. Debbie Sease (Sierra Club): He's had a strong serve, and a weak follow through, and a very impressive finish. His record is good on playing defense.

Ms. Carol Aten (National Parks and Conservation): President Clinton has recognized the power of the environment as a message and something that reaches the people.

O'Neil: He may understand politics more than he understands the environment?

Ms. Aten: They work together.[7]

From identification as America's "environmental president" to his use of "the power of the environment as a message," the public witnessed Clinton in a political drama that unfolded from "great expectations" through "disillusionment and betrayal" to a portrayal of Bill Clinton as "defender of the faith," standing against would-be destroyers of the environment in the 104th Congress.

Great Expectations

The Clinton/Gore '92 campaign clearly raised expectations for, and promised a new embodiment of, U.S. environmental policy. From the opening sentence of their 1992 platform on environment in *Putting People First,* the candidates seized this issue to distinguish their campaign: "For all its rhetoric, the Bush Administration has been an environmental disaster." By contrast, candidates Clinton and Gore invited a set of identifications against which they would presumably hold their own rhetoric—and administration—accountable: "We want to give America a real environmental policy," they assured voters. "We will renew America's commitment to leave our children a better nation—a nation whose air, water, and land are unspoiled, whose natural beauty is undiminished, and whose leadership for sustainable global growth is unsurpassed."[8]

In announcing his selection of Al Gore as his vice presidential running mate, Clinton evoked the senator's persona as a knowledgeable leader in environmental affairs and pledged, "together we will finally give the United States a real environmental presidency." For his part, speaking at Clinton's side at the governor's mansion in Little Rock, Gore assured voters, "I know from conversations that the two of us have had that Bill Clinton is speaking from his heart when he says together we can offer the leadership our world needs to save the earth's environment."[9]

Although Bill Clinton would be clear about the core vision of his candidacy—the centrality of jobs, education, and competitiveness in the global economy—the environmental scaffolding of his campaign would also be clear. In addition to promises to reduce pollution and toxic waste, preserve places of natural beauty, and pursue efforts toward a healthier global climate, candidates Clinton and Gore pledged, in an implicit rhetorical undertaking, to "[s]hatter the false choice between environmental protection and economic growth." "The task of saving the earth's environment," Gore asserted in his 1992 acceptance speech in New York City, "must and will become the central organizing principle of the post–Cold War world." By the time of the first inauguration, expectations for a successful Clinton presidency overall were very high. A poll early in his presidency showed that "Americans [are] generally confident that he will be successful in meeting many of the nation's most pressing challenges."[10]

In many ways, Clinton had, indeed, perfected a persona of a "real environmental president." The new nominee of his party integrated the promise of environmental protection within a larger vision of a "new covenant" of opportunity, responsibility, and community. Long overdue initiatives appeared from newly appointed Interior Secretary Bruce Babbitt to reform grazing on public lands and the archaic 1872 Mining Act, from new EPA administrator Carol Browner to speed cleanup of toxic waste sites, and from the president himself bold promises to resolve tensions over logging in old-growth forests of the Pacific Northwest. And in consolidating administration efforts in a new White House Office on Environmental Policy, President Clinton pledged "a new way of thinking [and] a new, more efficient and effective way to craft policies that work."[11]

Within his first eighteen months in office, the president had issued executive orders on energy efficiency, federal pollution prevention, compliance with federal right-to-know laws, conversion of federal vehicles to alternative fuels, the purchase of recycled paper, and directives to agencies to acknowledge concerns over "environmental justice" (the impact of proposed actions on low-income citizens and communities of color.) Clinton also signed the newly passed Colorado Wilderness Act and the California Desert Protection Act, as well as an international biodiversity treaty that had been ignored by the Bush administration.

One incident, however, seemed to embody the early promise of a committed Clinton environmental presidency more powerfully than others. Within weeks of his inaugural address and his allusion to posterity in the image of "a child's eyes wander[ing] into sleep," the president appeared in a televised Children's Town Hall at the White House. It was a convincing portrait. A young boy, Pernell, explains to the president, in his own words and in a compelling video, the effects of living in the polluted chemical corridor between Baton Rouge and New Orleans. Clinton listens as Pernell describes the toll that living under these conditions has taken on his family, including the death of his ten-year-old brother. "We've only got one planet," Pernell tells the president; then he adds, "We all believe very strongly that you, as an individual, have the know-how and the courage to go about and tackle this problem and many others we do have faith in you." The president responds to Pernell, "We'll do it for your brother."[12]

Disillusionment and Betrayal

Others' faith would not last as long. Even as the Clinton White House began to act on many fronts, it also began to stumble, badly. Within months of taking office, the Clinton administration backed off promises to reform mining and grazing, and it seemed to compromise too easily in the forest summit to resolve logging practices on federal lands. Environmental activists charged the administration betrayed a specific campaign pledge when Al Gore announced that a controversial toxic waste incinerator outside East Liverpool, Ohio, would be fired up. Others charged that "[b]y the end of that congressional session [1993–94], before the Gingrich take-over, the Clinton team had engineered the resumption of logging in ancient forests, sold out the Everglades and forced through the North American Free Trade Agreement." Nor did the president's efforts to explain these reversals seem convincing. On reform of grazing, Clinton appeared to abandon his own secretary of the interior: "The Interior Department made a mistake. They just made a mistake. They proposed raising the grazing fees too high in 1993. It was wrong. [A]fter strenuous objection by a number of people , we immediately dropped it, immediately."[13]

Equally difficult to explain was a Congress—from 1993 to 1994 under Democratic leadership—that produced "the worst environmental record in 25 years."[14] A loyal Al Gore blamed obstructionist Republicans bent on weakening environmental safeguards but others had begun to question the president's own leadership on environmental matters.[15] *Washington Post* writers Dewar and Cooper were generous in assigning blame: "Fast out of the starting gate, the 103rd Congress collapsed on the finish line. Bill after bill—[including] most environmental initiatives—fell before the GOP juggernaut, often with help from Clinton's missteps and disarray among Democrats."[16]

By the fall of 1994 the GOP was campaigning on a rhetoric of anti–big government and promises to overhaul burdensome (read "environmental") regulations. Reports of declining membership among the "big ten" environmental groups and the media's loss of interest in the environment appeared to give an opening to some who wished to dismantle the legislative legacy of Earth Day. The new 104th Contract with America Congress "unleashed an all-fronts attack on the very notion of environmental protection," Jessica Matthews wrote. "One of the leadership's first major bills would have had the government pay polluters not to pollute; Majority Whip Tom Delay (R-Tex.) introduced a measure to repeal the Clean Air Act, and the Republican [Utah] wilderness bill proposed to allow road construction, transmission lines, water projects, pipelines and the like in areas where, by law, man himself should be only a visitor." With the administration in apparent retreat, the way seemed clear for the most significant reversal of environmental policy in decades. Stuart Rothenberg summed up the change on Capitol Hill when he wrote in *Roll Call*, "The environment is now a political zero."[17]

Undoubtedly, the low-water mark for Clinton came when the president signed the 1995 Rescissions Act with its so-called salvage timber rider. The rider—a legislative device allowing an unrelated matter to be attached to a bill—

suspended relevant environmental laws regulating timber cuts on public lands and opened the way to what many believed would be abusive and unsustainable logging.[18] The Clinton reversal (he had weeks earlier used his first veto to block the bill) provoked immediate cries of "betrayal" from environmental organizations that had not previously criticized Clinton publicly, including Audubon, World Wildlife Fund, and Sierra Club.[19]

The president's signing of the salvage timber rider quickly became a powerful trope for the environmental movement's characterization of Clinton's record. "We thought a new day had dawned after the dark years of Reagan and Bush," said Dan Hamburg, a former Democratic member of Congress; "[Clinton is not] a friend of the environment but an enemy of the environment." Hamburg's comment mirrored a series of full-page ads in the *New York Times* denouncing Clinton and the salvage rider, charging "America Betrayed" and "Mr. President, you're giving waffles a bad name." (Earlier, Gary Trudeau had begun to depict Clinton with the icon of a waffle in his cartoon strip *Doonesbury.*)[20]

Defender of the Faith

By late summer and early fall 1995, however, the public had also become increasingly alarmed by the course on the environment the 104th Congress was taking. The excesses of the GOP Congress in attempting to roll back environment law, Matthews reports, had produced a "startling public backlash" even to environmental groups, a reaction so strong that the president would made environmental protection "a center-piece of his [reelection] campaign."[21]

At the same time, President Clinton began toughening his public rhetoric in the face of a number of bills that would repeal or weaken certain high-profile environmental laws. Over the course of several months, he would threaten to veto a measure gutting health provisions of the Clean Water Act, a so-called takings bill that would compensate polluters for forgone profits if they complied with federal environmental regulations, and a regulatory "reform" bill that would significantly delay or make more costly the ability of federal agencies to set forth or enforce new environmental or public health standards. And as a hostile Congress clashed with Clinton over the 1996 budget, the president vetoed appropriation bills that reduced funding for the EPA and Department of the Interior as well as the 1996 budget "reconciliation" act and a debt ceiling authorization whose attached riders would have opened the Arctic Wildlife Refuge to oil leasing, hastened logging in Alaska's Tongass National Forest, and extended a moratorium on listing of endangered and threatened species.

Jeffrey St. Clair and Alexander Cockburn suggest that, at the start of 1996, Clinton strategist Dick Morris "began telling his boss that enviro [sic] issues were political dynamite, particularly with Republican women." If true, the advice seemed to stick. Morris's would-be influence can be seen not only in the monotonously repeated Clinton campaign message of "Medicare, Medicaid, education and the environment" but also in Clinton's boldest actions on the environment, from the withdrawal of public lands for a proposed mine near Yellowstone National Park to his designation, two months before the election, of the 1.7-million-acre Grand Staircase–Escalante National Monument in southern Utah.[22]

While the origins of the Clinton "return" in the role of "defender of the environment" are variously argued, it is clear the president's newly found standing was aided by the Republicans themselves.[23] Frank Luntz, the GOP pollster who created the Contract with America, argued in a memo to House Majority Whip Tom Delay: "We [Republicans] have articulated environmental policies so badly for so long that virtually no one trusts us. Even the GOP faithful, who trust us implicitly on everything else, have conceded this issue to the Democrats. A recent national survey showed that 55% of Republicans don't trust their own party when it comes to the environment." Matthews, in fact, argues that the excess of the 104th Congress, "for the first time influenced— and sometimes determined—how people voted" in [the] November [elections]." "Eighty-five percent of defeated Republican incumbents," she pointed out, "had been on an environmental hit list."[24]

Yet even as Clinton moved to defend existing environmental laws, many viewed his efforts through a lens of suspicion. Some environmentalists refused to endorse the president for reelection.[25] And O'Neil's suggestion that Clinton "may understand politics more than he understands the environment" summed up the public's general ambivalence about the president's actions. Did Bill Clinton/Dick Morris discover that politics and the environment in fact "work together," or is this simply message-driven politics in a political culture that expects manipulation? Perhaps this is too easy. "This continual definition of policy in terms of [shifting] alliances," Hariman notes, "is easily criticized for sacrificing principle to expediency, but within the republican orbit, these outcomes are understood to be neither unacceptable in every case nor inevitable."[26]

Without committing to Hariman's claim, I go beyond stories of another Clinton "comeback" and inquire further into the possibilities of this president's "republican" style. I want to read Clinton's speeches—for a moment—not simply as a narrative of expectations, betrayal, and redemption but intentionally, as "promise" of civic talk, an invitation to speak of "civic mutuality" in the face of our contending interests. I want, tentatively, to suggest that Clinton's rhetoric invites a discursive community into being and, at the same time, subtly defers the rhetorical means for such a community to achieve its ends.[27]

Alternate Reading 1: Clinton as Republican Stylist

Interestingly, few environmental leaders actually criticize President Clinton's public rhetoric. Indeed, passages from Clinton's speeches are often cited by environmental groups as a promise or norm against which to hold accountable actions of his administration. This results, perhaps ironically, from the fact that the president perfected a certain style of constituting political authority. In his speeches and remarks during high-profile moments such as his 1993 forest summit in Portland, Oregon, Clinton appears to invite a fractured and divided nation to "come together" to deliberate and resolve differences during a "difficult process of change" in the country.[28]

An early promise of what the *New York Times* called Clinton's "politics of reconciliation" would come in the president's pledge to help resolve long-standing tensions between loggers and those wanting to preserve the old-growth forests of the Pacific Northwest. It is perhaps the clearest occasion on which Clinton would display the republican style he would attempt to perfect during his first term in office. In his statements during and after his April 2, 1993, forest summit, he would issue the invitation "come, let us reason together."[29]

The conference of loggers, salmon fishers, timber officials, environmentalists, and tribal leaders met ostensibly to share their concerns and to craft a solution to disputes over forestlands in Oregon, Washington, and northern California. Clinton attended the conference, and in his opening remarks he appealed for an exchange of views among participants and with the administration by composing the summit as a space for talk. "Together we can move beyond confrontation to build a consensus on a balanced policy to preserve jobs and to protect our environment." Speaking for the administration members with him, he assured conferees: "We're all here to listen and to learn from you." And, displaying his own listening competence, he shared what he had heard: "I remember the timber industry workers with whom I spoke in a town hall meeting in Seattle last July; . . . I remember the families from the timber industry whom I met last September in Max Groesbeck's backyard in Eugene. I was moved beyond words by the stories that people told me there; . . . [and] I was also inspired by Frank Henderson, who had lost his job as a timber worker."[30]

For Bill Clinton, agreement between loggers and environmentalists depended not only on creating the conditions for talk but also on displacing blame for divisive rhetorics in the past. A more distant agent, he suggested, may be responsible for some of the differences between environmentalists and timber workers: "For too long the National Government has done more to confuse the issues than to clarify them. The rhetoric from Washington has often exaggerated and exacerbated the tensions between those who speak about the economy and those who speak about the environment." If conflict lay not in the material tensions involved in resource extraction and the environment, Clinton suggested, but between people (even if misplaced), then it's solution was political, that is, it lay in the sphere of volition, not nature; disputes over the forest were amenable to talk among these same parties. Those gathered now in Portland "are meeting in a conference room, not a courtroom," Clinton asserted. They had only to recognize that "[t]his is not about choosing between jobs and the environment but about recognizing the importance of both and recognizing that virtually everyone here and everyone in this region cares about both." He appealed to them, therefore, "to end the divisions" and "arrive at a balanced solution."[31]

Though the expressed differences among those attending would be sharp, the president, nevertheless construed the discussions in ways that suggested a reconciliation: "One of the things that has come out of this meeting to me loud and clear is that you want us to try to break the paralysis that presently controls the situation, to move and to act." At the end of the conference, when conferees had failed to fashion a basis for a solution, Clinton announced, "I intend to direct the Cabinet and the entire administration to begin work immediately to craft a balanced, a comprehensive, a long-term policy to end this stalemate."[32]

Similar impulses toward a "politics of reconciliation" would appear in many of Clinton's other speeches on the environment. Speaking beside the banks of the Potomac River on the twenty-fifth anniversary of the founding of Earth Day, the president praised the efforts of communities in Virginia, Maryland, Pennsylvania, and the District of Columbia that were helping to clean up the polluted Chesapeake Bay: "The bay is coming back," he told them, "because people overcame all that divided them to save their common heritage."[33]

Hariman tells us in his superb study of Cicero's republican style that "[i]n place of comprehensive statement[s] of one's political precepts, the republican style emphasizes a more constitutive understanding of political discourse. . . . Cicero [as with Clinton, I suggest] is well aware that republican politics involves conflicts of interest . . . —the conditions for any successful negotiation have to be created in the act of negotiating. In other words, the point of persuasive discourse is more to form the virtuous civic community than to represent it."[34]

The composition of such a community requires that "public practices (such as the practice of oratory) and public figures (such as the president) cultivate a

moral sense in the citizenry that would result in decisions being made primarily with regard to the common good." And this requires, in turn, that its practitioners engage in, and sustain, a certain kind of political intercourse as a civic
practice, that is, that they continually strive "to overcome their private interests through common deliberation." Alongside (or despite) Clinton's perceived
wavering on the environment in his first term, his invitation to a fractured and
divided community to "come together" in a space composed for talk about
differences is a perfect synecdoche for the tropes of the republican style: that
the terms of judgment and political action are constituted in discourse; that
such discourse is validated by the consensus of those participating in the assembled political community; and that the ability of a rhetorician such as a
president to embody the virtues of the republic "brings the other elements of
republican composition into an aesthetic whole, and provides the audience with
a coherent definition of their civic order."[35]

Yet there is more. At the same time that the republican stylist invites the
civic community into existence, he or she must also provide the rhetorical resources whereby its members might perform their civic role. That is to say,
sensitivity to such a style supposes that governance requires more than the
announcement of a coherent doctrine or policy; "the full presentation of civic
republicanism only occurs when its doctrines are filled out rhetorically." It is
not sufficient that a president supported a certain policy (or failed to do so);
he must make accessible the terms of its composition to the community whose
assent is sought.[36]

On first reading, Clinton's speeches on occasions such as the forest conference and his annual Earth Day addresses excel in precisely this manner. Drawing on the themes of his new covenant of opportunity, responsibility, and
community, the president evokes a vision of civic mutuality and invites a nation's
concern for the environment in terms of a cornucopia of civic identifications,
from liberty, an expanding economy, and national security, to spiritual health
and beauty, and the nation's need to "manage a process of change."[37]

Throughout these and other remarks, Clinton uses pleas for preservation
of the natural world and for protection of communities' health as the context
and occasion for a call to "renew our national community."[38] Speaking to community members of Meridian Hills who had reclaimed a neighborhood park
in the nation's capital from neglect and crime, Clinton crafts his most fully
developed republican identification with the environment.

> In restoring a piece of nature, the people here have helped to restore a
> strong sense of place, of their own history a sense of purpose, a sense of
> pride, and a sense of hope for their children.

Preserving those things enables us to bring our communities and country back together.

There is clearly today a hunger in our national spirit not only for more security, for more economic opportunity but for something we can all be involved in that is larger than ourselves and more lasting than the fleeting moment. Reclaiming our rivers, our forests, our beaches, and our urban oases, like this one, is a great purpose worthy of a great people. The love of nature is at the core of our identity as individuals, as communities, and certainly as Americans and, increasingly, thankfully, a part of the community of all nations.

Preserving the environment is at the core of everything we have to do in our own country, building businesses, raising our children and restoring the fabric of our society. For we are here today to bear witness to a simple but powerful truth: As we renew our environment, we renew our national community.[39]

In his best oratorical moments, as this was, Clinton was clearly able to marshal eloquence and to embody a concern for the environment with a force similar to that displayed in his speeches on race.[40] Such speeches, however, largely display the president's skills in the first and third master tropes of republicanism, an articulation of the terms of civic mutuality and an ability, personally, to embody an ethic of caring and a willingness to listen, and a familiarity with those values that define our shared character. What is unclear from these, however, is whether Clinton's environmental texts move beyond the "inspirational" to a sustained argument or a "fill[ing] out rhetorically."[41]

Ironically, Clinton's very mastery of the stylistic elements of a politics of reconciliation and call for consensus also serves to obscure more contentious fault lines in Americans' disputes over the environment. And it is here that a Clinton environmental presidency falters rhetorically, as it defers a more sustained argument. So we return here to the thesis with which I began. Bill Clinton both invites but too often erases the possibilities of a more "complete" republican style.

Alternate Reading 2: Deferral and Erasure in the Presidential (Administrative) Body

If a republican style composes a basis for coordinating or judging among conflictive interests, then Bill Clinton is more often than not notably absent. "In a time when the overall framework is not clear," Clinton confessed, "explaining to the American people what our interests, our values and our policies are requires more systematic and regular explaining."[42]

Deferral and Erasure

Probably no president has reflected more openly in his speeches about such a need to articulate regulative principles and about the difficulties in doing so. "I think the trick is, from my point of view," Clinton admits in a roundtable discussion with farmers, when asked about conflicts between agriculture and the environment, "[the trick] is how to get the best environmental results and have some standard that will also deal with people that might abuse their privileges, and how to do it with fewer regulations." How to do this? He attempts to explain again: "Basically, what we're trying to do is to say, 'Look, here are the general standards in the law and the things that are necessary to preserve the land, water, and air over the next generation. But this rule book is not necessary if you can meet the standards however you please, if you can find some other way to do it.'"[43]

Interestingly, it is not that Clinton is unable to discover terms of civic mutuality, as Hariman had feared for the republican stylist today.[44] It is, rather, he appears to stop at precisely this point. Although his speeches assure us "a healthy economy and a healthy environment are not at odds with each other," Clinton rarely offers a "filling out," rhetorically, of ways and means, of metaphor or regulative principle, that enable audiences to negotiate between these and other tensions.[45] Tulis, like Hariman, agrees that a president's "rhetorical power is a way of constituting the people to whom it is addressed"; but it does so, Tulis insists, "by furnishing them with the very equipment they need to assess its use—the metaphors, categories, and concepts of political discourse."[46] In contexts that foreground potential conflicts between the economy and environmental protection, this absence too often eclipses or defers our ability to deliberate clearly about the latter. This tendency is abetted, rhetorically, by two features of Clinton's style: his metadiscourse of "balance," that is, his talk about the talk of balance between economic growth and the environment; and a rhetorical eclipse or "trump" of environmental claims by the constraints of the president's larger economic agenda.[47]

Perhaps the single most persistent feature of Clinton's discourse on the environment—born of his impulse to "bring people together"—is his plea for "balance," a balance among conflicting parties, a balanced solution, and, most importantly, his assurance that "a healthy economy and a healthy environment are not at odds with one each other." Clinton's appeal is clear. "Balance" is the very topos of equity in our judgments and a regulative principle in the face of conflict.[48]

Clinton's speeches also feature a more subtle subordination or trumping of environment claims by the president's economically driven first-tier goals. Indeed, from the beginning, Clinton coupled his environmental concerns with (and subordinated them to) his primary thesis of jobs, global competitiveness, and the economy: "What is our vision of a New Covenant? An America at the forefront of the global effort to preserve and protect our common environment—and promoting global growth." Such coupling too often seems to eclipse or trump the former (environmental) concerns.[49]

Interactions in California, a state critical to his 1996 reelection, illustrate his emphasis. When a developer in San Diego queried Clinton on what the president could do to release two hundred thousand acres "put on hold" by the Interior Department's enforcement of the Endangered Species Act, the president assured him this should not obstruct his plans. Interior Secretary Babbitt had "practical sense, he'd been in business, his family had been, and he believed in the environment," Clinton said. "But he had common sense about it." Clinton promised the real estate developer, "All I can tell you is I'll get on it." Similarly, in Oakland, the president confronted a long-standing conflict between dredging the Oakland port and the need for environmental study. Seizing this as an opportunity to boast of "our jobs-first policy," Clinton announced, "To make the port a magnet for shipping and commerce, we must deepen the channel. For years environmental concerns have slowed this process. I have directed the Army Corps of Engineers, the EPA, and all other concerned agencies to get on with it so that we can dredge the channel."[50]

From his first campaign ("It's the economy, stupid") through many of his speeches on the environment, Bill Clinton foregrounds the importance of the economy not simply as a preferred topic but as a basis for judgment or policy preference. "Most environmentalists are working people and business people themselves," Clinton tells the forest summit, "and [they] understand that only an economically secure America can have the strength and confidence necessary to preserve our land." In his 1997 state of the union address, the president justified his plans to designate ten American Heritage Rivers in terms of community economic development, "proving once again that we can grow the economy as we protect the environment."[51]

Ultimately, evoking a trope of balance (without categories for understanding) or offering assurances that we can have both a healthy environment and a healthy economy eclipse or defer more structured argument. The consequences are debilitating to republican governance if they aid a trend toward what Tulis has called "an increasing inability to talk intelligently about the basic principles that define [a presidency]."[52]

Resistance within the Presidential (Administrative) Body

But would a more sustained, coherent articulation of environmental policy itself be sufficient? On one level, it is easy to identify rhetorical gestures of "promise" in Clinton's rhetoric that contrast with Bush's ("an environmental disaster") or, conversely, to notice subtle erosions of such promises in the president's speeches, but this misses the deeper failures and sources within institutional culture that constrain any president. Focusing solely upon such personal enactment, Hariman cautions us, may "induce a corresponding incapacity to see impersonal determinants of political action [or] the causes of structural instability."[53]

Within a culture of republican politics, speech presumably is embedded in an institutional context and a set of deliberative assumptions that enable audiences to act as political agents, that sustain not only the bases for judgment but provide for norms of accountability and modes for civic redress capable of altering institutional behavior. Without this imbrication, republican discourse is disconnected from judgment and action. Indeed, it is precisely this disconnect in many areas of our culture that fosters cynicism and distrust of political institutions. The fact is that alongside the republican tendencies of Clinton's rhetoric are the more embedded formations of the corporate body of modern government and the deauthored nature of presidential speeches, that is, the internal struggles among agencies and departments to shape a president's policy, its rationale, and the contours and constraints of its implementation.

The rhetoric of the Clinton environmental presidency has both mirrored and furthered many of these same practices, practices that delink deliberation from action and presidential rhetoric from public judgment. Below are three instances—each featured in the media's coverage of Bill Clinton's comeback on the environment.

Curbing Noise from Air Flights over the Grand Canyon

In his 1996 speech for Earth Day in Great Falls National Park, Maryland, the president proudly announced, "We have done a lot of work since I became President to try to improve our national parks and to preserve them." Implicitly invoking his authority to enforce Public Law 100-91, which was passed to substantially restore natural quiet at the Grand Canyon, he declared, "We are dramatically cutting back on noise from aircraft flights over the Grand Canyon. . . . We are moving to restore a natural quiet in our parks."[54]

Within four months, however, the Federal Aviation Administration would release a "proposed action" that would frustrate the president's order at its core. The draft Environmental Assessment (EA), acknowledged: "The analysis presented here indicates that, within the initial impact analysis area, no appreciable change in aircraft noise levels is anticipated with the proposed Action." Environmental groups that filed suit to block the plan believed that, if anything, the final rule announced somewhat later, on December 31, 1996, was even worse than proposed in this draft. Dennis Brownridge wrote in *High Country News,* "You would never know it from the glowing news reports, but the Federal Aviation Administration has scuttled most of its plans for restricting aircraft over flights in Grand Canyon National Park."[55]

Reducing Global Warming

Global warming was an issue on which both Clinton and Gore criticized the Bush administration during the 1992 campaign. In his first Earth Day speech in 1993 the president declared that the United States must take the lead in addressing the challenge of global warming. "Today," he said, "I reaffirm my personal [commitment] and announce our Nation's commitment to reducing our emissions of greenhouse gases to their 1990 levels by the year 2000."[56] In his visit to Australia in November, 1996, the president asserted a greenhouse "is no place to nurture our children" and warned that the consequences of global warming "would be nothing short of devastating for children."[57] Nevertheless, when the White House released a position paper the following month in preparation for negotiations on a new global warming treaty, it proposed a delay in achieving the Rio Earth Summit's goal of stabilizing such greenhouse emissions. "Two weeks after President Clinton [in Australia] called for an aggressive international program to fight global warming," Gerstenzang reported, "his administration retreated from its goal of reducing gaseous emissions by the year 2000. The administration's new plan, if implemented, will delay until 2010 a deadline for an international reduction in the emissions of carbon dioxide and other pollutants."[58]

Relaxing Controls on Hazardous Waste Dumping

On September 18, 1996, American TV news programs showed a relaxed Bill Clinton as he stood on the edge of the Grand Canyon to proclaim the establishment of the new Grand Staircase–Escalante National Monument, a spectacular public lands preserve in southern Utah in the tradition of Teddy Roosevelt whom the president invoked several times in his remarks. Less noticed amid the coverage was a *Los Angeles Times* story of a proposed new rule by the EPA that would allow multiple categories of hazardous waste to be dumped in municipal landfills nationally. "Four years after criticism by presidential candidate Bill Clinton led the Bush administration to withdraw a plan relaxing controls of hazardous wastes," the *Times* reported, "the Environmental Protection Agency is quietly developing a similar program. Like the 1992 plan that never went into effect, the little noticed proposal relies on self-policing by companies seeking to dispose of potentially dangerous chemicals in ordinary landfills. [The Bush] plan, [EDF attorney Karen Florini] asserted, could have been characterized as 'throw the baby out with the bath water and tear out the central plumbing. . . . [The Clinton plan] is restricted to throwing the baby out,' she said."[59]

Thus charges that Clinton was, at the very least, an inconsistent "environmental president," have both a rhetorical and institutional basis—a deferral of more robust principles for mediating difference and also an eclipse of the republican voice in the face of institutional resistance and the deauthored (corporate) body of the presidency. Assurances of responsible logging emerge as unregulated "salvage timber" operations; a directive to the FAA to curb air flight noise above America's premier national park is translated as "no appreciable change in noise level"; and pledges to reduce greenhouse gases are delayed by a decade. Such assurances, directives, and pledges suggest a speaking voice that too often cannot "pierce [the] material density of the . . . institutions, rituals and practices through which a discursive formation is structured."[60]

The (Re)Making of the Environmental Presidency?

While Bill Clinton restored, to some extent, his persona as an "environmental president" during his campaign for reelection in 1996, the task for rhetorical scholars, I believe, is incomplete. Our challenge is not charting the president's political "return" but the recovery of the possibilities within his conflicted rhetoric for a relevant republicanism at the turn of the twenty-first century.

On the one hand, the republican style reminds us—even as environmental leaders wish for stronger leadership and clearer vision—that a rhetoric of civic mutuality must still sustain a consensus as the "essential condition of successful political action."[61] And, there were, in fact, signs that the Clinton administration may have been willing to take steps in a second term to test a new "center" and the political relations that could sustain a stronger consensus on the environment.

In December, after the 1996 election, the Clinton administration
canceled all remaining advertising of "salvage " timber sales.

The EPA proposed stronger standards for allowable levels of ozone
and small particulate matter in the air.

New wetlands rules for small acreage were proposed and stronger
reviews of compliance were targeted.

The annual "Economic Report of the President" released in February
1997 committed the administration once again to reform of
subsidies that encouraged exploitation of resources (mining,
grazing, etc.) from federal lands in the West.

And forest service chief Mike Dombeck told U.S. Forest Service
employees: "Our first priority is to protect and restore the health
of the land. Failing this, nothing else we do really matters."[62]

For all this, any reading of the public rhetoric of this president and of the
presidential (administrative) body will probably need to remain essentially
"frustrated" and of two minds: a reading that locates and celebrates this
president's impulse to invite disparate groups to come together as a national
audience but one that also acknowledges the aporias of dispersed power (both
in the representations of special interests and in internal struggles of the cor-
porate/executive body of the presidency). When framed by too shallow a reliance on reconciliation and eroded by the entrenched resistance of institutions,
the trope of consensus can too easily substitute for debate and disagreement.
Dissensus, Goodnight reminds us, is needed then to invite contestability and
to critique the terms of mystifying rhetorics when other forces threaten to
deflect or obfuscate.[63]

Both tasks—celebration and suspicion—then are still important, for there
are still choices to be made and an opportunity to frame the terms of consequential debates on a range of concerns: "forest health"; biodiversity and habitat
protection in the United States; alternatives to "command and control" approaches to environmental regulation; and steps needed to reduce global warming and the implications of such action for the U.S. and global economy.[64] These
challenges (and others) require more than a president's invitation to community and a "politics of reconciliation." They require an articulation of vision,
the rhetorical composition of a political community able to engage in and sustain serious debate, and constituencies forged in such moments that are com-
petent to hold institutional bodies accountable.

The results released in the Worldwatch Institute's 1997 annual state of the
world report on global environmental health are not encouraging. "Five years
after the historic U.N. Conference on Environment and Development in Rio

de Janeiro," it found, "the world is falling well short of achieving its central goal—an environmentally sustainable global economy."[65] Viewed from this perspective, debates that are to be relevant in coming years simply must be about more than regulatory reform or the easing of business costs under the Endangered Species Act.

Almost every survey of opinion among U.S. voters indicates strong approval for environmental values and an expressed willingness to support tougher measures to protect the public's health and the natural environment. Such support provides an American president the opportunity to initiate and nurture a vital debate about the conditions for an environmentally secure and just society. If engaged competently, such a debate would transcend (and critique the terms of) an often polarized discourse of "jobs versus the environment" and, in doing so, articulate a compelling principle of governance.

Thoughtful voices within the Republican Party have provided other opportunities. Noting that opinion polls indicate the environment is "the voters' number one concern about continued Republican leadership of Congress," Sen. John McCain (R-AZ) called on his colleagues to accept blame for negative perceptions of the GOP record. "We need to assure the public," he insisted shortly after the 1996 elections, "that in the 105th Congress the Republican environmental agenda will consist of more than coining new epithets for environmental extremists or offering banal symbolic gestures."[66]

And, it is more than simply a reassurance of the GOP record. If prudence and stewardship of the environment are civic virtues, then the vocabulary each requires also requires a continual, discursive renewal (as habits of the republic). The terms of such vocabulary are available as structures of motive only as we reaffirm them in moments of challenge, refine them in substantive debate, and renew them in civic celebrations. Concern for these practices is also our concern as rhetorical scholars. "By understanding republican politics as a discursive practice having its own rhetorical norms and aesthetic coherence," Hariman has urged, "we can nurture it as a means for improving public life." Our natural world, no less than our public life, depends increasingly upon our own competence as scholars who would understand and nurture this most fragile of political styles of governance.[67]

Notes

1. Rita K. Whillock, "The Compromising Clinton: Images of Failure, a Record of Success," in *The Clinton Presidency: Images, Issues, and Communication Strategies,* ed. Robert E. Denton, Jr., and Rachel L. Holloway (Westport, Conn.: Praeger, 1996), 128; K. M. Dalton, "President Clinton, You're No Teddy Roosevelt," *Los Angeles Times,* Jan. 26, 1997, M1; David Brower, "Why I Won't Vote for Clinton," *Los Angeles Times,* July 22, 1996, B5.
2. Bill Clinton, "Vice Presidential Announcement, July 9, 1992," in Bill Clinton and Al Gore, *Putting People First: How We Can All Change America* (New York: Times Books, 1992), 201.
3. Press statement, Dr. Robert Cox, president of the Sierra Club, Washington, D.C., July 28, 1995.
4. Philip Wander, "The Rhetoric of American Foreign Policy, *Quarterly Journal of Speech* 70 (1984): 357.
5. Clinton, "Announcement Speech, October 3, 1991," in Clinton and Gore, *Putting People First,* 192; emphasis added.
6. Although Vice Pres. Al Gore contributed an important and, in my view, principled voice to the Clinton administration, for the purposes of this analysis I focus on the rhetoric of the president only and the sources of institutional constraint for presidential public address. Robert Hariman, *Political Style: The Artistry of Power* (Chicago: University of Chicago Press, 1995), 110.
7. Roger O'Neil, "Bill Clinton Hasn't Kept All His Promises Dealing with the Environment," *NBC Nightly News* (Aug. 28, 1996), NTLN, DocID BRRL206467.
8. Clinton and Gore, *Putting People First,* 93.
9. Clinton, "Vice Presidential Announcement," 201, 204.
10. Clinton and Gore, *Putting People First,* 94; Al Gore, "A Vision for America, July 16, 1992," in Clinton and Gore, *Putting People First,* 212; Whillock, "The Compromising Clinton," 127.
11. Clinton, "A New Covenant," in Clinton and Gore, *Putting People First;* Clinton, "Remarks Announcing the Creation of the White House Office on Environmental Policy, February 8, 1993," in *Public Papers of the Presidents of the United States William J. Clinton 1993,* Book 1 (Washington, D.C.: Government Printing Office, 1994), 62.
12. Clinton, "Inaugural Address, January 20, 1993," in *Public Papers of the Presidents,* 2; Clinton, "Remarks at the Children's Town Meeting, February 20, 1993," in *Public Papers of the Presidents,* 155.
13. Jeffrey St. Clair and Alexander Cockburn, "The Greatest Environmental President. Really?" *Nature and Politics* [online journal], Sept. 5, 1996, retrieval date 9/12/96; Clinton, "Interview with Jim Gransberry of the *Billings Gazette* in Billings, Montana, May 31, 1995," in *Public Papers of the Presidents of the United States William J. Clinton 1995,* Book 1 (Washington, D.C.: Government Printing Office, 1996), 776.
14. Jessica Matthews, "Earth First at the Polls," *Washington Post,* Nov. 11, 1996, A29.
15. Perry Beeman, "Action Promised on Environment." *Des Moines Sunday Register,* Oct. 16, 1994, B7.
16. H. Dewar and K. J. Cooper, "103rd Congress Started Fast but Collapsed at Finish Line," *Washington Post,* Oct. 9, 1994, A1.
17. Jessica Matthews, "Prognosis for the Environment," *Washington Post,* Jan. 13,

1997, A17; Stuart J. Rothenberg, "How Times Change: The Environment Is Now a Political Zero," *Roll Call*, April 17, 1995, 41.

18. Environmentalists objected that the language of the act intentionally allowed nondiseased or healthy trees to be logged as "salvage" timber and relevant environmental regulations to be suspended for these sales. The act states: "The term 'salvage timber sale' means . . . removal of disease—or insect—infested trees, dead, damaged, or down trees, or trees affected by fire or imminently susceptible to fire or insect attack. *Such term also* includes the removal of associated trees . . . except that any such sale must include an identifiable salvage component of trees described in the first sentence [emphasis added]" (H.R. 1944 [Budget Rescissions Act], Title II General Provisions, sec. 2001.(a) Definitions [Washington, D.C.: Government Printing Office, 1995]). Federal courts later confirmed the fears of environmentalists that phrases such as "associated trees" could include live, green trees (often previously off-limit) for "salvage" logging sales. By early 1996 Clinton was publicly admitting he had made a "mistake" in agreeing to the salvage timber rider. See Joel Connelly, "Timber Rider 'a Mistake,'" *Seattle Post-Intelligencer*, Feb., 26, 1996, A4.

19. See Cox, press statement, and "President Clinton Flip-Flops on Protecting Forests," press release from the Sierra Club, Washington, D.C., July 26, 1995.

20. United Press International, "Clinton Disappoints Environmentalists," July 23, 1996, <C-upi@clari.net>, downloaded July, 23 1996; "America Betrayed," *New York Times*, May 16, 1996; and "Here's What President Clinton Said about Protecting Our National Forests," *New York Times*, August 7, 1995, A9.

21. Matthews, "Prognosis for the Environment," A17.

22. St. Clair and Cockburn, "The Greatest Environmental President. Really?"

23. The "Dick Morris" scenario does not alone explain the renewed saliency of the environment for the public at large. Throughout 1995 and 1996 several environmental organizations (including the Sierra Club, U.S. PIRGs, and the Natural Resources Defense Council) orchestrated a nationwide, community-based public media "accountability" campaign to spotlight actions of the 104th Congress in rolling back environmental law and to mobilize public anger in selected congressional districts. So-called wise use groups seemed to credit this factor, along with the president's newly found tough rhetoric, in halting the agenda of the antienvironmental "property rights" movement in the 104th Congress. See W. P. Pendley, "Whatever Happened to Property Rights?" *Blue Ribbon Magazine*, Dec., 1996, 4.

24. The poll referred to by Luntz on Republican distrust of the Republican party on the environment is by GOP pollster Linda DiVall. See DiVall, "Memorandum to the Superfund Reform Coalition Regarding National Survey Overview," American Viewpoint, Alexandria, Va., Dec. 12, 1995; Frank Luntz, "A Communications Manifesto," correspondence to Americans for a Republican Majority, Washington, D.C., Summer, 1996; Matthews, "Prognosis for the Environment," A17.

25. See Brower, "Why I Won't Vote for Clinton"; St. Clair and Cockburn, "The Greatest Environmental President. Really?"

26. Hariman, *Political Style*, 113.

27. Hariman observes, "For awhile . . . the republican style [still] . . . can be found in the presidency: William Jefferson Clinton provides a case study in its weaknesses and its strengths" (*Political Style*, 140).

28. Clinton, "Remarks Concluding the First Roundtable Discussion of the Forest Conference in Portland, Oregon, April 2, 1993," in *Public Papers of the Presidents of the United States William J. Clinton 1993,* Book 1 (Washington, D.C.: Government Printing Office, 1994), 387.

29. "Politics of Reconciliation," *New York Times,* Jan. 21, 1997, A18; Clinton, "The President's Radio Address, April 3, 1993," in *Public Papers of the Presidents of the United States William J. Clinton 1993,* 389.

30. Clinton, "Remarks on Opening the Forest Conference in Portland, Oregon, April 2, 1993," in ibid., 385.

31. Ibid., 386.

32. Clinton, "Remarks at the Conclusion of the Forest Conference in Portland, Oregon, April 2, 1993," in ibid., 388.

33. Clinton, "Remarks on the 25th Observance of Earth Day in Havre de Grace, Maryland, April 25, 1995," in *Public Papers of the Presidents of the United States William J. Clinton 1995,* Book 1 (Washington, D.C.: Government Printing Office, 1996), 563.

34. Hariman, *Political Style,* 110.

35. Ibid., 96, 121, 98.

36. Ibid., 98.

37. See Clinton's "New Covenant" address, accepting the Democratic Party's nomination as president, in New York City, July 16, 1992. On liberty see Clinton, "Remarks on Independence Day at Patuxent River Naval Air Station, Maryland, July 4, 1996," in *Public Papers of the Presidents of the United States William J. Clinton 1996,* Book 2 (Washington, D.C.: Government Printing Office, 1997); on an expanding economy see Clinton, "Remarks on Earth Day, April 21, 1993," in *Public Papers of the Presidents of the United States, William J. Clinton 1993,"* 468–72; on national security see Clinton and Gore, *Putting People First,* 93; on spiritual health and beauty see Clinton, "Remarks on Signing the Colorado Wilderness Act of 1993, August 13, 1993," in *Public Papers of the Presidents of the United States William J. Clinton 1993,* Book 2 (Washington, D.C.: Government Printing Office, 1994), 1377; on managing change see Clinton, "Remarks Concluding the First Roundtable Discussion of the Forest Conference," 387.

38. Clinton, "Remarks on the Observance of Earth Day, April 21, 1994," in *Public Papers of the Presidents of the United States William J. Clinton 1994,* Book 2 (Washington, D.C.: Government Printing Office, 1995), 741.

39. Ibid.

40. See especially Clinton's speech to the congregation of the Mason Temple Church of God in Memphis, speaking of the "values, the spirit, the soul, and the truth" of justice and moral responsibility, in "Remarks to the Convocation of the Church of God in Christ in Memphis, November 13, 1993," in *Public Papers of the Presidents of the United States William J. Clinton 1993,* Book 2 (Washington, D.C.: Government Printing Office, 1994).

41. Jeffrey K Tulis, *The Rhetorical Presidency* (Princeton, N.J.: Princeton University Press, 1987), 36.

42. D. Goodgame and M. Duffy, "Blending Force with Diplomacy," *Time,* Oct. 1, 1994, 35.

43. Clinton, "Remarks in a Roundtable Discussion with Farmers and Agricultural Leaders in Broadview, Montana, June 1, 1995," in *Public Papers of the Presidents of*

the United States William J. Clinton 1995, Book 1 (Washington, D.C.: Government Printing Office, 1996), 785.

44. Hariman, *Political Style,* 139.

45. The one area in which Bill Clinton most deliberately sought to lay out a clear explanation and to provide a more layered account of the basis for a new principle came in his approach to federal environmental regulatory authority. Targeted by the GOP leadership of the 104th Congress, regulatory "reform" became an opening for critics to restrain the EPA and other federal agencies charged with environmental protection. Shortly after the U.S. House of Representatives passed an encumbering reform bill, in Feb., 1995, President Clinton outlined his own approach. It was perhaps his most skillful display of identification with the public's anxieties over and composition of consensual possibilities. See Clinton, "Remarks on Regulatory Reform, February 21, 1995," and "Remarks on Regulatory Reform in Arlington, Virginia, March 16, 1995," both in *Public Papers of the Presidents of the United States: William J. Clinton, 1995,* Book 1 (Washington, D.C.: Government Printing Office, 1996).

46. Tulis, *The Rhetorical Presidency,* 203.

47. Hariman's discussion of the "realist" style warns of this possibility, particularly in regards to the norms of republican discourse (*Political Style,* 44–48).

48. Clinton, "Remarks on Opening the Forest Conference," 386.

49. Clinton, "Remarks at a Town Meeting in Billings, Montana, June 1, 1995," in *Public Papers of the Presidents of the United States William J. Clinton 1995,* Book 1 (Washington, D.C.: Government Printing Office, 1996); Clinton and Gore, *Putting People First,* 225.

50. Clinton, "Remarks at Town Meeting in San Diego, May 17, 1993," in *Public Papers of the Presidents of the United States William J. Clinton 1993,* Book 1, 691; Clinton, "Remarks to the Community in Alameda, California, August 13, 1993," Book 2, 1374, both in *Public Papers of the Presidents of the United States, William J. Clinton 1993* (Washington, D.C.: Government Printing Office, 1994).

51. Clinton, "Remarks on Opening the Forest Conference," 386; Clinton, "Remarks by the President in State of the Union Address, February 4, 1997," text, Office of the Press Secretary, the White House, 8.

52. Tulis, *The Rhetorical Presidency,* 180.

53. Hariman, *Political Style,* 119.

54. Clinton, "Remarks by the President on Earth Day, Great Falls National Park, Great Fall, Maryland, April 22, 1996," text, Office of the Press Secretary, the White House, 2. In a separate executive order, President Clinton stated, "I hereby direct the Secretary of Transportation . . . to address overflights for Grand Canyon National Park . . . to reduce the noise immediately and make further substantial progress toward restoration of natural quiet" ("Additional Transportation Planning to Address Impacts of Transportation on National Parks," *Federal Register,* 61, no. 81 [1996]: 18229).

55. Federal Aviation Administration, "Conclusions," *Draft Environmental Assessment: Special Flight Rules in the Vicinity of Grand Canyon National Park* (Aug. 20, 1996), sec. 4, 1; Dennis Brownridge, "It Will Be Noise as Usual in Grand Canyon," *High Country News,* Jan. 20, 1997, 3. Brownridge further reported: "Three of the four new 'flight-free zones' the agency proposed in July . . . have been effectively deleted in [the] new rules"; the FAA, he wrote, also "drops the idea of capping

the number of air tours flights at their current level," and despite the announcement of some curfews, "for 80 percent of the flights over the Canyon, which originate in Las Vegas, there are no time restrictions" (1).

56. In their joint 1992 campaign book, *Putting People First,* Clinton and Gore pledged to "[l]imit U.S. carbon dioxide emissions to 1990 levels by the year 2000" (97). Gore argued in 1993 that "the Bush administration threatened to torpedo the entire Earth Summit [in Rio] in order to prevent the adoption of targets and timetables for reductions" (Gore, *Earth in the Balance: Ecology and the Human Spirit,* [New York: Plume, 1993], xiv); Clinton, "Remarks on Earth Day, April 21, 1993" 470.

57. See "Sierra Club Blasts New Administration Global Warning Plan," press release, Sierra Club, Washington, D.C., Dec. 6, 1996.

58. James Gerstenzang, "Pollution Program Delayed," *Raleigh (North Carolina) News and Observer,* Dec. 8, 1996, 19A.

59. Clinton, "Remarks by the President in Making Environmental Announcement, Outside El Tovar Lodge, Grand Canyon National Park, Arizona, September 18, 1996," text, Office of the Press Secretary, the White House; James Gerstenzang, "Hazards Seen in New Plan to Ease Toxic Waste Rules," *Los Angeles Times,* Sept. 17, 1996, A5.

60. Ernesto Laclau and Chantal Mouffe, *Hegemony and Socialist Strategy: Towards a Radical Democratic Politics* (London: Verso), 1985.

61. Hariman, *Political Style,* 113.

62. Mike Dombeck, "Sustaining the Health of the Land through Collaborative Stewardship," text of directive to Forest Service employees, U.S. Forest Service, Washington, D.C., Jan. 6, 1996.

63. G. Thomas Goodnight, "Controversy," in *Argument and Controversy,* ed. Don Parson (Annandale, Va.: Speech Communication Association, 1991), 1–13.

64. St. Clair and Cockburn observed, "The Clinton Forest Plan called this [salvage] logging strategy 'forest health'; it became a way to confiscate the whole logging issue from public scrutiny" ("Environmythology: The Democrats' Thin Green Line Didn't Break, It Was Never There," *Texas Observer,* Jan. 26, 1996, 9).

65. Christopher Flavin, "The Legacy of Rio," in Lester R. Brown, Christopher Flavin, and Hillary French, *State of the World, 1997: A Worldwatch Institute Report on Progress toward a Sustainable Society* (New York: W. W. Norton, 1997), 3–22.

66. John McCain, "Nature Is Not a Liberal Plot," *New York Times,* Nov. 22, 1996, A31.

67. Hariman, *Political Style,* 140.

7 Colliding Ironies and Clinton's Salvage Rider Rhetoric in the Northwest Timber Controversy

Mark P. Moore

In 1995 a timber salvage rider passed in a budget bill, signed and endorsed by President Clinton, to block legal challenges to old-growth and salvage logging under existing environmental protection laws. Ostensibly, Republicans introduced the salvage rider to reduce the threat of fire and restore "health" to forests plagued by disease, particularly in the West. But the rider was also designed to override environmental laws like the Endangered Species Act without due regard to environmental damage from logging practices, which had been severely restricted by federal court since 1990.[1] The results were predictable. Timber sales dating as far back as 1989 were finalized at a feverish rate. By the spring of 1996, Clinton criticized logging practices under the rider for damaging the watersheds and nesting grounds of such threatened birds as the spotted owl and the marbled murrelet. However, the rider that Clinton signed and endorsed permitted such damage. By objecting to the salvage rider after signing it into law, it appeared that the president was trying to please everyone by talking the environmentalist talk, while walking the timber industry walk, or saving the forest by giving the industry a quick fix. As a result, the salvage rider and President Clinton's rhetoric surrounding it reignited the longstanding controversy in the Pacific Northwest over the logging practices in old-growth forests.

In this chapter I examine President Clinton's discourse on the salvage rider as a rhetorical strategy that attempted to appease first the timber industry and then the environmentalists during a critical time period leading up to and including his reelection campaign. I argue that Clinton's rhetoric was a strategic response constrained by clashing ironic perspectives held by the timber industry and environmentalists, perspectives with divergent social realities that prevent resolution of this forest conflict. In essence, the timber industry's ironic perspective grows out of the belief that protecting nature leads to human extinction; by saving the spotted owl or marbled murrelet, loggers must perish. Environmentalists, on the other hand, express irony by claiming that the success that led to the rise of the timber industry will ultimately be the cause of its failure. That is, technological fixes from a salvage rider only lead to greater destruction. I also argue that these perspectives are not the product of what is known as verbal irony, that is, irony portrayed by an ironist (leader, spokesperson, advocate of a group) who is intentionally being ironic. These ironic perspectives do not reflect a pretense of ignorance or a suspension of belief, or convey the opposite of literal meaning for humorous or sardonic effect. In short, the ironic perspectives are not forms of rhetorical deception or trickery. What they reveal is how each group views the other, through discourse, as arrogant, complacent, blindly self-confident, and most of all, unaware of its own irony. Each group views the other as an ironic victim, not simply because it is being deceived by someone or something, but because it should know better than to behave the way it does, but does not do so.

Both of the ironic perspectives held by the competing interest groups are situational and tragic. They reveal what D. C. Muecke identifies as a "Situational Irony" in which there is "no ironist but always both a victim and an observer" of the situation. Thus one group identifies a tragic, "ironical personified Fate" unfolding from the actions of the other, but it does so as the "observer" of the situation, not as an "ironist" who is intentionally being ironic. This type of irony can also be considered "Unintentional or Unconscious," but the discourse itself represents an ironic perspective of the situation for the competing groups, one that serves a strategic and rhetorical purpose in the controversy at hand.[2] Each group observes the other's situation and each group is characterized ironically by the other as the source of the tragic fate. However, since the ironic perspectives hold tragic endings for everyone, each group can only avoid tragedy (that is, the tragedy they see caused by the other group) and survive by eliminating the other group. The perspectives constrain Clinton because they are mutually exclusive. They solidify each group through division, and they would appear to eliminate opportunities to create or restore middle, or common, ground. Under these circumstances Clinton merely fueled the fire and alienated himself from both groups in the conflict. But in doing so, an opportunity arose for him to do what he perhaps does best, that is "reinvent" himself on the issue. I identify irony as constraint in the timber controversy, examine President Clinton's response to that constraint as a "rhetorical reinvention," then consider implications of irony and reinvention as functions of presidential rhetoric.

Irony as Constraint in the Timber Controversy

From a mere figure of speech, irony has become a phenomenon of considerable cultural and rhetorical importance. Perhaps the most sophisticated weapon at the disposal of satire, irony typically produces a masterful blend of both comic and tragic awareness. When viewed as ironic, life situations, either real, invented, or reinvented, can be presented to audiences as a corrective device that exposes ignorance, pride, vanity, and hypocrisy. For this study, irony is considered in general as an incongruity between the actual result of a situation, or a sequence of events, and the normal or expected result. As David Kaufer notes, "irony has come to signify a split perspective of appearance and reality in all its forms." More specifically, situational irony, the type of irony expressed by the timber industry and environmentalists, points out incongruities between appearance and reality but without the deceit, the pretense, or the suspension of a belief. Though there is no ironist or mocker, who is intentionally ironic, there are victims and observers. Victims of such situational irony are singled out and distinguished as "in the wrong" as opposed to those observing the wrongdoers who are, at least in this one particular case, "in the right."[3]

But a search for irony in the paradoxes, contradictions, and ambiguities of life does not always lead to a sympathetic understanding of that life or generate a greater sense of cooperation among its listeners. On the contrary, irony usually creates and depends on a sense of detachment from and superiority over audiences and intended victims. This "dissociative" function, which is common in situational irony, has been identified by Kenneth Burke as well as Muecke and others in what is called "romantic irony." With romantic irony, as Burke states, the ironist has no "kinship with the enemy" but stands apart from and superior to the role being rejected.[4] It is this dissociative function of romantic irony that surfaces most clearly in the situational ironies of competing groups in the forest controversy to constrain Clinton's rhetoric. However, with no ironist purposely trying to be ironic, the rejection of and superiority over one group by another is sincere. Thus, the situational ironies in the controversy are dissociative like romantic irony, but not deceptively so.

The dissociative and unsympathetic attitudes that Burke identifies in romantic irony also combine with those of preference and aloofness. Soren Kierkegaard believes irony by definition contains a "certain exclusiveness" and "looks down . . . on plain and ordinary discourse immediately understood by everyone; it travels in an exclusive incognito . . . and looks down from its exalted station." In *The Ironic Temper* Haakon Chevalier notes that "the ironic spirit has always inclined toward detachment," and the "ironist is committed to the search of a more and more exterior point of view, [one in which] nothing else is superior." Alan Reynolds Thompson observes in *The Dry Mock* that unlike other types of discourse "one must be detached and cool" to perceive irony. Northrop Frye states, "the ironist is most like the poet in the sense that they both turn their back on the audience." And finally, Muecke notes that all irony features an element of detachment or disengagement that creates a sense of distance among victims and audiences. Thus romantic or situational irony, which is identifiable in the discourse surrounding the forest conflict by introducing it with the implied phrase "isn't it ironic that" (isn't it ironic that protecting nature means human extinction; isn't it ironic that success means failure), serves as constraint for Clinton because it separates the very people he intends to bring together. Each group shares within itself the knowledge of an opposing situational irony and that knowledge reinforces the belief that each group, in its own eyes, is superior to the other.[5]

The structuring of the colliding ironies that constrain Clinton lends itself to an atmosphere of arrogance, antagonism, and perhaps even futility, but ironic discourse in itself does not have to be divisive or tragic. As opposed to the sense of superiority produced by knowledge shared among ironic observers, Burke prefers those forms of irony that stress humility toward and consubstantiality with the victim. In doing so, Burke builds on the notion that the relationships formed in irony come not from absolute statements (what he calls relativism, seeing everything in one set of terms) but from the developmental process of interaction among terms. Chevalier alludes to this humble perspective by saying that irony is a product of certain "radical insufficiencies of character [and] an escape from the fundamental problems and responsibilities of life, [but] what is a loss for the man [or woman] may be a gain for the artist, though the two beyond a certain point cannot be separated."[6]

By distinguishing between the associative and dissociative in general, it is possible to identify how irony functions as a rhetorical strategy for the competing groups in the forest controversy and as a constraint for President Clinton. If, as Burke suggests, romantic irony induces a sense of dissociation, division, and superiority, then it would also appear to harden attitudes, polarize groups, and limit Clinton's ability to appeal to both groups at the same time. In fact, the atmosphere created by such colliding ironies offers little, if any, hope for resolution, not to mention consensus. But before examining this "ironic constraint" that surrounds the salvage rider, I consider briefly the ways in which the forest controversy has been informed by a sense of irony over the past two decades.[7] In the salvage rider controversy, ironic discourse disperses over time, in fragments, from environmentalists and timber industry representatives to construct and reinforce competing social realities about what the forest is and how it should be used. The ironies comprise a critical commentary based on the tragic loss of cherished yet divergent lifestyles that have now thrown America's most fundamental ideological commitments of life, liberty, and the pursuit of happiness into fierce competition.

The ironic perspective expressed by the timber industry over the last two decades involves the notion of sacrificing humanity to save nature. This irony came to the forefront of public consciousness in the late 1980s and early 1990s with the spotted owl controversy.[8] Although the spotted owl became a national celebrity at the time, scientific knowledge about the bird in the Pacific Northwest, before 1970, was rather speculative. Scientists first declared the owl a Northwest resident in 1893, but only seven nests were found over the following seventy-five years. Knowledge of the owl increased significantly in the mid 1970s, when, in his master's thesis research, Oregon State University biologist, Eric Foresman, identified eighteen nesting sites and reported significant discoveries on spotted owl habitat needs and threats to the species from timber harvests that render habitat loss.[9] The owl's habitat, the old-growth forest, is an unlogged and natural forest, with large conifers that are more than two centuries old, combined with younger trees from at least two other species. Old-growth forests also have uneven canopies, broken treetops, standing dead snags, and many fallen, decaying logs. The spotted owl evolved in these old forests over thousands of years and remained undisturbed until the last half of the twentieth century, when extensive clear-cutting began to fragment old growth in a serious manner. After record timber harvests in the 1980s that covered seven hundred thousand acres of old growth in the Northwest,[10] and with diminishing amounts left (an estimated 5 to 10 percent in the continental United States), the owl as a victim of habitat loss became an ironic "protector" of the forest for environmentalists and an ironic cause of death for the timber industry.

As the spotted owl controversy grew in the early 1990s, the timber industry used their "protecting nature means human extinction" irony as a prominent rhetorical strategy to dramatize incongruities between what they believed to be the actual as opposed to the expected result of owl protection, one that rendered humans as victims of environmental efforts to save the spotted owl. For example, Frank Backus, a forester with the SDS Lumber Company, argued, "we'll be going out of business because of the northern spotted owl " Roger Kimble, a log loader from Canyonville, Oregon, said that "the hooty owl has finished us." Oregon state representative and timber industry supporter Bob Smith was "shocked that the courts are so concerned about owls and so unconcerned about people." In this way, the irony of courts being more concerned about owls than humans would shock America into "new" awareness of the problem. Oregon senator Bob Packwood stressed the point when he declared that the owl crisis will result in "catastrophic failure for the region."[11] The media also played on the industry's ironic sense of the controversy with such headlines as "Economic Woes Blamed on Owl" and "Saving Spotted Owl Seen as Threat to Schools."[12] But perhaps the most extreme case came in a joint Forest Service/Bureau of Land Management study that said the spotted owl, if protected under the Endangered Species Act, would cause "severe cases of community disfunction, . . . increased rates of domestic disputes, divorce, acts of violence, delinquency, vandalism, suicide, alcoholism," and other serious problems.[13]

By arguing that success or technological advancement in the timber industry ultimately leads to failure with more destruction, the environmentalist's ironic perspective is no less vivid. Jack Ward Thomas, who in 1990 headed a research team for the federal government that produced "A Conservation Strategy for the Northern Spotted Owl" (the Thomas plan), said continued fragmentation of old-growth forests from the economically efficient and technologically advanced clear-cutting practices would lead to the owl's extinction. He opened the report by asserting, "the owl is imperiled over significant portions of its range, because of continuing losses of habitat from logging and natural disturbances. . . . Moreover, in some portions of the owl's range few options remain open, and available alternatives are steadily declining throughout the bird's range." In *Ancient Forests of the Pacific Northwest*, Elliot Norse claimed that fragmentation from "logging of the ancient forests is without question the biggest threat to the survival of the spotted owl." Biologist Chris Maser described the spotted owl as "*an indicator species for the planned extinction of the old-growth forests*," in other words, "the planned liquidation of old-growth forests for short-term economic gain." In his book *Saving Our Ancient Forests* Seth Zuckerman stated ironically that the owl and logger are "endangered for the same reason—they're running out of habitat."[14] In 1991 religious practitioner Rip Lone Wolf described one low cloud formation below Enola Hill, a sacred ceremonial ground for Native American Tribes in Oregon, as a "veil being put on now because the spirits don't want us to see the desecration that's going on." Finally, the environmentalist Mitch Friedman stressed that heedless timber harvests cannot continue just to preserve the culture of Northwest logging communities. "We've fouled it up. . . . We've throttled evolution. There isn't enough genetic material, there isn't enough habitat, and at the same time we're changing the climate. Something's got to give. It's like tapping the brakes when we're headed ninety miles per hour towards a brick wall."[15]

The conflicting goals expressed in the competing perspectives on the forest are, of course, economic on the one hand and ecological on the other. And rather than view the controversy as a both-and contradiction (to have your cake and eat it too), the groups construct situational ironies that spell doom for themselves based on different sides of an either-or dilemma: economics *or* ecology. With the economic irony an environmental perspective grows from a logical assumption that the success that has risen in time for the industry will fall in time through the course of its own development. Conversely, the ironic perspective on environmental concerns suggests that the human effort to protect species, which stands in the way of economic advancement, will, if left unimpeded, render humans extinct. Thus the "ecological irony" and the "economic irony" seem to cancel each other out, but do they? Although the economic irony of the timber industry falling through the course of its own development appears to justify, at least on face value, the attempt on the part of environmentalists to transform or alter economic interest through such legislation as the Endangered Species Act, the ecological irony of humans becoming an endangered species from environmental efforts to save a bird seems to lack the anticipation and fulfillment found in the inevitability of the ironic condition. However, anticipation and fulfillment are enhanced by the economic irony: since the planet is finite its natural resources can presumably be exhausted.

What this suggests is that the strategic, situational ironies can be "assessed" in the timber controversy according to the type of anticipation and fulfillment that they hold for the audience. In other words, in a compelling irony, audiences would have reason to believe that the condition described in the ironic situation is in fact "real," and for that reason the ironic outcome would be more believable or more likely to be considered as an inevitable one. This would amount to what might be viewed as a "test" for situational irony based on the way the irony corresponds with the knowledge that an audience has about the controversy and the social reality constructed with that knowledge. The legitimacy that is established from this test not only reflects upon the situational irony itself, but also on the group's social reality out of which it surfaced. And based on the way that the groups anticipate and fulfill the necessary or inevitable conditions of their predicament, the environmentalists would seem to have a more compelling irony at this time. That is, their economic irony has more appeal as a rhetorical strategy, because it's inevitable fulfillment seems to follow consistently from common sense and scientific knowledge about the consequences of their ironic condition (quite simply, overconsumption on a finite planet).

With regard to the ecological irony constructed by the timber industry, anticipation and fulfillment are quieted by what would seem to be a lack of inevitability in the situational irony. There can be no doubt that an end to the timber industry would have an impact on more than just the economy, but it does not necessarily follow, as suggested in their irony, that a tragic end for the industry represents a tragic end to life. Nevertheless, even if environmentalists have what is perhaps a "more logical" or more compelling argument with their economic irony, they have not stopped the timber industry from logging old-growth forests, as witnessed during the period of the salvage rider. This may only reflect the way that economic conditions are ultimately more important than environmental concerns, but the ironies themselves emphasize a tragic outlook for both groups, groups that constitute an incompatible, bifurcated audience for Clinton to address. Therefore, what is most significant about the ironic perspectives is the constraint they represent for presidential discourse and policymaking. The constraint is in essence a no-win situation for the president, which is why rhetorical reinvention will become not only an attractive strategy but also perhaps a necessary one. And with it, Clinton does not choose between the long- and short-term views of an either-or situation, instead he joins them in a both-and contradiction. But before any reinvention takes place, a position must be developed.

Clinton Enters the Forest

During his 1992 campaign Clinton promised that, as president, he would not only give high priority to the forest controversy but also actually come to the Pacific Northwest, develop a plan, and resolve the problem in a way that would save both trees and jobs. In other words, he would make everyone happy. In April 1993 President Clinton kept the first part of his campaign promise by attending a forest conference in Portland, Oregon. For all practical purposes, the conference is where Clinton enters the forest (all ears and no bias). His intentions were to gather information and to hear about the problem, from all points of view. He began the conference by saying, "We're here to discuss issues whose seriousness demands that we respect each other's concerns, each other's experiences, and each other's views. Together, we can move beyond confrontation to build a consensus on a balanced policy to preserve jobs and to protect our environment."[16] From the outset, then, Clinton established himself as a president who can help everyone and intended to do so. To him there is no either-or dilemma.

Establishing Ground for the Initial Position (Invention)

As a consensus builder, Clinton identified with both interests to avoid the dilemma that had sustained the controversy in recent years. He said, "Coming from a state, as I do, that was also settled by pioneers, and which is still 53 percent timberland, we have an important timber industry and people who appreciate the beauty and the intrinsic value of our woodlands. I have often felt at home here in the northwest." Whatever he might have meant during his election campaign when he called himself an environmental president now showed early signs of reinvention, as he furthermore suggested that "[f]rom the trailblazers and the pioneers to the trappers and the hunters, the loggers and the mill workers, the people of the northwest have earned their livings from the land, and have lived in awe of the power, the majesty, and the forests, the rivers, and the streams."[17] Thus Clinton immediately turned the attention away from the jobs or trees dilemma and set all sights on how to keep both.

After encouraging the expression of all views, Clinton asked the disputants to answer the longstanding question that sustains the forest controversy, a question that would seem rhetorical if it were not the very point of clash in the conference. He queried, "How can we achieve a balanced and comprehensive policy that recognizes the importance of the forests and timber to the precious old-growth, which are part of our national heritage and that, once destroyed, can never be replaced?" Then, Clinton indicted the federal government. "For too long," he said, "the national government has done more to confuse the issues than to clarify them. . . . To make things worse, the rhetoric from Washington has often exaggerated and exacerbated the tensions between those who speak about the economy and those who speak about the environment." Dissociation from Washington and identification with the competing interests allowed Clinton to remain both separate and attached, neither part of the mess in Washington nor partial in the hearing, but connected with the grieving parties. His rhetorical leverage, if not apparent at the time, was the both-and contradiction he offered as an ideal for both groups. In closing, he asserted, "This is not about choosing between jobs and the environment, but about recognizing the importance of both. . . . A healthy economy and a health[y] environment are not at odds with each other. They are essential to each other." Clinton then gave one final appeal to unity: "We're all here because we want a healthy economic environment and a healthy natural environmental [sic]. . . . If we commit today to move forward together, we can arrive at a balanced solution and put the stalemate behind us."[18]

Pleasing everyone was Clinton's solution, and it set the agenda for discussion in both-and contradictory terms. For everyone to be pleased, everyone must sacrifice. There will be fewer trees to harvest and fewer trees to save. But by this time, both sides believed they had already sacrificed too much. Even as Clinton asked conference members to "stay at the table and keep talking and trying to find common ground," timber industry workers and environmentalists were outside reinforcing the situational ironies with protest.[19] Mill worker Benito Najera said he was demonstrating because "people are putting birds before families." Ted Rabern, representative for the Western Council of Industrial Workers, stated, "I'm sick and tired of seeing my neighbors beg for crumbs to feed their kids." And Phillip Britt, a contract logger, noted, "There's a lot of timber worker suicides, a lot of broken families, there are people losing their homes."[20] At the same time, the environmentalists were chanting, "Earth first, profits last!" and "Corporate scum, here we come." The singer Carole King told the crowd that it was "too late" for Clinton's "balanced solution . . . the compromises have been made a long time ago." Finally, the northwest environmentalist Lou Gold declared that the "balance must stop," because "it has created victims of everything from loggers to salmon."[21]

During the conference, Clinton heard testimony that merely reinforced these views. For example, Buzz Eades, a sixth-generation logger, admitted, "I'm scared. I'm afraid of the future that faces my family [and] I represent thousands and thousands of timber workers just like me . . . modern Paul Bunyans who are hiding in the car while their wife buys groceries with food stamps." Conversely, Bill Arthur, of the Sierra Club said, "We are at the edge of the Pacific Ocean and the timber frontier is over. . . . We have cut our forests like there is no tomorrow, but tomorrow caught up with us yesterday."[22] With each side defending its own position, the desire for common ground was not readily apparent. But after an extraordinary day of testimony about abandoned sawmills and dwindling old-growth forests, President Clinton buoyed both sides of the conflict by promising that the federal government would, in fact, draft a balanced solution in sixty days. As a result, the *Oregonian* called the conference a "smashing success" but also observed that despite all the "flowing rhetoric over 'balance' and 'ecosystem management,' . . . neither side has budged all that much."[23]

The Initial Position and Early Signs of Reinvention

Sixty days later, Clinton kept his promise and delivered his forest plan, dubbed "Option 9." Unfortunately, neither group liked it. Option 9 protected roughly 80 percent of the remaining old-growth forests in the Northwest and the spotted owls that live in it as a threatened species. In addition, the plan called for federal assistance in creating an estimated, eight thousand jobs over a two-year period (by 1994), to offset the estimated loss of six thousand jobs in the timber industry during that time. Finally, Option 9 set the annual timber cut at about 1.2 billion board feet, which was one-fourth as much as the Forest Service and Bureau of Land Management sold on spotted owl forestland during the record years of the 1980s but three times as much as any other new forest plan allowed with owl protection. So what was the problem? Well, Clinton anticipated a most striking one in an exclusive interview with the *Oregonian* after he introduced the plan. Clinton first explained that he was stunned by the scientific reports that indicated how little timber could be cut under owl habitat protection: "The first thing I said was, 'Can't we harvest some more timber and save some more jobs consistent with the law?'" But then, he added, "I became convinced that we could not get a higher yield that was legal and scientifically defensible in the court."[24] Loggers and mill owners criticized the Clinton plan because it reduced federal timber supplies in the Northwest and eliminated another six thousand jobs in addition to the nineteen thousand lost since 1990.

Although Clinton offered hope to the environmentalists and the timber industry, Option 9 reinforced the tragic irony of a temporary fix leading to further destruction for all concerned parties. It was by no means considered a solution by either party in the dispute, but it did privilege the timber industry in the sense that it allowed for the largest cut allowed by law. The plan favored the industry in other ways as well. Given the fact that Option 9 set aside 80 percent of the remaining old growth, environmentalists would have to argue that the plan was ecologically unacceptable, and they would not only have to make that case in public but more importantly in court. Here, then, is another irony that is worth mentioning because it has a direct bearing on the larger, tragic irony of temporary fixes leading to long-term disasters. Environmentalists, who, in court, waged war against and won temporary victories over the timber industry during the late 1980s and early 1990s, now felt the effects of their increasing dependence on litigation-driven strategies, foundation funding, and professional lobbying. What started out as a grassroots position held by volunteer activists against what they believed to be environmentally destructive logging had become a cautious, money-conscious movement, increasingly pragmatic and increasingly willing to compromise. Many grassroots activists in the Northwest, like Michael Donnelly, felt that the "friendly" Clinton administration had "coopted their movement by winning symbolic concessions that weaken their position with Congress and the American people." Larry Tuttle, of the Oregon Natural Resources Council, who fought for the old forests during Bush and Clinton administrations, said that his own lawyers from the Sierra Club Legal Defense Fund were putting "unreasonable pressure" on plaintiffs to cut "a deal" rather than buck the system.[25]

Four months after Clinton announced his plan, one deal to be cut by environmentalists became quite clear: either go along with the Clinton administration or Interior Secretary Bruce Babbitt would recommend a rider to release timber from the court injunctions. In addition, six months after announcing Option 9, Clinton proposed relaxing logging restrictions for spotted owl protection and allowing increased logging on state and private lands. According to Assistant Interior Secretary George Frampton the proposal eliminated most restrictions on nonfederal land affected by owl protection and would open thousands of acres to logging in the Northwest by March, 1994. The proposal echoed with the "temporary fix" irony. Guidelines for protection at the time required a minimum five-hundred-acre buffer circle around most nesting sites; some areas required two-thousand-acre buffers to comply with the Endangered Species Act (ESA). Clinton's new proposal, however, reduced buffers to seventy acres. Phil Carroll of the U.S. Fish and Wildlife Service noted, "the assumption is they'll [the owls] either move on or die, . . . because 70 acres is not enough to keep them alive."[26] With the threat of a rider hanging overhead, environmentalist's seemed to be outmaneuvered by their environmental president. As Lou Gold of the Siskiyou Project said, "the ability to go to court and win means something only if we can defend against riders."[27]

Clinton and the Salvage Rider

In an attempt to end the logjam, or what the Clinton administration called the "fragile peace," House Republican Charles Taylor of North Carolina introduced an amendment to the rescissions bill that would "dramatically increase annual timber harvests on federal lands through two years of emergency 'salvage sales.'"[28] Taylor's amendment came in March, 1995, one month after a congressional hearing about timber salvage on public lands affected by insects, disease, and fire in order "to develop a strategy to expedite the preparation of salvage sales and actions that will help solve the forest health problem in the West."[29] The issue of the hearing involved forest health and how to restore dead, diseased, and dying trees by removing them. Proponents and opponents responded to the amendment with the ironies already established by environmentalists and the timber industry. Timber interests argued that the salvage rider would "create thousands of jobs for workers who have been displaced by restrictions on tree cutting [as well as] provide forest health," whereas the environmentalists claimed "the bill also would allow cutting live, healthy trees as part of a salvage operation."[30] As such, the salvage rider further reinforced the constraint of colliding ironies.

From Opposition to Concession (Reinvention No. 1)

Over the four months leading up to the signing of the rescissions bill and salvage rider, Clinton continued to respond to the constraining ironic perspectives with the hope of saving both jobs and trees. In doing so he took a firm stand against the Republican-backed congressional effort to reduce environmental protection while supporting legislation that would in fact override federal laws on environmental protection. Clinton wanted it both ways, and his position could hardly be criticized, as he stated it in April, 1995, to the American Society of Newspaper Editors: "A big part of my New Covenant was protecting our environment *and* promoting our natural resources. It's something we can all give to our children whether we die rich or poor. And it is our obligation to our future economic health, because no nation, *over the long run,* succeeds economically unless you preserve the environment. . . . [But] the environment cannot protect itself. And if it requires a presidential veto to protect it then that's what I'll provide." With regard to timber, a veto was eminent. Clinton explained a month later that the appropriations and rescissions bill being drafted by House Republicans "will essentially throw out all of our environmental laws and the protections that we have that surround . . . timber sales. . . . So it would seem to allow to cut more timber, but actually it means lawsuits and threats to the environment."[31]

The president took his commitment to the environment into a congressional battle over the rescissions bill in general and the salvage rider in particular. After returning the bill (H.R. 1158) to the House without approval in early June, he said, "I continue to object to language that would override existing environmental laws . . . to increase timber salvage. . . . [I]ncreasing timber salvage and improving forest health are goals that my Administration shares with Congress. . . . [But] It is not appropriate to use this legislation to overturn environmental laws." In this, his first presidential veto, Clinton objected to the heavy cuts in education and national service as well as environmental protection, nevertheless, he repeated his message concerning trees and jobs, saying that the House should join with his administration to work "on an initiative to increase timber salvage and improve forest health."[32]

Clinton objected to the salvage rider in the original rescissions bill because it required, with language that would override existing environmental laws, the Forest Service and Bureau of Land Management to sell 6.23 billion board feet of salvage timber over a two-year period.[33] After the veto, the rider was amended in a way that eliminated requirements to sell a specific amount of timber, with the Forest Service agreeing to sell roughly 4.5 billion board feet over a two-year period. As such, Clinton signed the budget rescissions bill on July 27, 1995, (Public Law 104-19) and gave the following statement about the salvage rider: "On balance I am very pleased with this bill. The timber provisions are not exactly what I wanted, but they are better than they were, and I believe we can and should carry out the timber salvage plans and that we can do it consistent with our *forest plan and existing environmental laws.*"[34]

Three weeks after the veto, he reaffirmed his commitment to forest health by telling Congress, "I still do not believe this bill should contain any of the provisions relating to timber. I opposed the timber salvage rider because I believe that it threatens once again to lead to legal gridlock and to impair, rather than promote, sustainable economic activity. I continue to have that concern."[35] Clinton followed this assertion, however, with a subtle shift that allowed him to concede on the rider without actually conceding:

> But the conferees did accept important changes in the language that preserve our ability to implement the current forest plans and their standards and to protect other resources such as clean water and fisheries. Furthermore, Chairman Hatfield insists that the timber salvage provisions provide complete discretion for the administration to implement these provisions according to our best judgment.
>
> I take Senator Hatfield at his word. Therefore, after signing the rescissions bill into law, I will direct the Secretary of Agriculture, the Secretary of the Interior, and all other federal agencies to carry out timber salvage activities consistent with the spirit and intent of our forest plans and all existing environmental laws.
>
> We will abide by the balanced goals of our forest plans, and we will not violate our environmental standards. Both are too important to protecting our quality of life and our economy.[36]

The same day Clinton repeated his concern for environmental protection in a letter to House Speaker Newt Gingrich, saying, "I do appreciate the changes that the Congress has made to provide Administration with the flexibility and authority to carry this program out in a manner that conforms to our existing environmental laws and standards."[37] Exemptions remained, but Clinton did not address them specifically until after he signed the bill. In doing so, he shifted (as a function of reinvention) from objection to reluctant approval of the rider, as evidenced in his statement on the legislation one week before he signed it:

> To be sure, I do not support every provision of this bill. For instance, I still do not believe this bill should contain any of the provisions relating to timber. But the final bill does contain changes in the language that preserve our ability to implement the current forest plans and their standards, and to protect other resources such as clean water and fisheries.
>
> Therefore, after signing the rescission into law, I will direct the Secretary of Agriculture, the Secretary of the Interior, and all other Federal

Agencies to carry out timber salvage activities consistent with the spirit and intent of our *forest plans and existing environmental laws.*[38]

From Concession to Objection (Reinvention No. 2)

Three days after signing the bill, the president again shifted his position on the salvage rider. In an August 1 memorandum to the secretaries of the interior, agriculture, and commerce, and the administrator of the Environmental Protection Agency, he stated that he "most particularly" did not support the salvage rider. Although Clinton initially hoped the rider would end court battles over timber, he now said he was "concerned that the timber salvage provisions may even lead to [more] litigation that could slow down our forest management program." But he also compromised on environmental protection, saying he would now "carry out the objectives of the relevant timber-related activities authorized by Public Law 104-19 . . . in ways that, to the *maximum extent allowed,* follow our current environmental laws and programs." In effect, the bill he signed into law had limited his power to enforce environmental laws.[39]

Since the rider specifically allowed timber to be sold without court approval, the so-called maximum extent to which environmental laws would be followed, would be minimal. Three days after his concession, Clinton once again said that he objected to the salvage rider but that, overall he was "pleased that bipartisan leaders of Congress worked with me to produce a good bill."[40] Overall, it seemed the president had found a way to oppose and support one piece of legislation at the same time. But as soon as the salvage rider was signed into law, the timber industry went to court for the release of green sales blocked previously with the Endangered Species Act. Many of these sales were approved under the salvage rider, and by October, 1995, Clinton expressed his regret:

> I am deeply disappointed in the court's decision to force the Forest Service and the Bureau of Land Management to release these sales of healthy ancient timber. My administration's agreement with the Congress on this issue was significantly different from the interpretation upheld this week by the courts. We agreed that the administration would not have to violate our standards and guidelines for our *forest plan, and for forest management in general,* but only speed up sales that met those standards. We do not believe that this extreme expansion of ancient timber sales was authorized by the 1995 rescission act. . . .
>
> At this time, however, there is no choice but to comply with the court's

decision. The decision forces the release of timber that may lead to *grave environmental injury* to Chinook salmon and other wildlife and damage our rivers and streams. This could *jeopardize the livelihood* of thousands of people who depend on the Pacific Northwest's vibrant commercial and sport Fisheries.[41]

One way to interpret this statement is to say that in an attempt to please everyone affected by the forest crisis President Clinton, by his own admission, approved a public law that would probably hurt everyone affected by the forest crisis. Though he said he had not anticipated this eventual outcome, he certainly heard such predictions during the salvage rider debate. While the timber industry decried federal actions that blocked the harvesting of "dead" or "damaged" trees, environmentalists warned that this "forest health crisis" was exaggerated by the industry and served as mere pretense for increasing harvests in general. In September, 1995, only one month after Clinton implemented the new standards, federal judge Michael Hogan ruled that the salvage rider applied to all unawarded timber sales in Oregon and Washington and ordered the government to release an additional 250 million board feet of timber. What this meant, as Kathie Durbin noted in *Tree Huggers,* is that the environmentalists stood to "lose everything they fought for" in the forest. What Clinton offered as a have-your-cake-and-eat-it-too solution quickly turned into a question of whether the president knew that the rider would allow logging of healthy old growth and release timber sales blocked by court.[42]

As the industry resumed limited logging of the remaining old growth, environmental protesters returned to the woods in western Oregon, and the timber industry resumed their accusations of environmental terrorism. Familiar issues and rhetorical appeals arose from both groups as the federal land managers pleaded for a sympathetic ear and lawyers dashed from court to court with new lawsuits. Mike Miller of the Associated Oregon Loggers said, "Five, eight years ago, the fight was over old-growth forests . . . . Today, they are against cutting any trees period. Alive or dead." Howard Sohn, president of the Suns Studs mill in Roseberg, Oregon, lamented, "Suddenly, it has become morally wrong to cut green trees." Tim Hermack of the Native Forest Council of Eugene, Oregon, argued that "they've taken our rights to court action and comment. Our only course is to have a Boston Tea Party." Hermack also said the rider moved the environmental movement "below square one" in its attempt to save the old forest: "I hate to think that the worst predictions I made are going to come true, but here we are, back to defending the best of what's left." After five years at the bargaining table, the timber antagonists were back where they started.[43]

Local antagonism widened to include other resource concerns as well. David Bales of the Pacific River Council noted that under the salvage rider loggers were "cutting right across live streams and leaving no buffers whatsoever. . . . It's nothing but old-fashioned clear-cutting, the exact kind of logging that brought us all these problems in the first place." Steve Moyer of Trout Unlimited asserted "we really feared the worst when it [the rider] passed. . . . And it turned out to be a disaster." Glen Spain, Northwest representative for the Pacific Coast Federation of Fisherman's Association, explained, "This could spell destruction for vast sections of the Northwest's remaining salmon populations . . . a direct assault on the fishing industry." Democrats and environmentalists in Washington felt they were misled into thinking that the salvage rider would be limited only to salvage timber sales. Yet Heidi Kelly, a spokesperson for Slade Gorton, Republican senator from Washington and an original sponsor of the rider, said, "For them to claim ignorance at this late date simply doesn't wash. . . . We had days and weeks of negotiations with the administration on every apostrophe, every comma and every dotted 'I.'"[44] Republican senator Mark Hatfield of Oregon, who supported the salvage rider, added that "we all discussed it thoroughly. . . . They [Democrats] understood every detail of that bill."[45]

From Objection to Unresolved Silence (Reinvention No. 3)

Exactly who knew what depended on who was talking, and the ambiguity left considerable space for reinvention. Clinton, who began as an active opponent of the rider (and its exemptions to environmental laws), endorsed the bill with what Republicans called full knowledge of the implications, only to oppose it again with a claim of ignorance soon after logging began. Whether Clinton knew or not, the timber industry would get their logs. Nevertheless, in December, Democratic House Representatives Peter DeFazio and Ron Wyden of Oregon urged the president to modify the rider, while Senate Democrat Elizabeth Furse of Oregon drafted a bill to repeal it altogether. In doing so, Furse reinforced the belief that timber interests and Republicans misled Democrats by saying, "Taken together, this [rider] is the ultimate unintended nightmare. . . . No one ever had a clue this would happen."[46] But by the end of 1995 Clinton had little more to say about the rider except that the outcome was neither desirable nor intentional. In February, 1996, for example, he told a group of college students in Seattle, Washington, that, while he intended to make environmental issues a cornerstone of his reelection campaign, "We've made one or two mistakes under the law of unintended consequences. . . . [O]ne of them was the unintended and unwarranted consequence of the way that timber rider has been carried out."[47] But with his record on the salvage rider, it came as no surprise that neither the forest nor the environment were prominent issues in his 1996 campaign. To win environmentalists back, Clinton would have to exercise whatever power he had to end what had become known as "logging without laws."[48]

To appease environmentalists during the election campaign, the Clinton administration, via Secretary of Agriculture Dan Glickman, first admitted in July, 1996, that the Forest Service lost much credibility over the salvage rider and then announced that, as a result, strict new guidelines would be implemented. Specifically, the administration cut roughly 12 percent of harvests under the rider by blocking salvage logging in roadless areas, which reduced the harvest by an estimated 75 to 80 million board feet.[49] Republicans accused Clinton of trying to win over environmentalists with political games, but Clinton continued. In September he struck a deal with fifteen Northwest timber companies to spare forty-four timber sales covering thirty-eight hundred acres in Oregon and Washington, in exchange for younger forests with less environmental impact.[50] He then convinced western Republicans in Congress to drop two more environment-threatening riders from the 1997 appropriations bills, with veto threats.[51] However, as Clinton took such steps to win favor with environmentalists, he quietly removed himself from the public debate (with Glickman and the Forest Service speaking for the administration by June, 1996), which served as an admission of guilt to environmentalists. Furse, whose attempt to repeal the rider failed over the summer by two votes in the House, said the president's effort merely suggests that the "White House sees there's been real political trouble with the rider, and it's trying to contain the damage."[52]

Irony, Presidential Rhetoric, and Environmental Policy

Four general implications of the salvage rider debate in the timber controversy arise from this study with regard to presidential rhetoric and environmental policymaking. The first of these involves the manner in which the colliding ironies presented by competing interest groups function as constraint for the presidential rhetoric surrounding the salvage rider in particular and the forest controversy in general. Since environmentalists and loggers identify each other as *the* threat to the other's life and lifestyle in such a divisive manner, the ironies essentially solidify as a no-win rhetorical constraint for presidential discourse. Both economic and environmental ironies circumvent resolution because they are dissociative in nature: they externalize; create enemies; present victims as inferior; define the inferior as the "cause" of the problem. In other words, the dissociative ironies serve as scapegoat mechanisms for each group.

Together they constrain presidential rhetoric by forcing a choice between two tragic alternatives for the region, a choice Clinton could not make.

With the colliding ironies as constraint, a second implication of the study involves the function of Clinton's rhetorical strategy on the salvage logging legislation. In essence, Clinton responded to the dissociative ironies with an irony of his own, based on a have-your-cake-and-eat-it-too rhetorical appeal that would, in fact, please everyone by saving jobs and trees. With this, the president rejected the idea or reality of tragedy altogether with a win-win solution to the problem. In doing so, he created a bargaining situation, on the assumption that all parties wanted to save jobs and trees, in which he could counter the *dissociative* ironies constructed by the two groups with an *associative* one that suspended the anticipation and fulfillment of the tragic ironies of both groups.[53] In this sense, the "true" irony of the salvage rider was that economy *needs* ecology and ecology *needs* economy. It suggested a "fundamental kinship" between timber workers and environmentalists.[54] They are not exclusive of one another, but contain each other within. Clinton argued that trees and jobs must be saved, for environmental health and economic well-being could only survive as a team. With his associative irony, he thus encouraged a suspension of judgment about two dissociative ironies that, when taken individually, meant a tragic ending to at least one group, and when combined, spelled doom for all parties involved.

At the heart of this conflict, then, is a problem informed by a tragic irony: two groups in need of each other must, instead, fight against each other. As such, Clinton asked each group to end the court battles and come together. But while Clinton emphasized the "reality" of mutual indebtedness, there was little expressed by the competing interests. It goes without saying that economy, or economic well-being, depends on a healthy environment; natural resources generate capital. Conversely, ecology, or ecological well-being, depends on a healthy economy. As Oregon senator Mark Hatfield, a coauthor of the Endangered Species Act observed, when faced with a choice between economic hardship and the environment, Americans will compromise environmental protection.[55] Given such an axiom, Clinton in his salvage rider rhetoric provided something for everyone in the spirit of mutual indebtedness (setting aside some old growth while allowing some to be cut) and apologized for not being able to do more. But soon after the rider went into effect, mutual indebtedness turned to a sense of alienation as he dissociated himself from the industry for their exploitation of the rider and the environmentalists dissociated themselves from Clinton for his abandonment of environmental commitments to old growth and endangered species. Finally, Clinton characterized himself as having been unwittingly manipulated by timber interests, while timber and environmental groups accused him of playing "political games with timber policies."[56]

As reinvention, Clinton's irony, albeit associative rather than dissociative, carries a third implication for presidential rhetoric and the presidency in general. Although Clinton appealed to timber and environmental interests in the salvage rider controversy by arguing that they indeed need each other and must therefore come together to end the conflict in the forest, the irony itself served more as a way to keep these two incompatible groups at bay. The salvage rider presented itself as a rhetorical situation in which two groups (audiences) represented more of a threat to the president than the "neighbor" or "coworker" that he so fondly characterized them as at the 1993 Forest Conference in Portland. With their incompatibility, Clinton could not appeal to one group without alienating the other. As such, he used an irony that addressed the needs and interests of both. Taken together, the two groups in this controversy constitute a bifurcated audience and the audience bifurcation is a critical factor in explaining Clinton's reinvention strategy and the ironic messages to which it lends itself. That is, audience bifurcation in itself presents a situation where ironic strategies are particularly useful, if not necessary, because the president must address the needs and interests of incompatible audiences. With special interests and special interest politics creating incompatible audiences as a rule, a question arises as to whether or not irony has become a necessary strategy for the modern president who must please everyone when the "everyone" is at odds with one another.[57] If so, perhaps the president must now take the form of a modern-day *eiron,* whose very survival in politics still depends on bargaining, as Neustadt observes, but bargaining through an arsenal of clever tricks and illusions that sacrifices ethos for the sake of political survival.

A final implication of this study, therefore, involves Clinton's reinvention as a function of his presidential rhetoric on the rider during the critical time period leading up to and including his reelection campaign. From Lance Bennett's perspective on Clinton's campaign rhetoric as reinvention, negative judgments about Clinton and the rider could have been suspended until after the election by inducing the public and competing interests to consider the salvage rider not so much as a problem as an occasion for him to come back continually from an endless flow of criticism. Such rhetorical space or "psychological margin created by . . . an eternal comeback," as Bennett described it, "fit nicely with 'reinventing Bill' as the underlying psychological strategy of the entire campaign."[58] As such, he opposed the rider when it first came along, in favor of more environmental protection, which warmed the hearts of the environmentalists. Then he signed the rider, which alarmed the environmentalists, but raised hope for the timber industry. Then during implementation of the salvage rider, Clinton became the environmental president who was misled by the industry, which, of course, did not sit well with loggers. Thus if the Northwest could not have their cake and eat it too, Clinton would try to make it appear as if it did. While the industry got their timber (roughly 4.5 billion board feet under the rider), he eventually blocked salvage logging in roadless areas, struck a deal with timber companies that saved four thousand acres of old growth, and then halted salvage logging two weeks before the rider expired.[59]

Clinton's comeback from the salvage rider eventually rested on the perception that he would never *knowingly* have allowed (as, for example, an ironist would have known) the rider to damage the environment. And when he said that he was in fact misled, he introduced new and conflicting information from which he could reinvent himself on the issue. In doing so, he tried to encourage environmentalists, once again, to suspend negative judgment about a decision that Vice President Al Gore admitted during the 1996 election campaign was "the worst mistake" of the Clinton administration's first term.[60] This statement, which was often repeated by the Pacific Northwest's media during the election campaign, came at a time when Clinton could do little else: he signed the bill; the rider was in effect; the trees were falling; the deal was done. To acknowledge that he knew the extent to which the rider would create environmental damage would make him environmentally insensitive, to say the least. On the other hand, acknowledging that he was in fact misled was an admission that he was outsmarted and outbargained by industry interests. In this way, his willingness to admit being both uninformed and duped on the matter was a self-inflicted blow to his credibility that allowed him finally to survive the issue. With his associative irony, then, Clinton not only lost the faith of timber and environmental interests but also oversimplified the salvage issue, damaged his credibility, and ignored such demands as made, for example, by U.S. Forest Service chief Mike Dombeck, who called for extensive "ecosystem restoration . . . with broad opportunities and complex solutions."[61]

Implications of this study on Clinton's salvage rider rhetoric with respect to environmental policy and policymaking are not very promising. The dissociative ironies that Clinton confronted represent a paradox all to familiar to modern (rhetorical) presidents, that is, being all things to everyone. It is the all-too-familiar paradox of power characterized by Richard Neustadt in *Presidential Power,* Thomas Cronin in *The State of the Presidency,* and Godfrey Hodgson in *All Things to All Men,* to name just a few. With respect to the salvage rider, this paradox was a particularly alluring one for Clinton, who seemed to proceed initially as if the possibilities for harnessing and commanding this issue were unlimited, when they were not. Indeed, the salvage rider, as a policy that was intended to restore forest health, induced a kind of presidential "impotence," as Hodgson called it, brought about by the belief that the best (indeed only) way of resolving the conflict was to please everyone, which was beyond the scope of Clinton's presidential power. The presidency, as an institution, did not allow Clinton to do what he said he wanted to do for the environmentalists or the timber industry, as he argued throughout the life span of the rider. What then became more crucial was Clinton's reelection. The salvage rider was an administrative failure, the worst, as Gore said repeatedly during the campaign. As a result, Clinton, the Comeback Kid, adopted his old campaign strategy, constant reinvention, to deal with his own salvage, hoping that the environmentalists, the loggers, and the general public would suspend judgment until after the election. And apparently, enough of them did.[62]

Notes

1. For a general discussion, see Mark P. Moore, "Constructing Irreconcilable Conflict: The Function of Synecdoche in the Spotted Owl Controversy," *Communication Monographs* 60 (Sept., 1993): 258–74; Frank Church, "Mill Owners Struggle to Survive," *Oregonian,* Oct. 24, 1990; "No Peace for the Owl," *Newsweek,* July 9, 1990, 63; for views on logging restrictions and timber industry practices in the Northwest by the federal district court judge who ruled in favor of the logging restrictions and blocked timber sales due to violations of the endangered species act, see Judge William Dwyer, "The Owl and the Land," *Congressional Record* (June 26, 1991): S 8699–S 8700.

2. For distinctions between "verbal irony" and the type of "situational irony" constructed by timber and environmental interests in this controversy, see D. C. Muecke, *Irony: The Critical Idiom* (Fakenham, Norfolk: Methuen, 1970), 28.

3. David Kaufer, "Irony and Rhetorical Strategy," *Philosophy and Rhetoric* 10 (Spring, 1977): 92; Muecke, *Irony,* 66–67.

4. See Kenneth Burke, *A Grammar of Motives* (Berkeley: University of California Press, 1969), 514–17, and Muecke, *Irony,* 20–21, 77–81.

5. Soren Kierkegaard, *The Concept of Irony, with Constant Reference to Socrates,* trans. Lee M. Capel (New York: Harper, 1965), 265; Haakon Chevalier, *The Ironic Temper: Anatole France and His Time* (New York: Oxford University Press, 1932), 44, 47; Alan Reynolds Thompson, *The Dry Mock* (Berkeley: University of California Press, 1948), 5; Northrop Frye, *Anatomy of Criticism: Four Essays* (Princeton, N.J.: Princeton University Press, 1957), 271; D. C. Muecke, *The Compass of Irony* (London: Methuen, 1969), 42.

6. Chevalier, *The Ironic Temper,* 12.

7. During this time period, timber and environmental antagonism reached new heights and solidified what can be viewed overall as "audience bifurcation" marked by antipathy. This lends itself quite well to the development and increased dependency upon ironic discourse as a way to express the social reality of each group in a rhetorically strategic manner. The bifurcated audience (made up of timber and environmental interests) continually reinforces divisive attitudes and beliefs through the tragic ironies it conveys. This audience offers no "common enemy" for Clinton, making it difficult for him to affiliate with either the whole audience or even a bifurcated part of it. This, then, encourages Clinton to "waffle" or continually reinvent himself; he has no true affiliation, no victim to single out and victimize, only an "incredible" plan to make everyone happy, a plan that ironically and unintentionally victimizes everyone. For a discussion of irony and audience bifurcation, see, Kaufer, "Irony and Rhetorical Strategy," 94–98.

8. See Moore, "Constructing Irreconcilable Conflict," 258.

9. Eric Foresman, "A Preliminary Investigation of the Spotted Owl in Oregon," master's thesis, Oregon State University, 1976, 8, 102.

10. See Kathie Durbin and Paul Koberstein, "Survival Hinges on Old-Growth Habitat," *Oregonian,* Sept. 20, 1990.

11. Backus cited in Rick Bella, "Woodsmen Chop Plans to Bar Logging," *Oregonian,* May 25, 1991, E10; Kimble cited in Kip Hamburg, "Douglas County Reeling from the Economic Blues," *Oregonian,* April 5, 1992, R5; Smith cited in Paul Koberstein, "Northwest Timber Industry Rips Judges' Decision to Block Tim-

ber Sales," *Oregonian*, May 25, 1991, E10; Packwood cited in Paul Manzano, "Economic Woes Blamed on Owl, Timber Issue," *Oregonian*, Aug. 20, 1991, A11.

12. Manzano, "Economic Woes," A11; "Saving Spotted Owl" cited in Tim Gup, "Owl vs. Man," *Time,* June 25, 1990, 60.

13. Gup, "Owl vs. Man," 58.

14. Jack Ward Thomas, *A Conservation Strategy for the Northern Spotted Owl* (Washington, D.C.: Government Printing Office, 1990), 1; Elliot Norse, *Ancient Forests of the Pacific Northwest* (Washington, D.C.: Island Press, 1990), 78; Chris Maser, *The Redesigned Forest* (San Pedro, Calif.: R. and E. Miles, 1988), 152; Seth Zuckerman, *Saving Our Ancient Forests* (Los Angeles: Living Planet Press, 1991), 52.

15. Kathie Durbin, "Religious Rights vs. Land Management," *Oregonian*, Feb. 4, 1991, B1; William Dietrich, *The Final Forest: The Battle for the Last Great Trees of the Pacific Northwest* (New York: Penguin, 1992), 160.

16. William J. Clinton and Albert Gore, Jr., "The Forest Conference," Proceedings from the 1993 Forest Conference, Portland Convention Center, Portland, Ore., April 2, 1993, 6.

17. Clinton and Gore, "The Forest Conference," 6.

18. Ibid, 7–8.

19. Don Hamilton, Joan Laatz, and Brian T. Meehan, "Clinton Promises Quick Solution: Hope Offered in Forest Fuss," *Oregonian*, April 3, 1993, A15.

20. Foster Church and Cathy Kiyomura, "Timber Families Rally at Waterfront," *Oregonian*, April 3, 1993.

21. Barnes C. Ellis, "1,000 Call for an End to Cutting Old Growth," *Oregonian*, April 3, 1993, A15.

22. "Clinton, Gore Hear Pleas of Pain, Hope, Frustration," *Oregonian*, April 3, 1993, A15.

23. Kathie Durbin, "President Aims High for Forest Solution," *Oregonian*, April 4, 1993, A1.

24. Kathie Durbin, "Clinton Aims to End Logjam: He Introduces Plan to Manage Forests," *Oregonian*, July 2, 1993, A1.

25. Kathie Durbin, "Splitsville? Environmental Groups, 'Tree Huggers,' Find Themselves at Odds over Clinton Forest Plan," *Oregonian*, Dec. 5, 1993, C4.

26. See Joan Laatz, "Clinton Plan Would Ease Logging Limits," *Oregonian*, Dec. 1, 1993.

27. Durbin, "Splitsville?" C1.

28. George Hager, "Massive Spending-Cut Package Moves to House Floor," *Congressional Quarterly* (March 4, 1995): 676.

29. U.S. House Subcommittee on Resource Conservation, Research, and Forestry of the Committee of Agriculture, *Timber Salvage Situation on Public Lands Affected by Insects, Disease, and Fire.* 104th Cong., 1st sess., Feb. 10, 1995, 188.

30. Bob Benenson, "Environmental Laws Take a Hit," *Congressional Quarterly* (March 18, 1995): 797.

31. Bill Clinton, "We've Made Good Progress," *Vital Speeches of the Day* 61 (May 1, 1995): 422; emphasis added; Clinton, "Remarks on the First Anniversary of the School-to-Work Opportunities Act of 1994 in White Plains, Maryland," *Weekly Compilation of Presidential Documents* 31, no. 20 (May 17, 1995): 845.

32. Clinton, "Message to the House of Representatives Returning without Approval Legislation for Emergency Supplemental Appropriations and Rescissions for Fiscal Year 1995," *Weekly Compilation of Presidential Documents* 31, no. 23 (June 12,

1995): 994; "President Clinton's Veto of Rescissions Bill," *Congressional Quarterly* (June 10, 1995): 1669.

33. Clinton, *Veto of H.R. 1158. A Message from the President of the United States Transmitting His Veto of H.R. 1158, A Bill Making Emergency Supplemental Appropriations for Additional Disaster Assistance, for Antiterrorism Initiatives, for Assistance in the Recovery from the Tragedy that Occurred at Oklahoma City, and Making Rescissions for the Fiscal Year Ending September 30, 1995, and for Other Purposes.* 104th Congress, 1st. sess., July 7, 1995 (Washington, D.C.: Government Printing Office, 1995), 2.

34. Clinton, "Remarks on Signing Emergency Supplemental Appropriations and Rescissions Legislation and an Exchange with Reporters," *Weekly Compilation of Presidential Documents* 31, no. 30 (July 27, 1995): 1310; emphasis added.

35. Clinton. "Statement on Agreement with Congress on Budget Rescissions Legislation," *Weekly Compilation of Presidential Documents* 31, no. 26 (June 29, 1995): 1162.

36. Clinton, "Statement on Agreement with Congress," 1162–63.

37. Clinton, "Letter to the Speaker of the House on Emergency Salvage Timber Sale Legislation," *Weekly Compilation of Presidential Documents* 31, no.26 (June 29, 1995): 1170.

38. Clinton, "Statement on Budget Rescission Legislation," *Weekly Compilation of Presidential Documents* 31, no. 29 (July 21, 1955): 1282; emphasis added.

39. Clinton, "Memorandum on Timber Salvage Legislation," *Weekly Compilation of Presidential Documents* 31, no. 31 (Aug. 1, 1995): 1356; emphasis added.

40. Clinton, "Statement on Signing the Emergency Supplemental Appropriations and Rescissions Legislation," *Weekly Compilation of Presidential Documents* 31, no.31 (Aug. 4, 1995): 1378. Earlier in this statement he said, once again, "I still do not believe that this bill should contain any of the provisions relating to timber. But the final bill does contain changes in the language that preserve our ability to implement the current forest plans and their standards, and protect other resources such as clean water and fisheries" (1377).

41. Clinton, "Statement on the Court Decision on Timber Sales," *Weekly Compilation of Presidential Documents* 31, no. 44 (Oct. 28, 1995): 1954; emphasis added.

42. Kathie Durbin, *Tree Huggers: Victory, Defeat, and Renewal in the Northwest Ancient Forest Campaign* (Seattle: Mountaineers, 1996), 260.

43. Cited in Rob Eure, "Timber Antagonists Square Off Again," *Oregonian*, Sept. 24, 1995, A22.

44. Cited in Dana Tims, "Democrats Escalate Timber Salvage Fight," *Oregonian*, Dec. 23, 1995, A12.

45. Cited in Brent Walth, "Clinton Falls into Old-Growth Thicket," *Oregonian*, March 11, 1996, A6.

46. Cited in Tims, "Democrats Escalate," A12.

47. Walth, "Clinton Falls into Old-Growth," A1. See also, Peter D. Sleeth, "Clinton Points Ax at Salvage Logging Law," *Oregonian*, Feb. 25, 1996.

48. Durbin, *Tree Huggers,* 254.

49. Jeff Bernard, "Salvage Logging: Roadless Plan Will Trim Harvest by 12 Percent," *Corvallis (Oregon) Gazette-Times,* July 11, 1996, A1.

50. Bryon Denson and Peter D. Sleeth, "Deal Will Spare NW Old Growth," *Oregonian,* Sept. 18, 1996, A1.

51. Durbin, *Tree Huggers,* 286.

52. Hal Bernton and Brent Walth, "Salvage Logging Rules Change," *Oregonian,* July 3, 1996, C1. With Clinton silent on the issue, others in his administration drew heavy criticism for the salvage rider and forest management, like Interior Secretary Bruce Babbitt, who in March, 1997, was attacked by the timber industry for advocating prescribed fires to restore forest health (see Scott Sonner, "Igniting a Controversy in the Woods," *Corvallis [Oregon] Gazette-Times,* March 30, 1997, A6), and Agriculture Undersecretary James Lyons, who was ridiculed by environmentalists for denying their petition that would disallow the industry to bid on and log national forest timber sales (see Scott Sonner, "Environmentalists Contend for National Timber Sales," *Corvallis [Oregon] Gazette-Times,* May 16, 1997, A2). Suffice it to say, there is something ironic about saving a forest by cutting it down and burning it.

53. For a discussion of Clinton as ironist, see Mark P. Moore, "From a Government of the People, to a People of the Government: Irony as Rhetorical Strategy in Presidential Campaigns," *Quarterly Journal of Speech* 82 (Feb., 1996): 28–33.

54. Burke, *A Grammar,* 514.

55. Lynn Foster, "ESA May Be Stalled by Politics," *Oregon Scientist* (Summer, 1994): 1.

56. Scott Sonner, "Clinton Accused of Political Games with Timber Policies," *Corvallis (Oregon) Gazette-Times,* Aug. 2, 1996, A4.

57. For discussion of the increased use of irony as a rhetorical strategy by presidents and presidential candidates since 1964, see Moore, "From a Government of the People," 22–37.

58. W. Lance Bennett, *The Governing Crisis: Media, Money, and Marketing in American Elections* (New York: St. Martin's Press, 1996), 68.

59. Sonner, "Clinton Accused of Political Games," A4.

60. Bryon Denson, "Timber Law Troublesome to the End," *Oregonian,* Dec. 13, 1996, A1.

61. Scott Sonner, "Forest Chief: Move Restoration Dialogue beyond Stereotypes," *Corvallis (Oregon) Gazette-Times,* March 19, 1997, A1.

62. Richard Neustadt, *Presidential Power: The Politics of Leadership* (New York: John Wiley, 1960); Thomas Cronin, *The State of the Presidency* (New York: Little, Brown, 1975); Godfrey Hodgson, *All Things to All Men: The False Promise of the Modern American President* (New York: Simon and Schuster, 1980).

8

"We're Coming Clean"

Clinton, Public Advocacy, and the Human Radiation Experiments

David Henry

In December, 1993, representatives of the Department of Energy announced their intention to disclose details of America's secret atomic testing practices during the cold war. Secretary of Energy Hazel O'Leary opened a subsequent news conference by noting that she was "appalled, shocked, and deeply saddened" by what she had to report. O'Leary acknowledged that more than two hundred secret nuclear weapons explosions had taken place at the Nevada Test Site between 1963 and 1990. Perhaps even more disillusioning to a public urged to support the development of nuclear arms as a deterrent to Soviet aggression, American scientists had subjected more than six hundred citizens to medical experiments, actions associated far more with the enemy's "evil empire" than with the protectors of freedom. Without the subjects' knowledge, for instance, doctors injected at least eighteen patients with plutonium to study how quickly radioactive substances traveled through the human body. Revelations about such studies alarmed a public increasingly sensitive to the impact of nuclear research on environmental safety.[1]

Although medical experimentation and military testing in atomic science preceded Bill Clinton's assumption of the presidency, such revelations demanded a response. At her press conference Secretary O'Leary coupled her shock and sadness with an intimation of the campaign's initial discursive strategy. One of the graphics she used in her meeting with the press declared, "The Cold War is over. We're coming clean." To that end, she pledged, the data revealed in December would be followed every six months by the declassification of additional documents, the total of which exceeded 32 million pages. Antinuclear activists, however, were dubious. Heidi Carter, a spokeswoman for the American Peace Test in Las Vegas, expressed reservations about the extent to which government disclosures would constitute a full reporting of United States nuclear activity during the cold war. "I don't feel knowing about 204 tests does much to erase past lies," she said. "I hope this is the beginning of real accountability."[2]

In this chapter I examine the rhetorical dimensions of the crisis generated by demands for accountability in a democratic culture. My specific focus is on the strategy and tactics that underlay the Clinton administration's accounting of a research program grounded in suspect ethical practices. At the center of the strategy is a dependence on surrogate advocacy, wherein the president's position is advanced not personally but through individuals well suited to the task at hand. While the role of surrogates during election campaigns is well established, certainly of equal interest to critics of presidential discourse is how the chief executive employs carefully selected members of the administration to advance policy on potentially sensitive issues.[3] Surrogates may shield a chief executive by providing a level of "deniability" for ill-advised policy decisions, may serve as a "lightning rod" to attract attention on controversial issues and thereby move the chief administrator to the controversy's periphery, or may introduce ideas as "trial balloons," only to yield center stage should public opinion prove favorable.[4] Hazel O'Leary's centrality in the Clinton administration's disclosure of atomic secrets, however, affords an opportunity to explore a further function of surrogates. Neither shield nor lightning rod, O'Leary assumed the primary role in the government's campaign to restore public trust in the democratic process and the institutions of government.

The suasory choices made in pursuit of that goal thus constitute a study in presidential crisis rhetoric that promises to complement the continually expanding body of work focused primarily on an incumbent's personal place in the persuasive process.[5] Three inextricably linked features of the administration's accountability and openness campaign warrant attention.[6] First, studies focused on presidential leadership uniformly explore the rhetorician's power to define the grounds of public argument, and hence to shape perceptions and programs.[7] While O'Leary's place in public talk about nuclear policy was necessarily central, it is also the case that she assumed the posture of a facilitator. Rather than dictating the agenda to affected citizens, she initiated discussion in public forums by imparting information and then inviting "stakeholders" to respond. Second, the resulting sessions introduced a deliberative forum that was informed by but also expanded on Michael Halloran's conception of the rhetorical dimensions of the public proceeding. The potential consequence of the combination intimates a prospective formula for what Halloran terms "Doing Public Business in Public," a formula that may bode well for reviving faith in the political process. Finally, the intertwining of O'Leary's unique role and the primacy of the public in effecting decisions (or, at least, effecting decisions about decisions) suggests an ethical emphasis in public policy that fuses what Joseph Nye terms an ethics of consequences with an ethics of virtue. The significance of Nye's scheme for appreciating the unique dynamics at work in this case study is detailed in the chapter's conclusion. For while O'Leary's performance and the meetings with stakeholders merit analysis on their own terms, it is in what that analysis reveals about the interaction of ethics, rhetoric, and public policy from which this chapter derives its potential value for the study of public discourse. The remainder of the chapter attends to each facet of the campaign.

Hazel O'Leary as Presidential Surrogate

In November, 1993, investigative reporter Eileen Welsome produced a three-part series for the *Albuquerque Tribune* on the U.S. government's medical experimentation program in the wake of World War II.[8] The news at once shocked readers and confirmed suspicions about government deception. The *Bulletin of the Atomic Scientists* observed of the secretary of energy's press conference the following month, for example, that what she said was not "new information." Nevertheless, the *Bulletin* concluded, "Hazel O'Leary's discussion of experiments on civilians rocked the nation."[9] After researching Welsome's disturbing, often wrenching revelations, O'Leary called a news conference for December 7, 1993. She reported that during the period under investigation, the United States had conducted 925 nuclear tests, "204 of which were kept secret." Even more alarming than learning that more than 20 percent of the country's atomic tests had been concealed from affected communities, she noted in response to a reporter's question, was the extent of human experimentation: "On the health experiments, I'll have to tell you that my immediate reaction was that I was appalled and shocked and my, you know, it just gave me an ache in my gut and my heart." O'Leary's reaction in part characterized what made her the ideal surrogate for the administration.[10]

O'Leary's performance exhibited the traits of what Kathleen Hall Jamieson terms the "feminine style" of oratory that has evolved in the electronic age and that urges rethinking conventional wisdom about public advocacy.[11] O'Leary does not embody that style simply because of her gender; indeed, Jamieson contends that Ronald Reagan's mediated oratory epitomizes the "effeminate style" in contemporary political advocacy.[12] Jamieson's concept adapts Karlyn Kohrs Campbell's explication of the "feminine style" in oratory to the demands of a telemediated era. On Campbell's reading, "feminine rhetoric" is characterized by critics as inductive, working from example and personal experience; as grounded in proofs constructed from narratives or stories, rather than from deductive premises and models; and as personal and "somewhat tentative" in tone "rather than objective or authoritative."[13] Where such traits may have put their possessors at a disadvantage in an earlier age, Jamieson contends, they are ideally suited to mass-mediated communication. Additional benefits to the feminine style include an ability to convey emotion openly, a willingness to engage in self-disclosure, and a skill in maintaining harmony and well-being in a group.[14] Such a communicative style was not only an asset but also essential in attempting to restore public faith in a process responsible for experimental research practices that defied credulity.[15]

It was O'Leary's style from the outset, when she assumed the burden of leadership for the administration. Sen. Joseph Lieberman (D-CT) made clear O'Leary's prominence when she appeared before the Senate Government Affairs Committee on January 25, 1994, to testify on radiation experimentation. "I associate myself with the remarks that you've made," Lieberman said in his opening statement,

> and I think it's important for us to thank you and note your early and aggressive interest in this general subject of the effect of the nuclear age on people and particularly with regard to testing. You've been way out in front on this, and I'm glad that we finally have somebody on the other side of Pennsylvania Avenue who is equally concerned about this. I join with everybody in complimenting Secretary O'Leary on her leadership here. I think if they gave a Nobel Prize for guts in government, I would nominate you and I hope you would win it. You've given splendid and very moral public service here.[16]

Despite such praise, O'Leary approached her task with a clear sense of the enormity of the challenge. The "clear fact is," she said of the Department of Energy's past practices and her dissatisfaction with them, "that it doesn't change overnight just because a little old lady in tennis shoes at the top has decided that it should change."[17] Rather than saying what "should change," O'Leary set about to ascertain the extent of the challenge, to establish a clear line of response, and to work with affected parties to pursue the response. A facilitative leadership resulted, beginning with O'Leary's appearance at the December 7, 1993, press conference.

Graphs, illustrations, and charts accompanied the secretary's presentation. In addition to the thematic poster that defined the session—"The Cold War Is Over . . . We're Coming Clean"—seventeen topical visual aids reinforced the claims advanced. Each supporting visual carried a recurring heading, capital white letters on a dark background: BREAKING THE SILENCE. Perhaps none were as meaningful to O'Leary as two that came into play relatively late in her formal announcement. She called attention to the chart:

The secretary of energy's advisory committee, in the summer of 1992, did a survey on trust and confidence of the Department of Energy in regards to environmental restoration and waste management. . . . I'm not pleased to tell you that when the question was asked, "Do you trust and have confidence in the headquarters of the Department of Energy?" the only thing that kept us from being at the bottom of the barrel was the Congress of the United States of America. [scattered laughter] The media was [*sic*] a little ahead of us, and that's a good piece. . . . The true fact of the matter is where we want to be is on top. One of the ways we can get there is through this effort and others where we deliver what you need.[18]

Illuminating O'Leary's words was a bar graph labeled "Measuring Trust," which identified fourteen government agencies from "most trustworthy" to "least trustworthy." Rated on a five-part scale with levels of confidence ranging from "none" to "high," the National Academy of Sciences ranked first, and was the only agency with marks placing it between the two highest possible levels. A striking combination of the military, environmental groups, utilities, and banks completed the top five, and banks rated only between the second and third levels, a remarkable commentary on Americans' trust in public institutions. DOE Headquarters just edged Congress in the final two spots, both being judged at the lower end of the scale between the choices of "none" and "some."[19]

While vowing to bring forth the information necessary to improve the agency's credibility, O'Leary also employed visuals to establish the extent of DOE's task. "I want to leave you with a sense of what we're up against," she said, pointing to a sketch labeled "A Monumental Task." The "picture of the Washington Monument is to inform you that there are some 32 million pages of information documents being archived in the Department of Energy or at the National Archives or at other sites which are now subject to this review as we move through declassification." O'Leary gestured to the visual, on which two images dominated the left half. One image was the Washington Monument, surrounded by U.S. flags and carrying the caption, "555 Feet." Next to the monument were pages of documents piled atop one another, the top one marked "Secret" at both the top and bottom margins. The caption: "1 Million Pages." A three-part equation, in bold print, occupied the visual's right half: 32 Million Pages = 32 Washington Monuments = 3 Miles. "To put that in some perspective," the secretary noted, "it's 32 Washington Monuments, and it's three miles worth of data."[20] The goal established, O'Leary advanced the case in a fashion suitable for a facilitative leader, a fashion characterized by careful use of emotion, an emphasis on disclosure, and a reliance on proof by illustration and example.

O'Leary employed two tactics to engage directly the emotional feature of the "feminine style." First, in two early appearances she sought to establish a decidedly unsensational tone for her presentations. Second, at the same time, she turned the potential perceived negative of emotionalism into an asset. On December 7 she established a tone aimed at marking her role as a conduit of what DOE investigations revealed: "The idea here is to wrestle down what we know and then to give it to the public. I'm attempting not to be sensational. I'm also attempting to balance out the clear needs of the family involved and the public's desire to know." Despite her explicit intentions, however, the nature of the work could not help but affect compassionate beings, as she remarked before the Senate Government Affairs Committee the following month. In deciding to pursue the investigation, she testified, she considered the likely accusations that would follow. Yet the case itself demanded that she act. O'Leary "thought of the fact that in opening Pandora's Box, people would think that I was anti-science and technology, which could not be further from the truth, and [neither is it so], as has been the case mentioned often, that I'm far too emotional for this job. I believe that it is the emotion that leads to the very humanness that causes us all to be concerned about the allegations."[21]

O'Leary had expressed her own concern in December. "I would like to tell you," she announced at the initial news conference, "that what I've been told about these experiments, what I know and have processed with respect to these 18 citizens of our country, leave me both appalled, shocked, and deeply saddened." The humanness alluded to surfaced especially, she continued, in considering the impact of radiation tests on families. O'Leary was "constantly reminded of a comment by a daughter of one of the patients, who said her father would probably have known more—as much—about ice cream as he knew about plutonium if it was shared with him, as she believes, that he was to undergo plutonium experiments."[22] At issue was whether subjects had been administered tests with their consent, and even if consent had been obtained, whether the information provided truly constituted informed consent. By the standards of 1993, O'Leary concluded after DOE's research, consent followed the provision of partial information, at best. But the standards in place at the time of the experiments were exceptional, due to the exceptional circumstance of the cold war.

The cold war's demise, she maintained, demanded new standards. Part of her task was to disclose the benchmark from which DOE would operate henceforth. O'Leary demonstrated a facilitative leadership based in part on disclosure when she observed that the "startling fact is that so many, 20 percent of our tests, were unannounced. . . . There were 985 total nuclear tests; there were some 204, which were kept secret. And what I'm learning from people who were in the community is that that is a shock because, quite frankly, people thought there were 50 percent fewer." The secretary of energy thus acknowledged that even people in the organization had been deceived. While some might resist such openness for fear of being perceived as not in control, O'Leary used the revelation to link DOE's own interest with those of the public. We "have got to begin to start to grapple . . . as a nation" with the question of the ultimate disposal of plutonium in the United States, O'Leary said, noting that the issue was one on which "I intend to inform and to generate a lot of public debate . . . this year." An essential first step was to establish a benchmark of what information would be provided. In contrast to past practices of protecting all information, with the burden of proof falling to those who demanded disclosure, O'Leary intended to disclose information, with the burden of proof falling to those who would conceal data. The government, in O'Leary's words, ought to release "as much as we can to inform, to enlarge the debate and the opportunity for an energy source of the future, but not so much as to cause concerns about proliferation. So, look for that as a benchmark."[23]

With that starting point in mind, DOE had already commenced action. Although the atomic testing obviously preceded the Clinton administration's assumption of power, the issue's urgency compelled O'Leary and her staff to do "a great deal of both correcting the public perception and informing about what has occurred. Accordingly, we've had conversations with a world-renowned ethicist, Dr. [Ruth] Faden, and what she has agreed to do at the University of Maryland is to undertake to examine the records of these 18 people who were subject to experimentation over time, carefully review the records, ensure that we are releasing in detail after reviewing what actually happened." Inviting independent review thus reaffirmed DOE's pledge of disclosure and openness with the American people.[24]

Finally, induction and example constituted O'Leary's primary means of support as she took her case to the public. A first step was to place testing in the context of the cold war. "I guess those who've dealt with the Department [of Energy] over time would know the history, but let me weave it just a bit. One must go back to 1942 or 3 and certainly to the early days of the Atomic Energy Commission and remember where we were." Such recollection would reveal the United States "in a struggle for survival as a nation, and national security was at the heart of everything that happened in the Department. . . . The work to produce that atomic bomb was thought to be—and most of us understand was—the core, really, to ending World War II." Following the war, the goal was to retain superiority over the Soviet Union, and as a consequence DOE became "shrouded and clouded in an atmosphere of secrecy. And I would even take a step further—I would call it repression."[25] While historical example thus dictated extreme measures, the post–cold war age required a radical reversal of policy.

O'Leary turned to DOE's plan for "coming clean," a plan reinforced by the inductive practice of illustration. In documenting both the extent of the problem she and her staff encountered and the benefits arising from a policy of openness and citizen participation, O'Leary turned to illustrations to make complex data accessible. That the United States produced 89 metric tons of plutonium between 1945 and 1988, for example, would likely mean little to the vast majority of auditors. When visualizations reinforced the explanations, however, the information gained clarity. A map of the United States labeled "Total U.S. Weapons Plutonium Production (1945–1988)" not only identified production centers but also attached sheer figures to images (cities) with which auditors might better identify. Two cities were identified with the original project, Hanford, Washington, and Savannah, Georgia. The plutonium story continued with a second map labeled "Plutonium Inventories Today." The United States held 33.5 metric tons in December, 1993, at five locations other than Hanford and Savannah. Potentially affected regions in addition to the Northwest and Southeast included the Rocky Mountains, the Southwest, and the South. To make the metric ton figures meaningful, a chart showed that 1 metric ton of plutonium equals approximately 166 nuclear warheads, which is enough energy to power and light a city of 100,000 for a year.

Inductive argument by illustration thus merged with attention to emotion and a strategy of disclosure in her initial press conference to define O'Leary's facilitative leadership style. The style proved well suited for her initial encounter with nuclear stakeholders the following month.

O'Leary Meets the Stakeholders: Doing Public Business in Public

The demise of public trust in democratic institutions, leading to a cultural cynicism in which Americans have come to "hate politics," is well established.[26] That skepticism undoubtedly influenced Heidi Carter of the American Peace Test in Las Vegas. "I don't feel knowing about 204 tests does much to erase past lies," Carter observed in response to O'Leary's December 7 news conference. "I hope this is the beginning of real accountability." Carter's hesitation is understandable given the government's historic treatment of affected citizens, particularly those known as "downwinders."[27] O'Leary not only aspired to "real accountability" but also was determined that the stakeholders involved be instrumental in the accounting process.

Such instrumentality is informed by Michael Halloran's notion of the rhetorical dimensions of public proceedings. By a public proceeding, Halloran

> mean[s] an official business session of a representative body, including debate and decision on specific issues, conducted before an audience made up of members of the body's constituency. The body may be representative in a strict elective sense, . . . or in some wider sense. . . . In any event, the members of the audience have a real interest in the outcome of the body's deliberations. Because matters of consequence to them are at stake, they are rhetorically *available*. The public proceeding thus serves a dual purpose: it settles whatever matters are before the body, just as a similar proceeding held in closed session would; it shapes the views of the audience directly, as a proceeding held in private could not. [The primary function of the audience in this conception of a public proceeding is] to witness.[28]

In contrast to such a perspective on audiences as passive participants in the process, stakeholders' sessions sponsored by DOE aimed to establish a forum that, ostensibly, would lead to action. Participants were thus at once observers, as Halloran would have it, and active agents of change. What made the system appear to work, at least in the context of DOE sessions, was that Energy Secretary O'Leary listened. Because her leadership style aspired to facilitate and generate public discussion rather than to move deliberations to a predetermined conclusion, she deferred to those testifying, enabling the public to become advocates as well as auditors.

An essential first step for bringing the theory into action was to establish who the stakeholders were. O'Leary's was an expansive view of whom to define as affected agents. But by casting the net widely, DOE strategy ensured soliciting sufficiently diverse viewpoints that a close approximation to the truth might emerge from deliberations. "In order to make some sense" of the 32 million pages of documents to be examined, she said on December 7, "we need to focus on what stakeholders need and want, and a priority to be delivered." She continued:

> I've attempted to identify the stakeholders, and likely I've left some out. Clearly, historians. Clearly, people involved in issues involving the health and safety of people in nearby communities and our workers. Clearly those in the environmental community. Clearly those involved in issues of nonproliferation. And clearly, and clearly, a very broad group of people who have an interest in this information. We're going to have what I've

been calling a stakeholders' work session in February to try and outline, among all of those interests, how we prioritize the information that will now come forward to informed debate and to give us a correct posture as we move forward on nonproliferation.[29]

The first work session took place instead on January 11, 1994, at the Sheraton Palace Hotel in San Francisco. Sixty-three people spoke. DOE representatives opened the meeting, providing an overview of recent agency actions and proposing possible guidelines for the open discussion sessions. Throughout the introduction, staff members repeatedly emphasized the tentativeness of their suggestions and the process's openness to collective revision by the body. Then stakeholders were invited to speak. They included—in categories that are obviously not mutually exclusive—scientists such as Edward Teller, environmentalists, residents of communities near atomic research facilities, antinuclear advocates, and representatives from the Livermore Conversion Project and Psychologists for Social Responsibility, among others.

The focus here is on O'Leary's interactions with the stakeholders, which demonstrate how her leadership style facilitated moving the public proceeding from an informational forum to a potential deliberative body. What began as an inclusive session to solicit diverse viewpoints soon became a case study in collective agenda setting, wherein antinuclear advocates' concerns increasingly dominated both discussion and decision. Through what were intended as brief introductions, antinuclear stakeholders established their collective doubt about the need for nuclear research, delineated the impact of government programs on the environment, and narrated the human suffering created by radiation experiments. Once the participants' stories were in place, a designated stakeholder summarized results of preceding discussions. The summary constituted an action agenda to be carried out by DOE, an agenda O'Leary committed to in ways unanticipated by stakeholders. The result was a movement toward a restored trust in DOE, a result directly attributable to O'Leary's consultative style.

Because of scheduling conflicts, O'Leary arrived about a third of the way into the meeting, following the staff overview. Marylia Kelley of Livermore's Tri-Valley CAREs, working with DOE declassification director Bryan Siebert, introduced the meeting's procedural plan just prior to O'Leary's arrival. The public meeting, she noted, followed and **preceded small group sessions designed to foster citizen action. The objective, she stated, was to depend "on what's called the 'social contract' very strongly." Kelley elaborated the concept upon O'Leary's arrival. She told the secretary that a "number of citizens' groups and radiation survivors met last night and, if this meets with your approval, we would like to begin the meeting by going around the table, each person introducing themselves and maybe summarizing a main point in one sentence and rely on the social contract in terms of the number of people at the table and the number of minutes in an hour." That "seems fine," O'Leary responded. "I've come to listen." To complete the process, Kelley added, one person would "summarize some things at the end and then the idea is to go into a more broad roundtable discussion at the point. Would you like to begin?"[30]

The process ostensibly called for descriptive introductions, as with the secretary's own: "I'm Hazel O'Leary, recently of Washington, D.C., born in Newport News, Virginia, Secretary of Energy, 56- year-old widow, mother of one child, and off and on a servant of government." Two members of O'Leary's staff followed with similar introductions. The meeting's tenor gradually shifted, however, as subsequent speakers not only identified themselves but advanced the issues of primary concern to them. One urged consideration of how openness might reverse the economic decline attendant to extant secrecy policies, while Edward Teller, speaking fifth, called for an accelerated exchange of information with the Soviet Union and disclosure of the United States' open skies policies. Fred Allingham, executive director of the National Association of Radiation Survivors, followed by stating that his mission was to "be sure that all the citizens of this country who were exposed to radiation are represented in the declassification process."

Three of the next thirteen statements signaled the session's transformation from discussion session to a deliberative body driven by polemic. The three statements specified the doubts citizens had in the viability of the atomic energy program, the environmental harm attributable to atomic research, and the misery the nuclear enterprise caused test victims. David Hartsough of the Livermore Conversion Project followed Allingham. Members of the Livermore Project, Hartsough declared, "believe that the nuclear weapons mission is incompatible with openness and therefore we call on you to stop the research, design, testing and production of nuclear weapons [applause] and convert the labs from developing weapons of mass destruction to developing technologies that will prepare the United States and the world for an environmentally sound and sustainable 21st century. [applause]"

Ken Butigan of the Nevada Desert Experience spoke shortly after Hartsough. In an extremely long statement, given the intended function of the discourses, Butigan focused on the environmental impact of testing, and called for a "truth commission" to ensure that such deleterious policies were not repeated in the promised new era of disclosure. Butigan identified the Nevada Desert Project as an enterprise which has brought thousands of people to the Nevada Test Site to see for themselves the desecration of the land that belongs to the Western Shoshone Nation, and we call for the return of that land in a restored state, in cooperation with the Nation, to the Nation. We also call today, because, as we know, the United States government has lied about this process over the last 50 years—this 50-year human experimentation— and so we call for the creation of a "truth commission" which would be composed of citizens' groups, radiation survivors and the general public as well as disinterested scientists, that is, scientists, who have not worked at places like Livermore National Laboratory, to oversee and participate in the declassification of all documents related to health, safety and environmental impacts on U.S. citizens on the Western Shoshone Nation, and on people around the world. This, of course, will call for access and review of all documents in the DOE, the Department of Defense, and the CIA in order to find out what we really know about those impacts. [applause]

June Stark Casey added to the stakeholders' grievances with the story of her own experience. Observing that she thought she was the only direct radiation victim to testify, Casey concurred with an earlier claim that "we are all victims" of nuclear testing. Her specific role in San Francisco was to represent "several hundred thousand Hanford downwinders" who were subjected to 7,780 curies of radioactive iodine and 20,000 curies of xenon in the "green run" of 1949. Casey's story stood in symbolic representation of their collective experience:

> Also I would like to say . . . what happened to me when I was a student at Whitman College. I developed severe hypothyroidism. I began to lose my hair and, as a you can see, this is a photo the year before the green run experiment; now I have to wear a wig as a result of that. I had a breast lumpectomy. I've had skin cancer and lost two babies, a stillbirth and a miscarriage. And I did testify about this in 1989 at the U.S. House of Representatives almost five years ago. I did request at that time to learn the purpose of this experiment because some people believe possibly this experiment that was released on December 2–3, 1949, the purpose was to test the effects of radiation on local populations.

Yet Casey was not blaming Secretary O'Leary for the past. Rather she thanked her profusely for providing hope for the future. After mentioning two additional atomic controversies she hoped would be investigated—General Curtis Lemay's conduct of radiological warfare experiments at Hanford until 1954, and the alleged abduction of a woman in Delaware who was subjected to psychiatric tests that resulted in a twelve year memory loss—Casey closed with homage to O'Leary's leadership: "So, thank you again, you really are a living example of Gandhi's words, that one person can gently shake the world. Thank God for you. Thank you. [applause]" Four other stakeholders spoke after June Stark Casey, but the combined appeals of Hartsough, Butigan, and Casey crystallized the stakeholders' argument, at least from the perspective of nuclear opponents.

Marylia Kelley, who shared discussion coordination responsibilities, was the last to introduce herself before O'Leary attempted to summarize what she had heard and commented on what she hoped to accomplish. In her brief statement, O'Leary accepted responsibility for guiding what lay ahead but called on stakeholders to assume a share of the burden as well. Responding to Casey's contention that "we are all victims," O'Leary suggested that "we're also victims [of] our distrust of one another. Some have said—and I mean to speak to that directly—that this is a P.R. effort. It's not. It's about our future; it's about the survival of a nation; it's about the survival of our children; and it's about building a world that allows us to go forward." That can be done, she asserted, only if government agencies and affected citizens work in concert. O'Leary pledged that she and her staff would start the process, but she warned that without citizen involvement the efforts could not thrive. Participants will disagree, and may "be so spitting mad with each other that we won't be able to think or spit it out well. But we must continue and we must work [through] this process together." What drove O'Leary, she concluded, was an emotional fire that demanded action. "I've been accused of being emotional; I am. I'm very emotional about this issue and I think everyone in this room is, and what we must do now is build enough trust in order to work with one another . . . after the glare of these lights and these words [fades]."

Fred Allingham spoke for a majority of stakeholders, though his recitation of the diverse groups' calls for action reflected the dominance of antinuclear voices. Allingham thanked O'Leary, was interrupted by applause in the process, and then confided to the secretary that the group had "cautious optimism in our next step, and obviously a large dose of skepticism since our relationship with the DOE has not been good in the past." Eight action steps by the secretary might help diminish the skepticism: (1) an immediate moratorium on shredding, (2) an indexing of all documents held by DOE, (3) an increase in the number of staff positions assigned to declassification, (4) establishment of a "truth commission" for citizen oversight in the declassification process, (5) the release of current and projected budgets, (6) a broadening of the scope of DOE's radiation exposures program, (7) release of the "lead laboratory" plan, and (8) elimination of a DOE system in place that allowed for the sequestering of unclassified data. O'Leary's responses ranged from "I commit to do that" on demands within her charge to meet to "I can commit for me; I will negotiate with my colleagues" when decisions involved other agencies.

Two exchanges that occurred late in O'Leary's participation indicated both the extent to which stakeholders had become defined primarily as nuclear opposition and the level of identification that had developed between stakeholders and O'Leary. It was an identification, moreover, attributed directly to O'Leary's facilitative leadership style. That antinuclear activists dominated the session's proposed actions became clear when Fred Allingham concluded his presentation. Edward Teller spoke after Allingham. He contended that misinformation was as much an enemy of the process as the suppression of information. Although he agreed that citizens subjected to radiation tests should be so informed, he also believed that they should be advised that radiation within certain levels is no more harmful than what "everybody is exposed to every day." A telling exchange ensued:

> Voice, calling out: Liar!
> Teller: Thank you very much for your kind, unemotional remark!
> Voice: Liar!
> Teller: Thank you again. Miss Secretary, I think information is most important. Understanding of information is most important. I think comparison with background is a first step. But I think there has been as much damage done by misleading information through various people than there has been done by secrecy. I think openness and clarity of information must be pursued.

To the majority in attendance, openness was clarity of information. That Teller was a lone voice urging moderation and balance quickly became clear when participation was opened to audience members whose initial role had entailed only observation.

Anne Herbert, identifying herself as "a social change activist and a writer," directed her words to O'Leary's leadership style, a style grounded in compassion. Herbert cited a *New York Times* story shortly after the first revelations of medical experimentation appeared, a story quoting O'Leary as "heartsick" at the news. A second line from the story had O'Leary saying, "It seems to me that my position ought to be, what does it take to make these people whole?" Observed Herbert: "That's a style of leadership that could possibly save the world. It's coming from a different place and I really appreciate it." Following applause for O'Leary, Herbert continued, citing Carol Gilligan's work at

Harvard on leadership styles to help explain her point. What O'Leary offered was a "moral leadership" based on a concern for "what is actually happening to people." The secretary's predecessors, on the other hand, practiced a leadership that dictated that "it's morally okay if it follows the rules." There is, Herbert maintained, "a gender division here." And she concluded: "I couldn't imagine being morally inspired by the person who is in charge of the Los Alamos labs. I can't tell you how weird that is. And I really appreciate it and I'd like to support you not only in what you're doing but in your decision-making style, which I think is vital for the survival of the world. Thank you. [applause]"

Fittingly, O'Leary's participation in the stakeholders meeting closed as she expressed appreciation for Herbert's kind words. But both sides had exchanged more than words, for the ideas expressed led to a plan of action produced cooperatively in the public forum.

Ethics, Rhetoric, and Public Policy

The Clinton presidency thus engaged wisely the rhetorical crisis posed by revelations about America's secret nuclear testing program, assigning Hazel O'Leary to lead the government's response. The choice proved inspired, suggesting that surrogate rhetoricians may function constructively and actively in administrative rhetoric. O'Leary's temperament, discursive habits, and leadership style matched remarkably well the exigencies of the task at hand. She articulated the administration's distress with the breadth and depth of the government's cold war secrecy, vowed to act, and moved forward in cooperation with stakeholders to right a perceived wrong. An active role for stakeholders was essential to an effective response.[31]

Hence, beginning with the January 11, 1994, meeting in San Francisco, O'Leary assumed the role of a discussion facilitator, the better to generate constructive audience comment and argument. The strategy aimed to empower a public disaffected by democratic institutions, misled and misinformed by leaders entrusted with their welfare. Resulting stakeholder involvement commends the possibility of "doing public business in public," outside of the limited (and limiting) range of formal public proceedings. An empowered public of stakeholders and a nurturing leader in O'Leary combine, in turn, to reaffirm the mutual interdependence of the rhetorical, the political, and the ethical in the making of public policy. Joseph Nye is instructive in the ethics of political deliberation.

In *Nuclear Ethics* Nye engages the moral issues that in part divided, and continue to divide, participants in the debates over atomic testing. Nye, the Ford Foundation Professor of Security Affairs at Harvard and the director of the Center for Science and International Affairs at the Kennedy School of Government, bases his treatment of the complicated ethical problems on his research as well as his experience as a former undersecretary of state for Security Assistance. He thus brings to the task what might be termed the diplomat's penchant for the pragmatic and the academician's passion for the abstract ideal. The two impulses merit note, for they help explain the perspectives from which Energy Secretary Hazel O'Leary and the atomic age stakeholders operated, on the one hand, and the motivations that drove American science and technology during the cold war, on the other.

Nye proposes a "three-dimensional ethics" designed to accommodate two competing traditions in ethics and moral reasoning, an ethics of consequences and an ethics of virtue.[32] An ethics of consequences derives from the teachings of Jeremy Bentham and John Stuart Mill. Essential questions to determine the efficacy of a selected course focus on results: Did the policy achieve what was intended? In the process did the result equate to the greatest good for the greatest number? Practitioners of this social utilitarian ethics of consequences are not amoral or unethical. Rather, they weigh the ethical dimensions of their ideas and actions in terms that recognize that all policies may entail risks, may create harm as well as benefits, may prove counterproductive to the few while working to the benefit of the many.

An ethics of consequences clearly guided, or at least influenced, the thinking of cold war scientists, many of whom remained perplexed by the level of controversy generated by later revelations about nuclear testing. In June, 1994, Secretary O'Leary released the second wave of previously classified documents. In reporting her news conference statement and discussion of June 27, television network news turned to one group of stakeholders that had been represented in a distinct minority, at least in the January 11 public meeting. O'Leary intended for scientists and technologists to be part of the discussion from the outset, but as the vocal chastisement of Edward Teller at the first meeting revealed, antinuclear voices held sway. In contrast, CNN turned to scientists and their families in preparing viewers for the June 27 announcement.

CNN Daybreak, broadcast at 8:00 A.M. EST, carried a report by Miles O'Brien, who interviewed three participants in the testing program. Each indicated a trust in the doctors and researchers who urged their cooperation in the project, a trust that remained despite recent controversies:

> Miles O'Brien: When Julie Grilly first came to Los Alamos, birthplace of the atomic bomb, it was 1947. The nuclear genie was fresh out of the bottle and no one, not even the scientists who built the bomb, knew for sure what radiation might do to humans.

Julie Grilly: You know, we were at war and in the aftermath of the war, and I think they wanted to find out a lot of information.

O'Brien: The best way to do that? Conduct tests on human subjects. That's how Julie Grilly, a lab technician, became a nuclear guinea pig. A scientist was looking for volunteers to take capsules containing radioactive fallout particles. When you were approached, were you concerned about this in any way?

Grilly: Oh no.

O'Brien: Why not?

Grilly: Because I trust the people implicitly, no problem.

Glessie Drake, a lab technician who took a radioactive isotope, agreed. "Most of the doctors that I worked with took the same isotopes that I did," she recalled. "They were just doing science. Good science." Added Don Ott, "I don't think we did it for patriotism. We just did it 'cause we're in the business, science. Just part of a team." Philip Reilly, a lawyer and medical doctor offering authoritative testimony on the ethical issues raised by the subjects' uninformed consent, assessed the experimentation process from a decidedly consequential perspective: "The good derived from these experiments, in the context of the day, far outweighed any small criticisms I would make of the technicalities about how consent was or was not obtained." Affected subjects concurred with Reilly:

O'Brien: Everyone we spoke with at Los Alamos says they felt no ill effects from the radiation testing. Many of them are angry at the way the story has been portrayed.

Grilly: I'm sure any of us that participated the first time would participate again on them. In a moment.

Drake: You've taken my heroes and done bad things to them. These are my heroes.

O'Brien: They haven't gotten a fair deal.

Drake: That's right.

O'Brien: Heroes, villains, or just scientists doing their job. They say they should be judged in the context of those urgent times, not by the standards of today.[33]

Tom Smith proved less sympathetic to the researchers than Grilly, Drake, and Ott, however. More than thirty years earlier, while he was in the navy, Smith and other sailors witnessed at least seventeen nuclear explosions in the Pacific. Smith told WUSA-TV in Washington, D.C.: "I was 19 [or] 20 years old and it was a great time, to be perfectly honest. It was pretty neat. But no one ever explained to us that we were going to have these problems in later life."[34] Operating from an ethics of consequences, nuclear researchers coped with the admittedly serious effects of radiation on Smith and his shipmates by averring that the long-term benefits of scientific investigation more than countered the unfortunate losses experienced by the few.

Practitioners of what Nye calls an ethics of virtue, juxtaposed to the adherents of an ethics of consequences, are less willing to accept a moral vision that accommodates disadvantages, even to the few. This tradition, attributed to the influence of Immanuel Kant and focused on the participants' motives for action rather than the outcomes, inheres in the belief that rules and laws must guide what are acceptable human behaviors. Such rules dictate what constitutes good or bad behavior, right or wrong actions, just or unjust policies, and so on. Violations of the rules are unacceptable, regardless of the potential benefits to the majority. This perspective largely encompasses the worldview of the stakeholders and, at least in her public statements, the secretary of energy. O'Leary and others speaking on behalf of DOE consistently acknowledge that "20–20 hindsight" and the application of post–cold war morality to cold war practices are problematic. Nonetheless, her utterance in the first accountability press conference in December 1993 that she was "appalled, shocked, and deeply saddened" by what she had learned, intimates that she was not equally moved by the argument that there was enough to be learned from medical experimentation to warrant the secrecy practiced. The stakeholders' claims in public meetings, particularly those advanced by activists and residents of affected sites, indicate a clear public alliance with O'Leary.

Yet the ethical issues of the testing controversy are not easily resolved simply by differentiating the "good" from the "bad." Neither O'Leary nor ardent antinuclear advocates would likely condemn research essential to deterring the enemy in World War II or maintaining the peace in its aftermath. As Nye observes, both ethical traditions present puzzles not easily resolved by the simple rejection of one in favor of the other. Consider the quandary created, Nye explains, by a hypothetical case in which a gunman holds two hostages. Adherents to an ethics of virtue plead for the release of the hostages, arguing to the gunman that "killing is wrong." The gunman counters by offering to release one hostage, on the condition that one of those morally opposed to killing take the life of the other. While the proposition might be rejected if a single life is at stake, Nye continues, at what point does even the most vigorous proponent of virtue begin to consider consequences? What if the gunman's hostages numbered 100 or 1,000, and the proposition remained the same: one life taken for 99 saved? Or 999?[35]

Nye offers a scheme for engaging such dilemmas, one that aims to accommodate both ethical traditions. More importantly for critics and theorists of public communication, it is an analytical scheme consonant with the divergent rhetorics generated by the secret atomic testing controversy examined here. Those rhetorics entail, on one hand, the public communication style evinced in O'Leary's performances in news conferences, stakeholders meetings, and congressional hearings. That style consists in working inductively from the evidence of the cases at hand, employing narratives as proof, a willingness to share emotional responses to distressing data, and deferring to an active audience—particularly the stakeholders—rather than attempting to control the flow of information. On the other hand, scientists and other architects of the cold war take umbrage at negative depictions of their intentions and their work. Pointing to the exceptional circumstances that drove them, they hold that exceptional times required exceptional measures. The long-range impact of their studies, furthermore, promised benefits that clearly outweighed short-term harms.

Nye proposes a "three-dimensional ethics" designed to take advantage of the strengths of both ethical systems. Rather than juxtaposing consequences to motives, Nye incorporates both into a system that also requires attention to means. Thus, for any given controversy, the disputants' motives for action, means for pursuing their goals, and prospective consequences of their deeds must be taken into account. Essential to the scheme's success is appreciating its inexactness, understanding that each component must be weighed and assessed, while recognizing that a mathematically based or rational world solution to a dispute may not be possible. Although Nye does not address the issue in these terms, of course, it is a scheme that recognizes, perhaps even favors, the strengths of the public argument style evinced by Secretary O'Leary and in the stakeholders' discussions. And it is in this interface of rhetoric, ethics, and politics, finally, that the value of studying this telling moment in presidential communication resides.[36]

Notes

1. Kirkpatrick Sale, for example, identifies the tenuous link between technological progress and human health and safety as the second of three discernible dimensions of the environmental movement that emerged from 1960s activism. See Sale, *The Green Revolution: The American Environmental Movement, 1962–1992* (New York: Hill and Wang, 1993), 14–27. Also illuminating on the same point, albeit in quite a different fashion, are Robert Gottlieb, *Forcing the Spring: The Transformation of the American Environmental Movement* (Washington, D.C.: Island Press, 1993), 177–84, and Steven B. Katz and Carolyn R. Miller, "The Low-Level Radioactive Waste Siting Controversy in North Carolina: Toward a Rhetorical Model of Risk Communication," in *Green Culture: Environmental Rhetoric in Contemporary America*, ed. Carl G. Herndl and Stuart C. Brown (Madison: University of Wisconsin Press, 1996), 111–40.

2. This overview is drawn from data in Keith Rogers, "Critics Charge DOE Still Distorting Test Information," *Las Vegas Review-Journal*, Dec. 8, 1993, 3A; Keith Rogers and Tony Batt, "U.S. Discloses Nuke Tests," *Las Vegas Review-Journal*, Dec. 8, 1993; Martin Walker, "Racing toward Destruction," *Los Angeles Times*, Dec. 12, 1993, Book Review, sec., 1; and "Dirty Little Secrets of the Atomic Age," *Newsweek*, Dec. 20, 1993, 37.

3. Judith S. Trent and Robert V. Friedenberg provide a useful introduction to the use of surrogates in campaigns in *Political Campaign Communication: Principles and Practices*, 4th ed. (New York: Praeger, 2000).

4. Robert E. Denton, Jr., and Gary C. Woodward, *Political Communication in America*, 3d ed. (New York: Praeger, 1998).

5. Exemplary studies are Denise M. Bostdorff, *The Presidency and the Rhetoric of Foreign Crisis* (Columbia: University of South Carolina Press, 1994), and Amos Kiewe, ed., *The Modern Presidency and Crisis Rhetoric* (New York: Praeger, 1994).

6. The post–cold war emphasis on accountability, openness, and disclosure contrasts sharply with the rhetorical practices of administrations in place throughout the cold war, as Martin J. Medhurst, Robert L. Ivie, Philip Wander, and Robert L. Scott explain in *Cold War Rhetoric: Strategy, Metaphor, and Ideology* (New York: Greenwood, 1990). See also Martin J. Medhurst and H. W. Brands, eds., *Critical Reflections on the Cold War: Linking Rhetoric and History* (College Station: Texas A&M University Press, 2000), and Bryan C. Taylor and Stephen J. Hartnett, "'National Security, and All That It Implies . . .': Communication and (Post–)Cold War Culture," *Quarterly Journal of Speech* 86 (2000): 465–87.

7. Indicative are Jeffrey Tulis, *The Rhetorical Presidency* (Princeton, N.J.: Princeton University Press, 1987); Roderick P. Hart, *The Sound of Leadership: Presidential Communication in the Modern Age* (Chicago: University of Chicago Press, 1987); David Zarefsky, *President Johnson's War on Poverty: Rhetoric and History* (University: University of Alabama Press, 1986), esp. 8–11; and relevant chapters in *Beyond the Rhetorical Presidency*, ed. Martin J. Medhurst (College Station: Texas A&M University Press, 1996).

8. Three primary articles by Eileen Welsome, "Elmer Allen Loses His Leg—And All Hope," "Even in Death, Albert's Still Their Guinea Pig," and "'Do You Suppose the Stuff Did Anything to Me?'" appeared Nov. 15–17, 1993, in the *Albuquerque Tribune*. Overwhelming interest in the articles led the newspaper to combine them in a special publication, "The Plutonium Experiments." Additional

articles included "The Chronological Story, 1941–1991," "The Minds behind the Experiment," "Descriptions of 18 Patients Injected with Plutonium," "Radiation Killed Doctors Who Did Human Experiments," "Experiments Were Conducted in Shadow of Nuremberg Trials," and "`My God, Where's the Humanity?'"

9. Arjun Makhijani, "Energy Enters Guilty Plea," *Bulletin of the Atomic Scientists* (March–April, 1994): 18–28.

10. "News Conference with Energy Secretary Hazel O'Leary," Dec. 7, 1993, Federal News Service transcript, 7, 13. Transcript provided by the Department of Energy, July 13, 1994.

11. In similar fashion, Bryan Taylor's research on women in the nuclear weapons organization necessitates reconceptualizing both the dynamics of such organizations and the nature of nuclear history. See Taylor, "Register of the Repressed: Women's Voice and Body in the Nuclear Weapons Organization," *Quarterly Journal of Speech* 79 (1993): 267–85, and "Organizing the 'Unknown Subject': Los Alamos, Espionage, and the Politics of Biography," *Quarterly Journal of Speech* 88 (2002): 33–49.

12. Kathleen Hall Jamieson, *Eloquence in an Electronic Age: The Transformation of Political Speechmaking* (Oxford and New York: Oxford University Press, 1988), 89, 182–200.

13. Cited in Jamieson, *Eloquence,* 75–76.

14. Jamieson, *Eloquence,* 81–82. Jamieson addresses the issue of whether "men and women are naturally disposed to different communicative styles." She explains several reasons why this "is difficult to ascertain." Still, she concludes, "Whatever their cause, and despite the fact that the assertiveness of female speakers is on the rise, gender-associated differences remain" (81).

15. For an examination of how the feminine style can function to create audiences and thus "accord value to a feminist epistemology," see Sonja K. Foss and Karen A. Foss, "The Construction of Feminine Spectatorship in Garrison Keillor's Radio Monologues," *Quarterly Journal of Speech* 80 (1994): 410–26. From another perspective, O'Leary's leadership depended in part on a "communitarian language," which contrasted sharply with the "managerial language" of government regulators and the "pluralist language" of policy makers and academicians. Communitarian prose, write Bruce Williams and Albert Matheny, presumes "an enlightened citizenry capable of ruling directly through communal forms of democracy." Suspicious of the managerial and pluralist impulse alike, communitarian rhetoric rejects centralization of political authority and emphasizes returning government to the citizenry. See Williams and Matheny, *Democracy, Dialogue, and Environmental Disputes: The Contested Languages of Social Regulations* (New Haven and London: Yale University Press, 1995), 11–30.

16. "Capitol Hill Hearing on Radiation Experimentation," Senate Government Affairs Committee, Jan. 25, 1994, Federal News Service transcript, 4.

17. Hazel O'Leary quoted in "America's Nuclear Shame—Part 5," *CNN News Special,* March 13, 1994, transcript no. 293 (Denver: Journal Graphics), 6.

18. "News Conference with Energy Secretary Hazel O'Leary," Dec. 7, 1993, Federal News Service transcript, 11.

19. In a July 13, 1994, letter to the author, A. Bryan Siebert, director of the Office of Declassification and the Office of Security Affairs in DOE, provided copies of the eighteen visual aids used at the press conference. All data concerning graphics presented by Secretary O'Leary are based on these copies.

20. "News Conference with Energy Secretary," Dec. 7. 1993, 10.
21. Ibid.; "Capitol Hill Hearing on Radiation Experimentation," Jan. 25, 1994, 7.
22. "News Conference with Energy Secretary," Dec. 7, 1993, 9.
23. Ibid., 7–8.
24. Ibid., 9.
25. Ibid., 5.
26. See, for example, Nina Eliasoph, *Avoiding Politics: How Americans Produce Apathy in Everyday Life* (New York: Cambridge University Press, 1998); E. J. Dionne, *Why Americans Hate Politics* (New York: Simon and Schuster, 1991); Robert M. Entman, *Democracy without Citizens: Media and the Decay of American Politics* (New York: Oxford University Press, 1989); and Jeffrey C. Goldfarb, *The Cynical Society: The Culture of Politics and the Politics of Culture in American Life* (Chicago: University of Chicago Press, 1991).
27. Excellent introductions to the downwinders' experience are offered by Stewart L. Udall, *The Myths of August: A Personal Exploration of Our Tragic Cold War Affair with the Atom* (New York: Pantheon Books, 1994), Howard Ball, *Justice Downwind: America's Atomic Testing Program in the 1950s* (New York and Oxford: Oxford University Press, 1986), and Robert A. Divine, *Blowing on the Wind: The Nuclear Test Ban Debate, 1954–1960* (New York: Oxford University Press, 1978).
28. S. Michael Halloran, "Doing Public Business in Public," in *Form and Genre: Shaping Political Action*, ed. Karlyn Kohrs Campbell and Kathleen Hall Jamieson (Falls Church, Va.: Speech Communication Association, 1978), 119–20.
29. "News Conference with Energy Secretary," Dec. 7, 1993, 10.
30. "San Francisco Declassification Stakeholders Meeting," Jan. 11, 1994, Department of Energy transcript. All references to or direct quotation from Stakeholders Meeting discussion are based on the transcript from this session.
31. Throughout 1994 and 1995 O'Leary released updates every six months of DOE's progress in declassifying relevant documents. To verify the department's good faith, she solicited outside advice from the National Academy of Sciences, which formed a panel to evaluate the Openness Project. The panel applauded DOE's "clear commitment to openness" in a twenty-four-page report released in July, 1996: Panel on DOE Declassification Policy and Practice, Committee on International Security and Arms Control, *Review of the Department of Energy's Response to the Recommendations in the National Research Council Study of DOE Declassification Policy and Practice* (Washington, D.C.: National Academy of Sciences, 1996).

    Concurrent with the DOE meetings with stakeholders, President Clinton's Advisory Committee on Human Radiation Experiments examined four thousand documents and heard testimony from more than two hundred witnesses between the time of the committee's formation in April, 1994, and presentation of its final report in October, 1995. Though the committee conceded that the ethical costs of the experiments conducted between 1944 and 1974 were high, the report also found most of the tens of thousands of subjects cannot be located or came to minimal physical harm. See Advisory Committee on Human Radiation Experiments, *The Human Radiation Experiments: Final Report of the President's Advisory Committee* (New York: Oxford University Press, 1996). Danielle Gordon articulates a dissenting view in "The Verdict: No Harm, No Foul," *Bulletin of the Atomic Scientists* (Jan.–Feb., 1996): 32–40.

32. Joseph S. Nye, Jr., *Nuclear Ethics* (New York: Free Press, 1986), 16–21. For a wide range of explorations of parallel issues, see the collected essays in *Classical Virtue, Postmodern Practice,* ed. Robert Hariman (University Park: Pennsylvania State University Press, 2003).

33. *Daybreak,* CNN-TV, June 27, 1994, *Radio-TV Reports* transcript, 1–3.

34. *Eyewitness News,* WUSA-TV, June 27, 1994, *Radio-TV Reports* transcript, 2.

35. Nye, *Nuclear Ethics,* 18–19.

36. From the convergence of the virtue and consequences traditions, Nye proposes five guidelines for "judging moral integrity": (1) standards of clarity, logic, and consistency apply to the articulation of the case; (2) impartiality—respect for the interests of others—is practiced; (3) an initial presumption exists in favor of rules and rights; (4) procedures for protecting impartiality should be in place; (5) prudence is exercised in calculating consequences. These are delineated in *Nuclear Ethics,* 22–26.

PART IV

Presidential

Rhetoric and

Environmental

Governance for

the Twenty-first

Century

9

Topical Analysis and the Problem of Judgment in Environmental Disputes

The Case of Sustainable Forestry in New Hampshire

Lawrence J. Prelli

Forty years ago Richard McKeon contended that the central problem for rhetorical studies in our time is how to coordinate thought and facilitate collaborative action in the presence of pluralism. Given the diversity of value perspectives on almost any public issue, what standards best constrain judgments and adjudicate among differences? From McKeon's vantage, whenever people grapple with practical problems they must struggle to find situated answers to that question; when they do, they then confront the problem of judgment inherent to pluralism. Nowhere does this problem pervade more today than during policy deliberations about environmental issues.[1]

In this chapter, I initiate study of standard rhetorical practices that people deploy to address the problem of judgment when they deliberate about environmental policy issues. How this problem is handled will prove consequential with respect to participants' own interests and values. Hence, the term "stakeholders" commonly designates participants in processes of environmental policy formation. Stakeholders must address specific practical problems whose remedies demand confrontation of their respective differences. Thus this study is guided by the question, How do people handle the problem of judgment rhetorically in the absence of uniformly applicable and mutually acceptable standards?

The case examined here concerns New Hampshire's Forest Sustainability Standards Work Team (FSSWT). On June 27, 1995, John E. Sargent, then New Hampshire's state forester, convened FSSWT and charged the group with implementing the Northern Forest Lands Council's "principles of sustainability" within New Hampshire's forests.[2] I focus in this study on portions of FSSWT's discussions that culminated in a published collection of guidelines for foresters called *Good Forestry in the Granite State: Recommended Voluntary Forest Management Practices for New Hampshire.*[3] Those discussions afford a view of distinctive kinds of rhetorical practices that people deploy in response to the problem of rendering judgments in the presence of pluralism.

I approach FSSWT's deliberations from a perspective on argumentation that is rooted in practical reasoning. This requires a focus on questions of situated judgment rather than questions of universal validity. According to Toulmin, those questions include: "Are these the *right* (or relevant) arguments to use when dealing with this kind of problem, in this situation?—i.e., Are they of a kind appropriate to the substantive demands of the problem and situation?"[4] This perspective contrasts sharply with foundational understandings of argumentation: situated judgment directs attention away from worries about formal consistency and toward concerns about meeting practical demands that define a particular contingent situation.[5]

Toulmin extended this point when he argued that whenever people apply or criticize a conceptual framework they cannot usually meet practical demands with claims warranted by premises internal to that framework; instead, they must locate "trustworthy generalizations" external to that framework— generalizations that furnish standards of situated, practical relevance.[6] For instance, a scientific theory might be intrinsically intelligible. Yet we might criticize it with the extrinsic generalization that simpler formulations are better than those of greater complexity. Simplicity, then, would furnish a standard for the theory's relevance within a particular mix of circumstances that define the practical situation.

McKeon, and others who followed him, observed that the presence of pluralism makes the search for mutually acceptable practical standards for adjudication all the more complicated.[7] Indeed, what generalizations are "trustworthy" and which applications are "appropriate" are always potentially at issue whenever different perspectives are brought into contact. McKeon, more than Toulmin, stressed how pluralism gives rise to what I call here the problem of judgment.

McKeon, and later Toulmin, turned to rhetorical theory of invention for precepts with which to probe the operations and grounds of situated practical reason.[8] Similarly, I examine FSSWT members' rhetorical practices with a topical method of analysis. Topical method applies to any kind of discourse whatever; it is field invariant.[9] At its core, topical analysis brings into view standards that constrain and structure situated judgment.[10] A topical method of analysis is especially useful within pluralistic contexts because it allows us to move into any controversial arena and, without predetermining the outcome, discover the alternative organizing standards that disputants put into play. Such standards include often taken-for-granted value premises and general patterns of thought that structure decision making. Both shape how people deliberate about issues when in the mutually constraining presence of pluralism.

The following section offers a synopsis of the problem of judgment inherent to pluralism as manifested in deliberations about forest sustainability.

Forest Sustainability and the Problem of Judgment

"Sustainability" is invoked frequently during public deliberations about forestry issues. The term's currency gives rise to a range of different situated applications and interpretations. Appeals to sustainability can frustrate, confuse, and obfuscate issues; they often generate a fog of "sustainababble" rather than insight conducive to sound environmental practices.[11] Some treat the term as though it were the source of all meaning and goodness within the universe of environmental discourse, an "ultimate term" for the truly committed.[12] Pragmatic and less valorizing applications employ the term as a way to bridge commonplace divisions between economic and ecological interests and thereby foster greater collaboration on forestry issues. But even these relatively sober appeals conceal that sustainability is as much a focus of controversy as it is a vehicle for overcoming divisions.

Even clear, academic definitions of sustainability invite moral, economic, and ecological controversy. For example, consider this definition: sustainability is "the idea that the needs of the present must be met without jeopardizing the ability of future generations to meet their own needs."[13] What, then, constitutes "needs"? Are "needs" the same as "wants"? What practices "jeopardize" them? What "abilities" will future generations likely have? Such questions are commonplace loci for debate about environmental issues. And nowhere is the diversity of perspectives on sustainability better illustrated than during deliberations about the Northern Forests.

The Northern Forest region encompasses nearly 26 million acres that stretch from the eastern seashore of Maine, through New Hampshire and Vermont, and across New York almost to Lake Ontario. In 1990 the federal government and the state governments within the region established the Northern Forest Lands Council (NFLC). The purpose was to study and recommend alternatives to land and forestry practices that threatened the integrity of the northern forests and the human communities that depended upon them. The Lands Council recommendations looked to maintain "traditional patterns of land ownership and use" throughout the Northern Forest region.[14] Included were nine "principles of sustainability" and the recommendation that each state initiate a process to "define credible benchmarks of sustainability" for their successful implementation.[15] FSSWT was charged with finding ways to implement the nine sustainability principles within New Hampshire's forests.

FSSWT's membership was drawn primarily from the New Hampshire forest community's professional elite, nevertheless the group's composition exhibited a diverse range of interests. These included state conservation agencies (New Hampshire's Division of Forests and Lands; New Hampshire's Department of Fish and Game), federal agencies (U.S. Forest Service; White Mountain National Forest), forest products industries (Boise-Cascade; Champion International; James River Corporation), private timberland owners (New Hampshire Timberland Owners Association), environmental conservation organizations (New Hampshire Audubon; the Society for the Protection of New Hampshire Forests), recreational interests (the Appalachian Mountain Club), forest wilderness activists (editor of the forest advocacy newspaper the *Northern Forest Forum*), and University of New Hampshire scientists and cooperative extension workers.[16]

"Sustainability" quickly emerged as a contested term during the group's work.[17] At FSSWT's inaugural meeting, New Hampshire's state forester initiated the proceedings by noting that forest sustainability is controversial because the public fails to understand what professional members of the forestry community think about the relevant issues. When the public gets involved in FSSWT's work, he contended, they will gain that requisite understanding and public controversy will then subside. But preliminary discussions among the professionals themselves quickly demonstrated an absence of consensus. Some group members held markedly distinct standards for adjudicating the question, "What does and what does not constitute sustainable forestry practices?"[18] Early in that day's proceedings, a forest activist's apparently minor suggestion pointed to a fissure in the position that sustainability could serve as a transcendent value for uniting the divergent interests brought into contact within the group. He proposed that the group distribute the NFLC's nine randomly listed principles of sustainability under two directives issued in a Society of American Foresters Task Force Report.[19] FSSWT members agreed, and the formal framework on sustainability appeared in draft form as follows:

PRINCIPLES OF SUSTAINABILITY
Maintain the structural, functional, and compositional integrity of the forest as an ecosystem, through:
1. Maintenance of soil productivity.
2. Conservation of water quality, wetlands, and riparian zones.
3. Maintenance or creation of a healthy balance of forest size classes.
4. Conservation and enhancement of habitats that support a full range of native flora and fauna.

5. Protection of unique or fragile natural areas.

Meet the diverse needs of the human community, through:

1. Continuous flow of timber, pulpwood, and other forest products.
2. Improvement of the overall quality of the timber resource as a foundation for more value-added opportunities.
3. Addressing aesthetic impacts of forest harvesting.
4. Continuation of opportunities for traditional recreation.[20]

This structuring of sustainability principles into ecosystem and economic categories indicated that qualitatively different perspectives for adjudicating "the sustainable" would be at work during subsequent deliberations.[21]

Alternative perspectives on sustainability became more explicit when FSSWT members began articulating what they expected to achieve if the group succeeded in its work. The New Hampshire Timberland Owners Association (NHTOA) representative wanted a more concrete understanding of sustainable forestry practices: "Specificity and a greater certainty in terms of what to do on the ground to attain sustainability. There has been a tendency to use it recklessly, to ascribe to certain practices the term 'unsustainable' with absolutely no basis. . . . I would like us to come away from this process with very specific management prescriptions, concepts, strategies, that have meaning to people who own and manage land." The forest activist wanted an ecological understanding of sustainability from which to frame baseline standards: "I guess I'd like to get a grip on what is, from an ecological point of view, sustainable. And I'd like to see some kind of baseline standards that practitioners of forestry can meet. Hopefully, most [guidelines] can be voluntary, but there also [have] to be . . . standards below which one doesn't fall." The Boise-Cascade representative sought both to join economic and ecological understandings of sustainability and to advance how sustainability is measured: "The process will be successful if there are two outcomes. One will be recognition that both biological and economic sustainability is necessary. We need both elements. One without the other isn't going to cut it. Secondly, we need to develop a set of measures of sustainability and advance the measurement process." The New Hampshire–Audubon representative viewed both economic and ecological senses of sustainability as fluid with circumstances: "I don't think there's any consensus right now or likely to be on what sustainability really means. And I think society's understanding of the term is going to evolve over time and I think we need in our process to acknowledge that both our scientific understanding changes with time and economic realities change with time." Clearly the FSSWT members brought a plurality of perspectives on sustainability to its work, a plurality conducive to the problem of judgment.

I examine selected FSSWT deliberations for special value standards that constrained adjudication of sustainable forestry practices, and general structures for decision making. Of particular interest are three general structures that address differently the problem of judgment inherent to pluralism: the appeal to a foundational third standard, the bifurcation pattern, and the interdependence structure.

Appeal to a Foundational Third Standard

Anyone acquainted with resource policy deliberations has witnessed efforts to legitimate decisions with appeals that claim they are founded upon "the best available science." FSSWT participants made similar frequent appeals to science. Of interest here is how those appeals evoked science as a foundational third standard, which, purportedly, is impervious to partisan influence and human valuation and thus furnishes an impartial standard for settling differences. Such appeals attempt to avoid the burdens of judging between alternative value standards that characterize deliberation under pluralism.

On opening day, the four FSSWT "core" members presented proposals for the group's mission statement and protocols that incorporated the commonplace appeal to science.[22] The two-part mission statement began with the charge "[t]o identify practical, integrated, forest management practices, derived from the best available science, that address the NFLC Principles of Sustainability." The second of several protocols similarly declared that the group would "[b]ase work products on the best available science."

Some FSSWT members challenged the assumption that science would furnish definitive or even sensible answers to complex questions the group was likely to discuss. A forest geneticist expressed this point as follows: "It seems to me we ought to add 'and common sense and experience,' or something, there. Because I've seen a lot of science that doesn't make a lot of sense." Ensuing debate illustrated the contested rhetorical character of appeals to science as a foundational third standard for structuring decisions.

The Boise-Cascade member stressed the need for solid rather than malleable standards of judgment: "I'm a little uneasy about 'common sense.' What is 'common sense' to one person is 'madness' to another." Others quickly equated common sense and experience with politics and economics, and viewed science as a foundational third standard that could minimize the influence of both and afford impartial, correct answers. The NHTOA representative contended that the protocol says "that the best scientific understanding, for the purposes of this document, has to be first and foremost. And only secondarily is it compromised or tempered by economic or political constraints. If the product is based on good science that's what's wanted, even if it's controversial." A New Hampshire Department of Fish and Game representative argued "that the best available science forms the basis for this work. That sentence [the amendment] says to me: 'Yeah, that's OK, but we could also temper that with common sense and experience when we don't agree with the science.' I'm not sure that's our intent at all. I think it would be better said that 'in the absence of science we rely on common sense and experience;' but our intent was to establish a foundation of good science from which to operate. That would be the bottom line." To this, the Champion International member asserted, "Not to do that would make it arbitrary. So the emphasis is on science as opposed to economics or the social."

Throughout debate on this issue, forest products industry officials, in particular, appealed to science as a foundational third standard. They alluded to their own "economic interests" and implied that others harbored "political" interests. For them, science was insulated from both and thus afforded a foundation that, unlike so-called common sense and professional experience, yielded impartial decisions unsullied with partisan valuations or interests. Science, then, is deployed to shift discussion away from polarized clashes of interest and value toward a higher level of nonpartisan deliberation about truly sustainable forestry practices.[23]

Science, for some FSSWT members, furnished a stable foundation that allowed them to cut through transitory political influences and locate impartial answers to the questions that divided them. Others challenged the claim to impartiality and contended instead that science rhetorically constrains how partisan political judgments ultimately are rendered.[24] For example, the Appalachian Mountain Club (AMC) member pointed to the politics of judgments about where to locate burdens of scientific proof during debates on sustainable forestry:

> I do want to get back to my issue of burden of proof. You can say something is allowable unless the best available science says it's unsustainable, or that something is not sustainable unless the best available science says it is. So this is a spectrum, and the best available science can be used at either end. I think we have to realize there's going to be judgment involved. . . . I would not be comfortable saying anything goes unless we have 95% confidence that science tells us it's bad. I'm not comfortable with that. . . . This question of what the best available science actually tells us . . . will get some different answers depending on which end of the spectrum you're working on.

From this vantage, there is no foundational escape from burdens of judgment—even with science. How discussants locate and define burdens of scientific proof reveals their political inclinations on sustainable forestry issues. From the AMC member's position, foundational appeals to science are quite "interested" politically insofar as burdens of rigorous scientific proof are put upon those who claim some current forestry practice—such as clear-cutting—is "unsustainable" while similar burdens are not placed on those who argue such practices are sustainable. This position works to redirect deliberative efforts from adducing foundations and returns them to the inescapable burdens of judgment under pluralism.[25]

Questions about where to locate scientific burdens of proof are matters of judgment, but so, too, are qualities of thought and conduct that discussants believed constituted the "science" that addresses those burdens. Foundational appeals break down under pluralism, and when they do, value conflicts are transferred from matters such as sustainability to qualities of thought and conduct that constitute "real" science. Science was depicted during FSSWT deliberations as possessing qualities that were either foundational or judgmental, disinterested or interested, impartial or partisan, and so on.

Even mathematics and statistical measures failed to furnish means for avoiding this kind of impasse. Consider some of the debate about the second part of the mission statement proposal, which read: "Define the means by which we measure our achievement." The Boise-Cascade official defended the proposal: "I feel measurement is very important. I think we need to quantify what we're talking about as much as possible. . . . If we're going to be scientifically based in what we do rather than just based on opinion, I think measurement is real important to assess whether we're making progress or not." In contrast, the AMC member, an ecologist, contended: "We should have quantifiable goals whenever that's possible, but some of these things [i.e., the sustainability principles] are going to have to be addressed in some ways subjectively. If we limit ourselves to only those things that can be measured and put in a table, I think we're going to end up with a narrower sort of task. Even things that are measured involve some subjectivity in terms of what level of measurement. So I'm comfortable keeping some elements of subjectivity in here, and I think it's inevitable."

Here again we find tension over what qualities constitute science: Science is precise in measurement, with corollary associations of stable foundations and impartiality, or science admits subjectivity in measurement, with implications of partiality and judgment. Striking some situated balance among otherwise opposed qualities is prerequisite for meaningful use of science to address problems in the presence of pluralism. Often, however, polarity supplants situated proportion, integration, or balance.

FSSWT members also clashed over what value standards should adjudicate sustainable forest management practices. When individual value perspectives clash, they can generate a pattern for decision making that I call the bifurcation structure.

The Bifurcation Pattern

People often address the problem of judgment inherent to pluralism with arguments premised on assumptions deeply embedded within their own preferred individual value perspectives. The clash of individual perspectives culminates in a bifurcation structure when decisions are framed in terms of mutually exclusive and reciprocally related value preferences. Disputants are left to choose between corresponding but inverted standards for adjudicating the reasonable and unreasonable, the worthwhile and worthless, the good and bad.

A protracted exchange between a forest wilderness advocate and a forest products industry official illustrates how a bifurcated structure for decision making emerges from the clash of fundamental value perspectives. The exchange concerns whether "even-aged" management, otherwise known as clear-cutting, is a sustainable forestry practice. The activist developed the value of natural ecosystem integrity to divide economic and ecological interpretations of sustainability.

> The problem for me is what are we talking about in sustainability when we discuss clear-cuts, because a clear-cut of larger than maybe a couple of acres begins to remove an entire system or a portion of an entire system. And we may be able to sustain wood for mills using that on an overall statewide or region-wide basis, but what are we doing in terms of sustaining the integrity of the overall system that has effectively been removed for a period of time. And the other question that I have is that if presettlement forests showed an overstory or a dominant canopy dominated by trees of greater than a 130 or 150 years, what are we sustaining in terms of system integrity that way when we clear-cut an area?

For the activist, natural ecosystem integrity is the value standard for adjudicating what constitutes a sustainable forest; human interventions, such as clear-cutting, are irrelevant to that standard. Sustainable forest systems are forests that operate naturally without human alteration, as the Northern Forests presumably did before European settlement.

In response, the industry official used a topos common to ecosystem discussions, the variability of scale, to argue that the activist's standard was premised on arbitrary boundary distinctions.

> You can draw the system anywhere you want. When you remove a tree you're destroying a system, you're removing a system. . . . One tree. Removing a system. We can draw the line there. Why not draw it there? Because you have a system composed of all the xylem and cambial tissues and the leaves and the whole kit and caboodle. And that's a system, a functioning system that we're taking from the site.

For the industry official, the activist's appeal to natural ecosystem integrity is so arbitrary that it could justify complaint against removal of *any* amount of wood from the forest.

In direct response to those who advocated a natural ecosystem standard, the industry official invoked his own preferred standard for adjudicating sustainable forestry practices, the value of human utility. As he put it:

> This comes back to what standard that you use, because basically when you start removing material you're actually changing what the system is, and that may not be bad. You can change that system and how it operates, but if it's an operating system and doing what you want it to do, then it doesn't make any difference whether or not it's the *same* as the system before. I agree with you, you need to understand what the natural system is, OK, but because your system is different from the natural system doesn't necessarily mean it's a bad system.

For the industry official, human utility is the standard for judging a sustainable forest system and whether the system is natural and unaltered is irrelevant. Sustainable forest systems are altered systems that operate to serve human interests.

The forest activist then challenged the official's standard for sustainable forestry as itself arbitrary when weighed against the natural system: "But how does one sustain a system? A natural system can sustain itself. And the early successional species that maybe depend somehow on even-aged management somehow survived before you began clear-cutting and they were maintained naturally. Once we start altering the system, either we continue energy . . . inputs to somehow maintain that altered system, or the system eventually will revert in some form back to the more natural state." For the activist, the natural system is the standard for sustainable forest systems and human judgments founded in utility (for example, maintaining successional species through even-aged management) are the arbitrary standards.

This exchange exemplifies the classic clash between utilitarian and natural ecological valuings of sustainability. It also shows how judgments become bifurcated. Notice how the point for decision—whether clear-cutting is a sustainable forestry practice—is framed in mutually exclusive value terms: Sustainability is judged in terms either of human utility or of natural ecosystem integrity. From the vantage of human utility, even-aged management is fully consonant with sustainable forestry practices. From the vantage of natural ecosystem integrity, linkage of clear-cutting with sustainability is so inconsistent that it becomes virtually incoherent.

Viewed together, each position becomes the mirror image of the worst qualities it attributes to the other. From the vantage of utility, natural ecosystem integrity is based on arbitrary system boundaries that can be drawn at any scale to advance criticism of industry practices as unsustainable. From the vantage of a natural ecosystem standard, judgments of utility are so arbitrary that they can warrant any practices as sustainable forestry regardless of how much they disrupt that system's integrity. We are left with a bifurcated structure for decision about whether even-aged management is a sustainable forestry practice.

After this exchange one of the group's coordinators challenged the natural standard of ecosystem integrity by invoking the group's managerial mission: "But what we're talking about here are people who are managing their forests, that are having human influence on the forest, and that are going to be disturbing the forests. We're not talking about natural systems that are functioning on their own without human influence. What we're gearing this stuff towards is people who are manipulating the system. And if we don't have the accepted premise that people are manipulating the system, then we can't do our work." From her vantage, group deliberations are about forest management, and this presupposes that humans already altered the natural system. Natural ecosystem integrity posits an ideal standard for sustainability that is beyond the reach of foresters and landowners who manage forest systems "on the ground." To press that ideal upon them is hopelessly restrictive and impractical.

Nonetheless, the coordinator later yielded to natural ecosystem integrity as a standard for sustainability when she proposed that the group not call its management guidelines sustainable forestry: "I think what we're talking about here is just the first cut at management practices, but that we shouldn't be putting it out that this equals sustainable forestry." This spurred renewed debate. The industry official returned to the utilitarian standard to counter this tacit endorsement of the natural ecosystem integrity standard. Sustainability, in his view, depends on the managerial context: "If you look at the triad approach, OK, sustainability is defined differently than some of us might be thinking. In that case you take some areas and you're going to be clear-cutting, constantly, year after year, providing tremendous amounts of energy inputs. So you have to define the context in which you're talking about sustainability before you can talk about what's a sustainable practice."[26] Sustainability, then, is adjudicated within a dynamic managerial context of decision making; otherwise it becomes overly restrictive. Clear-cutting, for example, makes managerial sense as a sustainable forestry practice within the context of carefully planned, periodic rotations designed to grow stands of shade-intolerant species such as aspen or birch.

The activist challenged the triad approach as an exemplar of how science conceals political assumptions that maintain an unsustainable status quo:

> The triad is a perfect case of the muddling of science and politics whereby making a political assumption, they then are trapped into a fairly limited scientific "wiggle room" scenario. The assumption—and this is what Mack Hunter told me years ago—was that industry would continue to remove the same volume of fiber as it was currently removing from the Maine woods. . . . Given that assumption, what's the best science we can do to protect other values. That's not an assumption that I think is ecologically valid. In other words, "Is the current level of fiber removal from Maine ecologically sustainable?" is a question that didn't get asked. So we develop a whole system around an assumption that's basically politically driven.

For the activist, the political deployment of science restricts efforts to advance sustainable forestry practices far more than a natural standard of ecosystem integrity. Only a rhetorical sleight of hand could mask economically driven and ecologically unsustainable clear-cuts as sustainable forestry.

This exchange again shows how judgment becomes bifurcated. From the utilitarian perspective, natural ecosystem integrity cannot serve as the standard for sustainable forestry because any effort to "manage" a forest stand requires alteration of the natural system and thus violates that standard. From the vantage of natural ecosystem integrity, a system driven by economic utility cannot adjudicate sustainable forestry practices because it deploys science to conceal practices that perpetuate an ecologically unsustainable status quo. Again, when we view the two positions together, each mirrors the fatal flaw it attributes to the other: deployment of a sustainability standard that is so restrictive that it undermines meaningful intervention in current forestry practices on the ground.

The group coordinator sought to shift discussion away from this impasse over contested value terrain and toward on-the-ground practices that could foster some movement on issues regardless of values used ultimately to adjudicate sustainability: "I think that the answer at this point is that we just don't call it sustainable. And that as this project unfolds and we weave in everything else that we've got, that's when we begin to talk about what's really sustainable or not. But I think Geoff made the point a long time ago that if there were a lot of landowners out there doing some of this stuff already, we'd have a lot less concern about what's sustainable. So let's try to get this stuff out there and try to get some people doing it and then hopefully make the work about what is sustainable a little less onerous." These remarks reframe the focus of deliberations from bifurcated value judgments to principles of coordinated action that are acceptable regardless of value differences (see Moore, chap. 7, this volume, for a related discussion of bifurcation). How that reframing effort structured decision brings us to the third general strategy for handling the problem of judgment inherent to pluralism.

The Interdependence Structure

The interdependence structure frames decision making in terms of mutually agreeable principles of coordinated action that may allow people with different and often opposed value perspectives to address reciprocally related practical problems of respective concern to them.[27] Such principles are suboptimal from the vantage of individual value perspectives, but appeals to alternative value standards can culminate in a bifurcated structure for decision making. Principles of coordinated action become optimal foci for situated judgment whenever those who embrace different value perspectives need each other's cooperation to make progress toward resolving practical problems of respective concern to them or otherwise face the prospect of practical paralysis and inaction.

The coordinator started to establish an interdependence structure for decision making when she responded to the forest activist's appeal to a "natural" presettlement forest standard for adjudicating whether clear-cuts and other practices constitute sustainable forestry. The activist expressed the standard as follows: "But the question is if I want to look at the work I'm doing with my manipulated system to see how good a job I'm doing, it helps me if I have some kind of a control or a benchmark or some kind of independent system to measure it against, and that's where the presettlement, more natural kind of forest comes in." The coordinator's response shifts the grounds for decision from opposed values to mutually agreeable actions:

> But that's the crux of the discussion today. That information is not going to be available in 1996 from this group. It will be available ideally from a different group or this same group in a few years out. And so do we just say to all the people who have been involved in this process to date and who came out [to an earlier public meeting], "Sorry, we can't tell you there's anything that you should be doing today because we haven't been able to agree on it yet. We'll get back to you in four years, or three years, or whatever it is." Or are there some simple things that we can agree on now which are what we think people should be practicing on the ground today? And I don't think we're going to find in this group the answer to yes or no to clear-cut. . . . But the alternative, then, is to not talk about it at all, and leave it out, and is that what people want to do in this discussion?

Notice how the coordinator reframes the locus of decision making from a bifurcation structure of opposed values ("yes or no to clear-cuts") to an interdependence structure premised on the need for agreeable principles of coordinated action ("simple things . . . we think people should be practicing on the ground today"). Such an effort moves discussion onto a more constructive deliberative level.

Disputants who find themselves on opposite sides of value issues are motivated to structure decisions in terms of mutually agreeable principles of coordinated action when each perceives the others' cooperation as a prerequisite to addressing the problems that respectively concern them. From the vantage of individual value perspectives, those principles of action are suboptimal, but they become optimal given the mutuality of constraint on practical action that characterizes pluralism. Those principles of action allow some movement toward solutions to problems that otherwise would continue unabated if deliberations remained polarized over value differences.

For instance, FSSWT's emphasis on the voluntary nature of its recommended forestry practices is suboptimal from the vantage of some ecological values, but those guidelines could still help encourage better forestry and mitigate impacts of the worst on the ground practices. As the NH-Audubon representative put it, "I think we need to look at this as an incremental process. While you can say that practice A is controversial, we're not prepared to make a judgment on practice A. In the interim, people are going to be doing practice A, so are there things that we can do to encourage them to do practice A in a way that minimizes some of the potential negative?" What is the alternative to voluntary guidelines? For those with strong ecological concerns, the alternative is to wait for regulatory reform—a sober prospect in a state whose citizens include constituencies opposed to public regulation, government intrusion on private lands, or any action otherwise perceived as a threat to property rights. From the perspective of some, at least, this alternative amounts to doing nothing. Given such circumstances, influence on a voluntary basis is better than no influence at all.

Voluntary recommended forestry practices also are suboptimal given some economic values or property rights concerns. But recommended practices might reduce negative public perceptions of forest industry practices, which otherwise could culminate in greater demand for public regulation and intrusion on privately owned lands. Several industry officials and private timberland owner representatives were afraid that FSSWT's purported "voluntary" guidelines might become regulations. (This concern gained impetus when the state forester's public remarks seemed to espouse a future regulatory function for FSSWT's work.) The NH-Audubon representative sought to assuage this concern: "I would like to believe that if we do a good job with this, and come up with things that are doable and have a good rationale that people recognize, that they will be adopted voluntarily and that this document will actually reduce the need for regulation because peer pressure and public pressure will move this stuff toward standard practice and there will be less need for regulation." Those with concerns about regulation wanted more concrete assurances that the guidelines would remain voluntary.

> Coordinator: I just can't spend the next year operating under this mantle of fear because it's just too narrow a mind set for us to work under.
> Industry Official: I agree, we can't work under it. So we have to figure out a way to address it. . . . As you point out, yes we don't have control over it, but how can we sort of mitigate that fear in some way so that burden doesn't fall on us. We need to shift that burden somewhere else, and let somebody else screw up, not us.
> NH-Audubon representative: I think we're all in agreement that articulating our intent is a good thing. . . .
> Industry Official: But really showing the downfall; say, "If you just take these and put them into regulations you've really screwed up," kinds of statements.

This discussion over regulatory prospects clearly shows that from the vantage of timberland owners and industry officials the flexibility afforded with voluntary recommendations was superior to potentially inflexible regulations that would erode private control.

Reciprocally related practical problems drew some FSSWT members into an interdependent relationship. On the one side, the problem is the absence of meaningful regulation and thus lack of influence on forestry practices on private lands. On the other side, the problem is the threat of increased regulation and the corresponding loss of control over forestry practices on private lands. The two problems correspond but are inverted as we shift from one side to the other. The voluntary recommended forest management guidelines allowed FSSWT members on both sides to address problems of respective concern.

The voluntary guidelines furnished the principles of coordinated action for putting forest sustainability into practice on the ground. The guidelines were framed within an "options" format. For each management objective, landowners are offered a range of voluntary considerations and recommended practices that could bring their work closer into accord with the NFLC's principles of sustainability. FSSWT members appealed to this principled framework of practical options to show that it could mitigate one or the other of the reciprocally related problems that structured their interdependence.

For example, a forest products industry official stressed that the voluntary options approach would meaningfully reduce the practice of clear-cuts. He argued that when foresters read through the guidelines they would confront so many special ecological considerations pertinent to clear-cuts (e.g., regeneration, soil productivity, water quality, protected areas, scenic values, etc.) that they would elect easier managerial alternatives.

> If I was looking at trying to limit clear-cutting as much as I could, and doing it easily, I look at including and addressing it in each of these things: aesthetics, soils. Somebody looks at it and says, "Uhm, if I clear-cut I've got to think about this one. If I clear-cut I've got to think about this one. If I clear-cut I've got to think about this one. Geez, maybe I should really take a hard look at that management strategy, because it seems to have a lot of potential downsides and I'm taking a risk associated with clear- cutting. And it's just, kind of like, easier to comply with the standards if you don't clear-cut. . . ." So you really need to think, what it [i.e., the options approach] does is it [makes] people really think through this clear-cutting business before they do it because its got a lot of baggage attached to it. And so by incorporating it in each of these

sections [i.e., which correspond with the sustainability principles], you are in essence moving towards a no clear-cut policy.[28]

The options approach, then, promises to allow those with strong ecological values to influence foresters' decisions about clear-cuts to the point that the ultimate outcome could approximate the results of an explicit policy against clear-cuts.

The NH-Audubon representative stressed how the options approach, as a procedure, defies easy regulatory translation: "The other advantage I see in this sort of range of options presentation is that it makes it difficult for somebody to seize upon it as regulation because it's not saying just one thing. So that kind of gets us out of the bind of worrying about whether somebody's going to turn these into regulations or whether somebody else is going to accuse us of writing regulations." The options approach, then, assures private landowners that they will maintain power of decision over their lands and not become encumbered with additional regulation.

The voluntary forest management guidelines designate site-specific practices that are consistent with the NFLC's principles of sustainability. As such, they furnish the principles for coordinated action, which, although suboptimal from some individual value perspectives, could make for progress on reciprocally related problems that fostered interdependence in the presence of pluralism. From the vantage of those who strongly embrace ecological values, the voluntary guidelines are a unique opportunity to extend their influence over forestry practices on private lands in the absence of regulation. From the perspective of strongly held economic and property rights values, the voluntary guidelines will help reduce public perceptions that regulation even is needed and thus minimize potential loss of private control. Those who held each perspective needed those who held the other to address these reciprocally related problems. That is the mutual constraint of pluralism.

A topical method brings into clearer view special value standards and general structures of decision making that constrain situated judgments about forest sustainability. For instance, FSSWT members struggled to balance human utility and natural ecosystem integrity as standards with which to adjudicate whether clear-cuts constitute a sustainable forestry practice. FSSWT members also exhibited conflict in depictions of "science" as foundational or judgmental, disinterested or interested, impartial or partisan, and precise or subjective. These special topoi are among the multiple possible standards evoked during FSSWT deliberations to constrain situated judgments about forest sustainability.

At a more general level, topical analysis brought to conscious awareness three patterns that structured points for decision making during group deliberations: (1) the appeal to a foundational third standard avoids direct value clashes through resort to a third standard purported to yield impartial decisions about otherwise divisive questions; (2) the bifurcation pattern structures decision in terms of individual perspectives' mutually opposed values and thus polarizes judgment with dichotomously related categories of right and wrong, worthwhile and worthless, reasonable and unreasonable; and (3) the interdependence pattern structures decision in terms of mutually agreeable principles of coordinated action that, although suboptimal from the vantage of preferred individual value perspectives, become optimal as standards with which to address reciprocally related practical problems in the constraining presence of pluralism. These general topoi together illustrate some of the distinctive ways that disputants address problems of situated judgment when they deliberate in the presence of pluralism.

The insight of topical analysis is first and foremost applicable to the particular case examined. We saw sustainability break down as an overarching standard within the pluralistic context of FSSWT's deliberations. Sustainability took on sharply divergent meanings when adjudicated against a natural ecosystem integrity standard as opposed to a utilitarian standard. Moreover, foundational appeals to science afforded no escape from burdens of situated judgment and, indeed, became almost as bifurcated as efforts to adjudicate sustainability. Finally, we saw how a polarized debate about values was redirected toward principles of action that allowed disputants to address practical points of interdependence. Within this pluralistic context, "sustainability" then became shorthand for mutually agreeable principles of action that disputants forged collaboratively to address reciprocally related practical problems. Although suboptimal from particular value perspectives, those principles became optimal as standards for workable and mutually advantageous action under the constraint of pluralism. This shift toward interdependent judgment allowed FSSWT coordinators to minimize value polarization and move discussion onto a more deliberative problem-solving plane.

The FSSWT case is a study in how to manage the problem of judgment inherent to pluralism. FSSWT's organizers invited a plurality of stakeholders to come to the table and discuss forest issues. One could easily quarrel about sins of omission. For instance, FSSWT planners tried but failed to secure labor representation. However, they did bring forest products industry officials and forest activists to the same table. FSSWT's organizers invited rather than suppressed plurality; in terms of inclusivity, then they set an example worth following well beyond New Hampshire's borders.

Interdependence is no panacea for overcoming controversy or mitigating environmental disputes. As a topos, interdependence yields possibilities for arguments that may or may not prove useful in this or that particular mix of circumstances. I have noted repeatedly that burdens of situated judgment are inescapable. Value differences remain; they continually submerge and resurface in the ongoing flow of public deliberation about natural resource issues. Whether in New Hampshire or elsewhere, the problem is how to use plurality creatively and without paralysis to address environmental concerns. The interdependence topos offers one possible rhetorical option for addressing that problem.

Topical analysis and its results also are of particular relevance to classroom instruction in practical rhetorical reasoning about environmental issues. Usually, training in natural resource management acknowledges pluralism but does not explore the rhetorical dimensions of how multiple and arguable standards are deployed in particular, situated cases. General textbooks on environmental science and resource management textbooks specific to particular areas, such as wildlife or wetlands, teach students categories for sorting out different ways that people value aspects of the environment.[29] Students learn that people pursue such "goods" as ecology, science, recreation, economics, and aesthetics. Topical analysis of deliberations about natural resource issues can extend these valuable treatments through detailed examination of how values operate in particular cases to constrain situated judgments.

Exemplars of practical reasoning prepare students to discriminate among different standards for valuing, but topical analysis also yields insight into how those standards operate to structure decisions under pluralism. In the FSSWT case, topical analysis moved beyond location of specific ecosystem and utilitarian standards to explore how they clashed in ways that bifurcated points for decision. Foundational appeals did not avert such value clashes but shifted them from sustainability issues to issues about science. Finally, interdependence offered an alternative way to structure decisions in terms of mutually acceptable principles of action rather than purportedly shared values. From this and other similar cases, students move to a deeper level of analysis where they can examine how these (and other) structures of decision constrain discussion and debate of natural resource issues. Those who aspire to work in natural resource fields are thus prepared to grapple with problems of practical rhetorical reasoning within the pluralistic contexts they will encounter during their professional lives.

Results from topical analysis also can further practical instruction in environmental communication and advocacy. We can turn the standards for judgment into heuristics for invention of arguments about similar kinds of issues.

For instructional purposes, these topoi can then be arrayed as open-ended, flexible, heuristic lists. For instance, a list of special topoi commonly associated with ecosystem discussion would include the following: structural or functional integrity, system resilience or resistance, degradation or aggradation, variability of scale, positive or negative feedbacks, cycles (energy, nutrient, water). Another list headed "economic valuings" would include such standard themes of economic discussion as commodity production, production efficiency, profitability, employment opportunity, property rights, and centrality of markets. Still another list might be headed "aesthetic valuings" and designate such themes as balance, neatness, uniqueness, and fragility.

Students can use these topoi to generate practical arguments about particular questions. For instance, they might examine circumstances surrounding such questions as "should dock designs be restricted to restore declining eelgrass beds in New Hampshire's Great Bay?" or "should McDonald's locate a franchise on a local wetland?" They can then generate arguments to constrain situated judgments about these questions. For example, one student might invoke the aesthetic value of fragility to argue that dock design restrictions are desirable because they preserve fragile eelgrass ecosystems. Another might counter with the aesthetic standard of neatness to argue that landowners often desire sandy bottoms without eelgrass because they resemble neatly trimmed, weedless lawns of grass. Ensuing debate illustrates the problem of judgment inherent to pluralism.

Finally, topical analyses exhibit the kind of practical reasoning that could help improve the quality of public participation in environmental policy formation. Fuller called for "prolescience," in which the public participates in setting the scientific research agenda. Others examined rhetorical aspects of policy analysis and the policymaking process. In particular, Waddell underscored the importance of situated judgments of appropriateness.[30] Topical analyses add to these efforts because they bring into view the multiple grounds of situated judgment that are among the range of possible "goods" that citizens must deliberate about if they are to influence specific environmental policy agendas.

Citizens may lack proficiency in the many technical nomenclatures given expression during environmental deliberations, but that should not preclude their active participation. They can render policy decisions about even technically arcane research areas provided that they are framed as issues of value. For instance, FSSWT held public "scoping" sessions that illustrated that citizens with a stake in forestry issues were quite capable of arguing positions consonant with their interests and values. However, citizens will participate more incisively if they can discern the plurality of values that underpin alternatively argued positions and how they operate to constrain and structure situated decisions. Topical analysis brings forward those underlying and often tacit valuational grounds and patterns of situated practical reason. Once brought forward, citizens can deliberate quite efficaciously about comparative values, about alternative conceptions of the public good.

Environmental disputes exemplify a central problem for rhetorical studies in our time: the problem of judgment in the presence of pluralism. In the classical tradition, excellence embodied in *phronesis,* or practical wisdom, required wide experience and superior powers of discernment to grasp situated relationships between the good and the expedient, the ideal and the possible. Environmental disputes underscore the heightened difficulty of adjudicating among a plurality of goods and expediencies, of competing ideals and an ever-shifting array of situated possibilities. Topical analysis, at its best, could furnish concrete exemplars of practical reason within particular, problematic situations marked by pluralism. Such exemplars would afford opportunities to redeem the leading benefit of contingent human experience: the capacity to exercise foresight in circumstances of similar kind.

Rhetorical studies gain significance when they offer modes of inquiry that yield outcomes with practical consequence. In other words, rhetorical analysis would address practical concerns that practitioners confront as they deliberate about the plurality of goods and the most efficacious means to their attainment within particular, complex, problematic situations. Can this study of FSSWT's experience, for instance, guide other practitioners as they respond to questions of judgment—questions of relevancy and appropriateness—that demand they confront the potentially constraining presence of pluralism in each other while they strive to work out plausible remedies to pressing, situated problems? We learn from the FSSWT case that in particular circumstances of that kind, prudential rhetorical practice often requires a shift away from potentially divisive claims warranted exclusively with one's own preferred values and toward claims about collaborative action warranted by mutual perceptions of practical interdependence. Of course, the contingent circumstances that define a particular practical situation might not abide that shift. After all, situated judgment inescapably is involved; rhetorical study yields guiding exemplars, not formal algorithms. Even in situations where interdependence fails, however, the FSSWT exemplar still points to what often is the practical necessity of working to minimize polarization and establish collaborative pursuit of the best among available and achievable goods when in the constraining presence of pluralism.

Notes

1. Richard McKeon, "Communication, Truth, and Society," *Ethics* 67 (1957): 89–99.
2. Mr. Sargent has since retired.
3. New Hampshire Forest Sustainability Standards Work Team [FSSWT], *Good Forestry in the Granite State: Recommended Voluntary Forest Management Practices for New Hampshire* (Concord, N.H.: Society for the Protection of New Hampshire's Forests, Sant Bani Press, 1997).
4. Stephen Toulmin, "Logic and the Criticism of Arguments," in *The Rhetoric of Western Thought,* ed. James L. Golden, Goodwin F. Berquist, and William E. Coleman, 3d ed. (Dubuque, Iowa: Kendall-Hunt, 1983), 398.
5. W. M. Sullivan, "After Foundationalism: The Return to Practical Philosophy," in *Anti-Foundationalism and Practical Reasoning: Conversations between Hermeneutics and Analysis,* ed. E. Simpson (Edmonton, Alberta: Academic Printing and Publishing, 1987), 21–44.
6. Stephen Toulmin, "The Recovery of Practical Philosophy," *American Scholar* 57 (1988): 347–48.
7. Wayne C. Booth, *Critical Understanding: The Powers and Limits of Pluralism* (Chicago: University of Chicago Press, 1979); Donald P. Cushman and Phillip K. Tompkins, "A Theory of Rhetoric for Contemporary Society," *Philosophy and Rhetoric* 13 (1980): 43–67; McKeon, "Communication, Truth, and Society," 89–99; and W. Watson, *The Architectonics of Meaning: Foundations of a New Pluralism* (1985; Chicago: University of Chicago Press, 1993).
8. Richard McKeon, "The Uses of Rhetoric and Philosophy: Invention and Judgment," in *The Classical Tradition: Literary and Historical Studies in Honor of Harry Caplan,* ed. L. Wallach (Ithaca, N.Y.: Cornell University Press, 1966), 365–73; Richard McKeon, "The Uses of Rhetoric in a Technological Age: Architectonic Productive Arts," in *The Prospect of Rhetoric,* ed. Lloyd F. Bitzer and Edwin Black (Englewood Cliffs, N.J.: Prentice-Hall, 1971), 44–63; Gerard A. Hauser and Donald P. Cushman, "McKeon's Philosophy of Communication: The Architectonic and Interdisciplinary Arts," *Philosophy and Rhetoric* 6 (1973): 211–34; and Toulmin, "Logic and the Criticism of Arguments," 391–401.
9. Lawrence J. Prelli, "Rhetorical Logic and the Integration of Rhetoric and Science," *Communication Monographs* 57 (1990): 320, and Lynn M. Stearney, "Sex Control Technology and Reproductive 'Choice': The Conflation of Technical and Political Argument in the New Science of Human Reproduction," *Communication Theory* 6 (1996): 390.
10. Lawrence J. Prelli, *A Rhetoric of Science: Inventing Scientific Discourse* (Columbia: University of South Carolina Press, 1989), 19. In this book, I laid out central precepts and methods that, I believe, characterize a peculiarly rhetorical way of thinking about practical communication problems. That perspective, in my view, can help guide analysis and evaluation of communication problems as they arise during controversies in both technical and public forums.
11. Emily M. Bateson, "Sustaining Our Forest—Crafting Our Future," in *The Future of the Northern Forest,* ed. Christopher McGrory Klyza and Stephen C. Trombulak (Hanover, N.H.: University Press of New England, 1994), 138.
12. Richard M. Weaver, "Ultimate Terms in Contemporary Rhetoric," in *Language Is Sermonic,* ed. Richard L. Johannesen, Rennard Strictland, and Ralph T. Eubanks (Baton Rouge: Louisiana State University Press, 1970), 87–112.

13. Bateson, "Sustaining Our Forest," 134.
14. A major breach with tradition occurred in 1988 when nearly 1 million acres formerly owned by Diamond International was put up for sale on the open market. Historically, large land sales were transacted between timber companies, but these properties were marketed at least partly for their development value. Conservation and timber interests eventually purchased most of this acreage, including 790,000 acres in Maine, but two developers bought nearly 200,000 acres in New Hampshire, Vermont, and New York with an eye toward selling them off as residential and recreational properties. The three state governments secured half that acreage through direct purchase or easements, while some remaining lands were sold for development or short-term timber liquidation.

    These events generated the concern that the breakup of large private land holdings would threaten the largely forest-based economy in the region and reduce valuable public spaces for outdoor recreational activities such as hunting and fishing. In 1988 Congress responded by initiating the Northern Forest Lands Study, which was to be carried out by the U.S. Department of Agriculture's Forest Service and the Governor's Task Force on Northern Forest Lands (appointed by the governors of the four states within the Northern Forest Region). This study was intended to identify potential strategies to deal with threats to the forest. The Governors' Task Force compiled its own report in which, among other strategies, it recommended to Congress that it create a regional Northern Forest Lands Council to continue work initiated by the Northern Forest Lands study.

    See Northern Forest Lands Council [NFLC], *Finding Common Ground: Conserving the Northern Forest: Recommendations of the Northern Forest Lands Council* (N.p.: n.p., Sept., 1994), 4–7, and app. D, "Expanded Northern Forest History and Process." For an analysis of trends and events that culminated, among other consequences, in the formation of the Lands Council, see Christopher McGrory Klyza, "The Northern Forest: Problems, Politics, and Alternatives," in *Future of the Northern Forest,* Klyza and Trombulak, 36–51.
15. NFLC, *Finding Common Ground*, 42, 44.
16. Eighty-five percent of New Hampshire's forests are privately owned, with 10 percent in federal lands (the White Mountain National Forest), and the remainder distributed among state, county, and town properties. Of the total private holdings, individuals hold 84 percent; forest products industries hold 16 percent. Both individual and industrial owners are represented in the New Hampshire Timberland Owners Association. Susan Francher, New Hampshire Division of Forests and Lands, telephone interview with the author, Feb. 26, 1997.
17. Discussion of the term "sustainability" occurred during the group's first "operational" stage of its work, which ended when *Good Forestry in the Granite State* went to press in the spring of 1997. During this phase, FSSWT engaged issues of forest sustainability with "on the ground" management guidelines that could help foresters address problems such as soil erosion and how to protect fragile areas. The second phase, which got under way during the spring of 1997, was to deal with potentially more controversial issues, such as population growth and developmental encroachment on forestlands. I examine selected discussions that transpired during the first stage.
18. I attended the first seven months of the group's sessions and secured documents generated from all subsequent meetings, including drafts of *Good Forestry* until the final version went to press. This analysis centers on two of those sessions:

discussions about sustainability and about the nature of science transpired during the inaugural session, held on June 27, 1995, and debate about clear-cuts took place on Jan. 19, 1996. All references to or direct quotation from FSSWT discussions are based on taped recordings of those sessions.

19. Society of American Foresters, *Task Force Report on Sustaining Long-Term Forest Health and Productivity* (Bethesda, Md.: Society of American Foresters, 1993), xiii.

20. FSSWT, *Good Forestry*, 7. The first directive was amended slightly with insertion of "compositional" integrity.

21. Even concern about aesthetics is linked to the economically important tourism industry. New Hampshire's scenic beauty and opportunities for outdoor recreational activities are major attractions for both in-state residents and out-of-state visitors. Forest harvests could, of course, erode scenic qualities, so measures have been sought to minimize impacts and conceal them from the traveling public's view.

22. FSSWT's four "core group" members structured and coordinated group deliberations. They were drawn from the Society for the Protection of New Hampshire's Forests, the New Hampshire Timberland Owners Association, the New Hampshire Department of Fish and Game, and the New Hampshire Department of Forests and Lands.

23. I am not suggesting that forest products industry officials or those who otherwise have economic interests in the Northern Forests are alone when they deploy the foundational third standard. Environmental activists do so as well. For example, Trombulak, a professor of biology and Northern Forest activist, argued that a "scientific perspective" can be used to evaluate economic and political positions advanced during debate about Northern Forest policy. Forest industry employees often bemoan environmentalists' appeals to impossible scientific standards. As Wood implied, environmentalists sometimes insist that one cannot harvest trees without "knowing everything" about the forest ecosystem. The appeal to science as a foundational third standard is, therefore, quite commonplace and is often evoked on both sides of forest sustainability issues. Stephen C. Trombulak, "A Natural History of the Northern Forest," 12, 24–26; Stephen Trombulak and Christopher McGrory Klyza, "The Future of the Northern Forest: Putting All the Pieces Together," 231–33; and Jonathan Wood, "A Sustainable Resource for a Sustainable Rural Economy," 160; all in *Future of the Northern Forest*, Klyza and Trombulak.

24. Ultimately, the proposed amendment later appeared as a separate protocol subordinate to the "best available science" protocol: "In the absence of science, use experience and professional judgment."

25. International policy deliberations are replete with efforts to ease or shift burdens of scientific proof so that a firm, company, or government is expected to change or reduce practices purported to harm the environment. Such efforts are now expressed formally as the "precautionary principle," a principle endorsed as an element of international environmental law in such important agreements as the UN Framework Convention for Global Climate Change and the Agreement for the Implementation of the Provisions of the United Nations Convention on the Law of the Sea Relating to the Conservation and Management of Straddling Fishstocks and Highly Migratory Fishstocks. According to the precautionary principle, judgments must err on the side of caution whenever there is reason to believe current practices contribute to environmental degradation—even in the

absence of "certain" scientific evidence. This principle not only challenges nearly impossible scientific standards for discharging burdens but also works toward shifting burdens from proof of environmental harm toward proof of environmental safety. See United Nations, "Agreement for the Implementation of the Provisions of the United Nations Convention of the Law of the Sea of 10 December 1982, Relating to the Conservation and Management of Straddling Fish Stocks and Highly Migratory Fish Stocks," 34 I.L.M. (1995), 1542–80; and United Nations, "Framework Convention for Global Climate Change," in *Negotiating Climate Change: The Inside Story of the Rio Convention*, ed. I. M. Mintzer and J. A. Leonard (Cambridge: Cambridge University Press, 1994), app., article 3, 340.

26. Malcolm Hunter, a professor of wildlife at the University of Maine at Orono, developed the triad approach. Generally, this approach would divide forestlands into equivalent thirds that correspond with three distinct categories: intensively managed forests, multiple use forests (recreational and less intensively managed), and forests totally set aside from managerial interventions. Francher, telephone interview.

27. For more detailed elaboration of the interdependence topos, see Lawrence J. Prelli, "Empirical Diversity, Interdependence, and the Problem of Rhetorical Invention and Judgment: The Case of Wife Abuse Facts," *Communication Theory* 6 (1996): 406–29.

28. The last draft document outlined both legitimate uses of clear-cutting as a management tool *and* concerns about its impact at the site and landscape level. The former, for example, included regeneration of early successional species, while the latter included such negative impacts as reducing soil productivity and increasing erosion. The discussion emphasized use of this technique only when other techniques could not meet objectives and with due regard to recommended mitigating practices. At this writing, only one forest products industry official was dissatisfied with that draft version.

29. Daniel Botkin and Edward Keller, *Environmental Science: Earth as a Living Planet* (New York: John Wiley, 1995), 10–12; James H. Shaw, *Introduction to Wildlife Management* (New York: McGraw-Hill, 1985) 14–18; William J. Mitch and James G. Gosselink, *Wetlands* (New York: Van Nostrand Reinhold, 1993), 507–27.

30. Steve Fuller, *Philosophy, Rhetoric, and the End of Knowledge: The Coming of Science and Technology Studies* (Madison: University of Wisconsin Press, 1993); James A. Throgmorton, "The Rhetorics of Policy Analysis," *Policy Sciences* 24 (1991): 153–79; Giandomenico Majone, *Evidence, Argument, and Persuasion in the Policy Process* (New Haven, Conn.: Yale University Press, 1989); Craig Waddell, "The Role of *Pathos* in the Decision-making Process: A Study in the Rhetoric of Science Policy," *Quarterly Journal of Speech* 76 (1990): 381–400.

10 Global Gridlock

The American Presidency and the Framing of International Environmentalism, 1988–2000

Martín Carcasson

From its beginnings with the presidency of Theodore Roosevelt, through its expansion after the publication of Rachel Carson's *Silent Spring,* to its move to the mainstream in the 1990s, the American environmental movement has typically focused on recycling, endangered species, conservation of natural lands, and the reduction of various pollutants. Although these issues are salient worldwide, the international environmental movement tends to focus more on fears of overpopulation, limited food supplies, global economic inequalities, catastrophic climate change, and depletion of critical resources.[1] The eighteenth-century English economist Thomas Robert Malthus was the first to propose the basic theory of "limits" to the earth's ability to sustain the exponential human demands on its riches. In the twentieth century a series of books, such as *Our Plundered Planet* (1948), *The Limits of the Earth* (1953), *The Population Bomb* (1968), *Man's Impact on the Global Environment* (1970), *The Closing Circle* (1971), and *World Dynamics* (1971), made similar apocalyptic predictions.

The 1972 report from the Club of Rome entitled *Limits to Growth,* perhaps the most influential of the genre, had three basic conclusions: (1) if existing trends continued, the limits to growth would be reached within one century, resulting in ecological catastrophe; (2) it is possible to alter the growth trends and establish ecological and economic stability, if society is designed to satisfy the basic material needs of each person on earth; (3) the sooner the world chose the second path, the more likely the chance of success. These predictions of global devastation, based on unsophisticated modeling techniques, were clearly exaggerated and were considered unnecessarily alarmist by many at the time. Nonetheless, as the new century dawned the "existing trends" mentioned in *Limits to Growth* not only continued but also increased in many ways. In 1995 Mark Dowie outlined a few of the threats to sustainability that are "widely acknowledged to be undeniable":

Human beings—only one of between 5–30 million species on earth—
currently consume 40 percent by mass of the plant material
produced each year by photosynthesis—the [Gross Domestic
Product], as it were, of the earth. The rate of increase of human
use is about 2 percent per year. At that rate human consumption
will double in 36 years.

Thirty-five percent of the land on the planet is degraded, much of it
irreversibly. Soil loss currently exceeds rates of soil reformation 10
to 1. Fifty-five percent of the tropical rainforests on earth have
been destroyed.

Species extinction rates currently exceed 5,000 per year. Compared to
the previous known spasms of mass extinction, this rate is disturb-
ingly high—10,000 times higher than pre-human extinction rates.

Despite a quadrupling of economic output since 1950, the percentage
of humans living in poverty has continued to grow, even in the
industrialized countries of the North, where over 100 million are
classified as poor.[2]

Though the conclusions of Limits to Growth presented above may have been
exaggerated, the basic logic that argues, "the sooner the unsustainable trend
of expansion and growth is altered, the better," does seem viable.

In this chapter I examine how the American presidency has responded to
these international environmental issues, focusing on the rhetoric of the Bush
and Clinton administrations from 1988 to 2000. I argue that, despite a trend
toward a more proactive stance, the degree to which the American presidency
has called for a serious confrontation with global environmental issues has been
severely limited. Although Clinton's rhetoric represented a significant improvement over that of the Bush administration, both presidencies exhibited a clear
avoidance of the most difficult issues of the international crisis and a continuing reliance on both a nationalistic and economic paradigm. As a result, neither administration was able to call for, much less enact, concrete proposals
designed to confront international environmental concerns. Further analysis
reveals that many of these deficiencies are likely the result of significant inherent and ever-increasing constraints in modern economic and political systems.
As a result, the issues need to be reconceptualized by both activists and politicians if any significant progress is to be made. Due to the importance of the
president to the agenda-setting process and the framing of policy issues, such
a reconceptualization would most likely require the active involvement of the
chief executive in order to be widely disseminated.

My analysis draws from the work of Niklas Luhmann, who identified six "function systems" that work as terministic screens to limit how issues are understood in modern society: the economy, law, science, politics, education, and religion.[3] An application of Luhmann's framework includes two important steps: the first is to realize the limited nature of the conversation by identifying which function systems tend to dominate an issue, and the second, perhaps even more important, is to then examine issues through the function systems that have been neglected in order to discover new possibilities that could transform the debate. The primary intent of this analysis, therefore, is to uncover which function systems have been used by the Bush and Clinton administrations, how those function systems have operated, what constraints are evident within them, and what any disregarded functions could potentially add to the debate.

The principal finding of the analysis is that the primary function systems used by these two presidents when discussing global environmental issues were politics, economics, and science, all of which are hampered by constraints to action that are unlikely to be significantly overcome in the near future. The frames of law, education and religion were generally lacking in the presidential rhetoric, and offer some potential for a rhetorical transformation of the issue. Overall, some reframing is necessary before significant progress is likely. This chapter concludes with some preliminary suggestions for such a reframing.

International Environmentalism

The scientists, economists, academics, and industrialists who wrote the various global warnings from the 1940s to the early 1970s realized that their conclusions were not "infallible." According to John McCormick, the authors of *Limits to Growth* provided their conclusions in part to "open the debate on accelerating global trends to a wider community." Although the theories were significantly flawed and overstated in various ways, they did raise important questions that others set about to answer more systematically, which was the authors' primary goal from the beginning.[4]

Numerous issues are included under the banner of international environmentalism; however, this analysis focuses primarily on the interrelated concerns over global warming, overpopulation, and poverty. The basic concepts of global warming are well known. Certain gases, primarily carbon dioxide, methane, chlorofluorocarbons, and nitrous oxide, are argued to be altering the chemical composition of the earth's atmosphere with their heat-trapping properties. Since the beginning of the industrial revolution, for example, carbon dioxide levels in the atmosphere have increased nearly 30 percent. These increases are due primarily to the burning of fossil fuels, though the use of aerosols, refrigerants, and fertilizers also contribute, as do deforestation, landfills, rice paddy cultivation, and bovine and sheep ruminants. Some possible effects of global warming include the melting of polar ice, which raises the overall sea level and floods coastal areas; changes in weather patterns due to an increase in evaporation rate, which results in more frequent flooding, increases in violent storms, and increases in desertification processes; and changes in ecosystems as they migrate into new areas.[5]

EPA estimates cite a global mean surface temperature increase of 0.6–1.0 degrees F since the late nineteenth century, with a corresponding four- to eight-inch rise in worldwide sea level. Current estimates expect an acceleration of the rate of climate change. Scientists expect that the average global surface temperature will rise 2.2 to 10 degrees F by 2100, which would result in a two-foot rise in sea level to the U.S. coast.[6] Despite these estimates, much uncertainty and controversy concerning global warming remain. Whereas it is generally undisputed that the percentage of these gases in the atmosphere and the average global temperature have risen during this century, some scientists continue to dispute the *cause* (what proportion of the change is caused by human actions, and what proportion is caused by natural cycles?), the *danger* (how serious are the problems caused by global climate warming?) and the *solutions* (can anything actually be done to stop the process?) proposed by mainstream scientists. One of the most important issues to examine, therefore, is how the American presidents depict the scientific information concerning global warming.

Although the scientific debates are sufficiently complex on their own, the major difficulties arise when the issue is considered within the frame of international politics. In 1998 Stephen Hopgood outlined an important development of internationalism as the diminishment of the national-international distinction. He identified two dimensions to this decline: one of autonomy (loss of effective control) and the other of sovereignty (loss of authority). The *intra*national aspect of environmental problems—the fact that nations must share the same air, ocean, and atmosphere, that pollution tends to drift, and that the causes and effects of climate change do not recognize political boundaries—erodes autonomy, whereas the creation of international governmental bodies and the signing of international treaties and conventions impairs national sovereignty.[7]

Global warming is a transnational issue that tends to inflame passions as sovereign countries argue over who is to blame for the problem, who should be responsible for the solutions, and what those solutions should be. The primary fault line has developed between the developed countries (usually labeled as the "North") and the developing countries (the "South"), and revolves around several difficult paradoxes.

The North's consumption patterns and industrial infrastructure are currently the main source of the emissions, with the United States, despite having only 5 percent of the world's population, contributing 25 percent of the world's emissions. The South, on the other hand, owns most of the sprawling rainforests that act as "sinks" for these dangerous gases. Unfortunately, these same forests are one of the South's most critical resources: they are cleared to make room for agriculture, harvested to sell as exotic woods, and consumed as a primary, and dirty, source of fuel. The North, suddenly keenly aware of the environmental dangers, is calling for the South to conserve the resources the world needs. The South, struggling to match the standard of living enjoyed by the North, demands the sovereign right to exploit its resources to achieve the North's lifestyle. As stated by a Malaysian diplomat at the 1992 Earth Summit: "we are certainly not holding our forests in custody for those who have destroyed their own forests and now try to claim ours as a part of the heritage of mankind."[8]

As development continues, the situation is likely to get much worse. An article in the *Economist* captures this new dynamic vividly:

> As economic growth has accelerated, and as more countries, with more people, have joined in, so its environmental side-effects have increased. . . . [T]he environment is what poor countries live off. Typically, primary production—farming, forestry, fishing, mining—accounts for more than a third of their GNP, more than two-thirds of employment, and over half their export earnings. Their natural resources are their main assets. From them, they must feed a billion more mouths every 13 years. . . . *As the poorer countries industrialise, buy cars, get richer, their capacity for damage will overtake that of the rich world—because they have more people.* China alone, by burning its dirty coal and making polluting refrigerators, could torpedo everybody else's efforts to stop the build-up of atmospheric carbon and damage to the ozone layer.[9]

In other words, what occurs within the borders of the United States is immaterial if something is not done concerning developing countries such as China, Malaysia, and Brazil.

Several possibilities exist to help the South, all of them difficult and costly. What is clear is that the poorer southern countries are understandably more concerned with their short-term survival than long-term environmental consequences. As explained in a 1992 *Newsweek* article:

Essentially, the Third World wants the West to save it from the consequences of industrialization. The corollary is that otherwise the trees of
Peru and Indonesia will go the way of the ones of Woodside, Queens.
Nobody was thinking about these questions when the West had its Industrial Revolution—that's how it got so rich. Now it wants the rest of
the world to follow different, more stringent, rules. This is the global
application of the well-known phenomenon that one's willingness to
make 'sacrifices' for the environment goes up in proportion to the number of Volvos one already owns. . . . Speaking for many poor countries,
"The Chinese have made the choice that if there is a decision to be made
between development and environment, they'll go for development,"
says a Western diplomat in Beijing. "If the West wants a better environment, they'll have to pay." If the West doesn't want China to burn its
coal, the West can pay for the alternatives. If the alternatives involve
technology that the Chinese don't have—more efficient electrical generating plants, say—the West should provide it.[10]

The South, in other words, believes if the North is concerned, it should provide not only monetary aid, but also technological aid.

Another critical issue that further complicates matters is human population.
The difficulty in this issue concerns what is perhaps the most fundamental right
of all organisms: the right to reproduce. Population growth rates in the South
far exceed the growth rates in the North, thus, once again, a self-perpetuating
cycle will lead to greater problems unless changes are made. More people leads
to more consumption and more clear-cutting, adding more pollution and leaving fewer sinks for it. In 1992 Maurice Strong emphasized this issue by remark-
ing, "Since 1972 world population has grown by 1.7 billion people. . . . 1.5 billion
of these live in developing countries which are least able to support them."[11]

Issues of population control are also tied directly to poverty. Poverty leads
to high population growth because, "in a subsistence economy, children constitute a valuable additional workforce," and provide "the best form of insur-
ance for the parent's old age." The tribulations of poverty and overpopulation,
in turn, rationalize deforestation and the use of dirty technologies. As Indira
Gandhi said at the Stockholm UN Conference on the Human Environment
in 1972: "poverty is the biggest pollution." Despite such pleas, world poverty
and overpopulation were hardly mentioned at the historic Earth Summit
in 1992.[12]

One last problem is a catch-22 that confounds matters beyond conceivability.
If world poverty is somehow overcome, the threat of overpopulation may be
less and the destruction of rainforests may decrease, but then the inhabitants of

the developing countries would have access to more products that increase the stress on the environment. Prosperity leads to a higher per capita consumption of water, energy, fossil fuels, minerals, biomass, and land use, and an increase in waste, water and air pollution.[13]

In sum, the global environmental crisis is one that involves numerous overlapping issues, and is complicated by paradoxes that evade simple answers. Addressing one problem often exacerbates another. Nonetheless, the problems are real and call for a significant response and strong leadership. In the following section, I turn to an examination of the rhetorical response (or lack thereof) to these issues offered by two U.S. presidents.

The Presidency and the Global Environmental Crisis

A focus on the U.S. presidency is certainly warranted in this case because in the post–cold war world, it plays one of the most important public roles worldwide and speaks with perhaps the world's most influential voice. As Norman Vig wrote in *Environmental Policy in the 1990s,* "the importance of presidential leadership [in environmental policy] can scarcely be exaggerated. In our system, the president alone can exert unifying moral leadership in time of crisis, and he alone can lead in foreign affairs. The magnitude and complexity of the environmental problems we face at the close of the twentieth century are likely to require stronger leadership than we have seen from any president thus far—including Teddy Roosevelt."[14]

In addition, the United States is the worldwide leader in environmental issues, in both a positive and a negative sense. The United States leads the world in environmental activism, at the same time it leads the world in production of emissions and waste. As the most affluent nation in the world, the United States is often considered the envy of developed and developing countries, who hope to emulate the standard of living enjoyed by the U.S. population. That standard of living is twice that of most developed countries in Europe, and several times that of the developing countries. Simply put, if the maxim that "one's willingness to make 'sacrifices' for the environment goes up in proportion to the number of Volvos one already owns," Americans own the most Volvo, or, perhaps more appropriately, the most gas-guzzling SUVs. Indeed, if any serious movement concerning the international environment is proposed, it seems clear that it must entail both active participation and encouragement from the United States, in general, and its president, in particular.

The international environment first developed into a sustained presidential issue during the Carter administration. In 1980 Jimmy Carter commissioned a study of environmental problems—the *Global 2000 Report to the President*—that was released in the midst of the presidential campaign. The report concluded, among other things, that "unless nations of the world take prompt, decisive action to alter the trends . . . the next 20 years may see a decline in the earth's capacity to support life." Rejecting the "pessimistic" conclusion of Carter's report, the Reagan administration abruptly terminated much of the momentum of the environmental movement by preaching antiregulation and claiming that the excessive legislation imposed unnecessary limits on business and industry (see chapter 5, this volume). In what some environmentalists term "the Lost Decade," the Reagan administration reduced requirements and cut government spending on environmental protection. In 1988, as part of a political strategy to differentiate himself from Reagan and win back the moderate votes Reagan had alienated, Bush adopted the label of the "environmental president" for the presidential campaign, attacked Dukakis's environmental record as governor, and won the presidency.[15]

The Presidency of George H. Bush

Early in his presidency, George Bush sent an encouraging statement to environmentalists around the globe when he named William K. Reilly as the administrator of the Environmental Protection Agency. Reilly, the widely respected former president of the Conservation Foundation and the World Wildlife Fund, became the first professional environmentalist named to the post. In the days following the ceremony, the Bush administration vowed to fulfill campaign promises concerning the environment. Turning away from the eight years of Reaganesque antiregulation and environmental inaction, Bush called for a new acid rain bill, stricter amendments to the Clean Air Act, a ban on all ocean dumping of sewage sludge, a "no net loss" policy on wetlands, and the acquisition of more lands for the national park systems.[16] The apex of Bush's environmental record was reached with the passage of the Clean Air Act of 1990. From that point on, however, his environmental rhetoric revealed a significant conservative turn, due primarily to the recession and the influence of skeptical advisers such as John Sununu. The low point occurred in 1992 when Bush was denounced by the world for his antienvironmental stance at the Earth Summit in Rio de Janeiro, Brazil.[17]

The following themes from Bush's rhetoric are especially relevant to the international environment: (1) an attempted "balance" between economic and environmental concerns, (2) a reliance on scientific uncertainty as a justification for inaction and scientific innovation as the solution to the crisis, and (3) a distinct focus on the national environment over the international.

ECONOMIC VS. ENVIRONMENTAL CONCERNS

The most obvious and frequent argument made by Bush throughout his term was the need to balance economic and environmental priorities, which is one of the fundamental dilemmas of the environmental movement. The traditional view of this dichotomy was of two mutually exclusive competing values: for the environment to improve, economic development must be reduced—clearly a difficult policy to sell in capitalistic societies. Bush argued that the two could, and indeed must, be satisfied simultaneously. Essentially, Bush rhetorically advocated a policy of "sustainable development," though he rarely used the term. Bush entered the presidency after eight years in which the White House, citing economic concerns, attempted to dismantle, weaken, or delay efforts at improving the environment at the expense of industry and business. At the beginning of his term, likely in an effort to smooth the transition from Reagan, Bush focused mainly on selling the idea that environmental issues can be addressed "without stifling the economy" or "without compromising our record of unprecedented economic growth."[18]

Once the recession hit, however, environmental issues quickly began to drop from the Bush agenda. On September 18, 1991, at the signing ceremony of some minor environmental legislation in Arizona, the balance between economics and environmentalism had clearly tilted rather markedly toward the economy. Employing a telling metaphor, Bush announced that the country "could not afford a policy that makes the American worker an endangered species." On May 30, 1992, Bush participated in a question-and-answer session with agricultural leaders in California, and made several references to the Earth Summit, which was set to begin in less than a week. His remarks reveal his continuing shift toward economic protectionism rather than environmental activism: "You may have read about the Rio conference on the environment. . . . [W]e cannot permit the extremes in the environmental movement to shut down the United States on science that may not be as perfected as we in the United States should have it. . . . [W]e cannot shut down the lives of many Americans because of going to extremes on the environment. So that's my philosophy, and that's what we're trying to do. . . . But we can't do it and throw an awful lot of people out of work, especially when it's not based on sound science."[19]

The references to the "extremes" in the environmental movement was repeated in Rio—ironically, considering the United States was the only industrialized nation refusing to sign the climate-change convention—and a somewhat derogatory reference to "you who are environmentalists" elsewhere in the speech was quite removed from the 1988 campaign, where Bush professed to being one of those environmentalists. In the end, evidenced by the administration's position at the Earth Summit, political and economic concerns were clearly a higher priority than the environment for Bush.

THE ROLE OF ENVIRONMENTAL SCIENCE

Science played two important roles in Bush's environmental ethic: as a savior and as a procrastination device. The role of science in environmental issues is a complicated one. For some, science and technology are the cause of most environmental problems; therefore the solution is to stop the advancement of science and return to a more "natural" life. To others, such as Bush and later Clinton, future technology is viewed as the potential solution to current problems. Bush was optimistic and believed in the power of the market and of American ingenuity, and he felt that if given the necessary support, technologies would be produced to solve most of the environmental problems. Bush was thus able to tie together the economic, scientific, and environmental. For example, in 1991 Bush said: "Recent world events make it clear that free markets and economic growth provide the firmest foundations for effective environmental stewardship. People tend to forget that environmental stewardship is a high-tech business, and it requires great ingenuity and insight. Science and technology give us tools for cleaning up our environment and keeping it clean. They help us identify our problems precisely and develop efficient solutions. Our genius will open up new frontiers of clean energy: nuclear power, solar power, geothermal power, and others that exist only in the imagination of our dreamers and [innovators]." Later in that same speech, Bush solidified his point of view, saying, "We want to use science to help us solve our chief environmental problems. And Bill Reilly put it best in a recent newspaper piece that he wrote, 'The environmental debate has long suffered from too little science. There has been plenty of emotion and politics, but scientific data have not always been featured prominently in environmental efforts and have sometimes been ignored even when available. . . . Good science hastens our progress toward a cleaner environment, and we ought to use it to our best advantage.'"[20]

The second role of science for Bush was as a procrastination tool. The tactic was not uncommon. John McCormick argued that "[i]nconsistent and incomplete scientific data [have] been repeatedly quoted by governments and industries opposed to action on environmental problems." Often the issue hinges on the difference between prevention and cure, with governments acting hesitantly to committing major funding to the more abstract prevention of future problems if the science is not clear, often preferring to "wait" until the scientific data are more concrete. In a study of various international environmental issues, Porter and Brown concluded that "scientific evidence has helped galvanize international action on some issues (acid rain and ozone depletion) but has been secondary or irrelevant in other issues (whaling, hazardous waste trade, tropical deforestation, Antarctic minerals, and trade in African ivory)." Science is clearly a critical issue in international debate regarding global warming.[21]

Bush's stance on science was evident during his address to the Intergovernmental Panel on Climate Change (IPCC) in Washington in February, 1990. Bush's remarks were preceded by a series of scientific reports warning about the dangers of global warming. Included in the reports was an appeal by the Union of Concerned Scientists, endorsed by forty-nine Nobel laureates and seven hundred members of the National Academy of Sciences, that urged Bush to take action immediately.[22] The scientists, agreeing that continued research was necessary, nonetheless argued that uncertainty was "no excuse for complacency."[23] Despite the growing evidence, Bush disappointed the panelists from ten European countries by urging prudence: "Our responsibility is to maintain the quality of our approach, our commitment to sound science, and an open mind to policy options."[24] News reports filtered out a few days later concerning the inner struggle between Reilly and Bush chief of staff John Sununu concerning the tone of Bush's speech. A *Newsweek* article explained that "Sununu substituted the phrase 'climate change' wherever 'global warming' appeared in the draft Reilly submitted. Sununu also struck out some paragraphs advocating debate on the advisability of regulating fossil-fuel consumption. . . . Sununu also inserted into the speech a passage suggesting that Congress not jump headlong into global-warming policymaking until the scientists draw firmer conclusions." In the end the Bush administration's response to global warming "failed to impress environmentalists." Events at another White House conference on the science and economics of global climate change, held in April, mirrored the earlier meetings, with Bush touting the merits of "more research" and international environmentalists walking away disappointed.[25]

For Bush, the mention of "too little science" and calls for a commitment to "sound science" were characteristic appeals, especially as the Earth Summit neared. This distrust of science—somewhat contradictory to his optimistic view of science as savior—was likely a product of John Sununu's influence. Sununu, Bush's chief of staff until he resigned early in 1992, was an engineer by trade and opposed any U.S. commitments concerning global warming. Stephen Hopgood explained how the conservatives and environmentalists in the Bush administration used "scientific ammunition" to argue their point of view, and that Sununu and "other skeptics could usually find, and could even promote, respected scientific support for their arguments. . . . In other words, 'science' is not simply an objective commodity within policy deliberations, it serves as a resource for state officials to argue their respective cases."[26]

In sum, under the banner of "prudence," Bush called for increased funding for scientific research on climate change—which was less politically and economically expensive than committing to regulations to lower the level of greenhouse gases emitted by American industries. Bush's optimism concerning science as the savior even improved the rhetorical effect of his call for more research. In the end, Bush could reject the environmentalists' proposals by appearing proactive and prudent, all the while protecting American business interests.

NATIONALISTIC FOCUS

Unless speaking to an international audience, Bush rarely discussed international environment issues. At Reilly's swearing-in ceremony, Bush mentioned that "many of the problems that we face in the environment are global problems," but most of his comments during the speech focused on national issues. The international environment was not addressed again until the climate change conferences in February and April, 1990. At the first conference, Bush pledged that he "sincerely believe[d] we must do everything in our power to promote global cooperation. . . . The stakes here [at the IPCC conference] are very high: the consequences, very significant." Two months later, Bush demonstrated that he did have a grasp on some of the difficult international issues, though this comprehension would not be evident in Rio: "Let me focus for just a moment on the developing world. In a climate of poverty and persistent economic struggle, protecting the environment becomes a far more difficult challenge. Cold statistics don't begin to capture the harsh realities that are at stake. Development doesn't mean just another point in the gross national product, the GNP; it's measured in human lives, an end to hunger, lower infant mortality, longer life expectancy—not just quality of life but life itself. Environmental policies that ignore the economic factor, the human factor, are destined to fail."[27]

During a speech the next day, however, Bush used his optimism for the future to diminish the gravity of the situation and thus the corresponding call to action: "A growing sense of global stewardship prompted us to host this conference. . . . We also recognize that ours is an increasingly prosperous planet, with greater hopes now than ever before that more of our people in every nation may come to know an enduring peace and an unprecedented quality of life. So, we're called upon to ensure that the earth's integrity is preserved and that mankind's prospects for prosperity, peace, and in some regions, even survival are not put at risk by the unintended consequences of noble intentions." Bush's argument concerning "an increasingly prosperous planet" clearly contradicts the growing disparity between the global haves and have-nots. The excerpt also reveals his belief that economic development, rather than environmental protection, will lead to the global improvement of the quality of life.[28]

Bush definitely exhibited no sense of urgency concerning global environmental problems, likely due to his optimism about the future—which was based on his intertwined belief in science and the marketplace—and his political position, which required him to tend to the conservative end of the spectrum. Bush's political position concerning the environment was evidenced more by his silence than his rhetoric. Simply put, Bush rarely spoke on environmental issues to any large audiences. The "environmental president" did not mention the environment in his inaugural address, and the issue was barely mentioned in his state of the union addresses. For example, in the 1992 state of the union address—with the Earth Summit, the largest international environmental conference in history, looming only half a year away—not a word was said concerning environmental issues.

Bush chose to focus instead on national antipollution and conservation efforts. Even when he did comment on international issues, he emphasized economic concerns, not the difficult North-South problems of poverty, population control, and inequality. Bush did discuss the need to adjust the economy to allow for more environmental sustainability early in his administration, but by the time of the Earth Summit, he was clearly focused on the U.S. economy.

THE PRESIDENCY OF BILL CLINTON

In 1992 Bill Clinton and Al Gore defeated Bush and Quayle in the presidential election. Gore was the author of *Earth in the Balance,* a book that called for environmental issues to become the central organizing principle for civilization. Environmentalists the world over were overjoyed at the prospect of a "real" environmental presidency. Unfortunately, once again the environmentalists would be disappointed. This review of Clinton's environmental rhetoric focuses on the 1997 Kyoto treaty, Clinton's approach to science and the free market to develop solutions, and the increasing focus on the international environment.[29]

THE KYOTO TREATY

The primary global environmental event during Clinton's administrations was the Kyoto Conference held in December, 1997. In June of that year Clinton gave a major environmental address to a UN special session on the environment. There, he explained how the environment had "moved to the top of the international agenda." During the speech, he acknowledged that the United States "must do better" with its environmental record and even mentioned that the United States produced more than 20 percent of the world's greenhouse gasses, while representing only 4 percent of the world's population. These admissions were significant. During his administration, Bush had praised

America's positive leadership in environmental technology and air quality but never acknowledged America's negative leadership in greenhouse gas emissions and waste production.[30]

Four months later, Clinton spoke at the White House Conference on Climate Change. There he presented his administration's four principles on climate change: (1) he firmly established that the science of climate change was "real;" (2) he promised to show leadership at the upcoming Kyoto Conference and be prepared to commit to "realistic and binding goals" on emissions; (3) he called for solutions that "will allow us to continue to grow our economy as we honor our global responsibilities and our responsibilities to our children;" and (4) he said that "we must expect all nations, both industrialized and developing, to participate in this process in a way that is fair to all." The four principles represent clear progress from the Bush administration, though Clinton still fell short of the necessary sacrifices. One important development, however, was Clinton's perspective on the science of climate change, which had been the primary barrier to progress for Bush. During the speech, Clinton said: "for me the bottom line is that, although we do not know everything, what we do know is more than enough to warrant responsible action. . . . I know not everyone agrees on how to interpret the scientific conclusions. I know not everyone shares my assessment of the risks. But I think we all have to agree that the potential for serious climate disruption is real. It would clearly be a grave mistake to bury our heads in the sand and pretend the issue will go away." Though, the definition of "responsible action" is quite flexible, Clinton had displayed an ability to get beyond the uncertainties of science. In 1998 he went so far as to admit that, "there is virtually unanimous—not complete, but virtually unanimous—opinion among scientists that the globe is warming at an unacceptably rapid rate."[31]

At the Kyoto Conference, the United States was called to commit to reducing emissions to 7 percent below 1990 levels by 2008. But the United States did not sign the Kyoto agreement at that time, citing the lack of participation by developing countries. Not until Argentina broke ranks from the developing countries and signed the document in November, 1998, did Clinton agree to sign, though he never actually sent the Kyoto agreement to Congress for ratification (given statements from Congress that, unless more developing countries participated, the Republican Congress would not ratify the treaty). In other words, the United States' global leadership had again faltered.[32]

SCIENCE AND THE FREE MARKET AS SAVIORS

Although Clinton did not explicitly use science as a procrastination device, he did reveal the same optimistic faith in science and the U.S. market to spark disaster-saving technologies as had Bush. In 1997 he told a crowd of climate scientists, "Despite the complexities of these challenges, we have good reason to be optimistic, beginning with our 220-year record of making all manner of difficult problems solvable, and, importantly, a very good record in the last generation of environmental progress." In a 1998 radio address he first told the audience that there is "no excuse for delay" but then explained, "We have the tools, we have the ingenuity to head off this threat."[33]

Clinton's optimism was linked to his belief in the free market to lead to new products. In October, 1997, he called for the "unleashing [of] the full power of free markets and technological innovations to meet the challenge of climate change" and proposed a package of "strong market incentives, tax cuts, and cooperative efforts with industry." His plan was designed to "play to our strengths—innovation, creativity, entrepreneurship."[34]

Clinton's rhetoric, much like Bush's, revealed an optimistic belief in science and technology. Unfortunately, such optimism can discourage activism. If someone else will inevitably figure out the problem and fix it, why should sacrifices be made now? Indeed, optimism may be necessary—otherwise the task may seem too daunting and overwhelming to undertake—but a fine line exists between optimism that encourages continued participation and optimism that justifies inaction.[35]

THE DEVELOPING INTERNATIONAL PERSPECTIVE

Clinton did seem somewhat more willing than Bush to discuss international environmental issues. In his inaugural and first two state of the union addresses, the environment was only mentioned casually along with lists of other issues. In the 1996 state of the union address, Clinton devoted three paragraphs to the environment, but they were all focused on domestic issues. The environment played a minimal role in the 1996 election, primarily because with only a conservative, probusiness Republican as an opponent, Clinton could rely on the environmental vote without working for it.

In his 1997 state of the union address, Clinton devoted one sentence to the global environmental crisis.[36] In the 1998 speech, he spoke much more extensively on the subject:

Our overriding environmental challenge tonight is the worldwide problem of climate change, global warming, the gathering crisis that requires worldwide action. The vast majority of scientists have concluded unequivocally that if we don't reduce the emission of greenhouse gases, at some point in the next century we'll disrupt our climate and put our children and grandchildren at risk. This past December, America led the world to reach a historic agreement committing our nation to reduce greenhouse gas emissions through market forces, new technologies, energy efficiency. We have it in our power to act right here, right now. I propose $6 billion in tax cuts and research and development to encourage innovation, renewable energy, fuel-efficient cars, energy-efficient homes.[37]

The paragraph was significant, but closer examination reveals its limitations. In general, Clinton continued to exhibit the same procrastination tools evident since 1988. By explaining that the United States "led the world" in reaching a historic agreement—*without explaining that the agreement had not been even sent to, much less ratified by, Congress*—clearly Clinton did not attempt to use the powers of the rhetorical presidency to appeal to the American people to pressure Congress to ratify the treaty. By offering tax cuts and calling for more research as solutions, Clinton did not attempt to use the bully pulpit to mobilize the American people to action. By warning that "at some point in the next century we'll disrupt our climate," Clinton was contradicting the conclusions of many scientists who claim the increasing number of floods, storms, and droughts are *current* results of climate change brought on by global warming.

In the 1999 state of the union address Clinton avoided the subject of the environment altogether. The word "environment" was not even used in the address, though it was one of the longest on record. In 2000 Clinton labeled global warming the "greatest environmental challenge of the new century" but again did not mention the unratified Kyoto treaty, and focused on the development of new technologies.

SUMMARY OF CLINTON'S ENVIRONMENTAL APPEALS
Clinton's environmental rhetoric revealed some advances from that of the Bush administration. Clinton admitted that the United States was the world's foremost polluter, that the science on global warming was practically unanimous, and that global warming should be at the top of the international agenda. Nonetheless, Clinton's avoidance of the Kyoto agreement and his optimistic focus on the ability of the market and technology to alleviate the crisis reveal that significant barriers to action remained in place.

The 2000 Election and the Early George W. Bush Administration

Neither major party candidate in 2000 made the international environment an issue. Republican G. W. Bush did make a campaign pledge to reduce carbon dioxide emissions by power plants but blasted the proposed Kyoto treaty early in his campaign, warning that it would "cost the U.S. jobs." In *Earth in the Balance* Democratic candidate Al Gore had attacked the "tendency [of politicians] to put a finger to the political winds and proceed cautiously."[38] As he prepared for the 2000 campaign, Gore seemed to succumb to the same tendency. A 1999 story in *Time* magazine claims that if Gore became president, even he would be unable to muster the ability to call for significant action. The following excerpt captures the constraints to action that afflict U.S. environmental politics. Gore was speaking to a group of CEO's from leading environmental groups who had just presented proposals for cutting car and coal-fired power plants emissions, when

> [t]he room grew suddenly frosty, and Gore, who in previous months had been speaking out on climate change and fighting internally for more antipollution funding, said "Name a Senator who would support me." He then gave a lecture on global warming's vexing politics—the Senate would soundly reject the treaty in its current form—and abruptly ended the meeting. The green lobbyists concede that the public isn't yet ready to back painful measures to combat global warming, but contend that a political donnybrook led by the Vice President, even a losing cause, would raise awareness. Not so, says Gore. . . . "Losing on impractical proposals that are completely out of tune with what is achievable does not necessarily advance your cause at all," and could set it back by convincing politicians that the issue is too risky to revisit. Stronger policy proposals, Gore argues, have to go with public awareness and political support. "You cannot have one without the other," he says. A presidential campaign might be a good place to stir up a tempest about climate change, but so far, it appears unlikely that Gore will do so.[39]

Gore never did try to establish the international environment as an issue in the campaign, and after a historic election, Bush became president.

Bush was presented with two new UN-sponsored reports on global warming within his first weeks in office. Less than a week later, when Bush addressed a joint session of Congress to lay out his agenda, global warming was not mentioned. Reports were leaked to the media that the speech originally had one sentence devoted to carbon dioxide emissions controls, but as Robert D. Novak reported, the sentence "sent conservatives into a frenzy that apparently resulted in losing the sentence from the speech." Finally, on March 13, 2001, Bush sent a letter to four Republican senators explaining that he had reversed his campaign position on the reduction of emissions from power plants due to "important new information." In other words, the early days of the Bush administration provide further support for the argument that the crisis will not be addressed in its present frame.[40]

Framing International Environmentalism

Niklas Luhmann. argued that environmental issues can be considered through six function systems: politics, economy, science, law, education, and religion. Luhman further explained that each function system can be understood through a pair of binary codes: in/out of office (politics); ability/inability to pay (economy); truth/falsity (science); legality/illegality (law); better/worse (education); and immanence/transcendence (religion). I consider each of these function systems in turn, focusing on if and how George H. Bush and Bill Clinton invoked them, what constraints seem associated with each, and what potential there is for reframing within or among the function systems.

The Political Frame

The function system of politics is perhaps the most important to consider in the context of the American presidency and in this case reveals considerable barriers to action. In many ways, the U.S. political system is simply not geared to confront problems such as those of the international environment. First of all, most of the proposals for responding to these problems involve high short-term costs with uncertain long-term benefits. The U.S. political system inherently levies heavy disincentives to politicians to lobby for action in such situations, especially when opposing politicians dismiss the long- term threat and promise lower short-term costs. The notion of running a national campaign based on higher taxes to assist developing countries, higher energy prices to reduce consumption, and fear appeals concerning environmental catastrophe is clearly far-fetched, and the possibility of such a politician getting elected is unfortunately absurd. The environmental rhetoric of the Bush and Clinton administrations provides support concerning the political constraints evident in dealing with the international environmental crisis. The strongest evidence is simply the avoidance of the issues, especially in major speeches.

The fact that the industrial lobby can greatly outspend the environmental lobby in campaign funding only exacerbates these constraints.[41] The focus of both the Climate Change Convention at the Earth Summit and the Kyoto treaty was greenhouse gas emissions, especially of carbon dioxide. This issue is especially politicized because automobile manufacturers, oil and mining firms, and electrical utilities are all fervently against the forced reduction of emissions, which would raise their costs and reduce the demand for their products. As

John Judis reported in 1999, a coalition of such companies formed the Global Climate Information Project, a $13 million national media campaign focused on attacking the Kyoto treaty. Riders were even placed on appropriation bills that barred the EPA from educating the public concerning global warming. It seems clear that as long as the focus of international environmental concerns is placed specifically on emissions, the political power of industrial corporations will continue to hamper any progress.[42]

The Economic Frame

The economic frame is critical to the international environmental movement and was used extensively by both Bush and Clinton. Traditionally, economics and the environment are considered antagonists in a zero-sum game. Both Bush and Clinton attacked this notion, arguing that both ends could be sought simultaneously. Bush argued for finding the right balance between them, but that balance clearly suffered when a recession hit late in his term. The recession pushed Bush back to a more economically protective position during the Earth Summit and the 1992 election.[43] The primary flaw with the balancing frame, therefore, is that environmental concerns nonetheless remain conceptualized as low- priority luxury items to be brushed aside when the economy falters. With the numerous uncertain measures of economic performance, it is likely that a politician would always be able to find some distressing sign of economic trouble to justify reducing environmental activism, as the George W. Bush administration has demonstrated.[44]

Clinton's rhetorical framing of the economic-environment balance improved upon his predecessor's. Rather than simply arguing for a balance, Clinton, in typical New Democrat fashion, argued for using economic means to meet environmental ends. The development of a market for "pollution credits" represents perhaps the primary example of this framework, along with Clinton's optimistic vision of the technological innovations that would be developed to save the world from environmental catastrophe. Whereas pollution credits have had some success in national markets, their usefulness for international markets has been questioned, primarily due to the difficulty in monitoring and the inequities between the developed and developing countries.[45] And although technological innovation will be necessary in addressing the environmental crisis, it will not be sufficient, especially if the poorer developing countries are expected to pay for the new technologies. The manner in which Clinton optimistically turned to future innovation has the unfortunate side effect of justifying procrastination and challenging any call for sacrifice.

In summary, the economic frame holds some promise for improving the situation, especially in terms of developing incentives to reduce pollution and develop cleaner technologies but is not likely to be sufficient in the long run and on a large enough scale. Unless suggestions for a sustainable environment such as those offered by Daly and Cobb are enacted, the economic system will likely continue to oppose environmental measures rather than support them.[46]

The Scientific Frame

The scientific frame is perhaps the most interesting rhetorical frame, as well as the frame dominating environmental issues, especially concerning global warming. At one time, the scientific frame was thought to be the frame that would catapult the environmental movement to the forefront of international politics. Activists believed that the growing evidence of global warming, for example, would overpower the economic and political constraints of the past, and in the words of Daniel Sarwitz and Roger Pielke, Jr., "[they] fell head over heels in love with science." Unfortunately, despite mounting evidence that human activity is a significant cause of global warming, the uncertainties inherent to science leave plenty of room for continued political and economic hegemony, as evidenced by the analysis of Bush's and Clinton's rhetoric. Considered from the rhetorical frame of science, the problems are understandable. Luhman claims that science is based on the dichotomy between truth and falsity. The complicated nature of climate science continues to evade strict claims of "truth" and inevitably leads to calls for more science. As Sarwitz and Pielke argued, the science has paradoxically led to more questions, rather than clear answers, and more scientific research remains the primary American response to climate change. This problem is disastrous to arguments that call for present action for possible future benefit because it is easily trumped by the alternative, quasi-progressive argument of calling for "more" or "better" science. In the end, both Bush and Clinton used science as a justification for inaction, rather than as evidence of the urgency of the situation. The frame that activists once thought would be a bonanza for the environmental cause has in many ways become a trap.[47]

The Frame of Law

The frame of law was secondary in the rhetoric of Bush and Clinton. Nonetheless, the frame will likely grow in importance as the issue of international governance continues to develop. Confronting international environmental problems will probably require international monitoring and relinquishing power to entities such as the United Nations. In the current antigovernmental environment, such actions will be exceedingly difficult to support in the United States. Bush's experience at the 1992 Earth Summit—where the United States was the only industrialized nation not to sign some of the documents—and Clinton's inability to send the Kyoto treaty to Congress for ratification demonstrate the difficulty encountered when U.S. sovereignty appears to be questioned. The political frame, in other words, precedes the law frame, because any progress would require the development of new laws, not just the enforcement of current law. Once laws or treaties are in effect, the frame of law may grow in importance, but for the near future, it will likely remain secondary.[48]

Potential Reframing: The Frames of Education and Religion

Whereas the first four frames were used to various degrees by both Bush and Clinton, education and religion were generally absent from their discourse. Consequently, rather than explain their use, I focus on their potential. Both Bush and Clinton spent precious little time discussing issues of environmental importance when addressing the American people as a whole in venues such as inaugural address or the state of the union address. If U.S. presidents chose to use the bully pulpit to "educate" the American people about these issues and essentially help develop their understanding and salience, perhaps more options could be created. Rather than simply appealing for specific policies that would face difficult congressional constraints and the mobilization of opposing biases, the president could attempt to raise national consciousness concerning the issue, perhaps providing a foundation for more activism in the future. Clinton's admissions concerning the "virtual anonymity" of global science and of the high percentage of the world's pollution the United States emits are important in this context. Such claims—considering they are backed by strong evidence—are difficult for opposing political actors to dismiss. Such a role fits an image of an "educational presidency" rather than a "rhetorical presidency" but nonetheless may be the most we can expect.

Perhaps a route with even more potential would involve the president "educating" the public concerning the constraints to acting on the global environmental threat, rather than simply the science. Clinton supported the Kyoto agreement, but it was politically unfeasible for him to send the treaty to Congress. If he had addressed the nation directly—without necessarily focusing on the actual treaty—and explained to the American people that the global environmental crisis was real, but due to the short-term costs and long-term benefits, the uncertainty of the science, and the high political stakes, any serious confrontation faces immense constraints, perhaps the framing of the issue would have begun to change and open new possibilities. The president would have to avoid blaming the opposing political party, the media, or special interests, and focus instead on a political system that works well with many issues but is simply not designed to handle a problem of this nature. Such an appeal seems to hold some promise, though the level of public cynicism may be too high to overcome assumptions of ulterior motives.

Luhman's last function system—religion—was also absent from the presidential discourse but offers some possibilities. The label of "religion" is somewhat misleading, for Luhmann did not limit religion to organized religious theology, which—considering the world's conglomeration of established religions and the moral conflicts that rage between them—seems hardly the domain for progress. If Luhmann's function system of religion, which he described through the binary codes of immanence versus transcendence, is taken out of the specific context of established religions, it offers possibilities similar to those exhibited by Theodore Roosevelt (see chap. 1, this volume). The new focus, therefore, must be on language that adds the concept of transcendence to the conflict. This need is similar to Pearce and Littlejohn's call for "transcendent discourse." In their examination of the role of communication in moral conflicts, the authors wrote that transcendent discourse focuses on "constructive dialogue, new contexts in which to understand differences, and new ways to compare and weigh alternative choices." Essentially, alternative metanarratives must be developed that would work to reconceptualize the other five function systems and build a frame that is more conducive to environmental progress.[49]

Examples of the necessary sort of transcendent discourse are already in circulation. In 1997, for example, Clinton briefly hinted at the potential of transcendence:

> Nearly three decades ago when the Apollo astronauts first went to the Moon, we gained an entirely new perspective on the global challenge we face today. For looking down on Earth from the vantage point that revealed no political boundaries or divisions, the astronauts had the same chilling sensation. They were simply awestruck by how tiny and fragile our planet is. . . . [E]very astronaut since has experienced the same insight, and they've even given it a name—the Overview effect. It has instilled in each new astronaut a passion to convince people we must work together on Earth's behalf. . . . I challenge everyone in this room to rise to a vantage point high enough to experience the overview effect. It will enable us to reach common ground.[50]

Unfortunately, this message was delivered to a small audience at the White House Conference on Climate Change, not to a national audience. Nonetheless, Clinton did lay some foundation for a transcendent perspective that could bear fruit.

On one hand, it seems clear that a serious confrontation with international environmental issues will likely require a rhetorical appeal that runs counter to the enduring notions of individualism and consumerism that currently dominate the American mythos. As President Carter discovered during the energy crisis, messages based on sacrifice are a difficult sell to American audiences. On the other hand, however, the rhetorical appeal of American civil religion—complete with the myth of Americans as the "chosen people" and the United States as the "city on a hill"—seems to have remarkable staying power and could be tapped to confront these global issues. Perhaps the narrative could be successfully adapted to involve the United States' leading the world in overcoming the immense obstacle of global warming and environmental degradation.[51]

Such a myth would have several advantages. Unlike other myths, it would not divide. The enemy, rather than being personified in the Native American, the fascist, or the communist, would be conceptualized as pollution or wastefulness. It could also tap into many of the traditional American myths. The "hero," fitting the form of Thomas Edison, would be the inventor who develops the technologies that aid the effort. The effort would require the participation of all the people, not just government or industry, and could thus revive democracy and, as Neil Postman has argued, education. Perhaps most importantly, it would provide a transcendent goal for all Americans to focus upon beyond the individualism and consumerism of the free market, without requiring the destruction of those impulses. The global environmental crisis would, in a sense, merely represent the next of the series of mythic challenges the American people have overcome. Overall, it could provide some basis for a positive message concerning the American experience.[52]

Unfortunately, serious constraints to the development of such transcendent discourse remain. The overriding cynicism toward government action is clearly a hindrance, as is the combined influence of the economic liberalism of the free marketers and the social liberalism of the postmodern turn. The two latter movements focus on individualism and emancipation, respectively, and reject the grand narratives that bind people together to ideas that transcend the individual. However, I am not arguing that the narrative offered here would come to dominate the American experience and be wholeheartedly accepted, but it would rather be a vehicle through which *the president* could rhetorically construct a serious response to the global crisis. The U.S. president, more than any other political figure, can serve the role of moral leader and mythmaker, and this type of narrative could work to re-create the discourse surrounding the global environment, overcoming many of the current constraints. Working from within the tradition of American civil religion, in other words, the president could help provide a more solid basis for addressing the crisis.

From 1988 to 2000 George Bush and Bill Clinton, both surely aware of the growing global crisis, primarily either avoided the topic or provided only cursory examinations of its repercussions and limited proposals for action. The rhetoric of both presidents continued to revolve around the economic paradigm of cost-benefit analysis, which is inadequate for dealing with international environmental issues. Both called for "more research" as the primary response, despite the fact that scientific evidence had begun to coalesce into "virtual unanimity." Both tended to calm, rather than inspire, the American people with optimistic claims that science in the service of the free market would solve any future problem. Both presidents were reluctant to relinquish any national sovereignty to international governing bodies, and neither president discussed the related issues associated with world poverty, overpopulation, income redistribution, or technology transfer. Both presidents tended to celebrate American's global leadership, without much clarity regarding where America was leading the world.

The debate concerning the international environment has revolved primarily around the economy, politics, and science, none of which offers much promise for advancement. Due in part to inherent barriers to addressing issues with short-term costs and long-term benefits, the U.S. political system is a difficult landscape within which to articulate significant progress concerning international environmental issues. The economic frame has allowed limited progress, but that progress will always be checked by recessions, and the international viability of the market-based solutions seem unclear. Science also offers some promise, but with the continuing uncertainty surrounding scientific endeavors, a reliance on science remains a frightening gamble susceptible to the justification of procrastination. The system of law is limited primarily due to the problems of international sovereignty and the divide between the North and the South. Modern society's two remaining systems—education and religion—have generally been overlooked and offer potential areas for issue redefinition that could lead to progress. Whether the dominant frames are adjusted with the current function systems or whether alternative function systems are brought into the mix, to overcome the current gridlock a significant rhetorical transformation will clearly be necessary. The active involvement of the U.S. president—the world's most powerful rhetorical icon—will almost certainly be critical to any such transformation.

The point of this chapter is neither to blame nor to absolve Bush and Clinton (or any other U.S. president) for their failures to confront the difficulties of the global environmental crisis. As Cox suggests in chapter 6 (this volume), the easiest reaction would be to blame them for their lack of initiative in confronting the crisis. Indeed, Bush was called "the anti-Christ," "Uncle Grubby," the "Grinch who stole the eco-summit," "cranky Uncle Scrooge," and "eco-wimp" for his position at the Earth Summit.[53] Such criticism may be cathartic, but it is hardly effective. Blaming the individual implies that a different individual with a more proactive stance would be able to confront these issues politically. Such assumptions are unfortunately rather unrealistic, at least from the frameworks that are currently active. In other words, the misdiagnosis of a rhetorical situation leads to the misapplication of rhetorical remedies. If environmentalists truly want to change the way the world works—and more and more evidence seems to point toward that inevitable necessity—their rhetoric must strategically consider the constraints, assumptions, and beliefs, however valid or invalid they may seem to be, of their intended audience. Rather than taking the easy road of arguing past their opponents, environmental activists must take the hard road and seek to discover viable rhetorical strategies that could lead to real progress. At some point in time, international environmental issues will become *the* defining issue of global politics. As explained in *Limits to Growth,* the sooner that happens, the better.

Notes

1. John McCormick, *Reclaiming Paradise: The Global Environmental Movement* (Bloomington: Indiana University Press, 1989). The global environmental crisis and climate change politics are examined in detail in several works, including Gareth Porter and Janet Welsh Brown, *Global Environmental Politics* (Boulder: Westview Press, 1991); Joyeeta Gupta, *The Climate Change Convention and Developing Countries: From Conflict to Consensus?* (Boston: Kluwer Academic Publishers, 1997); Irving M. Mintzer and J. Amber Leonard, eds., *Negotiating Climate Change: The Inside Story of the Rio Convention* (New York: Cambridge University Press, 1994); Ranee K. L. Panjabi, *The Earth Summit at Rio: Politics, Economics, and the Environment* (Boston: Northeastern University Press, 1997); Ian H. Rowlands, *The Politics of Global Atmospheric Change* (New York: Manchester University Press, 1995); Matthew Paterson, *Global Warming and Global Politics* (New York: Routledge, 1996); and Ernst Ulrich von Weizsäcker, *Earth Politics* (Atlantic Highlands, N.J.: Zed Books, 1994).
2. Donella H. Meadows, Dennis L. Meadows, Jörgen Randers, and William W. Behrens, III, *The Limits of Growth: A Report for the Club of Rome's Project on the Predicament of Mankind* (New York: Universe Books, 1972). See also Mark Dowie, *Losing Ground: American Environmentalism at the Close of the Twentieth Century* (Cambridge, Mass.: MIT Press, 1995), 236.
3. Niklas Luhmann, *Ecological Communication,* trans. John Bednarz, Jr. (Chicago: University of Chicago Press, 1989). For an excellent application of Luhmann's theories to the issue of sustainable development, see Tarla Peterson, *Sharing the Earth: The Rhetoric of Sustainable Development* (Columbia: University of South Carolina Press, 1997).
4. McCormick, *Reclaiming Paradise,*76.
5. The material in this paragraph represents generally accepted positions from various sources (see n. 1, above).
6. Information originally acquired from Environmental Protection Agency on April 12, 2001, and in possession of author.
7. Stephen Hopgood, *American Foreign Environmental Policy and the Power of the State* (New York: Oxford University Press, 1998), 4.
8. Cited in Peterson, *Sharing the Earth,* 59.
9. "Costing the Earth: The Politics of Posterity," *Economist,* Sept. 2, 1989, 1, emphasis added.
10. Jerry Adler and Mary Hager, "Earth at the Summit," *Newsweek,* June 1, 1992, 20.
11. Maurice Strong, "Statement by Maurice Strong, Secretary-General United Nations Conference on Environment and Development at the Opening of the United Nations Conference on Environment and Development, Rio de Janeiro, June 3, 1992," printed in Stanley P. Johnson, ed., *The Earth Summit* (Boston: Graham & Trotman/Martinus Nijhoff, 1993), 50.
12. Weizsäcker, *Earth Politics,* 93. Gandhi cited in Weizsäcker, *Earth Politics,* 3. Prince Charles also captured the dilemma well in 1992 when he warned: "two simple truths need to be writ large over the portals of every international gathering about the environment: we will not slow the birth rate until we address poverty. And we will not protect the environment until we address the issue of poverty and population growth in the same breath." Prince Charles, at the World Commission on Environment and Development, April 22, 1992, cited in *The Earth*

Summit, ed. Stanley P. Johnson (Boston: Graham and Trotman/Martinus Nijhoff, 1993), 157.

13. Weizsäcker, *Earth Politics*, 3.
14. Norman J. Vig, "Presidential Leadership: From the Reagan to the Bush Administration," in *Environmental Policy in the 1990s*, ed. Norman J. Vig and Michael E. Kraft (Washington, D.C.: Congressional Quarterly Press, 1990), 54.
15. Weizsäcker, *Earth Politics,* 40. Nonetheless, Reagan was somehow able to keep a straight face during a 1982 press conference, when he told the gathered press, "let me remind you of something, I fancy myself an environmentalist." *Reagan Presidential Papers* (Jan. 21, 1982), 61.
16. Bush called for a new acid rain bill, stricter amendments to the Clean Air Act, a ban on all ocean dumping of sewage sludge, a "no net loss" policy on wetlands, and the acquisition of more lands for the national park systems. See David Corn and Jefferson Morley, "Bush's Environmental Thing," *Nation,* July 30, 1988, 84; Robert Sullivan, "A Kinder Environment," *Sports Illustrated,* Dec. 5, 1988, 122; Leslie Roberts, "Reilly Vows Environmental Activism," *Science* 243 (Feb. 10, 1989): 731; "Bush Stressing Environment in Sharp Contrast to Reagan," *Chemical Marketing Reporter* 235 (Feb. 13, 1989): 3; Dick Russel and Viveca Novak, "Environmental Tensions," *Nation,* March 27, 1989, 403.
17. See Hopgood, *American Foreign Environmental Policy.* For a rhetorical analysis of Bush's speech at the Earth Summit, see chapter 4 of Peterson, *Sharing the Earth*.
18. For a rhetorical discussion of the term "sustainable development," see Peterson, *Sharing the Earth.* George H. Bush, "Remarks at the Swearing-in Ceremony for William K. Reilly as Administrator of the Environmental Protection Agency," Feb. 8, 1989; Bush, "Message to Congress Transmitting the Report of the Council on Environmental Quality," June 23, 1989. All speeches from the presidency of George H. Bush were obtained online through the Bush Presidential Library at http://bushlibrary.tamu.edu/papers/index.html.
19. George H. Bush, "Remarks and Question-and-Answer Session with the Agricultural Community in Frenso, California," May 30, 1992.
20. Bush, "Remarks at an Environmental Agreement Signing Ceremony at the Grand Canyon, Arizona," Sept. 18, 1991.
21. McCormick, *Reclaiming Paradise*, 189. Porter and Brown, *Global Environmental Politics,* 104. See n. 1 above for works that focus on the international politics of global warming and climate change.
22. See "More Groups Address Climate Change," *Science News* 6 (Feb. 10, 1990): 95. Other reports included an EPA study concerned with the "migration" of trees northward due to warming trends and the impending rise in sea level, and a report from the International Energy Agency that identified economic and technological options for reducing emissions.
23. Colleen Shannon, "Washington Washout: Global Warming," *Chemistry and Industry* 4 (Feb. 19, 1990): 88.
24. Bush, "Remarks to the Intergovernmental Panel on Climate Change," Feb. 5, 1990.
25. Gregg Easterbrook, "Try to Follow the Pea," *Newsweek,* Feb. 19, 1990, 78; and *Chemistry and Industry,* Feb. 19, 1990, 88. See also Leslie Roberts, "Climate Extravaganza Bombs," *Science* 248 (April 27, 1990): 436.
26. A focus on the need and benefit of "sound science" was repeated throughout the

Bush presidency. Besides all the various speeches related to the Earth Summit, see Bush, "Remarks to the Intergovernmental Panel on Climate Change," Feb. 5, 1990; "Remarks at the Opening Session of the White House Conference on Science and Economics Research Related to Global Change," April 17, 1990; "Remarks at the Closing Session of the White House Conference on Science and Economics Research Related to Global Change," April 18, 1990; "Remarks at an Environmental Agreement Signing Ceremony at the Grand Canyon, Arizona," Sept. 19, 1991. See John Sununu, "The Political Pleasures of Engineering: An Interview with John Sununu," *Technology Review* (Aug.–Sept., 1992): 24–25; Maureen Dowd, "Who's Environmental Czar, E.P.A. Chief or Sununu," *New York Times,* Feb. 15, 1990, A1; and Hopgood, *American Foreign Environmental Policy,* 156–57.

27. Bush, "Remarks to the Intergovernmental Panel on Climate Change," Feb. 5, 1990, and Bush, "Remarks at the Opening Session of the White House Conference on Science and Economics Research Related to Global Change," April 17, 1990.

28. Bush, "Remarks at the Closing Session of the White House Conference on Science and Economics Research Related to Global Change," April 18, 1990.

29. Al Gore, *Earth in the Balance: Ecology and the Human Spirit* (New York: Houghton Mifflin, 1992).

30. William J. Clinton, "Remarks by the President in Address to the United States Special Session on Environment and Development," June 26, 1997. All Clinton's presidential addresses are available online through the Government Printing Office at http://www.gpo.gov/nara/pubpaps/photoidx.html. See also Martin Carcasson, "Prudence, Procrastination, or Politics: George Bush and the Earth Summit of 1992," in *Principles or Politics: The Rhetorical Education of George Herbert Walker Bush,* ed. Martin J. Medhurst, (College Station, Texas: Texas A&M University Press, forthcoming).

31. Clinton, "Remarks by the President at White House Conference on Climate Change," Oct. 6, 1997. Clinton, "Remarks by the President to Community Members on Climate Change," May 4, 1998.

32. John H. Cushman, "U.S. Signs Global-Warming Pact, but Has No Obligation to Abide by Agreement," *Houston Chronicle,* Nov. 13, 1998.

33. Clinton, "Radio Address by the President to the Nation," July 25, 1998.

34. Clinton, "Remarks by the President on Global Climate Change," Oct. 22, 1997.

35. A similar dynamic concerning optimism revolves around several issues in which the "power of the market" is assumed to cure all ills, such as those concerning American poverty and educational systems.

36. Clinton said, "We must also protect our global environment, working to ban the worst toxic chemicals and to reduce the greenhouse gases that challenge our health even as they change our climate."

37. Clinton did acknowledge the current effects on weather, saying that "growing evidence suggests that the extreme and erratic weather we're seeing in America and around the world is being intensified by global warming." See Clinton, "Radio Address by the President to the Nation," July 25, 1998.

38. Bush quoted in Todd Ackerman and R. G. Ratcliffe, "Bush Blasts Global Environmental Plan," *Houston Chronicle,* Sept. 2, 1999, 3A. Gore quoted in Jay Banegan, "Is Al Gore a Hero or a Traitor," *Time,* April 26, 1999, 67.

39. Jay Branegan, "Is Al Gore a Hero or a Traitor," *Time,* April 26, 1999, 67.

40. Bill Dawson, "Global-Warming Reports Put Hot Issue on Front-Burner for Bush," *Houston Chronicle,* Feb. 26, 2001, 1A; Robert D. Novak, "Stance on Global Warming Still Unspoken," *Houston Chronicle,* March 1, 2001, 26A; and George W. Bush, "Text of a Letter from the President to Senators Hagel, Helms, Craig, and Roberts," March 13, 2001. Acquired online at www.whitehouse.gov.

41. Mark Dowie, in an extensive history of the American environmental movement, vividly explained this inequality: "No matter how large, clever, and sophisticated in the ways of Washington the environmental movement has become, when it comes to lobbying Congress, it has remained a mosquito on the hindquarters of the industrial elephant. Corporations finance a lobby that is willing to spend almost unlimited time and money combating a process—environmental regulation—they claim costs them $125 billion a year. Chemical manufacturers, oil companies, big agriculture, timber interests, and their PACs will, unless campaign finance laws are reformed, always have greater access to the legislative [lobbyists] than environmental lobbyists." Dowie, *Losing Ground,* 85.

42. John Judis, "Global Warming and the Big Shill," *American Prospect* (Jan.–Feb., 1999): 16.

43. Hopgood, *American Foreign Environmental Policy.*

44. Michael Hedges, "Bush Rejects U.S. Role in Global Warming Pact," *Houston Chronicle,* March 29, 2001, 1A. A Bush spokesman was cited in the article as explaining that the Kyoto treaty was "not in the United States' economic best interest."

45. Ross Gelbspan, "Rx for a Planetary Fever," *American Prospect* 11 (May 8, 2000).

46. Herman E. Daly and John B. Cobb, *For the Common Good: Redirecting the Economy toward Community, the Environment, and a Sustainable Future* (Boston: Beacon Press, 1989).

47. Daniel Sarwitz and Roger Pielke, Jr., "Breaking the Global Warming Gridlock," *Atlantic Monthly,* July, 2000, 56.

48. Major works examining the Earth Summit include Steve Lerner, ed., *Beyond the Earth Summit: Conversations with Advocates of Sustainable Development* (Bolinas, Calif.: Common Knowledge Press, 1992); Caroline Thomas, ed., *Rio: Unraveling the Consequences* (Portland, Ore.: Frank Cass, 1994); Mintzer and Leonard, eds., Negotiating Climate Change; Johnson, *The Earth Summit;* and Panjabi, *The Earth Summit at Rio.*

49. W. Barnett Pearce and Stephen W. Littlejohn, *Moral Conflict: When Social Worlds Collide* (Thousand Oaks, Calif.: Sage Publications, 1997), 153, 81. Pearce and Littlejohn make many comparisons between their concept of transcendent discourse and Richard Rorty's "abnormal discourse." See Richard Rorty, *Philosophy and the Mirror of Nature* (Princeton, N.J.: Princeton University Press, 1979). The concept can also be linked to Daly and Cobb's appeal for a new, prophetic "religious vision," though the authors, as Christian theists, perhaps present a less inclusive vision. See chapter 20 in Daly and Cobb, *For the Common Good.*

50. Clinton, "Remarks by the President at White House Conference on Climate Change," Oct. 6, 1997.

51. See Richard Pierard and Robert Linder, *Civil Religion and the Presidency* (Grand Rapids, Mich.: Academie Books, 1988). "Civil religion," as a concept, began with Rousseau in the classic *Social Contract.* It was developed further by Robert Bellah, "Civil Religion in America," *Daedalus* 96 (1967): 1–18. See also James David Fairbanks, "The Priestly Functions of the Presidency: A Discussion of

the Literature on Civil Religion and Its Implications for the Study of Presidential Leadership," *Presidential Studies Quarterly* 11 (1981): 214–32.

52. Neil Postman, *The End of Education: Redefining the Value of School* (New York: Vintage Books, 1995). In chapter 5 Postman argued for schools to be reconceptualized around the metaphor of "Spaceship Earth" in order to stimulate students through a different grand narrative than the current consumption-based model.

53. See Charles P. Alexander, "On the Defensive," *Time,* June 15, 1992, 35; Sharon Begley, "The Grinch of Rio," *Newsweek,* June 15, 1992, 30; Sharon Begley, Mary Hager, and Brook Larmer, "And Now, the Road from Rio," *Newsweek,* June, 22, 1992, 46; Hopgood, *American Foreign Environmental Policy,* 191; Dowie, *Losing Ground,* 167; Albert Gore, Jr., "Success for World, Failure for Bush," *USA Today,* June 5, 1992, 13A.

Contributors

Vanessa B. Beasley (Ph.D., University of Texas) is assistant professor of corporate communication and public affairs at Southern Methodist University.

Martin Carcasson (Ph.D., Texas A&M University) is assistant professor of speech communication at Colorado State University.

J. Robert Cox (Ph.D., University of Pittsburgh) is professor of communication studies at University of North Carolina at Chapel Hill.

Suzanne M. Daughton (Ph.D., University of Texas) is associate professor of speech communication at Southern Illinois University, Carbondale.

Leroy G. Dorsey (Ph.D., Indiana University) is associate professor of communication at Texas A&M University.

David Henry (Ph.D., Indiana University) is director and professor of communication at the University of Nevada, Las Vegas.

Mark P. Moore (Ph.D., Indiana University) is professor of speech communication at Oregon State University.

Christine Oravec (Ph.D., University of Wisconsin) is professor emerita of communication at the University of Utah.

Tarla Rai Peterson (Ph.D., Washington State University) is professor of communication at the University of Utah.

Lawrence J. Prelli (Ph.D., Pennsylvania State University) is associate professor of speech communication and affiliate professor of natural resources at the University of New Hampshire.

C. Brant Short (Ph.D., Indiana University) is associate professor of speech communication at Northern Arizona University.

Micheal R. Vickery (Ph.D., University of Texas) is professor and chair of communication at Alma College, Michigan.

Index

Escalante–Grand Staircase National Monument, 164, 172

ethics 5, 26–27, 44, 66–69, 208, 221–25, 243, 249, 267; of consequences, 27, 208, 222, 224; of virtue, 27, 168, 208, 222, 224

Everglades, 162

evolution, 70–71, 73, 76

extermination, age of, 37

facilitation, 208, 210, 215, 220, 221

Federal Aviation Administration, 172

feminine style, 26, 209, 212, 220

Fifth Amendment, 135. *See also* private property

film career, Reagan, 141–42

Fish and Wildlife Service, 18, 85, 97, 192

Forest Lieu Land Act, 38

Forest Service, 38, 51–52, 186, 190–93, 198, 236

forest summit (conference), Pacific Northwest, 165–66, 170, 200

fossil fuels, 95, 261, 264, 268

free market, 270–72, 276, 280. *See also* capitalism

frontier myth, 21, 39, 62, 63, 135, 138–50. *See also* Frederick Jackson Turner

function systems, Niklas Luhman, 29, 260, 275

genetic research, 12

Gingrich, Newt, 162, 194

Glacken, Clarence, 30

Glickman, Dan, 198

Global 2000 Report to the President, 265

global warming, 29, 172, 260–61, 268, 271–75, 277, 280

Goodnight, G. Thomas, 174

Gore, Al, 23, 157–58, 160, 162, 172, 202, 270, 274

Gorton, Slade, 197

Governors' conference on conservation, 1908, 52, 65, 68–69, 71

Grand Canyon National Park, 38, 44, 56–57, 171–72

Grand Staircase-Escalante National Monument, 164, 172

Great Communicator, Reagan as, 21, 134

Great Depression, 86, 88

Great Falls National Park, 171

greed, 40, 46–48, 52, 55, 74

Green Culture: Rhetorical Analyses of Environmental Discourse, 4

greenhouse gases, 172, 270–71, 275

Gronbeck, Bruce, 8

Gunderson, Robert, 150

Halloran, Michael, 208, 215

Hariman, Robert, 158, 164, 166, 169, 175

Hart, Rod, 43, 53, 122, 127, 131

Hatfield, Mark, 194, 199

Hays, Samuel P., 63, 69, 114, 118, 125, 136

Herndl, Carl, 4

Hodel, Donald, 21

Hoff, Joan, 121, 128

Hoover, Herbert, 95

Humphrey, Hubert, 114

Ickes, Harrold, 104

indifference, sin of, 40, 46, 48–49, 55

interdependence, 238, 245–53

Intergovernmental Panel on Climate Change, 268

invention, rhetorical, 11, 234, 251

ironic perspective, environmentalist, 186; timber industry, 185–86

irony: associative, 184; dissociative and tragic, 183, 198–202; ecological, 187, 198; economic, 187, 198; rhetorical, 25, 26; situational, 181–84, 187–89

Ivie, Robert L., 8, 9, 14

Jaehne, Dennis, 56

Jamieson, Kathleen Hall, 209–10

judgment, 29, 171, 237–38, 240–41; bifurcated, 243–45; practical, 27, 233; situated, 27, 234, 250, 252–53

Kant, Immanuel, 224

Kennedy, John F., 19

Killingsworth, Jimmie, 4

Kyoto Protocol, 270–71, 273, 275–76, 278

Landmark Essays on Rhetoric and the Environment, 5

Legal Services Corporation, 113

Lemay, Curtis, 218

Leopold, Aldo, 96, 97

Rescissions Act of 1995, 23, 25, 162, 192, 193
risk, 11, 13
Ruckelshaus, William, 116–17, 137

Sagebrush Rebellion, 14, 137
salvage timber rider, 23, 25, 157, 162, 181, 184, 192–99, 201–202
science, 11, 223, 238–41, 244, 249, 251, 261, 271–72, 277; best available, 238, 266–67; burden of proof, 239–40; uncertainty associated with, 12, 265–68, 271, 278, 281. *See also* conservation: scientific basis for
Selzer, Jack, 11
Sharing the Earth, The Rhetoric of Sustainable Development, 5
Shenandoah National Park, 92, 93
Shoshone Nation, Western, 217–18
Sierra Club, 85, 95, 157–63, 190–92
Silent Spring, 19, 258
Society of American Foresters, 51, 236
Soden, Dennis, 56
soil conservation, 91
Soil Conservation Service, (SCS), 18
Soviet Union, 213, 217. *See also* cold war
spotted owl, 181–82, 185, 190–92
stakeholders, 13–14, 208, 214–16, 221, 225, 233, 250
stewardship, 22, 27, 146, 175, 267, 269
Sununu, John, 265, 268
Superfund, 137
sustainability, 5, 11, 28, 233, 235–42, 244, 250
sustainable development, 5, 66, 104, 238, 266
sustainable forestry, 238, 241–43, 245, 248
Symbolic Earth: Discourse and Our Creation of the Environment, 4

Taylor, Zachary, names first secretary of the interior, 85
technological optimism, 22; 272–73. *See also* technology: advances in, benefit to society
technology, 212, 276, 280; advances in, 11–13, 15–16, 19, 66; benefit to society, 129–30, 142–43, 267; destructive, 37; distrust of, 10; transfer, 263, 281

Teller, Edward, 216–17, 220, 222
Tennessee Valley authority (TVA), 18, 87, 104
Thomas, Jack Ward, 186
Thoreau, 30
timber industry, 23, 25, 28, 57, 181, 196, 197, 198–99; greed of, 15, 37–38, 46–48; ironic perspective of, 185–88
timber salvage rider. *See* salvage timber rider
Toker, Caitlin W., 13
Tongass National Forest, 163
topical analysis, 7, 234, 249–53
Toulmin, Stephen, 234–35
Trachtenberg, Alan, 63
Train, Russell, 114, 121
Trudeau, Gary, 163
Tugwell, Rex, 98
Tulis, Jeffrey, 5, 169
Turner, Frederick Jackson, 63, 66, 88, 138–39, 140, 142. *See also* frontier myth

Union of Concerned Scientists, 268
United Nations Conference on Environment and Development. *See* Earth Summit
United Nations Environmental Programme, 20
United States Department of Energy (DOE), 11, 26–27, 207, 213, 215; coming clean, 210, 214; Hanford Washington site, 214, 216, 218; Livermore National Laboratory, 217–18; Los Alamos Laboratory, 221; medical experimentation, 207, 209–10, 212–13, 218, 220, 224; nuclear tests, 26, 207, 209, 212–13, 218, 221; plutonium production, 214; public trust, 26–27, 208, 211, 214, 216, 219, 223
United States Department of the Interior, (DOI), 51, 85, 143, 163

Veenendall, Thomas, 4
Vietnam War, 113, 120
Vig, Norman, 136–37, 264

Waddell, Craig, 5, 11
Walden, 30
Wander, Philip, 158
Washington, George, 53

ISBN 1-58544-335-2

9 781585 443352   90000